PARTICIPATORY RURAL APPRAISAL
METHODS AND APPLICATIONS IN RURAL PLANNING

(Essays in Honour of Robert Chambers)

Studies in Rural Participation Series

No. 1. Participation Rural Appraisal : Methodology and Applications
– Neela Mukherjee

No. 2. Participatory Rural Appraisal and Questionnaire Survey (Comparative Field Experience and Methodological Innovations)
– Neela Mukherjee

No. 3. Participatory Rural Appraisal of Natural Resources
– Neela Mukherjee

No. 4 Participatory Learning and Action : With 100 field Methods
– Neela Mukherjee

No. 5 Participatory Rural Appraisal : Methods and Application in Rural Planning (Second Revised Edition)
– Amitava Mukherjee

No. 6 Participatory Learning & Action : Monitoring & Evaluation and Participatory Monitoring & Evaluation
– Amitava Mukherjee

About the Author

Prof. Amitava Mukherjee had a distinguished academic career, educated at Ranchi University, Ranchi, India, William Marsh Rice University, Houston; University of South Florida, Tampa; Department of Economics and the Graduate School of Business, Stanford University, Stanford, USA; School of Oriental and African Studies, University of London, London, and the London School of Economics and Political Science, London.

Dr. Mukherjee held the Chair in Economics and Planning, and co-ordinated the Faculty in the Centre for Micro-Planning & Regional Studies at the Lal Bahadur Shastri National Academy of Administration, Mussoorie; was Advisor and Project Head of the Planning Commission Project on decentralized planning. He has been a consultant to various international and UN agencies including FAO, Rome; UNDP and UNESCAP. He is currently the Chief Technical Advisor, Pro-Poor Public Private Partnership, United Nations' Economic and Social Commission for Asia and the Pacific, Bangkok.

He is a life member of the Indian Econometric Society, the Regional Science Association of India, the Indian Economic Association, and of the Royal Economic Society, England.

Dr. Mukherjee has numerous papers and over thirty books to his credit. His contribution to decentralized planning and participatory development is internationally

Studies in Rural Participation Series-5

PARTICIPATORY RURAL APPRAISAL
METHODS AND APPLICATIONS IN RURAL PLANNING

(Essays in Honour of Robert Chambers)

(Second Revised Edition)

AMITAVA MUKHERJEE

CONCEPT PUBLISHING COMPANY, NEW DELHI-110059

First Published in 1995 by Vikas Publishing House, New Delhi.

ISBN -81-8069-105-5 (HB)

Second Revised Edition 2004

Published and Printed by
Ashok Kumar Mittal
Concept Publishing Company
A/15-16, Commercial Block, Mohan Garden,
NEW DELHI-110059 (India)

Phones : 25351460, 25351794
Fax : 0091-11-25357103
E-mail : **publishing@conceptpub.com**

To all those who know that

"The heart that has never known sorrow itself will seldom be feelingly alive to the pains and pleasures of his fellow beings. It will seldom be overflowing with that warmth of brotherly love, those kind amiable affections, which dignify human character, even more than the possession of the highest talents."

– My Mother

PREFACE TO THE SECOND EDITION

The first edition of the book ran out of print in 1998. The book has been widely used in India and in several other countries like Vietnam, Bangladesh, Ethiopia, Eriteria and Pakistan. The 'feedback' received from different sources have been very encouraging. Several suggestions were made. The first edition of the book was also used extensively for training development workers from the development sector, government departments and academicians.

Though the book went out of print in 1998, due to pressing engagements, the revision of the book got delayed until 2002, when a major revision was carried out. The revision of the book has been both in terms of organisation of the chapters and the content.

In the first edition, the methodology for micro-level planning was discussed from the perspective for 'problem solving'. In applying the methodology at the ground level, I found that it proceeded to deal with planning for tackling a problem or set of problems. However, there were several occasions where the methodology had to be modified to apply to circumstance where problems did not exist, though micro-level planning was undertaken to "unprove" the well-being of the community, without there being any problem to solve. In planning lexicon, the methodology was robut when applied in the "problem solving" mode or where a "hard system approach" was adopted. The need for adopting the methodology for planning to improve the well-being of the community, irrespective of the existence of a problem or otherwise, emerged several times over. In this edition, therefore, two separate chapters have been included on methodology. *First*, dealing with the "Soft-system Approach", that is, a methodology for micro-level planning where no problem is assumed to exist; the *Second*, dealing with the "Hard-system Approach" to micro-level planning, where a problem has been identified and the process of micro-level planning initiated to tackle the problem.

The chapter on database for micro-level planning has been re-examined and rationalised. It has been seen that having a good database was essential for monitoring and evaluation but attempting at generating too large a database was costly and counterproductive.

Assessment, monitoring and evaluation are essential for any planning system. It was precisely for this reason that a separate chapter on assessment, monitoring and evaluation was included in the first edition. However, the 'science' of (or art of) assessing, monitoring and evaluating micro-level planning has undergone rapid transformation in recent years and the growing literature on the subject is daunting. One chapter in an entire book on assessment, monitoring and evaluation, could not do full justice to the complexity of a wide array of inter-related issues involved. Consequently, the chapter on assessment, monitoring and evaluation has been dropped in the edition. Instead given the pivotal role of "assessment, monitoring and evaluation" in micro-level planning, a companion volume entitled "Participatory Learning and Action in M&E and Participatory Monitoring and Evaluation" is being published, with a fuller treatment of the subject. Newer ideas have been brought in and several major examples of participatory methods being used for monitoring and evaluation have been included.

Thus the organisation of this edition of the book has been made compact and more focussed. Chambers' "Rural Appraisal: Rapid, Relaxed and Participatory", continues to be Chapter 1, classifying the conceptual issues involved in PRA, charting out the transition of Rapid Rural Appraisal (RRA) to Participatory Rural Appraisal (PRA) and providing the details of different disciplines and sources which have contributed to the evolution of PRA. It outlines the principles behind PRA and describes the different tools in the toolbox of Participatory Rural Appraisal. The incorrigible optimist that he is, Chambers misses no opportunity to exhort the readers to improvise, be adaptive, flexible, creative and always listening, always making midway corrections.

In Chapter 2, against the backdrop of the architecture of Participatory Rural Appraisal since re-divistened as Participatory Learning and Action (PLA) the symbiosis between micro-level planning and PRA/PLA has been demonstrated. It is hoped that this brief analysis would set at rest the misgivings about the compatibility of participatory methods and tools with micro-level planning. The chapter tries to establish a broad "consensus" about the similarities in the under-currents and foundations of PRA/PLA vis-a-vis micro-level planning. Since chapter one has dealt with several dimensions of PRA/PLA, in chapter two, only the symbiosis between critical elements of PRA/PLA and micro-level planning have been brought out up front. Thus, for example, the principles of PRA/PLA and the repertoire of PRA/PLA methods were not all re-opened in chapter two, but only representative clusters of these have been examined to provide a glimpse of the symbiosis between PRA/PLA and micro-level planning.

Like in the first edition, Chapter 3 deals with the conceptual issues and untangles the myraid methodological problems in micro-level planning in internalising PRA/PLA. Chapter three has been wholly rewritten. An attempt has also been made to conceptualise a methodology based on live experiences at developing micro-level planning in different parts of India, adopting what is called a "soft systems approach". That is, when the process of planning at micro-level is initiated, there is no presumption made of any problem or issue to be tackled. The analysis of the area (in terms of space, time, preferences, institutions and social and economic relationships) generates the issues and problems, if any, to be dealt within planning for the area. Chapter three then demonstrates how at every stage of such planning some of the "tools" in the "toolbox" of PRA/PLA described in Chapter 1 and 2 can be utilized, to inter-alia, improve the quality of planning both in terms of their content and in terms of their efficacy at involving the people in the adventure of economic development.

Two things need to be underscored here. Firstly, the suggested methodologies for micro-level planning are not cast in stone, in any sense of the term. There is no "one-methodology" for micro-level planning. Chapter 3 describes only one methodology adopted in several parts of India and Africa. The readers are strongly urged to improvise, adapt and developed newer ways of preparing micro-level plans. Second, the participatory "tools" indicated for different steps are also at best indicative. In practice, some of the tools may not work at all and indeed in many cases, may be, newer tools will be required for efficiently planning at the micro-level. Thus the indicative methodologies for micro-level planning and the indicative applicable tools for each step, in the planning processes are to provide some starting points for setting the agenda for a larger debate on the issue. These are not intended at churning out a prescription upon micro-level planners and practitioners of PRA/PLA. At the heart of PRA/PLA is the constant endeavour for improvising, experimenting and inventing newer tools, methods and approaches.

Chapter 4 is a counterpart of chapter three. In Chapter 4 an indicative methodology adopting what is called the "hard systems approach", has been presented. This chapter unlike Chapter 3, suggests a methodology for micro-level planning, where a problem is assumed to exist, such as low levels of income, poverty or what have you, and then proceeds to develop a suggested planning methodology to deal with the problem. The fundamental difference between the methodology of Chapter 3 and Chapter 4, lies in the approach to planning. The riders regarding suggested steps and tools applicable to the micro-level planning in Chapter 3, mutatis mutandis, also apply to Chapter 4.

The issue of lack of data has always been the bone of micro-level planning. It has traditionally been a centrist argument to stall the devolution of power for local level planning and its implementation. And the whole question of determining whether appropriate database for local level planning can be created through PRA/PLA required an adequate response. Chapter 5 is devoted to tackle these issues. The establishment of PRIs (Panchayati Raj Institutions, that is, local level elected bodies) all over the country has taken winds off the sails of those who have persisted with the argument that it is not possible to build a database through PRA/PLA methods for want of an institutional structure to handle the micro-management of tasks involved in building and updating database generated through PRA/PLA. Given that, Chapter 5 provides a broad contours of database that is necessary and that could be developed, without expending huge resources.

The final chapters laydown 4 actual plans for rural development prepared principally through PRA methods, two in Africa, in India and one in Indonesia. They demonstrate the realism of the use of PRA methods in local level planning. They are indicative.

There are certain unconventional terms that appear throughout most of the book. They require clear specification. ''Insiders'' are those who belong to the community. ''Outsiders'' (frequent) are field staff of agencies or departments engaged in local level planning, who visit the communities frequently. ''Outsiders'' (infrequent) are those who seldom visit the community.

The intention of this book is to encourage wider use of participatory methods in micro level planning for rural development and to ignite interest in micro level planning through PRA/PLA. As mentioned in the Preface to the first edition, nobody has as yet said the last word in PRA/PLA, and micro level planning as a discipline is still evolving. Indeed, the same is true of any discipline that is dynamic, evolving and open. That there is always room for improvement for experimentation and for improvising is undeniable. This book is, therefore, like the first edition far from complete, of which I am painfully aware. But given the turn of events overtaking us and resources available, continuing the attempt at removing the lurking doubts about PRA/PLA methods as applied to micro level planning, in the hope, as I said in the first edition that other runners in game would take it forward like a ''baton'' of an ''Olympic Relay Race''. If this edition of book could further accelerate that process, in some humble way, these efforts will be deemed more than amply rewarded.

Robert Chambers has helped me (like many others) immensely in more than one way since 1989, when I first met him on a bitterly cold day, in Mussoorie, India. I have, several times over offered him my big "Thank You", in silence. This book and its companion volume, are tokens of my salute to him for his stalwart support, over the years, to me.

Bangkok
June, 2003

AMITAVA MUKHERJEE

ACKNOWLEDGEMENTS

In the preparation of this book I have received, as always, help and assistance from a multitude of friends and well wishers. The list is too long to be paraded here, and though I wish to spell out some names only, it in no way detracts my grateful thanks to others whom I elect to keep anonymous.

My very best thanks to: Prof. Robert Chambers, Institute of Development Studies, University of Sussex, U.K. for Chapter-1 of the book; Prof. R.P. Misra, and Dr. K.V. Sundaram, for their advice and wise counsel in abundant measure; Prof. Graham Chapman, Professor of Geography, University of London, London, for his comments; Maria G. Quieti, Economist (Training), F.A.O. of the U.N., Rome for all the assistance provided; Prof. Y.K. Alagh, for sparing his time whenever I demanded it of him; to all those officers of the Indian Administrative Services (1991 Batch) who demonstrated the use of PRA in local level planning during their Professional Courses and in particular Ms. Ishita Roy, Dr. Jayatilak, Sri Ashok Khemka, Sri Satyabrata Sahu and Ms. Anu Agarwal; Prof. Neela Mukherjee for her collaborative efforts; and PRA Division, ACTIONAID India for providing me materials available with it. Best thanks are due to Food and Agriculture Organization of the United Nations, Rome for permission to quote parts of The Community Tool Box, Community Forestry Manual 2, by D'Arcy Davis Case *et al.* (Rome: FAO) 1990; Sustainable Agriculture Program, International Institute for Environment and Development and Ethiopian Red Cross Society for Chapter 8; and the Editorial Board of RRA Notes from which portions have been extracted for Chapter 5. My thanks are due to M.K. Tyagi, Centre for Micro-Planning and Regional Studies, L.B.S. National Academy of Administration, Mussoorie, for his help in preparing this work.

Thanks are due to Mr. Iskander, YAYASAN IBEKA, Jakarta; Mrs. Mumpuni Iskandar, YAYASA IBEKA; Hong Peng Liu, UNESCAP; Community Members in Cinta Maker, Indonesia and the Government of Indonesia.

AMITAVA MUKHERJEE

CONTENTS

Preface to the Second Edition *vii*

Acknowledgements *xii*

List of Figures *xvii*

1. Rural Appraisal: Rapid, Relaxed and Participatory 1
   – Robert Chambers

   Introduction, *1*
   Some Sources of PRA, *1*
   From RRA to PRA, *8*
   Definition of PRA, *11*
   The Principles of PRA, *13*
   The Menu of Methods of RRA and PRA, *15*
   Six 'Discoveries' of PRA, *18*
   Utility: Practical Applications, *28*
   Validity and Reliability, *32*
   Reversals and Reality, *41*
   Explaining Our Past Ignorance, *49*
   Dangers, *50*
   Frontiers, Challenges and Potentials, *53*
   The Paradigmatic Significance of PRA, *67*
   Abbreviations and Addresses, *71*
   Appendix-A : Sources of Information, *81*
   Appendix-B : PRA: Start, Stumble, Self-Correct and Share, *84*

2. Micro-Level Planning for Rural Development and Participatory Learning and Action Techniques: Similarities and Potential 87
   – Amitava Mukherjee

   Introduction, *87*

Micro-Level Planning for Rural Development in the Recent Decades, *88*
Relevance of PLA Methods as Tools to Local Level Planning, *89*
Comparison and Training Implications, *101*
Attitudes in Application on PLA, *102*

3. Micro-Level Planning for Rural Development in Participatory Framework : The Soft System Approach 108
– ***Amitava Mukherjee***

Introduction, *108*
PRA: Background and Features, *109*
PLA in Micro-Level Planning, *114*

4. Micro-level Planning for Rural Development in Participatory Framework : The Hard Systems Approach 143
– ***Amitava Mukherjee***

Introduction, *143*
Part I : Pre-Planning Stage, *145*
Part II : Planning Stage, *148*

5. Creation and Maintenance of Alternative Data Bases Through Participatory Rural Appraisal for Rural Development Planning 168
– ***Amitava Mukherjee***

Introduction, *168*
Functions of the Panchayats, *171*
Planning Functions at the Local Level, *172*
Data Requirement of Village Level for the Micro-level Planning, *175*
Data Requirement at Block Level for Planning, *212*
Data Requirement at District Level for Planning, *216*
People's Perception and People's Wisdom, *220*
Participatory Data, *222*
Participatory Methods in Government, *225*
Conclusions, *239*

6. Applications in Africa: Rapid Rural Appraisal for Local Level Planning Wollo Province Ethiopia 241
– ***Irene Guijt*** and ***Ian Scoones***

Introduction, *241*
Objectives and Activities, *241*
Preparation for the Fieldwork, *243*
Field Work Programme, *245*
History of Ancharo, *253*
Agricultural Production, *254*
Livestock Resources in Ancharo, *265*
Natural Resources, *271*
Nutrition, Health and Income Sources, *274*
Problems and Opportunities, *278*

7. Applications in Africa : Rapid Rural Appraisal in Amemo PA, Ambassel, Awraja 288
– ***Irene Guijt*** and ***Ian Scoones***

Introduction, *288*
Introduction to Amemo PA, *290*
Agriculture, *292*
Livestock, *301*
Natural Resources, *303*
Health and Nutrition, *309*
Income Generation, *313*
Problems and Opportunities in Amemo PA, *315*
Findings, *317*
Best Bets for Amemo PA, *318*

8. Application in India: Vikasnagar (Officers of the Indian Administrative Service, 1991 Batch) 326
– ***Amitava Mukherjee***

Introduction, *326*
Source of Finance, *335*
Drinking Water, *336*
Health, Family Welfare and Sanitation, *339*

Education, *350*
Forest – the Green Cover, *359*
Soil Conservation, *366*
Infrastructure, *371*
Sources of Renewable Energy, *373*
Agriculture, *374*
Horticulture, *384*
Vikasnagar Frozen Foods Limited, *387*
Animal Husbandry, *391*
Summary of Financial Allocation, *396*
Conclusion, *397*
Appendix A : Project Report – Vikasnagar Frozen Foods Limited, *399*

9. A Tactical Plan for Appropriation of Benefits from Development of a Mini Hydro Power Plant through Public-Private Partnership Project (At Cinta Mekar Village, Segalaherang Sub-District, Subang District, West Java Province, Indonesia) 406

Introduction, *406*
An Introduction to Cinta Mekar Village, *407*
The Participatory Planning Process, *413*
Some Analysis and Discussion of the Results, *438*
Summary, *441*

Index 445

LIST OF FIGURES

3.1	Search for a System	110
3.2	Social Mapping : This map was drawn by Villagers of Ramenahally village.	113
3.3	The Planning Cycle : Tactical Planning Stage : Stage-1 (Mukherjee methodology)	117
3.3A	Steps of Action Planning Stage	118
3.4	Johari's Window	121
3.5	Dream Map Diagram	123
3.6	Phase of Low Level of Facilitation Warranted	128
3.7	Phase of Low Facilitation and Moving to box – Three of Johari's Window	129
3.8	Activity-Sector Classification Matrix	134
3.9	MSC Analysis – Time Matrix	136
3.10	Project Benefit Matrix	138
3.11	Year-wise Sector-wise Budget Table	139
4.1	Social Mapping : This village resource map was Drawn by villagers of Godavellagudda village	147
4.2	Social Mapping : This map was drawn by Villagers of Ramenahall village	149
4.3	Typical transect from Manjakandriana region	150
4.4	Geographical Transects : This is a transect of a Village in northern Pakistan	151
4.5	Historical Transects of Ardanaryapura Village	154
4.6	Schematic Illustration of Triangulation used in PLA	156
4.7	PLA and the Project Cycle	159
4.8	Seasonal Diagrams : This chart was made by Basapura Villagers	160
4.9	Rapid Food Assessment	161
4.10	Rapid Fertiliser Consumption Assessment	162
4.11	Matrix Ranking in Godavellagudda Village done By the Village Women after First Selecting their own criteria	163
4.12a	to	
4.12e	Classic Illustration monitoring Project for Sal Forest regeneration	165

5.1	Transect through time illustration Land Use Trend In Harrawala Village in Block Doiwala	226
5.2	Transect	227
5.3	Social Map of a Village in Upper Egypt	228
5.4	Health Map, Krishna Rakshit Chak	229
5.5	Wealth Mapping, Village Berapal	230
5.6	Wellbeing Grouping Village Kalsigeriya	231
5.7	A Resource and Social Map of a Village	232
5.8	Mobility Map of Women from Qarara Area Gaza	233
5.9	Venn Diagram of Village Water Use Control in Sudan	234
6.1	Location of Anchard and Amemo Peasant Associations	242
6.2	Land Use in Ancharo	248
6.3	Transect diagram in Ancharo PA	249
6.4	Transect Diagram in Ancharo P.A.	250
6.5	Map of Ancharo (01) PA	251
6.6	Rainfall pattern in Ancharo	252
6.7	Seasonal Calendar of crops	255
6.8	Cropping patterns in good and inlow rainfall years	256
6.9	Seasonal calendar of pests and diseases	261
6.10	Crop rotation in Ancharo (4 years)	262
6.11	Possible irrigation sites in Ancharo	265
6.12	Seasonal calendar of livestock	268
6.13	Percentage of people owning oxen	269
6.14	Seasonal Calendar of disease, Food Supply and Income Sources	270
6.15	Labour calendar of men and women	275
6.16	Income sources in Sida Ager and Gerbi	276
7.1	Matrix for Assessment of Best bets for Ancharo P.A.	291
7.2	Map of Amemo Peasant Association	294
7.3	Land-use distribution of Amemo Peasant Association	295
7.4	Transect of Amemo P.A.	295
7.5	Transect of Amemo P.A.	296
7.6	Seasonal Calendar of crops and pests	297
7.7	Crop choice for Belg and Meher seasons	298

7.8	Crop choice for Meherseason 1983 E.C.	298
7.9	Presence of animals in amemo P.A.	301
7.10	Major soil types in Amemo	305
7.11	History of Abalfo; Geta mountains (wole-Agar) (as told by a 72 years old community member)	306
7.12	Area treated with soil and water conservation Measures	307
7.13	Fuel sources in Amemo P.A. 1983 E.C.	309
7.14	Food scarcity period and increased occurrence of Disease	311
7.15	Preparation of daily foods	312
7.16	Income generation in Amemo	313
7.17	Comparison of living standard (1978-1982 E.C.)	314
7.18	Division of harvest for sale and home consumption	315
7.19	Matrix for assessment of best bets for Amemo PA	324
8.1	District Dehradun	327
8.2	Block Vikasnagar	328
8.3	Social and Resource Map of Timli Village	329
8.4	Seasonal Calendar	331
8.5	Daily Routine of Men/Women	332
8.6	Muslim Basti village Kunja, Vikasnagar map drawn by group of Illiterate Muslim	333
8.7	Village Map of Health Facilities	342
8.8	Seasonal Calendar of Diseases causing Infant motality (Scoring by Seeds)	343
8.9	Seasonal Food Calendar (Consumption scored by Seeds grains)	344
8.10	Incidence of diseases (Scoring by Seeds)	346
8.11	Utility Ranking of Minor Forest Products	360
8.12	Forest Map of Vikasnagar	361
8.13	Soil Erosion Map	368
8.14	Retaining Wall or C.B. of a Check Dam	369
8.15	Dry Check Dam	369
8.16	Agricultural Map of the Block	376
8.17	Priority Ranking Matrix by Farmers	380
8.18	IRR of Project	389
8.19	IRR Project AV Selling Price (in Rs. Kg.)	389
8.20	IRR Project AV Procurement Price (in Rs. Kg.)	389
9.1	Well-being chart as used by participants to express the state of their wealth and expectancy	436
9.2	The present state of well-being and the expected impact of the project on Cinta Mekar Village	437

1

Rural Appraisal
Rapid, Relaxed And Participatory

– ROBERT CHAMBERS

INTRODUCTION

The past decade has witnessed more shifts in the rhetoric of rural development than in its practice. These shifts include the now familiar reversals from top-down to bottom-up, from centralized standardization to local diversity, and from blueprint to learning process. Linked with these, there have also been small beginnings of changes in modes of learning. The move here is away from extractive survey questionnaires and towards participatory appraisal and analysis in which more and more activities, previously appropriated by outsiders, are carried out by local rural or urban people themselves.

In these changes, a part has been played by two closely related families of approaches and of methods, often referred to as Rapid Rural Appraisal (RRA) which spread in the 1980s, and its further evolution into Participatory Rural Appraisal (PRA) which has come about fast and begun to spread in the 1990s. The purposes of this chapter are to outline the origins, principles, approaches, methods and applications of both RRA and PRA; and for PRA, to explore and assess its strengths, weaknesses, potentials and paradigmatic significance.

SOME SOURCES OF PRA

The approaches and methods described as PRA and evolving so fast that to propose one secure and final definition would be unhelpful. As PRA further evolves, there will be changes in what it can usefully mean. It has been called 'an approach and method for learning about rural life and conditions from, with and by rural people'. The prepositions have sometimes been reversed in order to read 'by, with and from'. PRA is, though, more than just learning. It extends into analysis, planning and action. PRA as a term is also used to describe a variety of approaches. To cover these a recent description is that PRA is: 'a family of approaches and methods to enable rural people to share, enhance and analyze their knowledge of life and conditions to plan and to act'.

PRA, as it exists in the early 1990s, has evolved from, draws on and resonates with several sources and traditions. Some of its methods do appear to be new; but some have been rediscoveries (see for example some described in Whyte 1977; Pelto and Pelto 1978; and Rhoades 1990). In understanding what has happened, it makes no sense to try to separate out causes, effects, innovations, influences and diffusion as though they follow straight lines. In a world of continuously quicker and closer communication, transfers and sharing have become more and more rapid and untraceable. So these sources and traditions have, like flows in a braided stream, intermingled more and more over the past decade, and each also continues in several forms; but directly or indirectly all have contributed to a confluence in PRA; and as with other confluence, the flow has speeded up, and innovation and change have accelerated to cover new ground.

Five streams which stand out as sources and parallels to PRA are in alphabetical order:

1. Activist participatory research,
2. Agroecosystem analysis,
3. Applied anthropology,
4. Field research on farming systems, and
5. Rapid rural appraisal.

Activist Participatory Research

The term 'activist participatory research' is used to refer to a family of approaches and methods which use dialogue and participatory research to enhance people's awareness and confidence, and to empower their action. Activist participatory research in this sense owes much to the work and inspiration of Paulo Freire, to his book *Pedagogy of the Oppressed* (1968), and to the practice and experience of consciencization in Latin America. The Freirian theme, that poor and exploited people can and should be enabled to conduct their own analysis of their own reality, has been widely influential, even though it has remained a minority view among development professionals as a whole. Two related schools have been known as participatory research and participatory action research (PAR).

Participatory research has been associated with the adult education movement since at least 1975 (Convergence 1975; 1981; 1988:3). Regional networks were set up. An African regional workshop on Participatory Research was held in Tanzania in 1979 (Kassam and Mustafa 1982). In India, the Society for Participatory Research in Asia (SPR in Asia 1982) has sought to spread the philosophy and practice of participatory research. Participatory research has been conducted in widely differing conditions (Rahman 1984). For example, in Bangladesh, as recorded in The Net (BRAC 1983), poor and powerless people took part in investigation and analysis of the power structure in ten villages, and of how benefits directed towards them by the Government were intercepted by the local elite. In the United States, the Highlander Centre in rural Appalachia has worked to enable underprivileged communities to gain confidence in their own knowledge and abilities, and to take political action (Gaventa and Lewis 1991).

For its part, participatory action research (PAR) has been parallel and overlapping with participatory research, and has had strong associations with industry and agriculture (Whyte 1991).

Activist participatory research has taken different forms and has been practised by people with a range of ideological positions, from radical crypto-paternalism to open-ended facilitation. Its special focus on the underprivileged and on political action has threatened established interests, whether political or professional, and limited its spread. In practice, much PRA has similarly been concerned with poverty and equity.

The contributions of the activist participatory research stream to PRA have been more through concepts than methods. Key commonly shared ideas and imperatives that stand out are:

(a) Poor people are creative and capable, and can and should do much of their own investigation, analysis and planning,
(b) Outsiders have a role as convenors, catalysts and facilitators, and
(c) The weak should be empowered.

Agroecosystem Analysis

Agroecosystem analysis (Conway 1985, 1986, 1987) was developed in Thailand from 1978 onwards, initially at the University of Chiang Mai, by Gordon Conway and his colleagues (Gypmantasiri *et al.*, 1980). It spread first through Southeast Asia and then elsewhere. Drawing on systems and ecological thinking, it has combined analysis of systems and system properties (productivity, stability, sustainability and equitability) with pattern analysis of space (maps and transects), time (seasonal calendars and long-term trends), flows and relationships (flow, casual, Venn and other diagrams), relative values (bar diagrams of relative sources of income, etc.) and decisions (decision trees and other decision diagrams). The approach was further developed by Conway and others with the Aga Khan Rural Support Programme (Pakistan) for cost-effective application in villages in Northern Pakistan, where it took a form which led quickly to identification and assessment of practical hypotheses for action.

Agroecosystem analysis was so powerful and practical that it quickly overlapped with and contributed much to RRA. In some cases, either or both labels could be used to describe what was done. Some of the major contributions of agroecosystem analysis to current RRA and PRA have been:

1. transects (systematic walks and observation);
2. informal mapping (sketch maps and drawn on site);

3. diagramming (seasonal calendars, flow and causal diagrams; bar charts, Venn or 'chapati' diagrams); and
4. innovation assessment (scoring and ranking different actions).

Applied Anthropology

Social anthropology in its classical forms has been concerned more with understanding than with changing, but especially in the 1980s, applied anthropology and development anthropology became more recognized as legitimate and useful activities. In the USA, the Institute for Development Anthropology established a network and a regular Bulletin. A very small number of social anthropologists found their way into the International Agricultural Research Centres, where they had an influence disproportionate to their tiny numbers, and the social anthropologists in aid agencies rose in numbers and status, though they were still few. Social anthropologists helped development professionals generally better to appreciate the richness of the validity of rural people's knowledge (e.g. IDS 1979; Brokensha, Warren and Werner 1980), and to distinguish the etic – the outsider's mental frame, categories and worldview, and the emic – those of the insider. And *The Art of the Informal Agricultural Survey* (1982), by Robert Rhoades, a social anthropologist at the International Potato Centre in Peru, was widely read and influential – far beyond the informal form of its publication.

In one methodological stream, the approaches of social anthropology were adopted in health and nutrition in rapid assessment procedures (RAP) (Scrimshaw and Hurtado 1987) and in rapid ethnographic assessment (REA) (Bentley *et al.* 1988), which variously used conversation, observation, informal interviews and focus groups.

PRA represents an extension and application of social anthropological insights, approaches and methods, cross-fertilized with others. Some of the many insights and contributions coming from and shared with social anthropology have been :

- the idea of field learning as flexible art rather than rigid science;

- the value of field residence, unhurried participant – observation and conversations;
- the importance of attitudes, behaviour and support;
- the emic-etic distinction; and
- the validity of indigenous technical knowledge.

Field Research on Farming Systems

Field research on farming systems, whether by social anthropologists, geographers, agricultural economists or biological scientists, has revealed the complexity, diversity and rationality of much apparently untidy and unsystematic farming practice, D.G.R. Belshaw at Makerere in the 1960s, David Norman and his colleagues at Ahmadu Bello University in Northern Nigeria in the 1970s, and Richard Harwood in Thailand (Harwood 1979) were among those who showed the good sense of practices like mixed cropping (e.g. Norman 1975). Farming systems research (FSR) and write up, inaccurate and unreliable in data obtained, leading to reports, if any, which were long, late, boring, misleading, difficult to use, and anyway ignored.

The third origin was more positive. More cost-effective methods of learning were sought. This was helped by the growing recognition of development professionals to the painfully obvious fact that rural people were themselves knowledgeable on many subjects which touched their lives. What became known as indigenous technical knowledge (ITK) (IDS 1979; Brokensha, Warren and Werner 1980) was then increasingly seen to have richness and value for practical purposes. One major question, as it seemed then, was how to tap ITK more effectively as a source of information for analysis and use by outsider professionals.

Towards the end of the 1970s, though most of those professionals, who were inventing and using methods which were quicker and more cost-effective than `respectable' questionnaire surveys, were reluctant to write about what they did, fearing for their professional credibility. They felt compelled to conform to standard statistical norms, however, costly and crude their applications, and obliged in their reports and publications to use conventional methods, categories and masseurs. In a classic statement, Michael Collinson (1980) described how he would take only a week to conduct an exploratory survey to identify agricultural research priorities, but would then feel obliged to follow this with a formal verification survey which represented the major commitment of professional time and funds. This more costly exercise had always confirmed the exploratory survey but the numbers which this formal survey provides are the only hard evidence produced by the diagnostic process. This is extremely important in convincing 'the Establishment' (*ibid.*:444). To convince, the researcher had to be conservative; but the process was costly and decisions and action were delayed.

Rapid Rural Appraisal

In the 1980s, in some places, the situation was transformed. The family of approaches and methods known as Rapid Rural Appraisal (RRA) gained increasing acceptance. It began to be seen that it had its own principles and rigour (Chambers 1980; Belshaw 1981; Carruthers and Chambers 1981). In the early 1980s, RRA was argued to be cost-effective, especially for gaining timely information, but still with some sense that it might only be a second-best. But by the mid-1980s, the RRA approaches and methods, when properly conducted, were more and more eliciting a range and quality of information and insights inaccessible through more traditional methods. Except when rushed and unself-critical, RRA came out better by criteria of cost-effectiveness, validity and reliability as compared to more conventional methods (see Validity and Reliability). In many contexts and for many purposes, RRA, when well done, showed itself to be not a second-best but the best.

In establishing the methods and principles of RRA, many people and institutions took part. No account can do justice to them, and with imperfect knowledge there is no way of avoiding significant omissions. An earlier attempt to list countries where RRA has been developed identified 12 in Africa, eight in South and Southeast Asia, three in Latin America, three in Australasia and the Pacific and one in Europe. Perhaps more than any other movement, agroecosystem analysis in Southeast Asia introduced new methods and established new credibility. In the mid 1980s, the University of Khon Kaen in Thailand was a world leader in developing the theory and methods, especially for multi-disciplinary teams, and in institutionalizing RRA as a part of professional training. The International Conference on Rapid Rural Appraisal held at University of Khon Kaen in 1985, and the published volume of papers which resulted on KKU 1987, were landmarks. The practical value of RRA was confirmed and its underlying theory outlined (Beebe 1987; Gibbs 1987; Grandstaff and Grandstaff 1987a; Jamieson 1987). Then in the latter 1980s, RRA was further developed and disseminated through extensive training by the International Institute for Environment and Development (IIED), based in London, working with colleagues mainly in Africa and Asia, and through its publications, especially the informal publication RRA Notes (1988).

In specialized fields, too, there were parallel and overlapping developments. In health and nutrition, for example, Rapid Assessment Procedures (RAP) (Scrimshaw and Hurtado (1987) were practised in at least 20 countries. In agriculture, some practitioners of farming systems research and extension innovated with higher, quicker methods in an RRA style. In irrigation, a small body of literature built up on RRA (e.g. Potten 1985; Groenfeldt 1989), and 'hard' journals published papers on RRA.

RRA began and continues as a better way for outsiders to learn. In answering the question–whose knowledge counts? – it sought, and continues to seek, to enable outsiders to gain information and insight from rural people and about rural conditions, and to do this in a more cost-effective and timely manner. It was, and remains, less exploitative than extractive questionnaire surveys where much is taken by outsider, and little or nothing is given back. All the same, like most past farming systems research, its normal mode entails outsiders obtaining information, taking it away and analyzing it. This is valid and useful activity which has and will continue to have its place. Depending on one's point of view and the context, the normal practice of non-participatory RRA can be described as extractive, or, more neutrally, elicitive.

FROM RRA TO PRA

In the mid 1980s, the words 'participatory' and 'participation' entered the RRA vocabulary. They already had a long history in rural development. We cite two examples. For some years in the 1970s and early 1980s, under the leadership of Norman Uphoff and others, Cornell University published the Rural Development Participation Review until USAID terminated its support, and participation was a recurrent theme in the contributions to Michael Cernea's book, edited for the World Bank, *Putting People First* (1985) which drew on experience from earlier years. It was at the 1985 Khon Kaen International Conference that participation began, albeit modestly, to be used in connection with RRA. Discussions at the Conference generated a typology of seven types of RRA (KKU 1987: 17) of which 'participatory RRA' was one. For this, the dominant purpose was seen as stimulating community awareness, with the outsider's role as catalyst. Later, in 1988, participatory RRAs were listed by the IIED team as one of four classes of RRA methodologies – the others being exploratory RRAs, topical RRAs and monitoring RRAs (McCracken *et al.* 1988).

In 1988, there were parallel developments in Kenya and India. In Kenya, the National Environment Secretariat, in association with Clark University, conducted an RRA in Mbusanyi, a community in Machakos district which led to the adoption in September of a Village Resource Management Plan (Kabutha and Ford 1988). This was subsequently described as a Participatory Rural Appraisal, and the method outlined in two Handbooks (PID and NES 1989; NES 1980). Around the same time in 1988, the Aga Khan Rural Support Programme (India) was interested in developing participatory RRA, and invited IIED to help. Jennifer McCracken carried out a four-week consultancy with AKRSP in Gujarat in September and October 1988 during which participatory rapid rural appraisals were conducted by and with villagers and AKRSP staff in two villages (McCracken 1988). In different ways, both the Kenya and Indian experiences were seminal for understanding and for the development of PRA.

Subsequently, there was an explosion of innovation in India (for which see *RRA Notes* 13) especially but not only in the NGO sector. MYRADA, based in Bangalore, trained its senior staff in PRA in early 1990 (Ramachandran 1990) and came to play a major role in training for other NGOs and for government.

AKRSP continued to innovate and broke new ground in showing how well village volunteers could themselves be facilitators of PRA. Action Aid, Bangalore undertook a networking role. Any listing of the NGOs that pioneered at an early stage would include (in alphabetical order) Action Aid, Bangalore; Activists of Social Alternatives, Trichy; the Aga Khan Rural Support Programme (India); Krishi Gram Vikas Kendra, Ranchi; MYRADA, Bangalore; Seva Bharti, Midnapore District; SPEECH, Madurai; and Youth for Action, Hyderabad. Government organizations that received and promoted training included the Drylands Development Board, Karnataka; the District Rural Development Agencies, Andhra Pradesh; and several Forestry Departments. PRA methods were adopted by the National Academy of Administration, Mussoorie for the fieldwork of its 300-odd Indian Administrative Service probationers each year, and by the Zavier Institute of Social Services, Ranchi, which introduced PRA for the fieldwork of its students.

At the same time, cross-fertilization and spread took place internationally. The small group of the Sustainable Agriculture Programme at IIED, with support from the Ford Foundation and SIDA, was decisively influential through its activities in Africa and Asia, and spread PRA and its methods through 30 substantial field-based training workshops in 15 countries and through publications and papers, especially RRA Notes: Manuals were written (e.g. McCracken *et al.* 1988; Gueye and Freudenberger 1990, 1991; Theis and Brady 1991). Among international NGOs, Intercooperation (Berne) and Action Aid (London) were prominent in seeking to promote PRA. Spread from India took place to Nepal from the initiative of Winrock International and to Sri Lanka on the initiative of Intercooperation. In early 1992, Action Aid, AKRSP and MYRADA were hosts in India to an International Roving PRA Workshop with 14 people from 11 countries in the South, and PRA or PRA-type activities were continuing to evolve independently in many countries.

A summary comparison of what are normally described as RRA and PRA is given in Table 1.1.

Table 1.1 : RRA and PRA Compared

	RRA	PRA
Period of major development	Late 1970s, 1980s	Late 1980s, 1990s
Major innovators based in	Universities	NGOs
main users	Aid agencies, Universities	NGOs, Govt. field organizations
Key resource earlier Overlooked	Local people's knowledge	Local people's capabilities
Main innovation	Methods	Behaviour
Predominant mode	Elicitive, extractive	Facilitating, participatory
Ideal objectives	Learning by outsiders	Empowerment of local people
Longer-term outcomes	Plans, projects, publications	Sustainable local action and institution

Now, in mid-1992, since activities described as PRA were spreading rapidly, taking activities described as PRA, stock of the principles of PRA, its methods, applications, strengths, weaknesses, potentials and paradigmatic significance is overdue.

DEFINITION OF PRA

It has been questioned whether it is useful to define PRA as separate from RRA. One view is that labels do not matter. There is a plethora of levels for approaches and methods of learning about rural life and conditions. Many of the sets of practices overlap. There is continuous innovation, sharing and exchange. In this view, the only importance of a label is the sense of pride of ownership and originality which it gives, so strengthening commitment, enthusiasm and good work among its practitioners. Otherwise, there would be no point in defining an exclusive territory of activities for PRA or any other set of approaches or methods.

The opposite view is that good PRA often implies radical personal and institutional change, and that the term should not be debased by being used for anything less than this. In this view, the claim that 'PRA is a simple methodology…' (PID and NES

1989: 1) is misleading, since personal and institutional changes are so rarely simple or easy. Moreover, if PRA becomes fashionable, many will label and relabel their work as PRA, though when in fact it is still extractive rather than participatory, and when their behaviour and attitudes are unchanged.

A balanced view may be that since we are concerned here with static terms – RRA and PRA –for combinations and fluxes of activities which are far from static, and which take different forms in different places, labels can help to define what belongs to where. This may serve to encourage better performance. The legitimating label of RRA has already been used quite widely to describe sloppy and bad work: see for example, a critique of a quick but heavily biased 'RRA' survey in Zambia (Pottier 1991), and some of the observations in a wide-ranging review of RRA activities in the Philippines (van Steijn 1991). The label of PRA could similarly be used to legitimate bad work; it could also be misused to describe RRA which is elicitive or extractive rather than participatory. In this view, then, it would make sense to have separate definitions, with RRA as a form of data collection by outsiders who then take it away and analyse it; and PRA as more participatory, meaning that outsiders and convenors, catalysts and facilitators to enable people to undertake and share their own investigations and analysis. There is, then, a distinction between 'an RRA' and 'a PRA'. An RRA is intended for learning by outsiders. A PRA is intended to enable local people to conduct their own analysis, and often to plan and take action.

In practice, there is a continuum between RRA and PRA. This can be understood through a description of methods. Some methods, like direct observation and semi-structured interviewing, have been emphasized in RRA but can be a vital part of good PRA. Other methods, like participatory mapping, where local people make their own maps, and participatory diagramming are emphasized in PRA but can also be used in an RRA mode. The continuum is illustrated in Table 1.2.

For both RRA and PRA, good performance requires that practitioners and facilitators follow basic principles. Some are fully shared and some have been additionally emphasized in PRA.

Table 1.2 : Continuum between RRA and PRA

Nature of Process	RRA ⟷	PRA
Mode	Extractive-elicitive	Sharing-empowering
Outsiders' role	Investigator ⟷	Facilitator
Information owned, analyzed and used by	Outsiders ⟷	Local People
Methods used	RRA ⟷	PRA

Most of these principles have been induced rather than deduced: they have been elicited by trying out practices, finding what works and what does not, and then asking why. Different practitioners would list different principles underlying RRA and PRA (see e.g. Grandstaff. Grandstaff and Lovelace 1987:9-13; McCracken, Pretty and Conway 1988:12-13; Gueye and Freundenberger 1990:10-19), but most might agree to include the following :

THE PRINCIPLES OF PRA

Principles shared by RRA and PRA

- *A reversal of learning :* to learn from rural people, directly, on the site, and face-to face, gaining from local, physical, technical and social knowledge.
- *Learning rapidly and progressively :* with conscious exploration, flexible use of methods, opportunism, improvisation, iteration and crosschecking; not following a blueprint programme but being adaptable in a learning process.
- *Offsetting biases :* especially those of rural development' tourism, by being relaxed and not rushing, listening not lecturing, probing instead of passing on to the next topic, being unimposing instead of important, and seeking out the poorer men and women, and learning their concerns and priorities.

- *Optimizing trade-offs :* relating the costs of learning to the useful truth of information, with trade-offs between quantity, relevance, accuracy and timeliness. This includes the principles of optimal ignorance – knowing what is not worth knowing, and of appropriate imprecision – not measuring more than needed. As Keynes is reputed to have said: 'it is better to be approximately right than precisely wrong'.
- *Triangulating :* meaning using a range (sometimes three), of methods, types of information, investigators and/or disciplines to cross-check (Grandstaff, Grandstaff and Lovelace 1987:9-10; Gueye and Freudenberger 1991: 14-16).
- *Seeking diversity :* this has been expressed in terms of seeking variability rather than averages (Beebe 1987:53-53)' and has been described in Australia as the principle of maximum diversity, or 'maximizing the diversity and richness of information' (Dunn and McMillan 1991:5, 8). This can involve sampling in a non-statistical sense. It goes beyond the crosschecking of triangulation; for defined broadly it deliberately looks for, notices and investigates contradictions, anomalies and differentness.

Additional Principles Stressed in PRA

To these shared principles, PRA adds others:

Facilitating – they do it : facilitating investigation, analysis, presentation and learning by rural people themselves, so that they present and own the outcomes, and also learn. This has been expressed as 'handing over the stick' (or pen or chalk). This often entails an outsider starting a process and then sitting back or walking away, and not interviewing or interrupting.

Self-critical awareness and responsibility : meaning that facilitators are continuously examining their behaviour and trying to do better. This includes embracing error – welcoming error as an opportunity to learn to do better;

and using one's own best judgement at all times, meaning accepting personal responsibility rather than vesting it in a manual or a rigid set of rules.

Sharing of information and ideas between rural people, between them and facilitators, and between different facilitators, as also sharing field camps, training and experiences between different organizations.

All these principles are behavioural, since they are applied in practice by people doing things. But those shared by RRA and PRA are more epistemological, while those of PRA are more personal. And this difference indicates the new emphasis placed in PRA on the behaviour and attitudes of outsiders in their interactions with rural people, an emphasis which could usefully be part of future RRA as well as PRA.

THE MENU OF METHODS OF RRA AND PRA

In its early days, RRA seemed to be largely organized commonsense. During the 1980s, though, creative ingenuity was applied and more methods borrowed, adapted and invented, many with a more participatory mode. A summary listing of headings can give some indication of the types of methods being used in mid-1992 without being exhaustive. All the methods can be used in both RRA and PRA, but some are more emphasized in one than the other.

Secondary sources : such as files, reports, maps, aerial photographs, articles and books.

Do-it-yourself : asking to be taught to perform village tasks – transplanting, weeding, ploughing, field-levelling, drawing water, collecting wood, washing clothes, thatching, etc.

Key informants : enquiring who are the experts and seeking them out.

Semi-structural interviews : This has been regarded by some as the 'core' of good RRA (Grandstaff and Grandstaff 1987b). It can entail having a mental or written checklist, but being open-ended and following up on the unexpected. Increasingly, it is using participatory visual as well as traditional verbal methods.

Groups : of various kinds (casual, specialist/focus, deliberately structured, community/neighbourhood). Group interviews and activities are part of many of the methods.

Sequences or chains of interviews : from group to group; or from group to key informant; or a sequence of key informants, each expert on a different stage of a process (e.g. men on ploughing, women on transplanting and weeding....) etc.

They do it : villagers and village residents investigators and researches: women, poor people, school teachers, volunteers, students, farmers, village specialists. They do transect, observe, interview other villagers, analyze data and present the results.

Participatory mapping and modelling : in which people use the ground, floor or paper to make social, demographic, health, natural resource (soils, trees and forests, water resources etc.) or farm maps, or construct three dimensional models of their land.

Participatory analysis of aerial photographs : (often best at 1:5000) to identify soil type, land conditions, land tenure, etc.

Transect walks : systematically walking with informants through an area, observing, asking, listening, discussing, identifying different zones, local technologies, introduced technologies, seeking problems, solutions and opportunities, and mapping and diagramming resources and findings.

Time lines : chronologies of events, listing major remembered events in a village with approximate dates.

Trend analysis : people's accounts of the past, of how things close to them have changed, ecological histories changes in land use and cropping patterns, changes in customs and practices, changes and trends in population, migration, fuels used, education, health, credit... and the causes of changes and trends.

Ethno biographies : local histories of a crop, an animal, a tree, a pest, a weed.

Seasonal diagramming : by major season or by month, to show days and distribution of rain, amount of rain or soil moisture, crops, agricultural labour, non-agricultural labour, diet, food consumption, types of sickness, prices, animal fodder, fuel, migration, income, expenditure, debt, etc.

Participatory diagramming : of flows, causality, quantities, trends, rankings, scorings – in which people make their own diagrams – systems diagrams, bar diagrams, pie charts, etc. *'Chapati'* or Venn diagramming is one form, method for identifying individuals and institutions important in and for a community and their relationships.

Well-being or wealth ranking : identifying clusters of households according to well-being or wealth, including those considered poorest or worst off (*RRA Notes* 15).

Analysis of difference : especially by gender, social group, wealth/poverty, occupation and age. Identifying differences between groups, including their problems and preferences. This includes contrast comparisons – asking one group why another is different or does something different, and *vice versa.*

Scoring and ranking : especially using matrices and seeds to compare through scoring, for example, different trees, or soils, or methods of soil and water conservation, or varieties of a crop.

Estimates and quantification : often using local measures, judgements and materials such as seeds, pellets, fruits or stones as counters, sometimes combined with participatory maps and models.

Key local indicators : such as poor people's criteria of well-being.

Key probes : questions which can lead direct to key issues such as – 'What do you talk about when you are together?' 'What new practices have you or others in this village experimented with in recent years?' 'What vegetable, tree, crop variety, type of animal, tool, equipment.... would you like to try out?' `What do you do when someone's hut or house burns down?'

Stories, portraits and case studies : such as a household history and profile, coping with a crisis, how a conflict was or was not resolved....

Team contracts and interactions : contracts drawn up by teams with agreed norms of behaviour; modes of interaction within teams, including changing pairs, evening discussions, mutual criticism and help, etc. (The team may be just outsiders, or a joint team with villagers).

Presentations and analysis : where maps, models, diagrams and findings are presented by villagers, or by outsiders, and checked, corrected and discussed.

Participatory planning, budgeting and monitoring : in which villagers prepare their own plans, budgets and schedules, and monitor progress.

Brainstorming : by villagers alone, by villagers and outsiders together, or by outsiders alone.

Short, simple questionnaires : (if at all) late in the process, designed to fill dummy tables which are by then known to be needed.

Report writing : at once, either in the field before returning to office or headquarters, or by one or more people who are designated in advance to do this immediately on completion of the RRA and PRA.

SIX 'DISCOVERIES' OF PRA

PRA has broken new ground, but every historian knows that there is nothing new under the sun, and what appear to be 'discoveries' are often only rediscoveries. Perhaps it is safest to express this personally, and to say that for me there have been discoveries, although some of them may be old hat for others. To understand more of the background, let us look further at the contrast between traditional extractive research and RRA on the one hand, and PRA on the other.

A major difference between research and RRA which are extractive, and PRA which is participatory, is in behaviour, attitudes and roles. In extractive research and RRA the outsiders – 'we' – are dominant. We determine the agenda, obtain and take possession of information, remove it, organize and analyze it, and plan and write papers and reports. We appropriate and come to own the information. We are collectors, processors and producers of outputs. In PRA, this is largely reversed. 'We' encourage and allow 'them' to be dominant to determine much of the agenda, to gather, express and analyze information, and to plan. We are facilitators, learners and consultants. Our activities are to establish rapport, to convene and catalyze, to enquire, to help in the use of methods, and to encourage people to choose and improvise methods for themselves. We watch, listen and learn. Metaphorically, and sometimes actually, we 'hand over the stick' of authority.

'They' then do many of the things we formerly did (and believed, often enough, that only we could do). They make maps and models; they walk transects and observe; they investigate and interview; they diagram and analyze; they present information; they plan. In consequence, they are more in command of investigation, they own and retain more of the information, and they are strongly placed to identify their priorities for action, and then to determine and control that action.

The participatory orientation of PRA has given new impetus to the development of methods. One of the delights of PRA has been the lack of a blueprint. Participation generates diversity; villagers play a part in interpreting, applying and sometimes inventing the methods themselves. Villagers and outsiders alike are encouraged to improvise in a spirit of play. What is done in different each time, the outcome of a creative interaction. In consequence, the three years to mid-1992 have witnessed many inventions, especially but not only in India and Nepal. Reviewing the participatory innovation of the past three years, six salient 'discoveries' stand out:

Villagers' Knowledge and Capabilities

The first discovery is that villagers have a greater capacity to map, model, quantify and estimate, rank, score and diagram than outsiders have generally supposed them capable of.

Participatory mapping and modelling (Mascarenhas and Kumar 1991) has been a most striking finding. An earlier work on mental maps (Gould and White 1974) did not reveal the richness of detail and discrimination expressed recently by villagers in India and elsewhere through participatory mapping. A working hypothesis is that in general rural people in the South have more extensive and detailed mental maps than urban people in the North; and that given the right conditions and materials, they can express this visibly on the ground or on paper, either as maps or as three-dimensional models (for example, of watersheds). They have now created many hundreds of such maps and models in at least 12 states in India, and in countries as different as Botswana, Burkina Faso (Hahn 1990). Cap Verde, Ethiopia, the Gambia, Honduras, Kenya, Nigeria, Pakistan, the Philippines, Senegal, Sri Lanka, Tanzania, Vietnam, Zambia and Zimbabwe either showing the huts and houses in a village (a social map) or the surrounding village area (a resources map), or combining both. Most recently, they have been indicating social details, using local materials such as seeds, stones and vegetables, or markers such as *bindis* (the small spots Indian women place on their foreheads). These are placed on cards or on the ground or on the maps or models to indicate for each household the numbers of men, women and children, assets owned, wealth/poverty, the handicapped, immunization status, education and other informations. With an informed group or person, a participatory census of a small village can be conducted in less than an hour, and then much other information added by 'interviewing the map'. Similarly, with quantification, estimating, ranking, scoring and diagramming, when the methods and materials are right, villagers have shown themselves capable of generating and analyzing information far beyond normal professional expectations.

To enable these capabilities to be expressed, the principle has been to assume that people can do something until proved otherwise. It has been following the principle that participatory mapping and modelling, Venn diagramming, matrix ranking and scoring, and other methods have been 'discovered' not as one-off achievements, but as near-universals, that people appear able to use largely independently of culture or literacy. They then provide people with the occasion and means to reflect on and rank problems and opportunities as they perceive them, and to express their preference – for improving their farming systems, for managing and using of common property resources, for better livelihoods, for health interventions, for species mixes in tree nurseries, for the qualities of new varieties of a crop, for amenities and their location, for development actions in their communities, and so on.

In all this, both methods and materials have been important in enabling villagers' capabilities to be expressed. But these in themselves are not enough.

Relaxed Rapport

The second discovery is that relaxed rapport between outsiders and rural people can and should be established early in the process.

Rapport is a key to facilitating participation. Relaxed rapport between outsider and villager, and some measure of trust are minimum predisposing conditions for PRA. In the past, two extreme types of interactions between outsiders and rural people have missed major opportunities: the rushed and unselfcritical rural development tourist had neither the time and nor the sensitivity to get far beyond formal mutual misunderstanding; and the pure social anthropologist has allowed so much time and shown such sensitivity that she or he has come to believe that only through prolonged residence can good rapport and good insights be gained. The two 'cultures' – of rushed visitor, and of resident expert – have conspired to conceal the potential for gaining rapport early and well, and early enough and well enough for the honest and accurate sharing of detailed knowledge and values. To a hardened 'old hand' at rural development tourism (the senior official: 'I was born and brought up in a village', 'I am a farmer myself' 'You can't pull the wool over my eyes') this might seem unnecessary: he (most are men) knows it all and has an automatic good rapport with all rural people. To a seasoned social anthropologist (the university professor. 'It took a year before they would tell me that....'), this might seem an affront: it would be unfair if others in a short time could achieve what had taken her (relatively more are women) so long. For anyone who has endured and struggled through months of residence and participant-observation to achieve rapport and insight, learning a new language and living a new life, it could seem unlikely and even unwelcome, that outsiders should find ways to establish rapport and glean good insights more quickly and with pleasure, participation and fun.

Empirically, though, the finding again and again with PRA is that if the initial behaviour and attitudes of outsiders are relaxed and right, and if the process can start, the methods of PRA themselves foster further rapport. Early actions by outsiders can include transparent honesty about who they are and what they are doing; and participation in village activities, especially being taught and performing village tasks. Personal demeanour counts, showing humility, respect, patience and interest in what villagers have to say and show; wandering around and not rushing; and paying attention, listening, watching and not interrupting. Then villagers quickly lose themselves in activities such as participatory mapping and modelling and matrix scoring. In contrast with questionnaires, they do not have a sense that information is being handed over, to be taken away. It is theirs. They own it, but share it. They often enjoy the creativity of what they are doing, and what they see and learn through it. The pleasure, fun and utility of what they have been helped to start doing express themselves in rapport. By reinforcing rapport, PRA methods thus sustain and strengthen the participatory process of which they are a part.

Diagramming and Visual Sharing

The third discovery is the popularity and power of participatory diagramming and visual sharing.

Diagramming and visual sharing are common elements in much of PRA. With a questionnaire survey, information is appropriated by the outsider. It is transferred from the words of the person interviewed to the paper of the questionnaire schedule where it becomes the possession of the interviewer. The learning is one-off. The information becomes personal and private, unverified and owned by the interviewer. In contrast, with visual sharing of a map, model, diagram, or units (stones, seeds, small fruits, etc.) used for ranking, scoring, counting or quantification, all who are present can see, point to, discuss, manipulate and alter physical objects or representations. Triangulation takes place with people crosschecking and correcting each other. The learning is progressive. The information is visible, semi-permanent and public, and is checked, verified, amended, added to and owned by the participants.

For example, in participatory mapping and modelling, villagers draw and model their villages and resources, deciding what to include, and debating, adding and modifying detail. Everyone can see what is being 'said' because it is being 'shown'. In shared diagramming, information is diagrammed to represent, for example, seasonal changes in dimensions such as rainfall, agricultural labour, income, indebtedness, food supply and migration. Paper can be used for diagrams, but the ground and other local materials have the advantage of being 'theirs', media which villagers, whether literate or illiterate, can command and alter with confidence. The diagram also presents a visible checklist or agenda which is theirs.

Sequences

The fourth discovery is the power and popularity of sequence of participatory methods.

Some of the participatory methods have been known and used in the past (Rhoades 1990). There are now some new ones, but perhaps more striking is the power of combinations and sequences which has been revealed (Shah 1991). To take some examples:

With participatory mapping, villagers draw not one, but several maps, which become successively more detailed and useful, or which present new and complementary information. (The same can apply with other methods).

Social mapping provides a basis for household listings, and for indicating population, social group, health and other household characteristics. This can lead to identification of key informants, and then to discussions with them (This is a useful sequence in many topic of RRAs and PRAs).

A participatory resource map leads to planning transect walks in which villagers, who made the map, act as guides for outsiders. The transects in turn lead to the identification and discussion of problems and opportunities, which then lead to listing and ranking options or 'best bets'.

A participatory resource map of an area of degraded forest, and a rootstock census of quadrats in the forest carried out by villagers leads to a calculation of numbers of trees to be planted; and debate and analysis lead to people's decisions about the proportions of different trees to be planted and the numbers required in tree nurseries (M. Shah forthcoming).

A village social map provides an up-to-date household listing which is then used for well-being or wealth ranking of households which leads, in turn, to focus group with different categories of people who then express their different preferences, leading to discussion, negotiation and reconciliation of priorities (combining Mukherjee 1992 and Swift and Umar 1991).

Matrix scoring or ranking elicits villagers' criteria of goodness and badness of a class of things (trees, vegetables, fodder grasses, varieties of a crop or animal, sources of credit, market outlets, fuel types...) which leads to discussion of preferences and actions.

Longer sequences have been devised and used in full PRAs. In Kenya, these have been part of a stepwise sequence (PID and NES 1989). In India, for example, with the Aga Khan Rural Support Programme, the sequences have been less codified and more in a style of systematic improvisation, though with specialized sequences; for example, appraisal, planning and action with degraded forests, or with identifying and working with the poorest.

The power of such sequences is four fold. First, the commitment of participants increases, making further action more likely, more spontaneous and more sustainable. Second, sequences triangulate and reveal errors or omissions in earlier presentations (see Pretty *et al.* 1992). Third, the different activities interact cumulatively, each activity adding a dimension and details which qualify and enrich others, so that, taken together, the whole becomes more than the sum of the parts. Fourth, all concerned learn through the process, through people sharing what they know, through observation and through analysis. In such ways as these, participatory methods fit well with a flexible learning process approach which is even more open-ended and adaptable than much earlier RRA; and they have the advantage that they usually enable villagers to use their own categories and criteria to generate their own agenda, and to assess and indicate their own priorities.

Training and Reorientation for Outsiders

The fifth discovery is that for some outsiders, initial training and reorientation need not take long before they can go off and practise.

The duration of training or familiarization covers a wide range. To date, universities have usually taken longer and NGOs and government shorter periods. RRA training conducted at the University of Khon Kaen in Thailand in 1990 took six weeks, which was considered inadequate (Grandstaff *et al.* 1990). PRA training at Egerton University in Kenya in 1990 took three weeks, and is being repeated. At the other extreme, in one case in India, slides of participatory mapping and 'handing over the stick' were shown for about an hour, and both were then adapted and adopted by a large NGO. In between these extremes, there have been workshops and training of half a day, a day, two days and so on upto ten days.

Face-to-face field experience is the key. The classroom insulates and inhibits; the field exposes and liberates. No one can learn to swim without entering the water. Participants in training often say they are not ready, that they need another day, more practice, before starting. But, applying the principle of optimal unpreparedness, it is usually best to start sooner than seems safe or sensible to newcomers; not to wait, but to start, stumble, self-correct, and then share.

On these lines, much PRA training in India has taken three to five days spent camping in or near a village (e.g. Ramachandran 1990; Devavaram *et al.* 1991; Jayakaran 1991; Joseph and Joseph 1991; Kumar 1991; Mascarenhas 1992). The camp usually entails two processes : training and learning for the team of outsiders, using various methods; and a participatory process which is 'for real', leading to plans developed by and with villagers. Staying a number of nights in the village intensifies and concentrates the experience. Attention is paid to outsiders' behaviour and attitudes. Villagers are encouraged to map, diagram, participate in transect walks and plan. The major aim of the training for the outsiders is to facilitate changes in perception and action, listening not lecturing, learning progressively, embracing error, being critically self-aware and themselves participating. For example, reversing roles by being taught by villagers to perform village tasks. For some outsiders, especially those who have had a strictly formal professional training, this can threaten trauma. They deserve sympathetic understanding, and no significant change may take place. For some, though, there opens up a new range of possibilities and a sense of freedom to experiment and innovate. It is then not necessary to be trained in all the methods. They can be tried, improvised and adapted subsequently, and new ones invented. The outsider's creativity is released, as well as that of the villager.

Another approach is to smuggle in participatory methods. Some professionals resist PRA approaches and methods, considering them unscientific and inappropriate. Methods which generate figures, matrices and tables can then sometimes help in getting started, and making other methods more acceptable. Robin Mearns found in Mongolia that wealth ranking was useful in this context as part of a 'hidden agenda' by giving 'every appearance of being the kind of 'hard' statistical method that Mongolian researchers and bureaucrats, like their counterparts in many parts of the world, have been professionally socialized to use and expect' (Mearns *et al.* 1992:37). Similarly, matrix scoring for varieties of a crop provides not only fascinating information but also good-looking tables with figures. The question is whether scientists and others will be so impressed by farmers' criteria, judgments and abilities as demonstrated in matrix scoring, and by the resulting matrices, that they will go on from this method to others, and progressively become more participatory.

Sharing and Spread

The last discovery concerns the importance of sharing in the culture and spread of PRA.

PRA in practice is recognized now to have three foundations: methods, behaviour and attitudes and sharing. At first, the methods appeared the most important, then the behaviour and attitudes of outsiders were seen as primary, especially for rapport; and now the third foundation, sharing, is recognized as having grown in importance. This is partly because it has become the mode in which PRA spreads. PRA in India has a culture of sharing which owes much to MYRADA and also to other NGOs. Village camps have been open to people from other organizations. Typically, a training camp organized by an NGO will include not just its own staff but also people from other NGOs and from government. Sharing is part of the experience of the camp: sharing of information by villagers, presenting it to each other and to outsiders; sharing of ideas and experience concerning approaches and methods between outsiders and villagers; sharing of self-critical appraisal of the process among outsiders; and sharing of food by all.

If PRA is spreading through the sharing of experience and mutual learning, it is also taking different forms in different places. People and organizations are inventing their own combinations and creating their own cultures. Some emphasize one set of methods; some another. Any one method – transect walks (Mascarenhas 1990), or well-being ranking (*RRA Notes 15*) for example – now has several variants. To share and exchange methods and experiences, interchanges of staff are efficient, with staff of one organization spending time with other organizations in their PRAs. In all cases, also, the creativity and inventiveness of villagers can come into play. In such ways, innovations can be continuously stimulated. It is then through all forms of sharing – training camps, trainers, ideas, experiences, methods, innovations – that takes place.

UTILITY : PRACTICAL APPLICATIONS

The case for RRA and PRA approaches is practical. It is the experience that they work. The experiential and anecdotal evidence for the utility of well-conducted RRA and PRA is now massive, but has not been adequately drawn together and analyzed.

To document the applications of RRA and PRA to date would require a separate paper and bibliography (but see for example Agricultural Administration, 1981 volume on PRA; IDS Bulletin (1981); KKU 1987, especially Gibbs 1987, and the bibliography; Lovelace, Subhadhira and Simaraks, 1988; PID and NES 1989; IIED publications including cases from Cap Verde, Chile, Ecuador, Ethiopia, Fiji, the Gambia, India, Indonesia, Kenya, Pakistan, Sri Lanka, Sudan and Zimbabwe; RRA Notes Passim, especially Number 13 reporting experience in India; and Forests, Trees and People News Number 15/16, 1992. There have also been many articles (for an earlier listing see Chambers 1985: 412-4 and numerous unpublished reports).

Regarding RRA, RRA approaches and methods have been used for appraisal, analysis and research in many subject areas. These include agroecosystems; natural resources, including forestry, fisheries and the environment; irrigation; technology and innovation; health and nutrition; farming systems research and extension; pastoralism; marketing; disaster relief; organizational assessment; social, cultural and economic conditions; and many special topics. As well as RRA, PRA has also been or could be applied to all these.

Regarding RRA, so much is being done so fast in so many places that any inventory of PRA applications made in mid-1992 will be incomplete and quickly out-of-date. However, most of the applications I know of can be separated into four types of processes and into four major sectors :

- participatory appraisal and planning;
- participatory implementation, monitoring and evaluation of programmes;
- topic investigations; and
- training and orientation for outsiders and villagers.

The four major sectors are the following. The sources are now so voluminous that only a few, and mainly very recent and accessible, references are given. For others see IDS 1992. A bibliographical review is overdue.

Natural Resources Management

Watersheds as well as soil and water conservation: For example, participatory watershed planning and management, including rapid catchment analysis (Pretty 1990).

Forestry: For example, social and community forestry; degraded forest assessment, protection, nurseries and planting; identification of tree uses; uses and marketing of minor forest products (See e.g. Case 1990; and for a strong PRA sequence M. Shah forthcoming).

Fisheries.
Wildlife reserve buffer zones.
Rural energy assessments, and fuel and fodder budgeting.
Village plans: preparing Village Resource Management Plans (PID and NES 1990), Participatory Rural Appraisal and Planning (as developed by AKRSP), and others.

Agriculture

Crops and animal husbandry : including farmer participatory research/farming systems research by farmers.

Irrigation : including rehabilitation of small-scale gravity flow irrigation systems.

Markets : investigating markets and small holder marketing potential.

Programmes for Equity

- *Women* : participatory appraisal of problems and opportunities.
- *Credit* : identification of credit needs, sources and interventions.
- *Selection* : finding and selecting poor people for a programme, and deselecting the less poor (e.g. Chandramouli 1991; PRA Notes 15 passim).
- *Income-earning* : identification of non-agricultural income-earning opportunities.

Health and Nutrition

Health assessments and monitoring (e.g. Appleton 1992; Francis, Devavaram and Erskine 1992; Joseph 1992). Applications include women's reproductive health (Tolley and Bently 1992; Cornwall 1992), disease problem ranking (Welbourn 1992), unemployment and health (Cresswell 1992), identifying major illness, healthcare providers and costs (Joseph 1992) (See also Heaver 1992 and PRA Notes 16: 101-106 for a fuller listing of actual or potential uses).

Food security and nutrition assessment and monitoring (Maxwell 1989; Appleton 1992; Buchanan-Smith 1992).

Water and sanitation assessment, planning and location.

These lists are to illustrate known applications. They are by no means comprehensive, and many more applications can be expected.

For several reasons, there are still (mid-1992) few case studies of the impact of PRA. First, PRA is recent, and many PRA processes are still in their early stages. Second, responding to demand and their own sense of priorities, experienced practitioners have been mostly engaged in training and appraisal rather than monitoring and evaluation, and this emphasis is reflected in the reports they have written. Third, academic researchers have been slow to recognize what has been happening and have rarely studied PRA.

These are conditions in which negative experiences are liable to be overlooked. More feedback is needed for whatever failures can be found, from those who have experienced PRA and not subsequently adopted it, and from organizations where attempts to introduce it have not been successful.

That said, positive evidence takes two main forms: the scale of adoption and use by organizations and individuals; and accounts of practical use.

First, the number of organizations which have to some degree adopted PRA is large and growing. The estimates which follow mainly concern agriculture and natural resources: I do not have a good sense of the scale of adoption and use in health, where PRA is also spreading locally, especially through UNICEF, NGOs which are in some places using PRA (mid-1992) must number at least a hundred, and perhaps several hundred. At least a dozen universities and training institutes have some staff who are exploring and using PRA (though almost everywhere they are a small minority) (See Section 12.8). government and parastatal organizations, all or parts of which have espoused PRA, are a similar number. Among these, a few have sought to introduce it throughout their programmes : among others, the Soil and Water Conservation Branch of the Ministry of Agriculture in Kenya, which has officially adopted PRA approach for its work in over 40 districts; the Drylands Development Board in Karnataka, India; and the District Rural Development Agencies, Andhra Pradesh, India. Government programmes with donor support are introducing PRA training and approaches, as with the ODA-supported Western Ghats programme in India, and the SIDA-supported Vietnam-Sweden Forestry Cooperation Programme in Vietnam. Actual spread and use in large field agencies, whether Government or NGO, is easily overestimated. Sometimes resistance can be expected. Much depends on personal orientation and choice, and on rewards. In smaller organizations, it is not by administrative fiat, but by consistent high-level support, widespread training of good quality and appropriate systems of rewards that actual spread will take place. With those caveats, the number of people who have now chosen to use PRA as approach and process, not just PRA methods, now numbers thousands, and is growing.

Second, accounts of practical use are innumerable but scattered in a large, inaccessible, grey literature. Not surprisingly, most of this is strongly positive. All the same, few PRA processes have yet been thoroughly researched and analysed. Recent evaluations, though, are showing that where the PRA approach has been used compared with just using T and V (training and visit), a range of agricultural and economic indicators are much more favourable, such as higher agricultural yields, greater diversity of crops, reduced soil erosion and sedimentation, greater net present value and benefit cost ratios, higher land prices and higher wage rates (pers.comm. Jules Pretty). Similar findings have been reported from the work of AKRSP in Gujarat.

A critical review of the other evidence and examples in the grey literature is overdue. There is also a huge research agenda to understand better the applications and potentials, the processes and impacts and shortcomings as well as strengths of PRA. Some of these can, however, already be assessed in terms of data validity and reliability.

VALIDITY AND RELIABILITY

Those who become involved with PRA tend to become enthusiastic. There can be an exhilarating sense of liberation and discovery. The presentation and analysis of detailed local knowledge in maps, models, matrices, diagrams and the likes by villagers can impress outsiders deeply in a personal way which challenges preconceptions, and affects beliefs and behaviour. This is reflected in remarks of NGO staff. After participatory social mapping "I have been working for eight years in this village, but I never saw it like this before."

After PRA experience : ——→ "I shall never go back to questionnaires."

After PRA training : ——→ "I have been trying to get this information from this village for six months and now we have it in two afternoons."

The experience behind these and similar statements are fact. For those who made them, the evidence of personal experience is enough. But questions can and must be asked about less personal and experiential means of assessing the validity and reliability of PRA approaches and methods.

Validity here refers to the closeness of a finding to the reality, and reliability refers to the constancy of findings. Highly valid findings are also highly reliable, but where there is a systematic bias, reliability can be high but validity low. Validity and reliability are not absolute values. There can be trade-offs, through optimal ignorance and appropriate imprecision, where lower validity and reliability can be more cost-effective, and can enhance utility through less cost or greater relevance or timeliness.

At the outset, most large questionnaire surveys present any assessment of PRA with low standards of comparison. (Certain routinised and repeated surveys like the National Sample Survey in India are at least partial exceptions to what follows.) Devastating critiques of rural questionnaire surveys have found them often badly designed, badly implemented and badly analyzed (see e.g. Moris 1970; Campbell, Shrestha and Stone 1979; Daane 1987; Gill forthcoming). All too often, questionnaire surveys are found wanting on many counts. And rarely are they subjected to full critical scrutiny.

Comparison should, though, also be made with rural questionnaire survey, which have been relatively well conducted. An example can illustrate. In 1973-74, I collaborated in a large questionnaire surveys in Tamil Nadu (reported in *Farmer* 1977:37-44). Since I was responsible neither for the training of the investigators who conducted the interviews, nor for the supervision of the survey, it is not immodest to say that the survey was well supervised, and the investigators were well trained and keen. There were eight investigators for 12 villages, each of which differed sharply from the other 11 (Chambers and Harriss 1977). Four investigators had only one village each, but the other four each had two villages. On the basis of the survey data, I wrote an article on agricultural extension and intended to submit it for publication. But the more I looked at it, the more I sensed something was wrong. Eventually, I took the results from the eight shared villages and paired them by investigator. The results from each village were more like those of its pair, shared by the same investigator than like any other village. It seemed likely that the main independent variable was the investigator; and the basis for the article collapsed. By occurring in a well supervised survey, this experience throws into question the credibility of other surveys which do not test for and report on individual interviewer bias. Few do. And the fact that the literature on this bias is so sparse may reflect that even those who do carry out tests, sin as I did in holding back from publishing the damning findings.

More generally, critical discussion of methodological problems so rarely accompanies publications of survey results that the validity of the findings of much of the survey industry is open to question. For our purposes here, the conclusion is that the quality of data from questionnaire surveys is often so poor that an improvement is not difficult to achieve.

This, though, is no reason for anything less than strict critical rigour in assessing the validity and reliability of RRA and PRA approaches and methods. The tests most readily applied concern measurements and numbers. Let us, therefore, examine the four main areas where RRA and PRA have generated numerical data which are available for assessment. These are farm and household surveys; wealth and well-being ranking; village censuses; and rainfall data.

Farm and Household Surveys

In five cases, comparisons have been made between the findings of an RRA approach and a conventional questionnaire survey.

Michael Collinson's (1981) Exploratory Survey of a farming system, involving some 20 professional person days, was never contradicted in any major way by the subsequent longer drawn-out and more expensive Verification Survey which represented the major commitment of professional time and funds.

Steven Franzel and Eric Grawford (1987) systematically compared a quick and light survey with a longer and heavier conventional survey in Kenya and found no significant differences attributable to the methods.

Diane Rocheleau and her team (Roflieleau *et al.*, 1989) working on agro-forestry in Kenya used a chain of informal in-depth interviews and group interviews, and compared the results with a survey of a formal randomized sample of 63 households. They found that the formal survey took three times as long and reproduced the same results as the group interviews and chain of interviews, with less detail and coherence (*ibid.* 21).

Andy Inglis (1990, 1991) led a team which used a repertoire of RRA techniques to gather local forestry knowledge in Sierra Leone in an area where a lengthy questionnaire with 278 questions had already been applied. The RRA results were presented four days after the last location was surveyed, but the questionnaire report was still not available six months after the completion of fieldwork. Comparisons of the questionnaire survey and RRA data showed sharp discrepancies in two localities where the questionnaire survey's findings were implausible and its validity had to be suspected. As Inglis points out:

> ..... if information is wrong to begin with, no amount of statistical manipulation will enable it to help the project staff make good decisions ... In contrast, the RRA survey was completed in a much shorter time, the results have been produced in specific locational reports that can be individually used as discussion papers in the field in follow up surveys. As research biases, mistakes and omissions are admitted and not lost in a mass of questionnaire codes, the decision maker can see how the information was generated, how important factors were revealed and how the best bests were arrived at (Inglis 1990:107).

C.N. Bernadas (1991) reports that in Eastern Visayas in the Philippines, highly structured questionnaire interviews identified declining soil fertility as the most pressing problem of farmers. Bernadas explains that the staff themselves had formulated the questions on the basis of what they felt to be priorities. The problem areas considered were predetermined based on the outsider's point of view. Two, needs and circumstances, as well as the developed technologies were not adopted by them. An

RRA approach was then used with informal discussions and dialogues and open ended interviews with guide topics. This led to the discovery that the most pressing problem facing farmers was not soil fertility but the long fallow due to the growth of a weed, called cogon (*Imperata cylindrica*). Relevant research could then begin.

In these five cases, then, the results of the RRA approach, compared with the more formal questionnaire, were variously more valid, less costly, more timely and more useful.

A cautionary counter example is a case of the worst of both worlds. This was a one-week survey through interviews of 30 farmers by a researcher in Northern Zambia, described as an RRA. Johann Pottier (1990) argues persuasively that in such hurried interviews an insensitivity to the context, to who is being met, to what is being said, and why, can lead to misleading conclusions, in this case that food security had been enhanced by growing maize. The investigation was, it seems, rushed and wrong. The lessons are many and include that hectic one-off individual interviews are bad practice whatever the label attached to them, and that respondents can reach by giving responses which, for reasons such as prudence, politenesses and favourable preservation of the self, are invalid but reliable, and thereby convincingly maintain myths and mislead.

Ranking

Ranking and scoring have long been part of the repertoire of social anthropologists. People in communities rank other individuals or households for characteristics as varied as aggressiveness, industriousness, or more commonly some concept of respect, honour, well-being or wealth (Pelto and Pelto 1978:82-87; *RRA Notes* 15, 1992).

The most common method is sorting cards into piles, carried out either by individuals in private, or by groups. Different informants often use a different number of piles for the same community, but evidence is consistent in finding close correlations in rank orders between informants. Sydel Silverman (1966:905) found that there was high agreement in the relative rank of most persons when three informants in an Italian community card-sorted households according to their criterion of rispetto (Approximately prestige). Polly Hill (1986:41,75) suggests that no villagers' relative household living standards can be a matter of passionate concern. On the basis of fieldwork in West Africa and India, she concluded that rural people (unless themselves too poor and disabled) are able to assess the relative wealth or well-being of members of their community far more accurately than are town people. This has been borne out by much subsequent wealth or well-being ranking. Barbara Grandin (1988) found that correlations (Spearman's Rho) across informants in 12 instances of wealth ranking (using a total of 41 informants) averaged .77 (range .59-.96). The correlations of each informant with final score average .91 (range .84-.98).

Silverman, Hill and Grandin are all social anthropologists and so might be expected to have developed good rapport before the exercise. The test is whether without a social anthropological training and relationship, the method can also be reliable and valid. Those who have facilitated such ranking exercises have found them easier than expected (see *RRA Notes* 15) and informally report high correlations between the rankings given by different informants or groups. Some triangulate rankings through discussion. Poly Hill's three informants in Nigeria thrashed out discrepancies between themselves (Hill 1972:59). In a PRA mode, on similar lines, MYRADA in South India has evolved a method of successive approximation in which separate groups rank households, and then meet to reconcile differences (per. Comm. Vidya Ramachandran), a procedure which is used in selecting households for anti-poverty programmes.

Another example is the ranking of the value of 30 browse plants as feed to their cattle by pastoralists in Nigeria (Bayer 1987, 1988). Ranking for the most important plants were found to correspond closely between different groups of pastoralists.

Not all ranking exercises can be expected to yield reliable and valid data, but these examples suggest close correlations between informants in three conditions: where information is common knowledge; where criteria are commonly held and well understood; and where what is ranked is a matter of intense interest.

Participatory Village Censuses

In participatory social mapping, villagers show the location of households. In India in 1991 this was extended by Sheelu Francis and others into participatory censuses. One variant is health mapping, in which symbols are used to indicate where people of different types and with different conditions live in a village. In a census, one common practice is for villagers to use seeds of different sorts to represent people. Another, invented by Anusuda and Perumal Maicker of Kethanayakanpatty village near Madurai in Tamil Nadu, is to have a card for each household and mark details with symbols on the card.

Triangulation of censuses took place in Ramasamypatti village, near Tiruchuli, in Tamil Nadu, in May 1991. In a PRA training organized by SPEECH, an NGO, four groups of between 5 and 15 villagers used different methods of analysis and presentation: two did social mapping direct onto paper; one made a ground model of the village with a card for each household; and one did a census onto a map drawn on a floor. All four independently generated a figure for the total population of the village. All four came to 355.

Rainfall Data

It has been found that farmers will often readily estimate rainfall by month. In 1988, two farmers in Wollo in Ethiopia estimated numbers of days of rainfall by month for the previous five years, and also indicate the pattern they remembered from their childhood (Conway 1988; ERCS 1988:50-52). The most common method now is for them to arrange a line of 12 stones for the months of the local calendar and then estimate rainfall using either broken sticks for relative volume, or seeds for numbers of days of rain by month, or both. Some farmers in India have preferred to indicate depth of soil moisture by month as being more relevant for agricultural purposes (pers. comm. J. Mascarenhas for Karnataka and Sam Joseph for Rajasthan). A refinement, invented by women in Galkada village, Badulla district, Sri Lanka, in January 1992, is to space the seeds to indicate the distribution of days of rain within each month.

The question is how valid are such data? Farmers' data on rainfall have several times been found to differ from those of nearby rainfall stations. At Nugu Dam in H.D. Kote, Karnataka, in August 1990, a discrepancy was found but not further analysed. In rapid catchment analysis in Kenya (Pretty 1990) when farmers' patterns of rainfall differed in six different catchments and also differed from the 'real' data from a nearby rainfall station, this was judged to reflect spatial heterogeneity, without ruling out the possibility that the farmers were wrong (per. comm. J. Pretty). The only detailed analysis of comparisons to date comes from Nepal. It was there in May 1990 near Lumle that farmers for the first time indicated volume and numbers of days of rainfall per month using seeds for days and sticks for Volume. 1 in 45 minutes, they presented first a normal year and then a pattern which they said occurred one year in five. Gerard Gill's (1991) painstaking analysis of their perceptions compared with 20 years of daily rainfall data at the nearby rainfall station defies brief summary. Suffice it to say here that what initially appeared as discrepancies about whether the farmers were 'wrong' turned out on closer examination to show respects in which the farmers' judgements were superior to the averaged met station data. Gill's title 'But how does it compare with the real data?' captures the irony of the assumption that 'scientifically' measured data are necessarily superior. More balanced conclusions are that there are different realities, that farmers' realities are likely to be linked to agricultural utility and weighted by recent experience, and that the issue is whose reality counts in what contexts and for what purposes.

These four sets of numerical evidence are all positive for RRA/PRA approaches and methods. To the best of my knowledge and belief I have not excluded any comparable negative evidence. All the same, a terminal caveat is in order. When all the four groups at Ramasmypatti came up with 355 as the population of the village, I was excited. I collected the reporting maps and diagrams, labelled and arranged them, and then photographed them. This positive evidence has since been disseminated through copies of the slides. Only later did I think to ask whether there had been any exchanges of information or of figures between the groups. In fact, I believe there was none. But had the groups come up with figures which differed the question is whether reaction too would have differed. The danger is selective and has been meticulously analyzed by Gill and published. But this was not done in the Kenya and Karnataka cases. Had those discrepancies been investigated further, they might, as in the Nepal case, have revealed a validity in the farmers' judgements; or they might not have. We do not know with any certainty.

The lesson is to remain critically aware at all times with a positive skepticism, and to probe, investigate, report and learn from negative as well as positive experience. With thjs caution, the finding from evidence available to data stands, that both qualitative and quantitative data elicited by RRA and especially PRA methods have usually proved more reliable and more valid than outsider professionals have expected.

As with all PRA, much depends on the behaviour and attitudes of the outsiders, and whether they have the time, patience and will to get closer to reality. A final example from Nepal illustrates a typical learning process through cross checking and successive analysis and approximation. After the use of PRA methods, presentations by two groups of outsiders on what villagers had shared with them on seasonality and trends in agriculture gave conflicting information. The response was for both groups to go back to their village the next day and reconcile the information, with their respective groups of informants forming one combined group, and with the statement 'We got the information from you yesterday and there seems to be some difference. Can you help us?' And, of course, they did. Information flowed, arguments and discussions took place among the villagers, among the outsiders and between both villagers and outsiders – as is typical of a good PRA exercise. Explanations were given, corrections made, and it was a much more satisfied group of researchers that returned to the base camp that night (pers. comm. James Mascarenhas). Discrepancies are, as here, welcomed, in the spirit of embracing error, as opportunities to learn and to get closer to the truth.

REVERSALS AND REALITY

The power and utility of RRA and PRA are, then, empirical facts; and as such, they demand explanation. Some explanations lie in the effective application of the principles outlined in section 5 above. But cross cutting these, there are other angles from which PRA experience can be examined and illuminated. So far, most of those who have innovated in developing PRA have been practitioners, concerned with what works, and what will work better, not academic theorists concerned with why it works. They have been searching not for new theories or principles but for new and better ways of learning and doing. The 'Why?' questions have been relatively neglected. There is now enough experience to allow us to induce some theory or explanations from practice.

The strongest explanations can be captured by the word 'reversals'. Reversal is used to describe a direction, away from normal practice and towards its opposite. The overarching reversal is from etic to emic, from our knowledge, categories and values to theirs. It answers the question 'whose reality counts?', initially with the reply 'theirs'. We start with their reality, not with ours.

Within the frame of the reversal, three clusters of reversal or change intertwine are mutually reinforcing; reversals of modes; reversals of relationships; and reversals of action. None is absolute; but all represent shifts from the normal in the reverse direction.

Reversals of Modes

From closed to open

Conventional investigations are preset. Almost all questionnaire surveys are designed by outsiders, with outsiders' concerns and categories. They seek to elicit responses to fill fixed boxes. Whatever the intentions that investigators shall prove under the category 'other', which lies at the end of the list of precoded responses on the sheet, they rarely do; and where they do, it presents problems later in coding and analysis. The convenient truth fits our familiar frame.

The reversal here is from etic to emic, and from closed to open. In contrast with questionnaire interviews, semi-structured interviews are more open, and conversations even preset sequence of questions. A value is set on probing, on pursuing leads, on serendipity. Moreover, with other methods common in PRA such as participatory mapping and modelling, matrix ranking, insiders are not only free to express their knowledge and values; they are encouraged and enabled to do so. The shift is from preset to participatory.

From individual to group

Questionnaire surveys require that interviews be with individuals or households so that commensurable data can be analyzed. In RRA, semi-structured interviewing can be with an individual or group, but with somewhat more emphasis on the individual 'interviewee' (see Grandstaff and Grandstaff 1987b: 135-7). In PRA, discussions with individuals can and do take place, but there is relatively more group activity. Cultural, social and other differences can be expected. Groups have well-known dis-advantages, such as dominance by one or more individuals. But the positive side, especially in PRA mode, when rapport is good they have strengths. Paradoxically, and contrary to common belief, sensitive subjects are sometimes more freely discussed in groups, when individuals would not wish to discuss them alone with a stranger. More generally, groups can build up collective and creative enthusiasm, especially with mapping and modelling, leading to an unselfconscious showing sharing and checking. Participants fill in gaps left by other and add or correct detail. Groups have an overlapping spread of knowledge, which covers a wider field and crosschecks.

From verbal to visual

With outsider-insider interactions, there is a scale of formality-informality from the structured interview with questionnaire, through the semi-structured interview with checklist of topics (Grandstaff and Grandstaff 1987b), to the conversation (Scrimshaw and Hurtado 1987). With the interviews, and sometimes also conversations, outsiders ask questions and probe. Eye contact is common the outsider maintains control, and largely determines the agenda and the categories. The interviewee responds, conscious of an interaction with a person who is seeking information. The transfer or exchange of information is verbal.

With PRA methods, in contrast, much of medium is visuals, through forms of participatory diagramming. This includes social and census mapping, resource mapping and modelling, seasonal analysis, Venn and Chapati diagramming, trend diagramming and matrix scoring. The many forms of participatory diagramming are all, by definition, often open to a group, not just to an individual or household.

With participatory diagramming, relationships change. The topic may be determined, or at least suggested, by the outsider, but the role is not to extract through questions but to initiate a process of presentations and analysis. The outsiders are facilitators, the insiders actors. The outsiders hand over control, and insiders determine the agenda, categories and details. The media and materials are often those of insiders – the ground, stones, sand, seeds as counters, sticks as measures, and so on. Eye contract, and insider's awareness of the outsider are low. Information is built up cumulatively, and cross checking is automatic. Often, several or many people are involved, knowledge overlaps. If half a dozen women diagram a census map of their village, showing women, men, children, handicapped persons and so on, not everything may be known by each; but two or more may know each item. Debate can be lively because everyone can see what is being said. It can then be the diagrams rather than the people who are interviewed.

Visual methods can also empower the weak and disadvantaged. Visual literacy (Bradeley 1992) is independent of alphabetical literacy, and appears to be near universal. Visual diagramming is thus an equalizer, especially when it is done using the accessible and familiar medium of the ground. On paper, too, the non-literate can diagram. In Kiteto district in Tanzania, in June 1992, a non-literate Maasai young man, though mocked by his literate colleagues, took a sheet of paper, and went off and quietly drew from his mind, very detailed map of a large village area and its settlements. In Pakistan, in March 1992, several non-literate women drew complex systems diagrams of their farms and households, with internal and external flows and linkages (pers.comm.Jules Pretty). Describing the experience of the Neighbourhood Initiatives Foundation (NIF) in the UK, Tony Gibson (1991) has pointed out that 'the talkers nearly always win'. But with a physical model of their neighbourhood to play with, timid people can physically put down their ideas. Often people, who put down an idea, wait for others to talk about it first and then say themselves: 'I agree with you'. Similarly, participatory mapping and matrices can enable marginalized women to express their preferences and priorities in a physical form, which does not entail personal confrontation with otherwise dominating men.

Some contrasts between verbal and visual models are presented in the table below:

	Verbal (Interview, Conversation)	Visual (Diagram)
Outsider's role	Investigator	Initiator and catalyst
Outsider's mode	Probing	Facilitating
Outsider's interventions	Continuous and maintained	Initial and then reduced
Insider's role	Respondent	Presenter and analyst
Insider's mode	Reactive	Creative
Insider's awareness of outsider	High	Low
Eye contract	High	Low
The medium and material are those of	Outsider	Insider
The poor, weaker and women can be	Marginalised	Empowered
Detail influenced by	Etic categories	Emic perceptions
Information flow	Sequential	Cumulative
Accessibility of information to others	Low and transient	High and semi-permanent
Initiative for checking lies with	Outsider	Insider
Utility for spatial, temporal and casual information relations, analysis, planning and monitoring	Low	High
Ownership of information	Appropriated by outsider	Owned and shared by insider

The shift from verbal to visual is one of emphasis in PRA. Diagrams are part of the repertoire. They can be facilitated on their own early in interactions. They can also be part of semi-structured interviews or conversations, introduced as a means for local people to express, share and analyze their knowledge. Diagrams then present an agenda for discussion. 'Interviewing the map', 'interviewing the matrix', and 'interviewing the diagram' are often the most fruitful and also most neglected stages of a discussion and diagramming process. With the visual, a whole new set of questions of discussions arises which does not in the verbal' (per. comm. James Mascarenhas). Combinations of visual and verbal, with early primacy to the visual, can be strong and stronger than either exclusively on its own.

From counting to comparing

Normal professional training is to make absolute measurements. So if trends or changes are to be identified, or conditions compared between households or between places, this is through measurements made either at different times or of different things or in different places. Our preoccupation with numbers drives us to ask 'how much?' For sensitive subjects like income, such questions commonly sow suspicion, wreck rapport, and generate misleading data.

Often, though, all that is needed for practical purposes is relative values. Comparing can be quicker. Comparisons without measurements have advantages. Involving reflection and judgement, they are easier to express than measurements. They can be elicited from trends and changes without baseline data. They are less sensitive, as has been shown by wealth and well-being ranking and by seasonal analysis: asking how income compares different months is both easier to judge and less worrying to give than are absolute figures. And comparisons, as with matrix ranking and scoring, can in a short time elicit a wealth of information and judgements of value inaccessible without great labour by other methods. Moreover, trends, comparisons and weightage lend themselves to visual sharing, with all its potential gains in participation, triangulation and progressive approximation and learning, comparing can be quicker, cheaper and more credible than counting.

Reversals of Dominance: From Extracting to Empowering

Both the traditional questionnaire survey and the classical social anthropological investigation are extractive, even though their means of extraction differ.

In questionnaire interviewing, it is with the interviewer that power and initiative lie. The questionnaire is 'administered to' the person interviewed. The interviewee is a 'respondent', a person who replies or reacts. The Latin responder means to return like with like. The questions and categories are those of the interviewer, who also records the 'response'. In their textbook, *Survey Methods in Social Investigation,* Moser and Kalton have only two entries for 'respondent', but 32 for 'response'. The professional concern is less with people – the respondents – and more with what they provide, the responses. It is the responses that matter more, for they are the raw material to be mined, packaged, transported and processed, the commensurable output to be collected, categorized, coded, counted and correlated.

The ultimate aim of the classical anthropologist too has been to obtain data which are then analysed and written up away from the field. Participant observation requires sharply different relationship to those in questionnaire surveys, but the basic aim is similar. There are, of course, qualifications to this. Development anthropologists aim to be useful through their work in a more direct manner; and many anthropologists intervene in their field for ethical reasons. But the motivation has usually been, and remains, that of a researcher. However useful and justified it may be, the consummation sought is to process the data extracted into Ph.D., articles or a book.

In contrast, the thrust of PRA is to reverse the roles of who is dominant. The objective is less to gather data, and much more to start a process. The initiative passes to 'them'. The stick is handed over. The prime actors are the people. The outsider is less the exctractor, and more the convenor and catalyst.

A PRA process also seeks to enable outsiders to learn, but through the sharing of information in a manner which enhances people's analysis and knowledge and leaves them owning it. The actual and the ideal, here as elsewhere, will rarely correspond exactly. But an ideal could be sketched as a process in which people are enabled to collate, present and analyze information, making it explicit and adding to what they already know. This happens, for example, through participatory mapping of a watershed where the map is used by villagers to plot current conditions and plan actions, and retained by them for monitoring action taken and changes made; or through mapping and surveying degraded forest, deciding how to protect it and what to plant, and then managing the resource; or through matrix scoring for varieties of a crop, which enables them to specify the characteristics of a 'wish variety they would like to try out'. The aim is to enable people to present, share, analyze and augment their knowledge as the start of a process. The ultimate output sought is enhanced knowledge and competence, an ability to make demands and to sustain action. Instead of imposing and extracting, PRA seeks to empower.

From Reserve to Rapport, From Tedium to Fun

The initial reserve of rural people towards outsiders and their careful responses in the hope of gaining benefits or avoiding loss are common place. RRA and more so PRA stress the process of gaining rapport. Some social anthropologists have expressed scepticism about the relative speed with which rapport can be established. For their deeper and more fully emic understanding, there is a case for lengthy 'immersion'. But it is a common experience with both RRA and PRA that when the outsiders' behaviour and attitudes are right, and participatory methods used good rapport usually comes quickly. This happens through not rushing, through showing respect, through explaining who you are, answering questions, being honest, and being interested and asking to be taught, being taught and learning village tasks.

The classical view of fieldwork is that it is painful, entailing long hours of collecting and checking data. Moser and Kalton (1971:296) observe about questionnaire surveys: 'A interviewer's interest is bound to flag after a time....' Pelto and Pelto (1978; 1978: 194-5) cite the case of an anthropologist, Kobben, who had to 'make a great sacrifice of time, during a year of fieldwork, to collect ... quantified data on a mere 176 persons' and even then he felt rather unsure of the validity of some of his data. The same authors go on to consider how extensive survey data from questionnaires needs to be checked and qualified by other methods, and conclude:

> Clearly, the quantified data of survey research or other standardized interviewing require close support from participant – observation and general informal interviewing. But the converse is equally true. The lesson in all this, as Kobben made clear, is that field research entails a great amount of tedious, time-consuming work --both qualitative and numerical (*ibid.* 194-95).

Earlier participatory research also suffered from being long-drawn-out. The pilot project in appropriate technology for grain storage in Bwakira Chini village in Tanzania involved an outside team residing in the village for eight weeks. This was considered a 'short period of dialogue', but even so the application of the dialogical methodology was 'time consuming and tiresome' (Mduma 1973: 203, 213).

The contrast with RRA is sharp. Professional conversations are mutually stimulating and interesting. Of cattle keepers in Nigeria, who ranked browse plants, Wolfgang Bayer (1988:8) wrote that 'Pastoralists were very willing to share their knowledge about browse plants with us and appeared to enjoy the interviews as much as we did'. Reflecting on the comparison between a topic RRA and questionnaire survey on forestry and fuelwood in Sierra Leone, Andy Inglis (1991:40) wrote that the RRA approach enabled respondents "to enjoy a professional chat about their livelihood or kitchen habits, instead of being subjected to an intrusive 278 question questionnaire by bored enumerators."

With PRA the contrast is even sharper. Data are not collected by outsiders, but presented by insiders. For outsiders, in John Devavaram's words (*RRA Notes* 13:10), "One doesn't get bored repeating field work. It is always interesting." What is shared is often unexpected and at times fascinating. For insiders, the creative act of presentation and analysis is usually a pleasure, as is the process of learning through the expression, sharing and augmenting of what they know. In matrix scoring for trees or varieties of a crop, using the ground and seeds, it is a common experience for the outsider to become redundant as the process takes off, as villagers debate and score on their own. After village participants had made and analyzed models (maquettes) of their first attempt at a map, villagers scrub it out and start again with concentrated enthusiasm. Again and again, villagers in India have lost themselves in mapping and modelling, and outsiders have had to learn not to interview, not to interrupt, not to disturb their creativity. There is pride in what had been made and pleasure in presenting it to others. So often PRA is fun.

EXPLAINING OUR PAST IGNORANCE

There remains a puzzle, why it has taken until the 1990s for all this to come together; for the confluence of streams (See under "Some Sources of PRA") to occur; for the principles (See under "The Principles of PRA") to begin to emerge; for the menu of methods to reach its present richness (See under "The Menu Methods of PRA and PRA"); for the practical applications to be made (See under "Utility : Practical Applications"); for the degree of validity and reliability of RRA and PRA to become evident (See under "Validity and Reliability"); for the power of reversals of mode and dominance to be recognized (See under "Reversals and Reality"); and for the potentials for empowerment, fascination and even fun to be expressed as they have. At a personal level, I am bemused to understand how for several decades I have been working in rural development without knowing about all this. More generally, it is a mystery why it has taken so long for the development o community as a whole to 'discover' the richness not just of the knowledge, but of the creativity and analytical abilities of villagers.

Some of the mystery disappears if we look for explanation in ourselves. The beliefs, behaviour and attitudes of most outsiders have been the same all over the world. Agricultural scientists, medical staff, teachers, officials, extension agents and others have believed that their knowledge was superior and that the knowledge of farmers and rural people was inferior; and that we, the professional outsiders, had a monopoly of powers of analysis. Most outsiders have then either lectured, holding sticks and wagging fingers, or have interviewed, machine-gunning with rapid fire questions, interrupting, and not listening beyond immediate replies. We have 'put down' rural people. Our reality has blanketed our beliefs, demeanour, behaviour and attitudes have then been self-validating. Treated as incapable, rural people have behaved as incapable, hiding their capabilities from us and even from themselves. Nor have we known how to enable them to express, share and extend their knowledge. The ignorance and inabilities of rural people have not been only an illusion, but an artefact of our own arrogance and ignorance.

For participatory approaches and methods to take off, a stage had also been reached when different conditions could come together: recognition of past error and inadequacy, as with agricultural research for resource-poor farmers; greater confidence and professionalism in rural NGOs; approaches like agro-ecosystem analysis which simply did not exist before the 1980s; and finally, the emergence of an international community of communication with a critical mass and momentum in which approaches and methods could be shared between disciplines, countries and organizations, as at IDS in 1979, Khon Kaen in 1985 (KKU 1987) and Bangalore in 1991 (Mascarenhas *et al.* 1992). Perhaps, in their many forms and with their many levels, are now clustering and coalescing more, as philosophy, approaches, repertoire and practice. Their time may have come.

DANGERS

Any such up-beat statement must at once be qualified. For RRA and PRA, five dangers stand out.

The first danger is faddism. Like farming systems research, RRA and PRA could be discredited by over-rapid adoption and misuse, and by sticking on labels without substance. The warning signs are there: demand for training which exceeds by far the tiny cadre of competent trainers; requirements that consultants 'use RRA' or now 'use PRA' and then consultants who say they will do so, when they do not know what RRA or PRA entail or are the wrong sort of people to be able to do them well; and the belief that good RRA or PRA are simple and easy, quick fixes, when they are not.

The second danger is rushing. The word 'rapid', necessary in the late 1970s and early 1980s, is now a liability. It has been used to legitimize brash and biased rural development tourism. Much of the rationale for RRA/PRA has been to make time to find the poorest, to learn from them and to empower them. Hurry and lack of commitment, compound errors and mean that the poorest are once again, neither seen, listened to, nor learnt from. The R of RRA stands better for 'relaxed', allowing plenty of time.

The third danger is formalism. In the long term, this may prove the most difficult. With any innovation, there is an urge to standardize and codify, often in the name of quality. Manuals are called for any composed. They can indeed be useful as compilations of experience, as cookbooks that widen the choice of recipes, as sources of ideas, especially for trainers. But manuals can also harm. With any new approach or method, manuals start short but grow fast. Paragraphs proliferate as intelligent authors seek to cater to every condition and contingency. Some farming systems research gave rise to manuals the weight and volume of which was itself a problem. (For example, the four volumes of *Farming Systems Support Project Manuals* (FSSP 1987) weighted, on our kitchen scales, approximately 3.6 kg). The dangers are evident. Training is based on the text, and takes longer. More time is spent in the classroom, teaching the theory and less in the field learning the practice. Spontaneity is inhibited and spread slowed, stopped or reversed.

The initial lack of manuals for PRA in India has then been an advantage. Would-be practitioners have been forced to learn, not from books, and not by rote, but from colleagues, through sharing, and from their own improvisations and experiences in the field. Many of the best innovations have happened when practitioners have not known or followed whatever rules for matrix ranking. The first guidelines for wealth ranking (Grand in

1988) presented individual interviews in private as the preferred method, but many practitioners have now found ways of using group interviews; by mid-1991, MYRADA had conducted over two hundred wealth ranking by group (per. comm. Vidya Ramachandran). Nor has the criterion for ranking remained some concept of 'wealth'. More commonly now, more complex and diverse concepts of well-being, as defined by rural people themselves, are used.

The largest and heaviest manual in India in mid-1992 was produced by Ravi Jayakaran of Krishi Gram Vikas Kendra. The reader opens it to find printed boldly on the first page:

Use Your own Best Judgement at all Times

The other pages are all blank.

The lesson is that practitioners must take responsibility for what they do. They must feel free to start, to make mistakes and to learn on the run. It is not books of instructions, but personal commitment, critical awareness and informed improvisation, which can best assure quality and creativity.

A linked, fourth, danger is role. Practitioners and trainers fall into habits and routines. There are many different ways of doing participatory mapping and modelling, transect walks, seasonal analyses, group interviews, ranking and scoring, identifying special groups of people and the like. But practitioners in any organization, or even region, show signs of slipping into unvarying standard practices overlooking other options. Of course, some routinization and repetition are inevitable, even desirable. But experimenting, inventing, testing, adapting and constantly trying to improve are part of the potential strength of PRA. To nurture and keep that spirit, one method is exchanges of trainers between organizations, countries and continents to share approaches, methods and experiences in the field.

A final danger or difficulty is rejection. Some of the many pioneers who contributed to the streams – participatory research, participatory action research, applied anthropology, agro-eco-system analysis, farming systems research and RRA itself, which have fed into PRA, feel that they have not received due recognition, when what they should really feel is pleasure and pride. Others, especially academics, may feel excluded, bypassed or threatened by the developments described in this chapter, and ject them. At worst, this will mean that students in colleges and universities, and staff in field organizations are denied access to and the opportunity to use PRA approaches and methods. At best, this will mean a positive contribution through constructive criticism which will sharpen the rigour and add to the repertoire of PRA. It can only be hoped that the spirit of sharing will encourage and allow all professionals to use and develop PRA approaches and methods, for this is the monopoly of no person or group. As it grows, PRA is, and should remain, an open access resource.

FRONTIERS, CHALLENGES AND POTENTIALS

The future presents many frontiers, challenges and potentials. The following eight stand out :

Beyond Farming Systems Research (FSR)

Farming systems research faces problems because of the diversity, complexity and uncontrollability of many farming systems, especially rainfed farming in the South. Participatory approaches, known variously as farmer-back-to-farmer (Rhoades and Booth 1982), farmer participatory research (Farrington and Martin 1988) and farmer to first (Chambers, Pacey and Thrupp 1989) have moved towards involving farmers to undertake their own analysis. This is potentially parsimonious in the use of scientists' time (Chambers and Jiggings 1986) but its methods are still in an early stage of development.

Pioneering work by many of those working in India, and by Jacqueline Ashby of CIAT, Clive Lightfoot of ICLARM, Jules Pretty of IIED and others has shown that farmers have diagramming analytical capabilities which were not hitherto suspected. In India and Malawi, Lightfoot and others have facilitated ground diagramming by farmers of nutrient flows on their farms and elsewhere, diagramming of their farming systems by farmers. Anil Shah of KRSP, in March 1991, facilitated the diagramming on paper by a farmer, Savasi Bhura, of Gadhechi village, Surendranagar district, Gujarat, of a complex flow and causal diagram of the impact of irrigation. Jules Pretty, in Pakistan in early 1992, found during a training exercise that illiterate as well as literate farmers could make detailed diagrams of flows and causality on their farms, including an impressive diagram by an illiterate woman. Elsewhere in 1992, in India and Bostswana, matrix scoring for varieties of a crop has been developed by asking analysts to add a 'wish' variety in which farmers specify the characteristics they would like extension and scientists to provide for them.

The challenge now is for outsider professionals to further develop and disseminate approaches and methods to help farmers do their own analysis and make their own needs and priorities known to scientists. If such efforts continue to be successful, the implications for activities, procedures, training, rewards and institutional cultures in agricultural education, research and extension will be little short of revolutionary.

Policy Research and Change

At a policy level RRA/PRA has recently begun to be a strong source of insights. Examples from Zimbabwe, Tanzania, Chad and Nepal illustrate the potential.

In Zimbabwe, in November 1991, RRA with PRA methods were used to investigate the effects on agriculture of structural adjustment policies. RRAs were conducted by a team of researchers over two weeks in two communal areas. Their findings and recommendations, in a report (FSRU 1991) completed straight after the fieldwork, provided immediate feedback from the field concerning marketing, transport, input supply, prices, food security and farmers' attitudes towards agricultural structural adjustment policies, and provided policy makers with insight into the farmers' eyeview and their intentions.

In Chad, in 1991, a survey was undertaken on a national scale using RRA techniques to try and understand how people perceived their food security problems, and what solutions they proposed (Buchanan-Smith 1992). Thirteen survey enumerators worked in 55 representative villages, spending about a day in each village. A group interview with a checklist as guide was followed by household interviews, particularly oriented towards women (who were rarely represented in the group interview). Three years of different weather conditions were used as reference points. Organizing and analyzing the mass of data was achieved despite difficulties, and lessons were learnt for improving this sort of survey. Three categories of administrative areas were found, each with a distinctive household food security strategy. The results challenged the conventional thinking in N'djamena which held that the key to raising production was promoting free market systems for agricultural produce. The survey showed that the local people knew methods and technologies to increase production but were constrained by lack of credit for ploughs, oxen, improved seeds and more efficient irrigation, and that more was needed than developing agriculture marketing alone.

Another striking example is provided by land policy in Tanzania (Johansson and Hoben 1992). As a contribution to a government reassessment of land policies, the Institution of Resource Assessment at the University of Dar es Salaam organized four RRAs for mid-level policy makers. Four villages were chosen to represent a range of conditions. Four teams were formed, each spending five days in one of the villages. Through the direct learning of the RRAs, they concluded that the government's top down approach was wrong, that communities and people were already doing land use planning, that imposing a land use map was misguided, and that new participatory approaches were needed. They presented their findings at a seminar with high-level policy makers. The resulting recommendations from the seminar entailed major reversals of policy, and seemed 'to indicate just how great an impression, such a short visit to a rural area can have and how effective an RRA can be in providing relevant insights for policy makers and planners' (*ibid.* 30).

These three examples were one-off efforts. A prototype for a more permanent facility is being tested in Nepal. There, eight small Rapid Development Teams have been trained in basic PRA methods and are in place at different locations in the terai (lowland). The intention is that they will simultaneously use PRA methods to investigate and report on aspects of policy and conditions, providing comparative insights for policy makers (pers. comm. Gerard Gill). A similar approach, but without PRA methods and without teams, was developed with ten representative villages in Sri Lanka in the mid 1970s (Senaratne 1976) but was not sustained. If the Nepal initiative is effective, it could represent a breakthrough for wide application in other countries.

The potential here appears vast. So often the state is self-deceiving through misleading information feedback through official channels (Chambers forthcoming). Perhaps in contrast, policy makers could now, through improved RRA and PRA approaches and methods, have available information and insights which are more immediately up-to-date, reliable and credible.

Personal Behaviour, Attitudes and Learning

All too often senior officials, scientists and academics, who pronounce and prescribe on rural development, lack recent direct knowledge, and base their analysis and action on ignorance or on personal experience in the name of science and modernity even in the 1990s.

It is not a new idea that rural development would gain if senior officials and policy makers were able to spend time unofficially living and learning in rural conditions, though little appears to have been done. An exception is the Exposure and Dialogue Programme of the German Commission of Justice and Peace, which for some years has been enabling senior outsiders to learn the life stories of village people (Kochendorfer-Lucius and Osner 1991; Osner *et al.* 1992). In a less structured manner, senior officials in India have appreciated the opportunities to spend time incognito in villages, with their interactions unconstrained by official protocol. At a personal level, the methods of PRA offer new scope, and make mini-sabaticals easier to envisage. PRA approaches and methods provide ways in which officials, scientists and academics can come face-to-face with rural people in an informal and non-threatening mode which both sides can find rewarding. They can also provide experience and learning which are intellectually exciting, practically relevant and often enjoyable.

Behaviour and attitudes can, though, be an impediment, sometimes irremediable. A senior government officer, an able scientist, a distinguished academic, an experienced NGO worker, a local-level extensionist or health worker – any of these, depending on personality, experience and circumstances, can either take to PRA with enthusiasm or reject it with passion. Much needs to be learnt about how, in the rural context, to facilitate changes in outsiders' behaviour and attitudes.

Some methods have already been devised, such as Anil Shah's 'shoulder tapping'. He has written that taking District Officers in Gujarat on a transect walk to see the problems of soil erosion, "I told them in advance that a transect in Participatory Rural Appraisal (PRA) is for observation and to understand the knowledge and perception of the farmers. We do not advise, but ask open-ended questions without implied advice. I told them that this was very difficult for educated people, more so for those in authority. Therefore, when I heard anyone giving advice or asking questions with implicit advice, I would tap this shoulder and if necessary offer my services to rephrase the advice or query into an open-ended question."

By the end of half a day, and several taps, a lot had been learnt that would otherwise have been missed (Shah 1992). More such methods, and much more experience with them, are needed.

The policy and personal potentials of RRA/PRA interlock. Their scope has scarcely begun to be tapped. The frontier here is to see how to scale up, how to enable many more policy makers at all levels, as well as others at the local level, personally to gain direct learning experience in the field from and with rural people, enabling them to fit policy and action more to local conditions and priorities and to the needs of the poor.

Spread with Quality Assurance

In strategic discussions about RRA and PRA, quality has been a recurrent concern. The term quality control has given way to quality assurance, since no person or organization can exercise control. Increasingly, the conclusion has been that assurance has to be personal, and that quality depends on the individual practitioner.

One dilemma here is how far to encourage would-be practitioners and trainers to start on their own. The danger is that bad performance will lead to discredit and disillusionment. The opportunity is for wider and faster spread. A problem is that capability depends on personality. Some people have a facility for using the 'right' language, especially at international conferences, but behave in the 'wrong' manner in the field, dominating, lecturing, interfering, interrupting and holding on to the stick. One solution may be for more shared field experience, for trainers to conduct training together, for more mutual 'shoulder tapping', and more learning from each other.

Appendix A, 'start, stumble, self-correct, share' is an attempt to encourage launching out and trying PRA approaches and methods, and learning by doing. Nothing in rural development is ever a panacea; and PRA faces problems of spread, scale and quality assurance. The potential realized will depend largely on practitioners and trainers. The questions are whether critical self-awareness, embracing error, using one's own best judgement at all times and constantly trying to do better can be built into the very genes of PRA; and if so, whether RRA and PRA can be not just self-spreading, but self-improving.

Empowerment and Equity

Good PRA empowers. Those who, through PRA, express and share what they already know, learn through that expression and sharing. Those who investigate and observe add to their knowledge. Those who analyze become yet more aware and reach new understanding. Those who plan and then implement what they have planned take command and further learn through the experience of action.

Whether empowerment is good depends on who are empowered and how their new power is used. If those who gain are outsiders who exploit, or a local elite who dominate, the poor and disadvantaged may be worse off. Whether PRA is equitable and good depends then on whom it involves. The 'natural' tendency is for this to be men rather than women, the better off rather than the worse off, and those of higher status groups rather than those of lower status. The challenge is, then, to so introduce and use PRA that the weaker are identified and empowered and equity is served.

Fortunately, tools available suit this task. Sequences such as participatory mapping, household listing, well-being ranking and livelihood analysis can identify groups distinguished according to local values. Focus group discussions can then identify the priorities and interests of different categories of people, including, or especially, those who are disadvantaged. The contrasts can be sharp. Drawing on application of PRA techniques in Sierra Leone, Ghana, Malawi and Bangladesh, Alice Welbourn (1991) has shown how significant can be differences of ethnic group, age, gender and economic status, and combinations of these. With pastoralists in Kenya, Jermy Swift and Abdi Noor Umar (1991:56) found marked and striking differences of priority: out of a possible maximum of 100, livestock management was scored 87 by the rich, but only 7 by the poor, and lack of livestock by the rich but 49 by the poor.

Differentiating groups and interests can empower the poorer in several ways. It can give them collective awareness and confidence to confront others and argue their case: Youth for Action, an NGO based in South India, has worked at first in some villages only with Harijans (untouchables), so that they gained in confidence and capability, before later the rest of the village was involved. AKPSP (India) convenes groups of women and men separately to choose the numbers of trees of different sorts they want in their nursery, and then helps them reconcile their difference.

Differentiation through wealth or well-being ranking can help an outside organization select and deselect those with whom it will work: Action Aid and MYRADA, both in South India, have used PRA methods to identify the poorer who then gain more from their programmes.

PRA methods, such as diagramming, can also be brought into play to clarify and resolve conflicts. Agroecosystem diagramming was used in the Philippines to make explicit, the differences of interests between groups after the construction of a small dam at lake Buhi and to achieve consensus about priorities (Conway, Sajise and Knowland 1989; Conway 1989). In the approach of the Neighbourhood Initiatives Foundation in the UK, a large model of a neighbourhood allows people to address conflicts by putting down suggestions and using markers to agree or disagree without needing to identify themselves. This 'depersonalizes conflicts and introduces informality where consensus is more easily reached' (Gibson 1991).

The identification, expression and resolution of conflicts of interests remain a frontier for participatory methods. The coming years will show what potential there is. The worst is that participatory methods may so enhance the awareness of the disadvantaged and encourage their organization and action that a backlash is provoked which leaves them weaker and worse off. One hope can be that diagrams can be used to defuse tension by focusing public debate. They can make differences permanently explicit, and can direct discussion to a visible thing rather than to individual people.

To explore this frontier demands sensitive commitment and time. PRA methods to identify differences of interests and priorities are well known. Methods for negotiation and equitable conflict resolution are less so. It is perhaps in this domain more than any other that there is need and scope for new participatory methods.

Substituting for Surveys

Rural questionnaire surveys are one of the largest rural industries. They are also one of the most protected and inefficient. They have hitherto not been subjected to a market challenge. Like Henry Ford's Model T automobile, mass produced, durable, and all the same colour, they are routinely turned out in a standard form. In the case of some repetitive national surveys, like the National Sample Survey in India, there may be no full substitute. But other ad hoc surveys are continuously being commissioned. Administering questionnaires is still the normal mode of rural research.

Donors and governments alike have maintained demand for questionnaire surveys through their concern for monitoring and valuation (M&E). Funds are set aside for baseline surveys so iat later progress can be monitored and projects evaluated. Few ich baseline surveys have ever been useful, let alone worth the sources invested in them. The reasons include difficulties in isuring comparability in subsequent surveys, in assessing the ounter-factual (what would have happened without the project), finding comparable controls and in identifying causality.

It is too early to say that the days of the standard iestionnaire survey are numbered. Like the Model T, it is bust and durable; the public is fond of it, and it employs many orkers who lack other skills. Some managers (academics, onsultants) like it because it keeps them off the shop floor (out f the field). But the market for the Model T declined, as better id more varied alternatives were developed, and with large iestionnaire surveys, there are similar straws in the wind, the all: the National Council of Applied Economic Research, obably the largest survey organization in India, apart from the ational Sample Survey, has been trying out rapid and articipatory methods as an alternative or complement to uestionnaire surveys, and with positive results, a leading PRA ractitioner and trainer, Sam Joseph, of Action Aid, Bangalore, hen challenged, was able to specify a more cost-effective PRA iethod for obtaining all the items of data in a standard baseline irvey; and as noted above eight teams of researchers in Nepal, ained in PRA methods, are attempting to generate simultaneous nd comparable insights from different locations.

> I trained the ... Soyabean project group in the use of PRA for monitoring of the project impact in 5 states of the Federation, i.e. Kaduna, Niger, Enugu, Anambra and Oyo States of Nigeria. The group of 16 researchers was amazed about how much easier it is to obtain in depth information through participatory mapping, in addition to other PRA techniques they have already known. We were able, through mapping, to obtain all relevant socio-demographic information we required for the project; for example, the number of households in a village, households involved in soyabean production, gender issues in soyabean production, utilization of soyabean and preference ranking of various

soyabean diets ... We gathered an incredible amount of information within an hour and a half visit to the village ... The researchers have been begging me to give more training in PRA ...

In cases such as this, PRA methods, used well, can be not only more cost-effective than questionnaire surveys; they are also more popular with all concerned, researchers and rural people alike.

The use of PRA methods in M&E research raises issues of comparability and causality. Comparability of information shared in different contexts may become a big question in the 1990s. Decentralized and democratic processes may generate disparate data which central planners cannot then easily add up or compare. More remains to be learnt about how and how well PRA methods can generate commensurable data (for example demographic, health and agricultural information) from different places; and to what extent central planners and officials can tolerate and manage incommensurability and variability in the form of locally shared information and locally generated plans.

With causality, PRA methods have advantages over questionnaire surveys. Statistical correlations and regressions do not establish causality. People who live in an area have a comparative advantage in knowing and interpreting what has happened there, and PRA now has relevant tools to help them conduct their own analysis.

The need now is to multiply and assess more tests, experiments and innovations, like those of the NCAER in India, of Winrock in Nepal and of Adjebeng-Asem in Nigeria, in order to learn how rapid, relaxed and participatory approaches and methods can substitute for, and improve upon, questionnaire surveys.

Spread by Villagers

A finding of the PRA experience has been (See under "Villagers' Knowledge and Capabilities", p. 20) that rural people can do much that outsiders have thought they could not do. One by one the dominoes have fallen as they have shown that they can map, model, rank, score, estimate, diagram and analyze more and better than expected. Often, too, they can do this better than outsiders. The working rule has become to assume that people are capable of something until it is proved otherwise.

One frontier then becomes the development and spread of PRA and related approaches and methods by villagers themselves. Extension has in recent decades been thought of as an activity for the field staff of government organizations or of NGOs, usually with high recurrent costs. The question is whether, and if so how, to 'hand over the stick' to farmers and villagers themselves, and whether this can be sustainable through local demand for the service provided.

Farmers' own extension has a long history, probably as old as farming itself. Deliberate training of farmers as extensionists, though, is more recent. As one example, in the 1980s in Central America, World Neighbours trained volunteer extensionists and gradually handed over responsibilities for experiments and extension to them (Bunch 1985). In India, both MYRADA and SPEECH have invited villagers who had already gained experience of PRA to take part as facilitators of training in other villages.

The Aga Khan Rural Support Programme (India) has taken this further. In the late 1980s, it developed village volunteers as an approach in which villagers were trained as facilitators both for their own and for other villages. The village volunteers were not just to be extensionists, but to facilitate the PRA approaches and methods (Shah 1989: Shah, Bharadwaj and Ambastha 1991). The village volunteers came to provide services for which people were prepared to pay, not only from their own but from other villages. They also were enabled to form teams to conduct PRA exercises in other villages. These teams are doing these exercises in a number of villages involving mapping, transect diagramming, interviewing, group discussions, prioritization and preparation of a village natural resources management plan. It is observed that they enjoy the process...' (Shah *et al.* 1991:87-88). In February 1992, a team of village volunteers demonstrated their skills as facilitators to an international group of visitors in Kabripather village, Bharuch district, Gujarat. In a day, the village volunteers enabled villagers to map their degraded forest, count and measure rootstock in five quadrats on the ground, assess numbers of nursery plants needed, and through matrix scoring, analyze needs and choose numbers of each species (M. Shah, forthcoming). In July 1992, it was reported that village volunteers conducting PRAs had told AKRSP staff that now 'they need not bother to attend'.

The question now is whether spread through village volunteers can become self-sustaining and self-improving. The incentive systems evolved by KRSP and villagers involve payment by results, rewarding good performance. Demand exists from new villages for the services of village volunteers. It remains to be seen whether village volunteers on their own will be able and willing to train village volunteers in new villages, who will then in turn be in demand. Were that to occur, and with market incentives for good performance, what began as programme initiated from outside, might become self-spreading. Were that not to occur, it might still be feasible for organizations like AKRSP to foster spread with a light touch, training volunteers and encouraging them to form teams that sell their services.

PRA in Institutions

Perhaps the biggest challenge is the establishment of PRA as a way of operating, even as a culture, in organizations. Normal bureaucratic tendencies to standardize, centralize and impose top-down targets at best impede and at worst prevent the open-endedness, flexibility, creativity and diversity of much good PRA. To establish PRA as the norm in an organization, therefore, requires reversals and change of culture.

Three main types of organizations have been involved: NGOs, government field organizations and universities as well as training institutes.

Those organizations, which have embraced and developed PRA have shared three characteristics. The leadership has been stable and committed to PRA; a substantial proportion of staff have personally wished to use the PRA approach and methods; and there has been recurrent training and reinforcement. Commitment of a director or principal of an institution is on its own not enough; nor is on its own repeated training. Nor does it seem useful to train at lower field level without a higher level commitment. It is critical that the middle-level managerial staff in any organization, genuinely, and not just verbally, wish to use or support PRA. If they do not, there are innumerable small ways in which their lack of support can undermine and finally eliminate PRA initiatives.

Not surprisingly, much of the initial innovation and spread has been among NGOs, since their organizational cultures quite often share values with PRA. Some, like IIED based in the UK and MYRADA and AKRSP in India, have undertaken training for government field organizations, and have defined or begun to redefine their roles to include PRA training for others. Adoption and use in government field organizations is more problematical (See under *Utility : Practical Applications* p. 28). To learn more from experience, already gained with strategy and tactics, is a priority that will be addressed in a forthcoming issue of PRA Notes.

In the long term, universities and training institutes are strategically vital. Currently, many of them disable those who pass through them, conditioning them with attitudes and behaviour of superiority, and teaching methods, which then have to be unlearnt. Rehabilitation can then be tiresome, painful, costly and far from always successful.

Globally, RRA and PRA have made little impression in universities and training institutes till date. The scale of adoption of RRA and PRA remains minuscule compared to the scope. The potential for applications in training and education remains vast and almost entirely unrecognized. Only when more universities and other tertiary institutions for education and training introduce RRA and PRA into their curricula, teaching and fieldwork, and a new generation of professionals are well versed in their principles, methods, behaviour and attitudes which go with them, will its acceptance and spread become truly wide.

To this absence in universities, four exceptions can be noted regionally :

First, in Southeast Asia, several universities in Thailand (notably the pioneering University of Khon Kaen) and the Philippines (including the University of the Philippines, Los

Banos) have been using RRA for years. A comparative study is overdue to understand why and how they came to adopt it, and their experience in legitimating, teaching and further developing it.

Third, in the early 1990s, some key training institutions in India and Nepal started to adopt and develop the PRA approach and methods. These include the National Academy of Administration at Mussoorie, the Indian Institute of Forest Management at Bhopal, the Xavier Institute of Social Service at Ranchi, and the Institute of Forest Management at Pokhara in Nepal. All these are believed to be using PRA methods in the village fieldwork of their students in place of questionnaire surveys. At the same time, a number of agriculture universities in India, including the Narendra Dev University of Agriculture and Technology, Faizabad and other Eastern Indian agricultural universities, the Tamil Nadu Agricultural University and the Hebbal Agricultural University, Bangalore, have invited lectures, workshops and training in PRA and related methodologies.

Fourth, staff in several Australian universities have taken up and practised RRA and PRA. Historically, this followed a paradigm shift in agricultural education to systems thinking and self-directed learning, in Hawkesbury Agricultural College (now the University of Western Sydney, Hawkesbury; the School of Crop Sciences at the University of Sydney (Ampt and Ison 1989; Ison n.d.); the School of Agriculture at Charles Sturt University, Riverina (Dunn and McMillan 1991); and the Law School, Mcquarie University (Voyce *et al*. 1989). One RRA in Australia identified intra- and inter-generational conflict and the transfer of the family farm as neglected topics of concern to many farmers (Ampt 1988; Ampt and Ison 1988; Ison 1990) and then RRA techniques were used to study the transfer of the family farm (Voyce *et al*. 1989). RRA has also been used for the identification of grassland research problems (Ampt and Ison 1989). In September 1991, participants from several institutions combined as a team to facilitate a PRA in the Kyeamba Valley which enabled landholders and their families to identify and analyze issues of concern, and to plan action (PRA Team 1991).

Pathways of dissemination are not easy to foresee, but this Australian example may be a pointer. With this form of global sharing, the normal direction of transfer of innovation is reversed and approaches as well as methods evolved in developing countries and adopted and adapted in rich countries.

THE PARADIGMATIC SIGNIFICANCE OF PRA

One contribution to be sought from universities is a better understanding of underlying theory. In Australia, RRA has been linked with soft systems theory (Checkland 1981) and contextual science (Russell and Ison 1991). In making these links, Australian researchers have begun to explore further the paradigmatic significance of RRA and PRA.

The word 'paradigm' is used with various meanings. Here I shall use it to mean a coherent and mutually active pattern of concepts, values, methods and action, amenable to wide application.

In his paper (Jamieson 1987) "The paradigmatic significance of RRA", delivered at the International Conference on Rapid Rural Appraisal at Khon Kaen in 1985, Neil Jamieson argued that RRA, with its rapid learning, fitted and supported a new and emerging paradigm of development. Despite ideological conflicts, Marxists, socialists and capitalists had shared evolutionary, unilineal, universalistic, positivistic and utilitarian assumptions, and a fervent belief in progress. Another view of development, he said, was of human evolution as problem-solving under pressure, as adaptive change. This fitted better with a cybernetic systems approach, which included the concepts of feedback, of lead time (the time between receipt of information and when it is too late to use it), and of lag time (the time between receipt of information and the completion of action based on it), (see also Joseph 1991). Jamieson argued that change had accelerated and unpredictability had increased, making accurate and timely feedback more than ever vital for effective adaptive change.

Much that Jamieson wrote not only still applies, but applies now with more force than in 1985. At a theoretical level, chaos theory has shown more clearly how patterns and directions of hange can be sensitive to small differences in starting onditions (Gleick 1987). At the empirical level, changes in local nd global conditions – ecological, social and political – appear ɔ be accelerating. In conditions of faster and faster change, and ɔf increasing unpredictability, it matters more even than before ɔ have timely, prompt learning and rapid adaptive responses.

Perhaps more significantly, parallel shifts of paradigm are ow occurring in three domains: in science; in business ıanagement; and in development itself.

In science, conventional approaches, using hard systems and eductionist assumptions and methods, are in crisis when face nany of our important problems (Means 1991; Appleyard 1992). Scientific methods are not competent to predict or prescribe for the complex open systems which matter most. Global environmental issues involve huge uncertainties and demand what Funtowicz and Ravetz (1990) call a 'second order science' in which judgement plays a more recognized part. Precise understanding prediction and prescription for local agro-eco-social systems can be similarly elusive. This is not a new discovery, Jeremy Swift wrote in 1981:

> ... a major World Bank livestock development project in Mali is based, for crucial calculations of sustainable grazing pressure, on the report of a highly competent ecologist in 1972; the calculations were redone in 1977-78 by a different, equally well-qualified ecologist, who halved the earlier carrying capacity. Nobody is to blame; the science is inexact. But the consequences could be disastrous for the project, and more so for the pastoralists involved (Swift 1981:487).

Perhaps, no one was to blame then. But now we know more about what is not knowable using the standard methods of 'disciplines'. When so much is so unknowable and so unpredictable, solutions have to be sought through methodological pluralism, through flexible and continuous learning and adaption, and through the exercise of judgement.

In business management, the parallel shift has been from the values and strategies of mass production to those of flexible specialization (see e.g. Kaplinsky 1991:7). Standardization has been replaced by variety and rapid response, hierarchical supervision by thrust, and punitive quality control by personal quality assurance at source. Much in Tom Peters' book of advice to American business managers, *Thriving on Chaos: Handbook for a Management Revolution* (1987), applies equally in PRA. He advocates, for example, 'achieving flexibility by empowering people', learning to love change, becoming obsessed with listening, deferring to the front line, and 'building systems for a world turned upside down'. A highly successful Brazilian manager, when he took over a company, abolished norms, manuals, rules and regulations, and put the company's employees in the demanding position of using their own judgement' (Selmer 1989: 79). It has been the discipline of the market and opportunities from new technology which have driven and drawn business management to decentralized flexibility, to diversification, and to finding and exploiting transient niche markets. For PRA and related approaches, the discipline is what works with people and communities, and the opportunities of the new approaches and methods, which drive and draw. In both business management and PRA, value is placed on decentralization, sharing knowledge, empowerment, diversity, and rapid change and feedback. So it is that the philosophy and approaches of PRA can be seen as one expression of a wider paradigm for effective action in the contemporary world.

In development theories of universal economic growth as the main means to a better life are less credible than ever (see e.g. Ekins 1992, Sachs 1992 passim). As economic growth ceases to be a simple, universal objective, as it is recognized as environmentally harmful among the richer, and as economic resources are recognized as finite, so it matters more to enhance the quality of life through other more sustainable means. For the rich, the question is how to be better off with less; for the poor, it is how to gain more and be better off with what they can gain, but without repeating the errors of the rich. These objectives can be served by enabling local people to identify, express and achieve more of their own priorities. In line with this, the emergent paradigm for human living on and with the earth brings together decentralization, democracy and diversity. What is local and what is different is valued. In this paradigm, the trends towards centralization, authoritarianism and homogenization are reversed. Reductionism, linear thinking and standard solutions give way to an inclusive holism, open systems thinking and diverse options and actions.

RRA, and more so PRA, are part of general paradigm shift. They resonate with the support methodological local people's priorities and democratic local diversity. Like 'future development', the future of PRA is unknowable; but the promise is there. How much of that promise is realized, how soon, and how well, will be determined by professionals in NGOs, government services, training and research institutes and universities. Closed or open, conservative or radical, reductionist or pluralist, timid or bold, as guardians of the old or as inventors of the new, they will determine this through personal choice.

ABBREVIATIONS AND ADDRESSES

Action Aid	Action Aid, 3, Rest House Road, Post Box 5406, Bangalore-560 001, India.
AKRSP	Aga Khan Rural Support Programme (India), Choice Premises, Swastik Cross Roads, Navarangpura, Ahmedabad-380 009, India.
IDS	Institute of Development Studies, University of Sussex, Brighton BN1 9RE, UK.
IIED	Sustainable Agriculture Programme, International Institute for Environment and Development, 3, Endsleigh Street, London WC1H ODD, UK.
MYRADA	MYRADA, 2, Service Road, Domlur Layout, Bangalore-560 071, India.
NCAER	National Council for Applied Economic Research, 11, I.P. Estate, New Delhi 110 002, India.
NIF	Neighbourhood Initiatives Foundation, Chapel House, 7 Gravel Leasowes, Lightmoor, Telford, TF 4 3QL, UK.
ODI	Overseas Development Institute, Regent's College, Inner Circle, Regent's Park, London NW1 4NS.
PRA	Participatory Rural Appraisal.
RRA	Rapid Rural Appraisal.
SPEECH	14, Jeyaraja IIlam, Kiruba Nagar, Madurai-625 014, India.

References

Action Aid, (1991) : Jamkhed: "Participatory Rural Appraisal in Identifying Major Illness", Healthcare Providers and Costs, Action Aid, Bangalore.

Ampt, P.R., (1988): "Rapid Rural Appraisal", Forbes Shire, February 1988, Initial Report, School of Crop Sciences, University of Sydney.

Ampt, P. R. (1989) : "Rapid Rural Appraisal for the identification of grassland research problem", *Proceedings of the XVI International Grassland Congress*, Nice, France, pp. 1291-92.

Ampt, P.R. and Ison, R.L., (1988) : "Report of a Rapid Rural Appraisal to identify problems and opportunities for agronomic research and development in the Forbes Shire, NSW", School of Crop Sciences, University of Sydney, December.

Appleton, Judith, (1992) : "Notes from a food and nutrition PRA in a Guinean fishing village", *RRA Notes*, 16, pp. 77-85.

Appleyard, B., (1992) : *Understanding the Present: Science and the Soul of Modern Man*, Picador, Published by Pan Books, London.

Ashby, J.A., (1990) : "Evaluating Technology with farmers: A Handbook", IPRA Projects, Centrol Interactional de Agricultura Tropical (CIAT), AA 6713, Cali, Colombia, December.

Bawden, R.J., Macadam, R.D., Packham, R.J. and Valentine, I., (1984): "Systems thinking and practice in agricultural education", *Agricultural Systems,* 13, pp. 205-25

Bayer, W., (1987) : "Browse quality and availability in a farming area and a grazing reserve in the Nigerian sub-humid zone", Report to the ILCA Sub-humid Zone Program, Kaduna, Nigeria, Gottingen, May.

Bayer, W., (1988) : "Ranking of browse species by cattlemeepers in Nigeria", *RRA Notes,* 3, pp. 4-10, December.

Bayer, W., (1987) : "Rapid Appraisal: The evolution of the concept and the definition of issues", in *KKU Proceedings,* pp. 47-68.

Belshaw, D., (1981) : "A theoretical framework for data-economizing appraisal procedures with applications for rural development planning", in R. Longhurst (ed.), *IDS Bulletin*, Vol. 12, No. 4, pp. 12-22.

Bentley, Margaret E., Pelto, Gretel H.; Straus, Walter L.; Schumann, Debra A., Adegbola, Catherine, de la Pena, Emanuela, Oni, Gbolahan A., Brown, Kenneth H. and Huffman, Sandra L., (1988) : Rapid ethnographic assessment: applications in a diarrhoea management program, *Social Science in Medicine*, Vol. 27, No. 1, pp. 107-116.

Bernadas, C.N. Jr., (1991) : Lesson in upland farmer participation: the case of enriched fallow technology in Jaro, Leyte, Philippines, *Forest, Trees and People Newsletter*, 14 October, pp. 10-11.

Biggs, S., (1980) : Informal R&D, *Ceres*, Vol.13, No. 4, pp. 23-26.

BRAC, (1983) : The Net: Power Structure in Ten Villages, Bangladesh Rural Advancement Committee, 66 Mokhahali Commercial Areas, Dhaka 12.

Bradley, Sarah Murray, (1992) : "Visual literacy: a review with an annoted bibliography", mimeo, IIED, London.

Brokensha, David W, Warren D.,. and Werner, O., (1980) : *Indigenous Knowledge Systems and Development,* University Press of America, Lanham, Maryland.

Buchanan-Smith, M., (1992) : "Finding out how people prioritize their food security problems in Chad: the challenges of RRA at national level", memeo, IDS, Sussex.

Bunch, R., (1985) : Two Ears of Corn: A Guide to People-Centred Agricultural Improvement, World Neighbours, 5116, North Portland, Oklahoma City, Oklahoma 73112.

Campbell, G.J. Shrestha, R. and Stone, L., (1979) : The Use and Misuse of Social Science Research in Nepal, Research Centre for Nepal and Asian Studies, Tribhuvan University, Kirtipur, Kathmandu.

Carruthers, Ian and Chambers, Robert., (1981) : "Rapid Appraisal for rural development", *Agricultural Administration*, Vol. 8, No. 6, pp. 407-422.

Case, D'Arcy Davis, (1990) : "The Community's Toolbox: The Idea, Methods and Tools for Participatory Assessment, Monitoring and Evaluation in Community Forestry, *Community Forestry Field Manual* 2, FAO, Rome.

Cernea, Michael (ed.), (1985) : *Putting People First: Sociological Variables in Development Project*, the Johns Hopkins Press, Baltimore.

Chambers, Robert, (1981) : "Rapid Rural Appraisal : rationale and repertoire", IDS Discussion Paper, No.155, IDS, Sussex.

____(1992), "The self-deceiving state", *IDS Bulletin,* Vol. 23, No. 4, IDS, Sussex.

Chambers, Robert and Harriss, John (1977) : "Comparing twelve South Indian villages: in search of practical theory", in B.H. Farmer (ed.), *Green Revolution? Technology and Change in Rice Growing Area of Tamil Nadu and Sri Lanka*, pp. 301-322.

Chambers, Robert and Jiggins, Janice (1986) : "Agricultural research with resource-poor farmers: a parsimonious paradigm:, IDS Discussion Paper 220, IDS, Sussex.

Chambers, Robert, Pacey, Arnold and Thrupp, Lori Ann. (eds.) (1989) : *Farmer First: Farmer Innovation and Agricultural Research*, Intermediate Technology Publications, London.

Checkland, P.B., (1981) : *Systems Thinking, Systems Practice*, John Wiley, Chichester.

Collinson, M., (1981) : "A low cost approach to understanding small farmers", *Agricultural Administration*. Vol. 8, No. 6, pp. 433-50.

Convergence, (1975) : Vol. 7, No. 2, 1981, Vol. 14, No. 2, and 1988, Vol. 21, Nos. 2 and 3; special issue on participatory research.

Conway, G., (1985) : "Agroecosystem analysis", *Agricultural Administration*, 20, pp. 32-55.

____(1986), Agroecosystem Analysis for Research and Development, Winrock International Institute for Agricultural Development, PO Box 1172, Nana Post Office, Bangkok 10112.

____(1987), "Rapid Rural Appraisal and Agroecosystem analysis: a case study from Northern Pakistan', in *KKU Proceedings,* pp. 228-54.

____(1988), "Rainbow over Wollow", *New Scientist*, 5 May.

____(1989), "Diagrams for farmers", in R.Chambers, A Pacey and L.A. Thrupp (eds.), Farmer First, pp. 77-86.

Conway, G., Sajise, P. and Knowland, W. (1989) : "Lake Buhi: resolving conflicts in a Philippines development project", *Ambio*, Vol. 18, No. 2, pp. 128-35.

Cornwall, Andrea (1992): "Body mapping in health RRA/PRA", *RRA Notes*, 16, pp. 69-76.

Cresswell, Teresa (1992): "Unemployment and health: the development of the use of PRA in identified communities in Staveley, North Derbyshire", *RRA Notes* 16, pp. 27-30.

Daane, J.R.V. (1987): "Quelle Methode poru l' Analyse de Ststems do Production en Zonal Rurale Tropicale: Le Dilemme entre Demarche Quantitative Peu Biable et Demarche Qualitative Peu Generalisable", Contribution au eme Seminaire d'Economie Rurale CIRAD, Montpellier.

Devavaram, John, Nalini, J. Vimalnathan, Abdul Sarkar, Krishnan, A.P. Mayandi and Karunanidhi., (1991): "PRA for Rural Resource Management", *RRA Notes* 13, pp.102-111.

Dunn, A.M. (1991): "New challenges for extensionists: targeting complex problems and issues' paper for the 10th European Seminar on Extension Education, Universidade de Tras-os Montese Alto Douro, Vila Real, Portugal, September.

Dunn, Tony and McMillin, Allan (1991): "Action research: the application of Rapid Rural Appraisal to learn about issues of concern in land care areas near Wagga Wagga, NSW", paper presented at a Conference on Agriculture, Education and Information Transfer, Murrumbigee College of Agriculture, NSW, September 30 to October 2, 1991.

ECRS, (1988): Rapid Rural Appraisal: a Closer Look at Rural Life in Wollo, Ethiopian Red Cross Society, Addis Ababa and the IIED, London.

Ekins, P., Hillman, Mayer and Hutchinson, Robert (1992): *Wealth Beyond Measure: an Atlas of New Economics*, Galia Books, London.

Farmer, B.H., (1977): *Green Revolution? Technology and Change in Rice-Growing Areas of Tamil Nadu and Sri Lanka*, Macmillan, London and Basingstoke.

Farrington, John (ed.) (1988): *Experimental Agriculture*, Vol. 24, Part 3.

Farringtonb, John and Martin, Adrienne (1988): "Farmer participation in agricultural research: a review of concept and practices", Agricultural Administration Occasional Paper No. 9, ODI London.

Francis, Sheelu, Devavaram, John and Erskine, Arunothayam. (1992): "Training workshop on participatory rural appraisal for planning health projects", *RRA Notes* 16, pp. 37-47.

Franzel, Steven and Crawford, Eric. (1987): "Comparing formal and informal survey techniques for farming research: a case study from Kenya", *Agricultural Administration* 27, pp.13-33.

Freire, Paulo. (1968): *Pedagogy of the Oppressed*, The Seabury Press, New York.

FSRU (1991): "Structural adjustment and communal area agriculture in Zimbabwe: case studies from Mangwende and Chivi communal areas: a report of a rapid rural appraisal exercise", Farming Systems Research Unit, Department of Research and Specialist Services, Ministry of Lands, Agriculture and Rural Settlement, Harare, Zimbabwe, November.

FSSP (1987): *Diagnosis, Design and Analysis in Farming Systems Research and Extension*, Volumes I, II and III, and trainer's Manual, Farming Systems Support Project, Institute of Food and Agricultural Science, University of Florida, Gainesville, Florida 32611, December.

Funtowicz, S.O. and Ravetz, J.R. (1990): Gloval Environmental Issues and the Emergence of Second Order Science, Commission of the European Communities, Luxembourg.

Gaventa, John and Lewis, Helen (1991): "Participatory education and grassroots development – the case of rural appalachia", *Gatekeeper Series* 25, IIED, London.

Gibbs, Christopher (1987): "Rapid Rural Appraisal: an overview of concepts and applications', in *KKU Proceedings*, pp. 193-206.

Gibson, Tony (1991): "Planning for real: the approach of the Neighbourhood Initiatives Foundation in the UK", *RRA Notes* 11, pp. 29-30.

Gilbert, E.H. Norman, D.W. and Winch, F.E. (1980): "Farming Systems Research: a critical appraisal", MSU Rural Development Paper No. 6, Department of Agricultural Economics, Michigan State University, East Lansing, Michigan 48824.

Gill, G. (1991): "But how does it compare with the real data?" RRA Notes 14, pp. 5-14 (also Research Report Series Number 16, HMG Ministry of Agriculture-Winrock International, Kathmandu, January 1992).

Gill, G., Forthcoming, "Participatory methods in policy analysis for natural resource management", in *Natural Resource Economics of India: A Guidebook for Researchers and Policy Makers*, Oxford and IBH, New Delhi.

Gleick, J. (1987): *Chaos: making a New Science*, Heinemann, London.

Gould, P, and White, R. (1974), *Mental Maps*, Penguin Books, Harmondsworth, UK.

Grandin, Barbara (1988): *Wealth Ranking in Smallholder Communities: A Field Manual*, Intermediate Technology Publications, 103, Southampton Row, London.

Grandstaff, Terry B, and Grandstaff, Somluckrat W. (1987a): "A conceptual basis for methodological development in Rapid Rural Appraisal", in *KKU Proceedings*, pp. 69-88.

____ (1987b): "Semi-structured interviewing by multidisciplinary teams in RRA", in *KKU Proceedings*, pp. 129-143.

Grandstaff, Somluckrat W., Grandstaff, Terry B. and Lovelace, George W. (1987): "Summary Report", in *KKU Proceedings*, pp. 3-30.

Groenfeldt, D. (1989): "Guidelines for rapid assessment of minor irrigation systems in Sri Lanka", Working Paper No.14, International Irrigation Management Institute, Sri Lanka.

Gueye, Bara and Schoonmaker, Freudenberger, Karen (1990): "Introduction a la Methode Acceleree de Recherche Participative (MARP)", Centre de Recherches pour le Development International, BP 2435, Dakar, Senegal, October..

Gueye, Bara and Schoonmaker, Freudenberger (1991): Methods Accelerr de Recherche Participative", IIED, London, August.

Guijt, Irene, and Manneh, Karafa, Martin, Mary and Sarch, Terri, (1992): "Reflections on the training: process and prospects", in *From Input to Impact: Participatory Rural Appraisal for Action Aid*, The Gambia, Action Aid, the Gambia and IIED, London, March pp. 1-19.

Guijt, Irene, and Pretty, Jules N., (forthcoming), *Participatory Rural Appraisal for Farmer Participatory Research in Pubjab*, Pakistan, IIED, London.

Gypmantasiri *et al.* and Conway, Gordon (1980): "An Interdisciplinary Perspective of Cropping Systems in the Chiang Mai Valley: Key Questions for Research", Multiple Cropping Project, Faculty of Agriculture, University of Chiang Mai, Thailand, June.

Hahn. H. (1991): "Apprendre avec les yeux, s'exprimer avec les mains: des paysans se forment a la gestion du terrior", AGRECOL, Oekozentrum, CH-4438 Langenbruck, Switzerland.

Harwod, R. (1979): *Small Farm Development: Understanding and Improving Farming Systems in the Humid Tropics*, Westview Press, Boulder, Colorado.

Hill, Polly. (1972): *Rural Hausa: A Village and a Setting*, Cambridge University Press, Cambridge.

IDS (1979): "Whose Knowledge Counts?', *IDS Bulletin*, Vol. 10, No. 2.

____(1992): "Some Sources on Rapid and Participatory Rural Appraisal".

Inglis, Andrew Steward. (1990): "Harvesting local forestry knowledge: a field test and evaluation of rapid rural appraisal techniques for social forestry project analysis", dissertation presented for the degree of Master of Science, University of Edinburg.

____(1991): "Harvesting local forestry knowledge: a comparison of RRA and conventional surveys", *RRA Notes* 12, pp. 32-40.

Ison, Raymond, I., (1990): "Rapid Rural Appraisal: A participatory 'problem' identification method relevant to Australian agriculture", School of Crop Sciences, University of Sydney, 2206.

Jamieson, N. (1987): "The paradigmatic significance of RRA", in *KKU Proceedings*, pp. 89-102.

Jayakaran, Ravi (1991): "PRA Camp at Mahilong, Bihar, 27-30, November 1990: Krishi Gram Vikas Kendra", *RRA Notes*, 13, 00. 118-122.

Johansson, Lars, and Hoben, Allan (1992): "RRA's for land policy formulation in Tanzania", *Forests, Trees and People Newsletter,* 14/15, February' pp. 26-31.

Joseph, S. (1991): "Lead time, lag time: RRA/PRA in Action Aid", Action Aid. Post Box 5406, 3 Resthouse Road, Bangalore-560 001.

____(1992), "Participatory Rural Appraisal in identifying major illness, healthcare providers and costs", *RRA Notes* 16, pp. 53-56.

Joseph, Thomas, and Joseph, Sam. (1991): "PRA in Malda District, West Bengal: report of a training workshop for Action Aid India and Tagore Society for Rural Development", *RRA Notes* 13, pp. 95-101.

Kabutha, Charity, and Ford, Richard (1988): "Using RRA to formulate a village resources management plan, Mbusanyi, Kenya", *RRA Notes* 2, October, pp. 4-11.

Kaplinsky, R. (1991): "From mass production to flexible specialization: a case study from a semi-industrialized economy", IDS Discussion Paper 295, IDS, Sussex, November.

Kassam, Yusuf, and Mustafa, Kemal (Eds.) (1982): *Participatory Research: An Emerging Alternative Methodology in Social Science Research*, Society for Participatory Research in Asia, 45, Sainik Farm, Khanpur, New Delhi 110 062.

KKU, (1987): Proceedings of the 1985 International Conference on Rapid Rural Appraisal, Rural Systems Research and Farming Systems Research Projects, University of Khon Kaen, Thailand.

Kochendorder-Lucius, S. and K. Osner (1991): "Development Has a Face: Life stories of Thirteen Women in Bangladesh on People's Economy", Results of the International Exposure and Dialogue Programme of the German Commission of Justice and Peace and Grameen Bank in Bangladesh, October 14-22, 1989, Gerechtigkeit and Frieden Series, Deutsche Kommission Justice et Pax, Kaiserstrasse 163, D-5300 Bonn 1.

Kumar, Alok (1992): "Trends in Health Care", *RRA Notes* 16, pp. 48-52.

Kumar, Somesh (1991): "Anantapur experiment in PRA training", *RRA Notes* 13, pp.112-17.

Lightfoot, Clive, *et. al.*, (1991): *Training Resource Book for Participatory Experimental Design*, Narendra Dev University of Agriculture and Technology, Faizabad, UP, India; International Centre for Living Aquatic Resources Management, Manila, Philippines; International Rice Research Institute, Manila, Philippines.

Longhurst, R., (ed.) (1981): "Rapid Rural Appraisal", *IDS Bulletin*, Vol. 12, No. 4.

Lovelace, Geroge W, Subhadhira, Sukaesinee and Simaraks, Suchint (eds.) (1988): "Rapid Rural Appraisal in Northeast Thailand: Case Studies", KKU-Ford Rural Systems Research Project, Khon Kaen University, Khon Kaen, Thailand.

McCracken, J.A. (1988): *Participatory Rapid Rural Appraisal in Gujarat: A Trial Model for the Aga Khan Rural Support Programme (India)*, IIED, London, November.

____(1990), "BOBP tries out RRA in Chinnamedu, Tamil Nadu", *Bay of Bengal News*, June 1990, pp. 2-5.

McCracken, J.A., Pretty, Jules N. and Conway, Gordon R. (1988): *An Introduction to Rapid Rural Appraisal for Agricultural Development, IIED*, London.

Mascarenhas, J. (1990): "Transects in PRA", PALK Series IV E, MYRADA, 2 Service Road, Domlur Layout, Bangalore 560 071.

Mascarenhas, J, and P.D. Prem Kumar (1991): "Participatory mapping and modelling user's notes", *RRA Notes* 12, pp. 9-20.

Mascarenhas, J, *et al.*, (1991): "Participatory Rural Appraisal: Proceedings of the February 1991 Bangalore PRA Trainers Workshop", *RRA Notes* Number 13, IIED, London and MYRADA, Bangalore, August.

Maxwell, Simon. (1989): "Rapid food security assessment : a pilot exercise in Sudan", *RRA Notes 5*.

Mduma, E.K. (1982): "Appropriate technology for grain storage at Bwakira Chini Village", in Kaswsam and Mustafa (eds.), *Participatory Research*, pp. 198-213.

Mearns, R. (1991): "Environmental implications of structural adjustment: reflections on scientific method", IDS Discussion Paper 284, IDS, Sussex, February.

Mearns, Robin, Shombodon, D., Narangerel, G, Turul, U, Enkhamgalan, A., Myagmarzhav, B. Bayanjargal, A. and Bekhsuren, B. (1992): "Direct and indirect uses of wealth ranking in Mongolia", *RRA Notes* 15, pp. 29-38.

Moris, Jhon R. (1990): "Multi-subject farm surveys reconsidered: some methodological lessons", paper for the East African Agricultural Economics Society Conference, Dar es Salaam, 31 March to 4 April, 1970.

Moser, C.A., and Kalton, G. (1971): *Survey Methods in Social Investigation*, second edition, Heinemann Educational Books Ltd., London.

Mukherjee, Neela (1992): "Villagers' perceptions of rural poverty through the mapping methods of PRA", *RRA Notes* 15, pp. 21-26.

NES, (1990): *Participatory Rural Appraisal Handbook*, National Environment Secretariat, Kenya, Clark University; Egerton University; and the Centre for International Development and Environment of the World Resources Institute, February.

Norman, D.W., (1975): "Rationalizing mixed cropping under indigenous conditions; the example of Northern Nigeria, Samaru Research Bulletin 232, Institute for Agricultural Research, Samaru, Ahmadu Bello University, Zaria, Nigeria (also Journal of Development Studies n.d. pp. 3-21.

Osner, Karl, Kochendorfer-Lucius, Gudrun, Muller-Glodde, "Ulrike and Warning, Claudia. (1992): Exposure-und Dialog program: Eine Handreichung fur Teilnehmer und Organisatoren", Justitia et Pax, Kaiserstrasse 163,5300 Bonn 1.

Palm Series 1-5, MYRADA, 2 Service Road, Domlur Layout, Bangalore 560 071.

Pelto, Pertti J, and Pelto, Gretel H. (1978): *Anthropological Research : The Structure of Inquiry*, second edition, Cambridge University Press.

PID and NES (1989): *An Introduction to Participatory Rural Appraisal for Rural Resources Management Programme for International Development*, Clark University, Worcester, Mass. And National Environment Secretariat, Ministry of Environment and Natural Resources, Nairobi, November.

Potten, D. (1985): "Rapid Rural Appraisal – emergence of a methodology and its application to irrigation: a bibliographical review", paper for the Review and Development Seminar on Selected Issues in Irrigation Management, International Irrigation Management Institute, Sri Lanka.

Pottier, J. (1991): "Representation and accountability: understanding social change through Rapid Appraisal, with reference to Northern Zambia", mimeo, Department of Social Anthropology, SOAS, University of London, April.

PRA Team (1991): The Kyeamba Valley: "Issues of Concern to Landholders and Their Families, identified in a Participatory Rural Appraisal by Members of the Kyeamba Valley Community, September 1991", compiled by a PRA team with the following connections: Landcare, Department of Conservation and Land Management, New South Wales Agriculture, School of Agriculture, CSU-R, Centre for Conservation Farming, CSU-R, School of Crop Sciences, the University of Sydney and Wagga Wagga City Council.

Pretty, Jules N. (1990): "Rapid Catchment Analysis for Extension Agents", Notes on the 1990 Kericho Training Workshop for the Ministry of

Agriculture, Kenya, Sustainable Agriculture Programme, IIED, London, November.

Pretty, Jules, Subramanian, S., Ananthakrishnan, D., Jayanthi, C., Muralikrishnasamy, S. and Renganayaki, K. (1992): "Finding the Poorest in a Tamil Nadu Village: a sequence of mapping and wealth ranking", RRA Notes 15, pp. 39-42.

Rahman Md Anisur, (ed.) (1984): *Grassroots Participation and Self-reliance*, Oxford and IBH, New Delhi.

Ramachandran, Vidya (1990): "A Workshop on Participatory Learning Methods, 8th to 12th January 1990", MYRADA Talavadi Project, PRA/PALM Series No.1, MYRADA, Bangalore.

Rhoades, Robert (1982): "The Art of the Informal Agricultural Survey", International Potato Centre, Apartado 5969, Limca.

____(1990), "The coming revolution in methods for rural development research", User's Perspective Network (UPWARD), International Potato Centre (CIP), PO Box 933, Manila,

Rhoades, R.E, and Booth, R., (1982): "Farmer-back-to-farmer: a model for generating acceptable agricultural technology", *Agricultural Administration*, Vol.11, pp. 127-37.

Richards, P. (1985): *Indigenous Agricultural Revolution*, Hutchinson, London and Westview Press, Colorado.

Rocheleau, Diane, Wachira, Kamoji, Malaret, Luis and Muchiri Wanjohi, Bernard (1989): "Local knowledge for agro-forestry and native plants", in R. Chambers, A. Pacey and L.R. Thrupp (eds.), *Farmer First*, pp. 14-24.

RRA Notes 1-16 and continuing, Sustainable Agriculture Programme, International Institute for Environment and Development, 3 Endsleigh Street, London WC 1 HODD.

Russel, David B, and Ison, Raymond L. (1991): "The research-development relationship in rangelands: an opportunity for contextual science", Plenary Paper for Fourth International Rangelands Congress, Montpellier, France, 22-26 April.

SPR in Asia (1982): *Participatory Research: an Introduction*, Society for Participatory Research in Asia, 435 Sainik Farm, Khanpur, New Delhi 110 062.

Sachs, Wolfgang (ed.) (1992): *The Development Dictionary: A Guide to Knowledge as Power*, Zed Books, London and New Jersey.

Scoones, I., (1988): "Learning about wealth: an example from Zimbabwe", *RRA Notes*, No. 2.

Scrimshaw, S. and Hurtado, E. (1987): "Rapid Assessment Procedures for Nutrition and Primary Health Care: Anthropological Approaches for Improving Programme Effectiveness", United Nations University, Tokyo; UNICEF/UN Children's Fund; and UCLA Latin American Centre, Los Angeles.

Semler, R. (1989): "Managing without managers", *Harvard Business Review*, September-October, pp. 76-84.

Senaratne, S.P.F. (1976): "A programme of micro-level studies in rural Sri Lanka" mimeo, no source given, 12 pages.

Shah, Anil C. (1991): "Shoulder tapping: a technique of training in participatory rural appraisal", *Forests, Trees and People Newsletter 14*, October, pp.14-15.

Shah, Meera, (forthcoming), "Participatory afforestation programmes' sequence adopted by Aga Khan Rural Support Programme, India.

Shah, Parmesh (1989): "Concept of people's participation in the watershed development-extension volunteer approach" mimeo, AKRSP, June.

____(1990), "Economic classification of a community using locally generated criteria", *RRA Notes*, No. 8.

____(1991), "Sequences in Participatory Rural Appraisal (PRA): Background Note for the 24 October 1991 joint IIED/IDA Workshop", IDS.

Shah, Parmesh, Bhardwaj, Girish, and Ambastha, Ranjit (1991): "Farmers as analysts and facilitators in participatory rural appraisal and planning", *RRA Notes* 13, pp. 84-89.

Sharner, W.W., Phillipp, P.F., and Schemehl, W.R. (1982): Farming Systems Research and Development: *Guidelines for Developing Countries*, Westview Press, Boulder, Colorado.

Silverman, Sydel F. (1966): "An ethnographic approach to social stratification: prestige in a central Italian community", *American Anthropologist*, Vol. 68, No. 4:899-921 (quoted in Pelto and Pelto 1978:82-4).

Swift, J. (1981), "Rapid Appraisal and Cost-effective Research in West Africa", *Agricultural Administration* 8, 6 November, pp. 485-92.

Swift, Jeremy and Umar, Abdi Noor (1991): "Participatory Pastoral Development in Isiolo District: socio-economic research in the Isiolo Livestock Development Project", Isiolo Livestock Development Project, EMI ASAL Programme, Isiolo, Kenya.

Van Steijn, T. (1991): "Rapid Rural Appraisal in the Philippines: report of a study on the application of RRA by Philippines NGOs, Gos and University Institutes", draft version for comment, Council for People's Development, 1758, Kamias Road, Quezon City, Metro Manila, Philippines, July.

Theis, J, and Grady, H. (1991): "Participatory Rapid Appraisal for Community Development: a Training Manual Based on Experiences in the Middle East and North Africa", Save the Children and IIED, London.

Tollery, Elizabeth and Bentley, Margaret E. (1992): "Participatory methods for research on women's reproductive health", *RRA Notes*, 16, pp. 63-68.

Voyce, M., *et al.*, (1989): "The transfer of the family farm", National Farmer (Australia), 10 March, 1989, pp. 1-17.

Welbourn, A. (1991): "RRA and the analysis of difference", *RRA Notes* 14, pp. 14-23, December.

____(1992): "A note on the use of disease problem ranking with relation to socio-economic well-being; an example from Sierra Leone", *RRA Notes* 16, pp. 86-87.

White, A.V.T. (1977): Guidelines for Field Studies in Environmental Perception, UNESCO, Paris.

White, William Foote (ed.) (1991): *Participatory Action Research*, Sage Publications, Newbury Park, London, New Delhi.

Wignaraja, Ponna, Akmal Hussain, Harsh Sethi and Ganeshan Wignaraja (1991): *Participatory Development: Learning from South Asia*, United Nations University Press, Tokyo and Oxford University Press, Karachi.

APPENDIX A

SOURCES OF INFORMATION

RRA Notes are a major source on PRA, and are free on request. RRA Notes 13 is recommended to any reader seeking a good introduction. RRA Notes are available on request from the Sustainable Agriculture Programme at IIED, 3 Endsleigh Street, London, WC1Ch ODD.

The interest in RRA Notes is growing fast, and the series will continue to be sent out to those on the mailing list. A growing number of requests are being received for the complete set of back issues. This is not only costly, but also means the occasional reprinting of backcopies. IIED have, therefore, started a system of charging for backcopies of RRA Notes. This will be on sliding scale as follows:

1. In future, IIED will send up to two backcopies free of charge.
2. For requests for more than 2 copies, IIED will charge pound 2.50 per issue. This includes the costs incurred for reprinting and for postage.
3. For a full set of 15 backcopies the charge will be pound 33.00.

For information about field experience and training opportunities contact:

Australia: A.M. Dunn
School of Agriculture,
Charles Sturt University,
Riverina,
PO Box 588, Wagga Wagga,
NSW 2650
Tel: 61-69-222385; Fax: 61-69-222812

Botswana: S. Nkhori
Production Systems Program,
Department of Agriculture Research,
P.O. Box 10, Mahalapye
Tel: 267-410677

India: Sam Joseph
Action Aid,
3 Rest House Road,
Bangalore – 560 001
Tel: 91-812-586682/586583; Fax: 91-812-586284
Telex: 845 2142 AAIN IN

Kenya: Mahesh Mishra
OXFAM
PO Box 40680
Nairobi
Tel: 254-2-442123/445168

Nepal: Gerard Gill
Winrock International
PO Box 1312
Kathmandu
Tel: 977-1-212987/222904;
Fax: 977-1-222300
Telex: 2305-APROSC NP

Nigeria: Selina Adjebeng-Asem
Technology Planning and
Development Unit,
Faculty of Technology,
Obafemi Awolowo University,
Ife-Ife
Tel: 234-36-230290

Senegal:	Bare Gueye ENEA BP 5589 Dakar Tel: 221-253176
Sri Lanka:	Mallika Sanaranayake Intercooperation, 92/2 D S Senanayake Mawatha, Colombo 8 Tel: 94-1-691215; Fax: 94-1-685 979 Telex: 22151 or 21208 HPT CE atten: Intercooperation
UK:	Sustainable Agriculture Programme IIED, 3 Endsleigh Street, London WC1H ODD Tel: 971-388-2117; Fax: 071-388-2826 Telex: 261681 EASCAN G
Vietnam:	Le Minit Tue Trung tana nghien unu lam nghiep, (FRC) Pteu Ninh, Phone Chau, Vinh Phu, Vietnam
Zimbabwe:	Saiti Makuku Natural Resources Department, Ministry of Environment and Tourism, PO Box 8070 Causeway, Harare Tel: 263-4-729`36/705661/705671; Fax: 263-4-720738 Telex: 26082 SIMTOUR

APPENDIX B

PRA: START, STUMBLE, SELF-CORRECT, SHARE

Participatory Rural Appraisal is a label. More and more people are adopting it, and calling what they to PRA. More and more influential organizations are requesting or requiring that PRA be carried out.

This brings dangers and opportunities.

The dangers are that the label will be used or claimed for activities where behaviour and attitudes are not participatory; that these activities will do badly; and that good PRA will be discredited. There is a danger too, that the demand for training in PRA will so outstrip good supply and that people will claim to be PRA trainers when they have no direct personal experience of good PRA. This has already happened.

The opportunities are hard to assess but look big. Time will show. Perhaps we have in good PRA one among a family of approaches for reversing centralization, standardization and top-down development; and for enabling and empowering rural communities take command more of their lives and resources, and to improve their well-being as they define it.

So what is the core of good PRA?

We will all have different answers. It is more important to ask the question and to puzzle about good answers than to have one right answer. It is more important for each person and each group to invent and adapt their own approaches, methods, sequences and combinations than to adopt a ready-made manual or model. Let a thousand flowers bloom (and why only a thousand?), and let them be flowers which bloom better and better, and spread their seeds.

Here is one personal set of answers. If you read them, criticize them, reject them. Think out your own, from your own ideas and experience.

In the words of the one-sentence manual: 'Use your own best judgement at all times'.

The core of good PRA is our behaviour and attitudes.

It involves:

being self-aware and self-critical,
embracing error,
handing over the stick,
sitting, listening and learning,
improvising, inventing, adapting,
using our own best judgement at all times.
So we can ask:
who lectures? who holds the stick? whose finger wags"
whose knowledge, analysis and priorities count?

Ours? Theirs, as we think they should be? Or theirs as they freely express them?

Good PRA is empowering, not extractive.

Good PRA makes mistakes, learns from them, so is self-improving.

Good PRA spreads and improves in its own.

So start. Do not wait. Get on with it. Relax. Try things. Learn by doing. Fail forwards. Experiment. Aṣk – what went well? What went badly? What can we learn? How can we do better? How can we help others to do better?

Remember the three pillars :

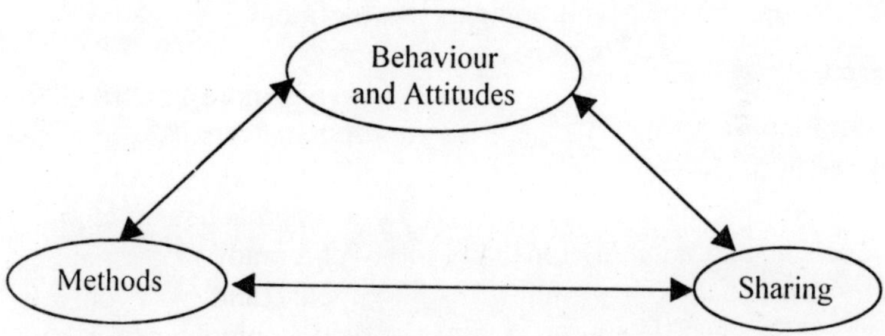

PRA becomes self-improving and self-spreading: self-improving through critical awareness, embracing error and learning what works; and self-spreading through sharing.

Start with behaviour and attitudes. Ours. And use the methods at once to help.

Or start with a method, and observe and reflect on your behaviour and attitudes as you use it. Relax. List. Keep quite. Allow fun. Learn. And learn how to do better.

PRA is what we make of it. It is a potential, not a panacea. If you do not like it, leave it. No one will mind. It is not for everyone. But if you like it and use it, share it and help others to share.

Have a go. Why not?

2

Micro-Level Planning for Rural Development and Participatory Learning & Action Techniques

Similarities and Potential

– AMITAVA MUKHERJEE

I. INTRODUCTION

There is no system of governance and planning that is completely centralized, but the system that most developing countries adopted in the fifties and the sixties, particularly those that came out of colonial rule, were characterized by a centralized bias. However, the current political imperatives in most countries, which include ideological stances and in some cases, competing social and group interests, coupled with administrative imperatives, emanating out of administering far flung areas (from the 'centre') with underdeveloped social and economic infrastructure, large and unevenly distributed populations, and diverse, often complex local conditions, have driven a number of countries to opt for a more decentralized system of governance and planning. Decentralized planning for rural development is, therefore, viewed as a political strategy directed towards, *inter alia,* the promotion of increasing people's participation in the initiation, planning and implementation of development programmes, equity in resource allocation and greater accountability of bureaucracy and public administrators to elected bodies. It is increasingly being recognized as a more effective system for developing local level economy, and for managing public affairs.

Fortunately for India, these ideas caught on fairly early in its experimentation with planned economic development, and given its federal democratic structure, decentralized planning and resource use was inherently embedded in its Constitutional framework.[1] Planning was decentralized to the state level very early in the fifties, which has stabilized in all the states, and several attempts were made to decentralize planning for rural development to the sub-state level up to the district.[2] These attempts had fluctuating fortunes because of a variety of causes, and has stabilized only in three states Gujarat, Karnataka and West Bengal.

With the IMF – World Bank designed structural reforms implemented in the country, the failure of the public sector to reach "commanding heights" leading to reducing the role of the state in the economic life of the nation and a realization that ensuring non-failure of livelihood entitlement is only possible by delegating the responsibility of economic management to the people themselves, has placed local level planning at the top of the agenda. We will use the terms local level planning for rural development and micro-level planning interchangeably throughout this discussion. For brevity, we would use the terms local level planning or micro level planning in this book, hereafter.

II. MICRO-LEVEL PLANNING FOR RURAL DEVELOPMENT IN THE RECENT DECADES

The Eighth Five Year Plan was commenced in April 1992, and at the time of writing this the Plan document was not available, but the Directional Paper for the Eighth Five Year Plan was available.[3] This chapter enjoins that "a genuine push towards decentralization and people's initiatives and participation should be made a key element in the process of development" (para. 4). Hark these words:

> "People's initiative and participation should be made key elements in the process of development, instead of people being passive observers. Change in the attitude that every target must be related to and be made proportional to the financial outlays of the plan not withstanding the decline in effectiveness of the outlays in achieving results over the years, and the reversal of the trends of rising cost of development at the margin in real terms, will be attempted

at. Improvement in education, literacy, health, family planning, land improvement, minor irrigation, recovery of waste land and afforestation, through people's movement with lesser costs to society, will be key elements in the forthcoming decade".[4]

Pronouncements such as these are not new in the Indian context, as we mentioned earlier.[5] But the time has arrived, it seems, to shed some scepticism in this regard because the government has also secured the passage of the Seventy Third (Constitution Amendment) Act 1993,[6] in the Parliament seeking to provide Constitutional safeguards towards the establishment of Panchayati Raj Institutions (local level bodies) at the district and sub-district levels, which would be mandated Constitutionally to plan for the area covered by their respective territorial jurisdictions. The new Article 243G of the Constitution of India reads thus:

"Subject to the provisions of this Constitution, the legislature of a State may by law endow the Panchayats with such powers and authority as may be necessary .....with respect to:

(a) the preparation of plans of economic development and social justice;
(b) the implementation of schemes for economic development and social justice as may be entrusted to them including those in relation to matters listed in the Eleventh Schedule".[7]

III. RELEVANCE OF PLA METHODS AS TOOLS TO LOCAL LEVEL PLANNING

When one surveys the micro-level planning landscape against this backdrop, it is manifested that the relevance of everything that is participative, people centred and based on informed judgement will be of material consequence in micro-level planning in India, namely, data base and use of community's wisdom and collective will. This has been so because the involvement of the common man in local level planning was poor. Both PLA and micro-level planning have features that make the two perfect match for each other in correcting these defects. We might evaluate, in these contexts, the compatibility of the two on the basis of six parameters:

(i) Why local level planning and why PLA is used?
(ii) What are the principles of local level planning and what are the principles behind PLA ?
(iii) What are the techniques for micro-level planning and what are the PLA methods ?
(iv) What uses micro-level planning and who uses PLA ?
(v) What is the context in which local level planning operates and what is the context in which PLA is used ?
(vi) What are the limitations of local level planning and what are the limitations in the use of PLA ?

Let us discuss each in turn. It is important to underscore here that a distinction is made between RRA, PRA and PLA. (See Chapter-1). However, for us there is considerable commonality between the three. The discussion to follow, thus, has to be read in the light of the foregoing.

Why Local Level Planning and Why PLA is Used ?

PLA is used to avoid the problems associated with long and costly formal surveys.[8] These problems include the following:

The problem of collecting too much data.
The problem of collecting irrelevant data.
The problem of generating results after inordinate delays.
The problem of producing inappropriate results.
The problem of little, if at all, association of the local people.

PLA is directed towards avoiding the risks that go with the use of quick and unstructured development tourism surveys, including the risks of

- obtaining only a partial and once-overall picture of the area or issue under investigation;
- relying heavily on previous assumptions;
- working without a framework to guide the collection and analysis of information.
- PLA is designed to help overcome the biases of the more accessible and well-to-do individuals and groups;
- working with only the quantitative, apparent data;
- ignoring the more qualitative, in-depth information and insights;
- disregarding the dynamics that lay behind innate quantitative figures; and
- interacting with the local population in a top-down manner.

PLA has an in-built mechanism to encourage participation of local people in the process of development by:

- investigating local insights gained by interfacing with the common man, resulting in more effective "research information" being located;[9] and
- involving local people in research and design of socio-economic endeavours so as to lead to increasing commitment and empowerment of the common people.

As against this backdrop of "Why PLA", What is the rationale of Micro-Level Planning/Local Level Planning for economic development ?

Local level planning obviates the difficulties of:

- collecting too much data, at a huge cost in terms of money and time, without knowing what exact data to collect[10] and what to make of the flood of data already collected;
- following from the above, huge cost of data collection, given that resources for local level planning are scarce;
- eliciting incorrect and often insufficient information, on account of, *inter alia*, pitfalls associated with long

surveys including respondent-fatigue, through extraordinarily long questionnaires;

- inordinate delays in obtaining data;[11]
- working out plans on the basis of irrelevant results[12] or by ignoring relevant details; and
- keeping the common man out from the process of planning, variously called as local level participation, participatory planning and so forth.[13]

Local level planning avoids the dangers associated with:

- working with solely secondary data, which at best provides a second hand picture of the area, its inhabitants and the economy being planned for;
- following the beaten track relaying on what has been done in the past, which is at once "insulated" from the excitement (and risks as well) associated with innovation and improvisation;[14] and
- attempting at working out a plan and devise projects and schemes for rural development without an intimate knowledge of local conditions, without knowing from the people themselves what they consider their problems and ignoring what solutions they may have for tackling those problems.

Local level planning ensures that the pitfalls that go with working out a plan for area development:

- based on the interaction that the planners, sitting at the "Centre", far away from the actual scene of action, have with groups who have access to them, or who have vested interest in meeting them;[15]
- by looking at only quantitative figures generated by impersonal methods with a long time lag;
- by adopting a "we-they" approach, where the distant planners (usually the bureaucrats, economists and technocrats) pose as the "benefactors" or the "saviours", and the common people are looked at as the "beneficiaries", as "problems", as "recipients"; and

- without local knowledge, local information, local insights and qualitative information and, therefore, without the benefit of indigenous knowledge and communal wisdom, leading (amongst other problems) to "targetitis", missing the target all the time, and wasting public resources in re-fixing targets over and over agair to match actions initiated (instead of the other wa) round) are avoided, without imposing further costs t(society.

Local level planning is based fundamentally on the premises that local level plans would reflect as much of the common wil and communal wisdom, as is possible and the people kno\ better than "outsiders" what their problems are and how best t solve these problems using local resources.

What are the Principles of Local Level Planning and Wha are the Principles behind PLA?

The principles of PLA *inter alia* are the following:

- Increase involvement of local people and increas people's participation throughout the exercise and lea ultimately to their empowerment.
- Learning from and sharing with the common peopl using local classifications and terminologies, so that tl repository of local knowledge and wisdom is optimall utilized for treating the issues at hand.
- Collecting as much information as is necessary to avoi getting into the problems of "data diarrhoeas", that i resorting to optimal ignorance.
- Exploring the range of circumstances, instead c restricting oneself to one outcome/possibility b resorting to statistical sampling.
- Investigating each issue at hand in different ways anc from different perspectives, or what has been callec "triangulation" so that alternative scenarios are examined, evaluated and decided upon.

- Following from the above, ensuring involvement of people in the entire process from different backgrounds and with different areas of expertise so as to make the PLA inter-disciplinary in character.
- Adopting an informal approach, which is flexible, amenable to change, alteration and amendment to suit changing circumstances and conditions.
- Affecting changes in the design, structure and content of the whole exercise as it proceeds. That is, the process is to be interactive.
- Greater part of the work is based in the field. That is, much of the exercise is carried out at the scene of action.

As against this, the principles of local level planning are, amongst others, the following :[16]

- Local level planning is a "down-down" exercise, to be undertaken locally, keeping in view what can be achieved through local action alone. That is, involvement of the local people to increase their participation in formulation and implementation of local level plans is the cornerstone of the arch of local level planning. This has been called by some as "empowerment of the people". Empowerment here, however, is not what it means in received theory. It is necessary to look into space specifities of the source and nature of power, noting that power should not be equated with political power which is transferable and retransferable. It reflects the fact that local level planning explicitly recognizes the celebrated truth, namely, that every human formation has its own way of creating and exercising power; it has its own long history of resistance and self defence; it has an unique experience articulated as traditions, conventions, modes of behaviour, folklores, usages, PLActice and customs. They are best adapted to each particular group's culture and opportunities, and they are not residuals which are outdated and replaceable by universal recipes.[17]

- Following from the above, local level planning should be a continuous process of learning (about the local area economy that would work and about what to plan for) and of applying what has been learned.
- These in turn lead to the third principle: local level planning must be informed of local customs, conventions, traditions, usages, PLActices and unwritten laws. There is a lot to be learnt from each of these, to prepare operable local level plans.
- Local level planning should be based more on informed judgment and qualitative data than on aiming at quantitative precision based fundamentally on quantitative data. It must avoid, all the more, (and it cannot illafford) creation of a costly and detailed data base.[18] That is, there should be economy in the collection of information for local level planning ("optimal ignorance" in PLA terminology). This is tantamount to enjoining that collection of data should be restricted to what is only necessary for the purposes of local level planning.
- Local level planning, being based on local knowledge and framed with people's participation, should consider a whole range of possibilities and choose that which is considered best. Unlike planning from above, it ought not to be embedded in only a rigid statistical framework and generate a solution based on results churned out of complicated models.[19]
- Local level planning, apart from being drawn up under local conditions and near the scene of action, should have the flexibility to admit mid-way corrections so as to include changes and assimilate lessons of experience, without causing wide disturbances in the system as the plan proceeds.
- Local level planning must essentially be locally undertaken and locally controlled, as it ought to have local participation as the key element. That is, most of the work of planning at the local level, as is true of its implementation, has to be carried out at the ground level ("in-the-field", to use PLA semantics) itself.[20]

- Projects identified under local level planning, with the help of the local people should be determined through the local level planning exercise, to be socially acceptable, strategically sound and environmentally and economically sustainable.[21]
- Local level planning has to be integrated and harmonized with other types of planning, such as the National Plan, State Plan, Regional Plan, or even sectoral plans like a Road Plan or Forest Plan, all of which affect the local area economy. The role of the different plans and different tiers of plans, their source of finance, their areas of concern and their timeframe, *inter alia,* have to be clearly demarcated, and wherever warranted should be properly aligned to achieve the goals of development.[22]

What are the Tool of Local Level Planning and What are the Techniques of PLA?

The PLA methods provide a range of choices of different techniques, as we have seen in the introductory chapter, which could be used individually or in any combination. Which of the techniques, and/or in what combination they are to be used will depend on ingenuity of the local level planner (PLA practitioner), the available resources, including time, and the output desired. The choices include, but not restricted to, the following :

- Secondary Data Review,
- Direct Observation, Observation Indicator Check-lists,
- Semi-Structured Interview and Sequences or Chains of Interviews,
- Focus Group Discussion,
- Preference Ranking and Scoring,
- Pairwise Ranking and Scoring,
- Direct Matrix Ranking,
- Ranking by Voting,
- Wealth Ranking or Well-being Ranking,
- Analysis and Group Discussion,

- Innovation Assessment,
- Construction of Diagrams,
- Mapping and Modelling,
- Participatory Mapping,
- Historical and Future (Vision) Mapping,
- Mobility Mapping
- Social Network Mapping,
- Social Mapping,
- Transect Walks,
- Historical Transect Diagram,
- Historical Transect
- Seasonal Calendar Seasonal Diagramming,
- Historical Seasonal Calendar,
- Time Lines and Trends Analysis,
- Historical Profile,
- Livelihood Analysis,
- Flow/Causal Diagram,
- Venn/Institutional Diagram,
- Thipparpur Method: An Alternative to Venn Diagramming,
- Systems Diagram,
- Force Field Analysis
- Empowerment Circle
- Anonymous Health Analysis
- Pie Charts,
- Histogram,
- Participant Observation (Do-It-Yourself and Learning By Doing),
- Oral Histories,
- Workshops and Workshopping,
- Group Walks,
- Stories,
- Folklore,
- Case Studies and Portraits,
- Proverbs,
- Indigenous Categories and Terms, Taxonomies and Ethno-classification,[23] and
- Participatory analysis of aerial photographs.

The techniques of local level planning include several options,[24] but there is no planning or social science research technique that cannot be applied to local level planning, as long as it can be adopted to local conditions. Typically, the following are the techniques commonly used in traditional local level planning.

- Interviews,
- Surveys,
- Group Discussions,
- Village Meeting,
- Problem Tree Analysis,
- Maps,
- Mapping of Resources,
- Scalograms,
- Schemograms,
- Activity Analysis,
- Ergographs,
- Relational Matrices,
- Simple Social Accounting Matrices (rarely),
- Area Income and Product Accounts,
- Simple Statistical Tools,
- Inter-Area Analysis,
- Intra-Area Analysis,
- Flow Studies,
- Resource Suitability Classification,
- Resource Depletability Analysis,
- Natural Resources and Hazards Inventory,
- User Origin Analysis,
- Settlement Typology Schemes,
- General Sectoral Analysis,
- Aerial Photographs,[25] and
- Land-Sat. Imagery,

A full range of newer tools will hopefully emerge as local level planning is put to more intensive use. Generally, all techniques, that help in understanding the local area and its economy, that increase people's participation and which encourage people to get involved in the process of planning, which elicit people's needs and solution, and which are simple, quick and easy, have applicability in local level planning. It is reiterated that "people centred", "simple", "quick and "replicability: (or some combination of these) are the key attributes which a technique has to have for being applied to local level planning. And PLA fortunately has all of them.

Who uses PLA and Who are the Principal Classes of Actors in Local Level Planning?

PLA is amenable to use by anyone involved in planning, development and research. It is best carried out by the local people, and where that is not possible, with the help of local people. The use of PLA methods is sought for by those who are interested in working out a symbiotic relationship between the common man and the processes that have a bearing on development and welfare of the masses.

Local level planning is essentially concerned with improving the quality of life of people, particularly so in the rural areas. Local level planning is resorted to by local governments, the local administration and by local level institutions, like the Panchayati Raj Institutions in India.[26] It is primarily a public means for improving public resources so as to expand the ability of the individuals or combination of individuals, in the local area to create value responsibly with their own resources. It is supported by those who have faith in collective-will and community's wisdom in making choices.

In several countries, the Central Governments use local level planning as outlets for implementing its schemes at the cutting edge level. Usually, this is common in India.

What is the Context in which Local Level Planning Operates and What is the Context in which PLA is used?

The use of PLA has mainly been confined : mostly to less developed countries, though it is, of late, been used in developed countries as well;[27] mostly in rural situations, but of late, use of PLA in urban situations as well, is very common,[28] mostly in agricultural field and to other areas like economics, health, nutrition,[29] energy and forestry, food security and even economic structural adjustment programme, and mostly at the village level but can be used on a larger scale also.

Local level planning has been used primarily for rural development.[30] In several countries, like in India, local level planning relates to rural areas, and local plans for urban areas are classified as urban planning, though they too are local level plans avoiding the pitfalls of a "top-down" approach. local level planning for rural areas is formulated and implemented by development administrators and local level elected bodies. Whereas local level planning for urban areas is administered by Municipal Boards/Councils or other specially created urban bodies like the Kolkata Metropolitan Development Authority, in Kolkata.

In the emerging Indian context, contingent upon the passage of the Seventy Third (Constitution Amendment) Act 1993, referred to above, local level planning will be used in the context of :

- mostly rural situations by the Gram Panchayats, the first tier (village level) local elected governments;
- mostly rural situations by Panchayat Samities, the second tier (block level) local elected governments; and
- mostly semi-urban and urban situations by the Zilla Parishads, the third tier (district level) local elected governments etc.

Though local level plans would be involved with economic activity, its use is critical in social sectors like basic health, family planning, nutrition, drinking water, primary education, non-conventional energy and rural roads. This has been explicitly recognized successive Five Year Plan Documents for India.

What are the Limitations of Local Level Planning and what are the Limitations of PLA?

Like all other techniques, PLA methods have their share of limitation. They may be catalogued as under :

- PLA methods are complementary to other research methods, like statistical surveys, long term anthropological studies and so forth. They do not profess to supplant other research methods.

- PLA methods may be rapid while the process of rural development may not be rapid, with the former abounding and the latter a rarer phenomenon in the history of rural development of most nations.

- PLA approaches to understanding real life situations, being a collaborative effort of the "outsiders" and the local people, may raise local expectations and, therefore, there is the need to take follow up action.[31]

PLA methods may not be always necessarily cross culturally transferable, that is, a PLA tool found suitable in one area may not always help necessarily in another environment. There is, therefore, the need to adopt PLA methods to local conditions.[32] Improvisation and development of newer methods are key elements in PLA.

For the correct use of PLA methods, it is necessary to train the facilitators and participants appropriately, noting near that PLA cannot be properly used by the uninitiated and untrained people. It should not, therefore, be surprising if ego-centric people after attending a half day workshop on PLA methods, try to apply them for 4 days in a village (punctuated with "bandobasti") and then deliver a thundering judgement against PLA methods.

PLA raises questions, produces hypotheses or 'best bets' for development but not the final answers.

PLA, unless carefully applied, may in a few cases lead to exacerbating hybernating social tensions.

Flowing from the above, PLA is best used in communities which share common knowledge, values and belief.

COMPARISON AND TRAINING IMPLICATIONS

If we compare the PLA methods and local level planning on the basis of the six parameters discussed above, striking similarities between the two, with regard to their rationale, underlying principles, their basic philosophy, users, context in which they are used and limitations, are revealed. The use of PLA in local level planning, therefore, looks like a harmonious blend of compatible means and ends. And the success rate is likely to be very high, particularly when viewed from the perspective of flexibility and leeway for improvisation, embodied in the two. It would be a rewarding exercise to explore further the use of PLA in local level planning.[33]

A prerequisite to widespread use of PLA in local level planning would be the availability of a wide cross-section of actors in local level plans, who are trained in the use of PLA in local level planning. This is especially so, since PLA can be used properly only by people who are trained in its use. In the Indian context, and similar other contexts, this would be particularly important. This would mean a large number of people will have to be induced to use PLA, which in turn brings up the question of training in PLA use. To assess the magnitude and scope of PLA in micro-level planning in India,[34] it would be necessary to turn to these issues in a separate paper. Suffice it to indicate for the present that according to one estimate the number of people to be trained would be above 4,00,000, noting that there are 2,17,910 panchayats (the number vary), 5,143 blocks and 463 districts, all of which have planning teams or actors involved in local level planning, without taking the panchayats and other development agencies like banks and NGOs into consideration, has been estimated at 3,12,568 by the Planning Commission.[35] This presumably would, at least, have to be the magnitude of quantitative training needs for PLA methods to be put to good use in micro-level planning in India.

ATTITUDES IN APPLICATION ON PLA

The number to be trained in PLA methods for micro-level planning is large and requires a long term training plan, but there are several qualitative aspects of PLA training that need to be kept in perspective. We cannot deal with all of them in this short space, nevertheless, we must mention here one aspect of training in PLA methods in the third world bureaucracy, such as the one in the Indian context, namely, behaviour and attitude. Imparting knowledge about PLA methods is not likely to be a greater problem that what one would encounter with regard to training in any other tool/technique. Indeed, similar methods have been fruitfully deployed for a long time by anthropologists, geographers and sociologists (economists are late comers in the game). The real crunch will be imparting the right kind of orientation attitude and behaviour to the different actors in the application of the PLA methods; this will be difficult. There are two problems that are basic to it. The first one relates to reorienting their understanding of the intelligence and knowledge base of the common man. There is a widespread understanding that the common man is very intelligent, and the storehouse of communal knowledge, what is good for the community, is beyond question, noting that there is a distinction between being educated and being literate (in the formal sense), and between being learned and knowledgeable. The success of PLA methods being accepted as a formal tool, for local level planning and for their deployment successfully, demands that the orientation of all the actors in local planning, from the Gram Panchayat level to the Zilla Parishad/District level functionaries, change from one of imparting to the people, information about what their problems are and the "shelf of solutions" to choose from, to one of knowing from the people, what their problems are and what solutions they can offer. The orientation has to change from the "lecturing mode" to the "participative mode". It is only then that use of PLA as a tool for grassroots planning would succeed and indeed, local level plans *per se,* programmes under such plans and schemes for operationalising local level plans under ground conditions, would have a sustainable foundation.

The second problem would be to inculcate in the actors, involved in local level planning, the ability to empathise with the common man for whom the plan "tolls". The actors in grassroots planning have not only to accept that the common man deserves to be respected for his intelligence and knowledge, but they (actors in local level planning) should imbibe an ability to look at the problem areas from a common man's perspective. For instance, when the local level planner is involved in understanding the extent of poverty in the local area economy, the criterion for judging poverty should be one which local people perceive, as correctly reflecting the extent of poverty in the area under reference. That is, those involved in local level planning and the potential users have to be trained to avoid the pitfall of the typical extension worker.

These are difficult things to do and they become almost intractable when it comes to bureaucrats and most government functionaries, who erroneously exude a feeling of having "arrived". It is not uncommon to find bureaucrats with bloated egos, with at times misplaced pride and at times vulgar motives, in charge of rural development. Affecting attitudinal changes in such functionaries is important, and, under the given circumstances, is a somewhat difficult proposition. It has, nevertheless, to be achieved. The solution to the problem of "people in charge" not willing to change attitudes (which die hard with flux of time) lies in, not throwing up hands in despair, but in more and more persuasive training.

Notes

1. In the federal structure of India there are clear division of powers and functions between the Central Government and the States, but entities below the States are not recognized in the Constitution of India for the devolution of powers, resources and functions for planning.
2. See Mukherjee, Amitava (1990). *Researches in Decentralization with Special Reference to District Planning in India* (New Delhi: Heritage Publishers) Chapter 1. One reason why local level planning, that is, planning at the sub-state level did not consistently stabilize is that it had no Constitutional sanction. It operated on executive fiats/State Legislation, subject to "machinations" at the state level.
3. Government of India (1991): Objectives, Thrusts and Macro-Dimension of the Eighth Five Year Plan 1992-97 (New Delhi: Planning Commission, Government of India).
4. *Ibid.*
5. Government of India (1984). Seventh Five Year Plan, Volume-II (New Delhi: Planning Commission, Government of India), pp. 417
6. Constitution (Seventy Third Amendment) Act 1993, being Bill No. 153 of 1991, introduced in the Parliament on 16th September, 1991, and approved by the Lok Sabha in December 1992.
7. Ibid.
8. See for instance Gill, Gerald (1991): "But How Does it Compare with the Real Data?", PLA Notes, No. 14, pp. 1-14, where he demonstrates how quickly rainfall data was provided by farmers in Nepal at much lower costs than the "met. station".
9. See Fairhead, James (1991): "Methodological Notes on Exploring Indigenous Knowledge and Management of Crop Health", *PLA Notes*, No. 14, pp. 39-42.
10. See the remarks of the Committee of the Study Group on Information Gap on pages 15-16, of its Report. Government of India (1989): Report of the

Study Group on Information Gap (New Delhi: Planning Commission), July.

11. For instance Census Data uptil the 1981 Census Operation were available with a lag of upto five years. The position for 1991 Census has slightly improved. See Minhas, B.S. (1990). *Data Base for Decentralized Planning,* Vol. I (New Delhi: Concept Publishing Co.), 1990.
12. There is a difference in perception about what is relevant and what is irrelevant between those who plan from distant offices and those who plan at the grassroots level. For example, results of a research into the institution of marriage in the Garhwal Hills of the Himalayan Range may be irrelevant for land consolidation planning for a planner in Planning Commission, New Delhi, or at Lucknow, but would be a critical input for the Block Planner in Chakrata, Garhwal. This is so because people in that part of the country PLActise "Polyandry-Polygamy" or "Polygamy-Polyandry " from one generation to another accordingly as the man-land ratio changes.
13. See Clayton, Barry Dalal (1990): "Confessions of a Reconstructed Planner", paper read at the Local Level Adaptive Planning Workshop held at London, jointly organized by International Institute for Environment and Development, London and the Development Administration Group, Institute of Local Government Studies, University of Birmingham. See also Chambers, Robert (1988): "Sustainable Rural Development", and the case study by Mishra, P.R. *et al;* (1988). "Social Security Fencing, Sukhmajri and Nada, North India" in Conroy, G. and Miles Litvinoff (eds.) *The Greening of Aid, Sustainable Livelihood* (London: Earthscan Publications) 1988 for example of the efficacy of people's participation in development efforts.
14. A common tendency is to refer back to the course of action adopted in earlier years, in case a precedent exists, and adopt it with or without modifications according to the expediencies of circumstances.
15. A noted scholar of Local Level Planning has beautifully put it, which bears repetition here" "When we look at the reality from the air (from the top), we get only a photographic image...the viewer gets the image he likes. The human world on the ground is thingified (*sic*)". Misra, R.P. (1990): *District Planning: A Handbook* (New Delhi: Concept Publishing Co.), p. 5.
16. See for details Mukherjee, Amitava (1991): *Methodology and Data Base for Decentralized Planning,* Vol. 2, Part C (New Delhi: Heritage Publishers), Appendix-A.
17. Mukherjee, Amitava and Yugandhar, B.N. (1991): "Decentralized Planning: Issues and Training Implications: An Analytical Framework", *IASSI Quarterly,* Vol. 10, No. 2, pp. 106-131.
18. For the better part of a total of approximately six years has been used to create a data base for Pauri District in the then Uttar PLAdesh, now in Uttaranchal, India at an estimated cost of over Rs. 10 million. See Pal, Devendra (1989): *Computerized District Data Base Centre Pauri Garhwal with then in U.P.* now in Uttaranchal (Dehradun: Wadia Institute of Himalayan Geology) for details.

19. Government of India (1984): Report of the Working Group on District Planning (New Delhi: Planning Commission, Government of India) Volumes I and II.
20. Bamberger, Michael, *et al,* (1990) : *Case Studies of Project Sustainability: Implications for Policy and Operations from Asian Experience* (Washington D.C.: Economic Development Institute of the World Bank).
21. Bendavidaval, Avrom (1990): *Rural Area Development Planning: Elements and Tools* (Rome: Food and Agriculture Organization of the United Nations, Training Service Policy Analysis Division).
22. See for details Sunderam, K.V., K.S. Ramesh and P.S. Tiwari (1989): *Essays on Space, Man and Society* (New Delhi: Heritage Publishers).
23. See McCracken, J.A., *et al.,* (1988) : *An Introduction to Rapid Rural ApPLAisal for Agricultural Development* (London: IIED) and the bibliography provided at Appendix-1 therein, and Chapter of this book, for a suite of PLA techniques.
24. See Weber, Karl et.al. (1986) : *Rural Development Planning in Pakistan* (Bangkok: Asian Institute of Technology) HSD Manual No. 4 of 1986, and Bendavid – val (1991): *Rapid Area Development Planning: Principles, Approaches and Tools of Economic Analysis* (Rome: F.A.O., Policy Analysis Division) for a suite of tools/ techniques of Local Level Planning.
25. Aerial photographs are also used in PLA. See Sandford, Dick (1989): "A Note on the Use of Aerial Photographs for Land Use Planning on a Settlement Site in Ethiopia", *RRA Notes,* No. 6, June 1989. Reference is also invited to Abel, Nick and Michael Stocking (1979). "Rapid Aerial Survey Techniques for Rural Areas", paper read at the RRA Conference at the Institute of Development Studies, University of Sussex, Brighton, from 4th to 7th December 1979, and to Caeson, Brian R. (1985). "Aerial Photography as a Base for Village Level Planning in Nepal", paper read at the Regional Symposium on Remote Sensing Applications of Socio-Economic Aspects of Environment, March 4-9, 1985 at the Economic and Social Commission for Asia and Pacific (ESCAP), Bangkok.
26. Panchayati Raj is a three tier system of locally elected councils at the village, block and district levels. Its earlier "incarnation" was in the fifties. See Krishnaswamy, P.B. (1987): *Micro-Macro Links in Planning* (Canberra: The Australian National University) Development Studies Centre Monograph No. 9, pp. 18-19 and National Institute of Rural Development (2001): *India Panchayati Raj Report,* Vols. I and II (Hyderabad National Institute of Rural Development).
27. See Ampt. Peter and Raymond Ison (1989): "PLA has a Role in Developed Countries", *RRA Notes,* No. 5, pp. 22-23.
28. See Davis-Case D'Archy (1989): "Community Forestry Rapid ApPLAisal", FTPP Community Forestry Note 3 (Rome: Food and Agriculture Organization of the U.N.).
29. An earlier paper on this is by Payne, Phillip R. (1979): "Assessment of Nutrition Problems: Who Do We Look at and What Do We Measure?", paper read at the RRA Conference, December 4th to 6th, 1979, at the Institute of Development Studies, University of Sussex, Brighton.

30. FAO (1985): Towards Improved Multi-Level Planning in Agriculture and Rural Development in Asia and the Pacific (Rome: FAO), Economic and Social Development Paper No. 52. See also FAO.
31. Two former trainee-officers of the Indian Administrative Service, Somesh Kumar and A. Shanti Kumari used PLA/RRA to find out the problems of villagers of village Thippapur, Andhra PLAdesh, India and prepared "an Action Plan based on what the villagers suggested" before leaving the village itself. This was possible because they were persons in authority, which indicates that PLA/RRA is a "safe" method for those in power and willing to help. See Kumar, Somesh and A. Shanti Kumari (1991): "The Thippapur Experience: A PLA Diary" in RRA Notes Participatory Methods for Learning and Analysis, No. 14, pp. 43-52. The term "outsiders" here include planners, bureaucrats, technocrats, economists, researchers and other development agents. Many such cases are reported in Mukherjee Neela (2002): *Participatory Learning and Action with 100 Field Methods* (New Delhi, Concept Publishing Co.).
32. See Fussell, Weyman (1990): "Participatory Rural ApPLAisal: Is It Culturally Neutral? Thoughts from PLA in Guinea-Bissau", *RRA Notes,* No. 9, pp. 31-33.
33. Maetz, M. and M.G. Quieti (1987): *Training for Decentralized Planning: Lessons from Experience* (Rome: Food and Agriculture Organization of the U.N.).
34. This has traditionally been one of the major arguments (though contentious) against decentralized planning in India. See Mukherjee, Amitava (1990): "Decentralized Planning, Apprehensions and Environment: An Analytical Framework" in Yugandhar, B.N. and Mukherjee, Amitava (eds.) (1990): *Readings in Decentralized Planning* (New Delhi: Concept Publishing Company), Vol. II.
35. Government of India (1989): Training for District Planning: Report of Study Group (New Delhi: Planning Commission).

3

Micro-Level Planning for Rural Development in Participatory Framework : The Soft System Approach

– AMITAVA MUKHERJEE

INTRODUCTION

Micro-level planning forms the foundation of the Five Year Plans for India and given the disillusionment that people at large have with top-down planning and top-down approach to development, micro-level planning or local-level planning has an important role to play for the development of this country. The Seventy Third Amendment of the Constitution as also the Seventy Fourth Constitution Amendment and the consequent State legislations have further added to the importance of micro-level planning by providing it a legal basis, and providing the framers of micro-level plans, a modicum of constitutional safeguards.[1] Since the basis of micro-level planning is that it is people centred and relies on people's decision, the role of Participatory Rural Appraisal (PRA) or Participatory Learning and Action (PLA) in this adventure can be significant from first principles. The principal concern of this chapter is to examine the emerging role of PRA or PLA in micro-level planning and how it could be done best, together with some reflections on the probable implications. In this Chapter (as in Chapter-2) the terms micro-level planning and local-level planning will be used interchangeably, in the generic sense, for connoting district and sub-district level planning, such as "Panchayat Level Planning" and "Village Level Planning".

PRA : BACKGROUND AND FEATURES

Background

In the fifties and the sixties there was a virtual unanimity amongst economists and development planners that capital and technology were the only required inputs for the development of the underdeveloped economies. Injecting capital and technology would do the trick. The chorus of cheers that Green Revolution received all round is evidence of that conviction. The subsequent turn of events, however, indicated that transfer of technology and the injection of successive doses of capital failed to do the trick in all cases. It was realized soon that the complexity of the interface between economic and non-economic factors, such as culture, tradition, environment, politics, practices, customs and usage, all had vital bearings on how the production system functions and that there can be growth (measured in some lifeless numbers) without there being any development. The need for taking care of the different dimensions of life as part of an integrated system came out in bold relief. There was a general acceptance that a system, such as the agricultural system found in several parts of India, develops with the flux of time through adaptive change which is fairly continuous rather than by linear progression, that this change is dynamic and that its parts interact by influencing each other. Fig. 3.1 depicts the sub-systems that operate within the agricultural system. The impossibility of changing one element of the whole system, to the exclusion of others, was realized. Thus in the system shown by Fig. 3.1 it is impossible to change the bovine-wealth sub-system, without impinging upon the other sub-systems such as the bio-mass sub-system. There was, therefore, a virtual consensus that the system as a whole has to be understood to identify problem areas and strengths, to bring about changes in the right direction.[2]

The foregoing change in the paradigm of development thinking led to a search for newer methods of understanding economies and societies, particularly the rural ones, which were stochastic and full of uncertainties. This search for newer systems led to the development of new research methods,[3] including **Rapid Rural Appraisal (RRA)** and its successor **Participatory Rural Appraisal (PRA)**, which assimilated som

THE THIRD APPROACH

A human being as a system?

Components and Interactions :

body, legs, arms, head, strong interactions of components; wrong focus might leave the human being without brain, blood, liver, heart, etc.

Boundry : the physical structure of the body

Inputs : food, air, water, sunlight, mental stimulation, etc.

Outputs : thinking, power, creativity, etc.

Larger System ; the population

Environment : natural conditions;

interactions with the human being as a system.

Objectives : to live, to create, co recreate, to enjoy, etc.

Management ; strong function to convert input to outputs

using resources as well as other systems

In case of ill bing:

1. diagnosis by general practitioner.
2. treatment by subject matter specialist

We have found another and more complex system

Fig. 3.1 : Search for a System

attributes of research methodology from other disciplines, such as Anthropology, Sociology, Geography, Economics and Ethnographic research. The emphasis on understanding people's own point of view and on the fact that different people perceive and understand reality differently came to be the distinguishing features of PRA. PRA was characterized by an applied, holistic and flexible approach to progressive learning, conducted by multi-disciplinary teams, emphasizing community participation and recognizing the primacy of people's knowledge, reality and wisdom. Since subsequently PRA was used in a wide variety of contact – urban, pari-urban, rural – all taken together, "R" for rural seemed out of place. And at once, PRA was used not only for appraisal but for planning, monitoring, evaluation, assessment, advocacy, implementation, research and human resources development. Additionally, there was a growing realization that greater emphasis on behaviour and attitudes was critical in successful use of the tools and methods advocated by PRA. Hence PRA came to be recognized as "Participatory Reflection and Action", and subsequently as Participatory Learning and Action, or PLA for brevity.

Participatory Rapid Appraisal: Important Elements

In Chapter 1, the different elements of PLA have been examined. It is, therefore, not necessary to deal with them here. Nevertheless, to impart completeness to the discussions of this chapter, we wish to emphasise certain salient features of participatory methods.

Of the various forms of participatory methodologies, PLA is a specific form. It is an alternative and complementary method to conventional sample survey methods of investigating problems and collecting data and information. PLA is a way of learning from and with a community's members to examine, "analyze and evaluate constraints and opportunities", and facilitate a process where the communities and development seekers make informed and timely decisions regarding their development projects.[4] PLA is a family of methods and approaches available to the people to systematically and efficiently collect information for the general analysis of a particular issue or problem or of their lives *per se*, for assessment of needs, for conducting feasibility studies, for identifying and prioritizing projects, for planning, for monitoring and for evaluation of projects and programmes and for taking action.

Clearly, by its design and intent, PLA is a system for understanding quantitative and qualitative nuances of an issue and for gaining insight and an understanding of the complexities or of the lives of the communities of the subject or of the lives of communities. It is not intended to generate only accurate statistics *per se* on a list of variables. PLA methods would be of use to "obtain a differentiated understanding" of the community's attitudes, "beliefs and behaviours" towards an issue or problem and planning, say planning for public health and sanitation and their lives generally. It is intended to give qualitative and quantitative data from the perspective of the community.[5]

The different methods available in the toolbox of PLA have been discussed in both Chapters 1 and 2 in this volume to which reference is invited and, therefore, they are not discussed here.

PLA versus Other Research Methods

Survey method is the most commonly used traditional method for analysing problem and issues relating to development of a community. Its foundation lies in formal and standardised research techniques which produce quantifiable, representative, verifiable and comparable data, admitting statistical manipulation. Generally, the field investigators are not required to take any decision while collecting primary data and can collect primary data irrespective of whether the principal investigator is taking part in data collection in the field or not.

The basic differences between participatory methods like PLA and the conventional approach are five. First, participatory methods like RRA and PLA as against conventional survey research encompass community participation, it is usually of short duration and there is economy in data collection. Being based on the principle of optimal ignorance, it avoids the pitfalls of what we call data diarrhoea. Fig. 3.2 is a cartoon, which succinctly drives home the basic point. It is quite likely that data collection by sample surveys may entail lesser time, but it is always the case that data processing and analysis, away from the field, would need a whole lot more time. Second, after the formal survey is completed, it becomes a costly affair to fill up data gaps that still remain or to correct data wrongly recorded. Third, survey research often suffers from the disadvantages of being inflexible and harbouring the danger of turning into a superficial

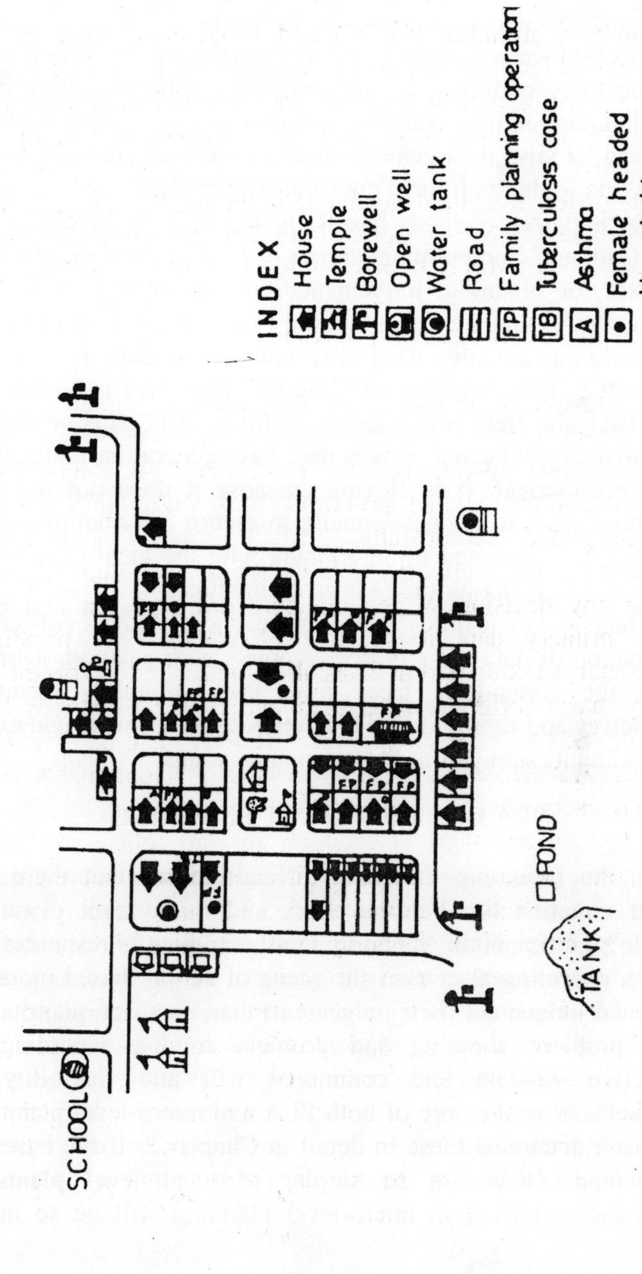

Fig. 3.2 : SOCIAL MAPPING : This map was drawn by villagers of Ramenahally village

exercise. Because it is pre-designed and it has a fixed questionnaire, it inhibits learning during data collection in the field and deeper understanding of social processes. Fourth, survey often leads to fielding a questionnaire which is very large, leading to responses being distorted. Respondents suffer from questionnaire fatigue. Finally, the problem of "moral hazard", can lead to false data generation and on erroneous view of the real world in the traditional questionnaire method.

Participatory methods like RRA and PLA by involving the field team and community members in all aspects of the study or analyses, or planning, implementation, monitoring, evaluation and action, virtually ensures that only such data will be collected as would be actually used. Redundancy in data is virtually eliminated. This, together with the fact that there is no need to send back the field investigators to fill in data gaps or correct data wrongly collected, makes data base generation under PLA more economical. It is flexible because it does not use any structured format or questionnaire to record information. Since data base is generated by interfacing with the local people, the process of learning-by-doing is on all the time.

Thus the key features of PLA are economy in data collection, elimination of data not required, people's parti-cipation, learning about the community faces from the community members themselves and trying to find a solution to problems if one exists or build on its strengths as the community wants.

PLA IN MICRO-LEVEL PLANNING

Given the foregoing, it is not difficult to see that there is a lot of commonality between PLA and micro-level planning. People's participation, economy in all activities as resources are scarce, operating at or near the scene of action, based more on informed judgement (best judgement) than on strict quantitative data, problem shooting and problem solving according to collective wisdom and communal will and flexibility in approach, form the core of both PLA and micro-level planning. We have discussed these in detail in Chapter 2. If the bases of PLA (and PRA) are so similar to local level planning, application of PLA in micro-level planning will be so much more easier and appropriate.[6] How and where PLA may be used in micro-level planning are issues we wish to examine now.

In order to do justice to the tasks at hand, we must look first at the steps in micro-level planning, but since micro-level plans have different space specificities, it is not possible to have one outline of a methodology. Based on our experience we give below a suggested methodology, which has steps that closely approximate the steps that could be common to most methodologies.[7] This methodology relates to a facilitated process.

"Nuts and Bolts" of Micro-Level Planning using PLA Methods

The Four Components of Micro-level Plans

Micro-level planning, has to encompass four dimensions of development. Like all plans, it must be a physical plan. That is, the plan must outline what physical elements will be included in the plan, such as the number of schools to be established, number of water harvesting structures to be created, the length of the "milk roads" to be laid out, acres of land over which, afforestation will be attempted and so on. In the aggregate it must provide an idea of where the area will migrate in terms of its state of development over a period of time. One has to underscore that a physical plan may also be in "negative" terms. For example, in an urban context it may include an estimate of the number of slums that may be cleared and the affected households relocated.

A physical plan in a micro-planning exercise, in order to be implemented, needs resources. A micro-level plan, therefore, has to project an idea of the quantum of resources required to carry out the physical plan worked out. A micro-level plan must, therefore, be a *resource plan* as well. Resources, in this context, have to be understood in its wider connotation, viz., human resources, social resources, political resources, natural resources, cultural resources and financial resources. Under current thinking, all forms of resources are necessary for an efficient implementation of a micro-level plan, though it is possible to substitute one form of resource by another, within certain broad limits, depending upon the technology adopted for implementing the various components of the physical plan. The elasticity of substitution, in economic terms, is nearly always less than unity. And where substitution is forced beyond the wide band, the results are second best.

The physical and the financial plans must have a timeframe. Depending upon the nature of plans (perspective, short term or long term etc.), the various components of the plan will be implemented within a timeframe and at various points in time within that larger timeframe. A micro-level plan (or for that matter any plan) must provide a road map of which element of the plan will be implemented when. A micro-level plan must, therefore, be also a *temporal plan*.

A micro-level plan is prepared with the people and by them, catering to their space-specific needs, unlike a macro-level plan where "one glove fits all" is the rule. A micro-level plan, therefore, indicates which of the physical elements will be grounded where. For instance, it must not only say that "x" number of water harvesting structures will be set up, but also indicate in which or on whose land will they be created and on which watershed, across which water course. Thus a micro-level plan, as distinct from a macro-level plan, must also be a *spatial plan.*

Therefore, a micro-level plan must be a physical plan, a resource plan, a temporal plan and spatial plan, all moulded into a coherent whole.

The Two Stages of Micro-Level Plans

There are generally two stages of micro-level planning. The first stage of a Micro-level planning process is the *Tactical Planning Stage* and the second stage is the *Action Planning Stage*.

Tactical Planning relates to or indicates the perspectives of the community, their hopes and fears. It provides a contemporaneous landscape of an area and its people. It gives "fleeting" glimpses into the resources, capacities and capabilities people have, as also the problems confronted by the community, their coping mechanisms and the ways and means identified to circumvent these problems. Judged at from that perspective a tactical plan provides the rationale and ball-path for the course of action contemplated to bring the community out of the quagmire of poverty, privation and deprivation. In fine, it provides the *raison' d'etre* for the plan, its perspective, its objectives, its goals and activities (projects) for achieving those goals. The Tactical Planning Stage is shown in Fig. 3.3.

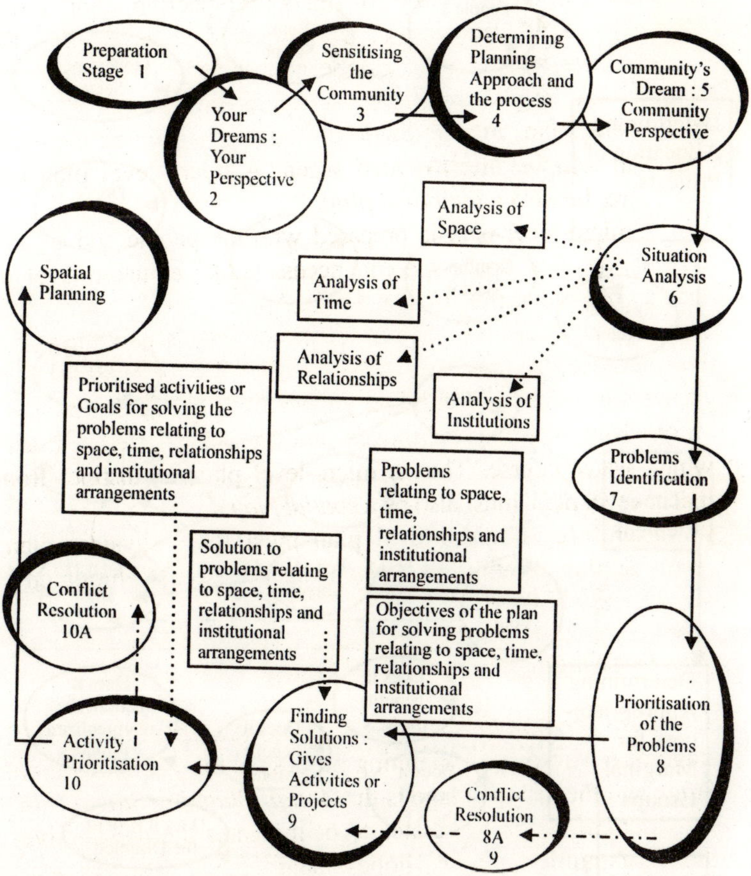

Fig. 3.3 : The Planning Cycle : Tactical Planning Stage : Stage-1 (Mukherjee Methodology)

The *Action Planning* relates to issues revolving around when and who will execute the plan. What will be the timeframe within which the implementation of the different activities will be affected? Action Planning is an exercise at identifying who does what and integrating the roles of different classes of development players in helping the community to accomplish its goals. Additionally, it classifies the activities within a timeframe. The steps of *Action Planning* in summary are shown in Fig. 3.3A.

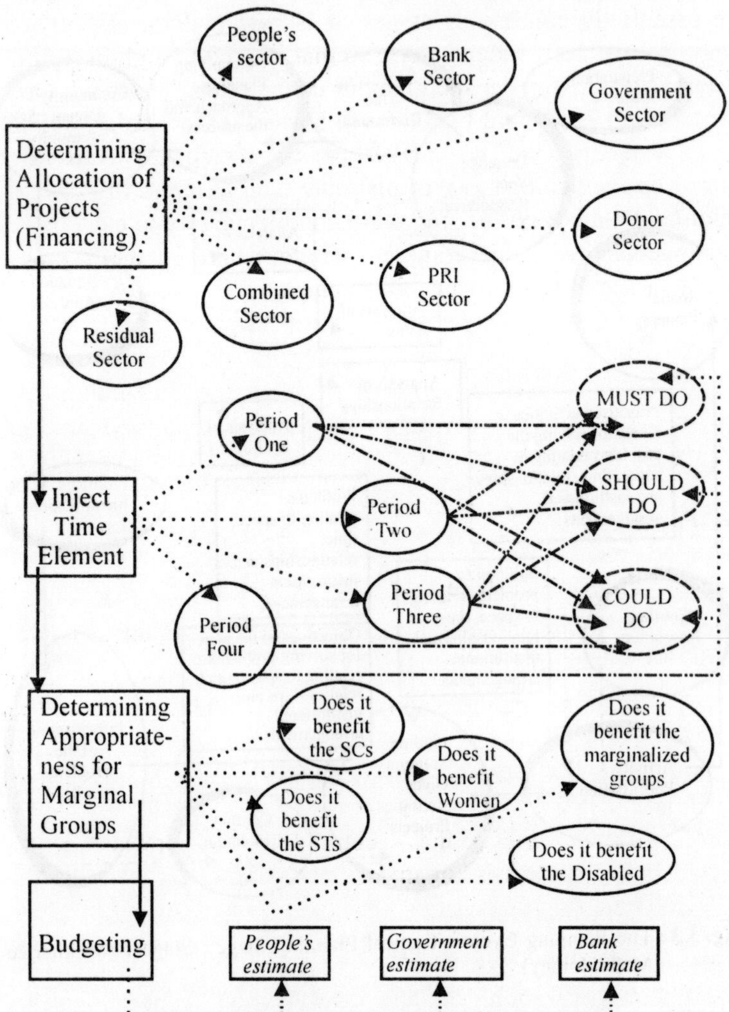

Fig. 3.3A : The Planning Cycle : Stage II : Action Planning : Steps of Action Planning Stage

The *Tactical Planning Stage,* therefore, shows the "how", "what", "where" and "why" of a micro-level planning exercise, the Action Planning Stage shows the "when" and "who" of the plan.

Although *Tactical Planning* and *the Action Planning Stages* are essentially continuous stages, it is best to look at the two stages as distinctly independent, so that the rigour and discipline of one is not lost under the glamour of the other. Those who are creative and have field bias tend to stress the Tactical Planning Stage, whereas those who have "positive personality" and are more into the "doing" part of planning tend to stress the Action Planning Stage. Both the stages are complementary to each other and together make one complete whole. There is, therefore, a need to achieve a proper balance in emphasis.

There are thirteen suggested and indicative Steps, in *Tactical Planning,* and five such steps in *Action Planning,* though most of the steps are consecutive, some of them can be prosecuted concurrently. The various steps of Tactical Planning and in Action Planning in a micro-level planning exercise are as under:

Pre-Planning

Step-1 : Preparation stage

Step-2 : Developing the facilitator's perspective: "Your Dream".

Step-3 : Sensitizing the community

Step-4 : Determining the planning approach and the process.

Planning Per Se : Tactical Plans

Step-5 : Determining the community's perspective : "Community's Dream".

Step-6 : Situation analysis

Step-7 : Problem identification

Step-8 : Prioritization of the problems : generating the objectives of the plan

Step-9 : Conflict resolution, if required

Step-10 : Finding solutions : generates activities or projects.

Step-11 : Activity prioritization : generates the goals.

Step-12 : Conflict resolution, if necessary.

Step-13 : Deciding on locations : Spatial planning

Planning Per Se : Action Planning

Step-14 :Determining allocation of projects to sectors

Step-15 :Injecting the time element : MSC analysis

Step-16 :Determining appropriateness of the plan for marginalized groups

Step-17 :Budgeting

Step-18 :System of monitoring and evaluation.

Let us now see the role of participatory methods in each of these steps.

The Use of Participatory Methods in the First Stage of Micro-Level Plan : The Pre Planning Stage

Step 1: Preparation Step

In the preparation step, the first issue to be tackled is review of existing literature and creation of a database. This will obviate the need to reinvent the wheel and prevent considerable headaches. While the issue of the kind and extent of data required for micro-level planning have been discussed in a separate Chapter in this volume, the sources of data and its quality warrant a few remarks. There is an incredible amount of literature revolving around the subject of database, especially on the quality of secondary data available in the developing countries. Whatever the veracity of these debates and discussions, it is worth remembering that it is beyond the role of a facilitator for developing a micro-level planning to test and verify the available data. The planner is neither the "policeman" nor a member of the investigating agency. The facilitator has to accept the data for whatever they are worth, make a marginal mental adjustment for the margin of error and form an idea of the area for which a micro-level plan is attempted. It is crucial to pay attention to the database for not merely appreciating the learning that would come from the participatory sessions but also for providing inputs to the community within the limits accepted by Box-3 of the *Johari's Window.* Reference is invited to Fig. 3.4.

In the Indian context, a huge mass of data is generated by a well-organized governmental system for generating data. Data available from the Population Census Operations especially the Village and Town Directory generated by it, the Agricultural Census Operation and the Livestock Census Operation are very useful. The data collected by the Central Statistical Organization (CSO) could also prove useful. The District Credit Plans developed by the Lead Bank of the area and the District Plans prepared by the district administration (often by the District Planning Officer/District Statistical Officer) come in very handy. These need to be studied carefully, particularly in the context of Action Planning to which we shall revert later. There are several private agencies, which also generate data, but much of it is macro-data and is useful for contextualising the micro--planning exercise than as inputs into the planning process.

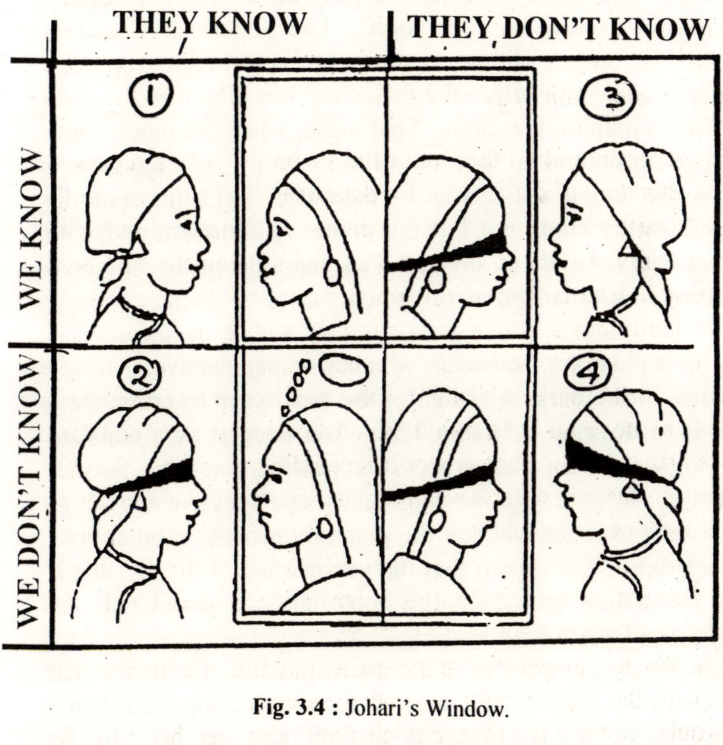

Fig. 3.4 : Johari's Window.

Step 2 : Your Dream: Your Perspective

The review of literature and secondary data provides a perspective of the "health of the area" as it were and its people. It gives insights into what all has been done, being done and planned to be done in the foreseeable future, by different development actors. At any given point in time a myriad of forces operate on any area or community and it stands to reason to understand these for forming a correct perspective. On that basis the facilitator must have a dream for the area: where does she like the area to move on 5 or 10 years down the line; how should the people look like ten years down the line etc. If a facilitator cannot dream for the community and its area, it is unlikely that she will be successful in facilitating a good micro-level plan.

One is reminded of the famous J F Kennedy (JFK) episode in the American Congress. When JFK sought budgetary support from the American Congress of some billions of U.S. Dollars, he was asked "For What"? He replied, "By the end of the decade, we will put a man on the moon". The American Congress approved the budget without demur and every major American newspaper had its headline the following morning that America would put a man on the moon. That night, when the moon came out Americans could all look out of the window, and imagine 'a man on the moon'. JFK was assassinated at Dallas, but the assassin's bullet could not kill the dream JFK dreamt and with him that every American dreamt. Ten years down the line Neil Armstrong indeed landed on the moon.

The facilitator's dream provides him with a perspective. A micro-level planning facilitator, who has no perspective, is trying to whistle in the dark. And one of the best ways to articulate a dream is to develop a Dream Map. And keep it as a constant guide to see where the process is leading to, how far her perspective differed with the community's perspective and act as a touchstone to judge whether the planning process is on course. And experience has shown that the perspective of the facilitator is the foundation on which the community is sensitized. An example of a Dream Map is at Fig. 3.5.

How far the perspective of the micro-planning facilitator will win community support will depend upon the personal attributes and capability of the facilitator. If the facilitator can listen to the

A typical wall painting in one of the KAWAD project watersheds. Unfortunately, such watershed development publicity is often misleading in that it suggests that there are quick fixes to water-related problems

Fig. 3.5 : Dream Map Diagram

voices of the poor, if he/she is concerned about the poor, if she/he is enthusiastic about the work, if she/he is clear about her/his motives, then the chances are that her/his dream will capture the imagination of the community.

Step-3 : Sensitizing the Community

Sensitizing the community is a composite of several steps. If the community being worked with is new to the micro-planning facilitators, the obvious thing to do first is to "build rapport". A large number of methods have been invented and used by development practitioners to build rapport with the community, beginning with "meet and greet" using their custom, talking to them in their language, walking through the area where the community lives, joint walk, giving a helping hand, doing it yourself or learning by doing or simply just listening to their stories.

An integral part of the sensitization process is telling the community, the purpose of the planning exercise, its scope, limitations and the parameters within which it must operate. Nothing serves the cause of micro-level planning through PRA/PLA methods better than an open and transparent beginning.

The sensitization must then entail managing the community's expectation. One need not labour the point that any participatory session builds the community's expectation, often dispropor-tionate to what could possibly be done. There is a need to temper down soaring expectations. While expectation acts as an elixir for community action (a hopeless community rarely acts), it must be realistic. The facilitators need to explain to the community the scope of the planning exercise, its parameters (including the size of the budget), implementability, what is expected of the community in implementing the plan and the chances of its success. A good sensitization effort acts as an aid to developing a good community perspective in Step 5 later. The role of sensitization of the community in a micro-level planning process in the current context, is enlarged because it increases transparency of the process.

Sensitization also involves making an assessment of the community's preparedness to participate in the micro-planning exercise. Are they willing to undertake a micro-level plan? How much support does the process have from the community? If necessary, "advocacy" for eliciting communal support may have to be mounted and information that the community may not have (filling in Box-2 of *Johari's Window*) may have to be supplied. Sensitization is thus an empowering element in any micro-level planning exercise.

Step-4 : Determining the Planning Approach and the Process

Given the data, information and knowledge that the facilitator will have from the foregoing steps, a series of decisions have to be taken. In deciding planning approach the following decisions have to be taken :

- Whether direction of local level plan will be from projects to strategies or form strategies to projects;
- Whether planning will be nested planning or combined planning;
- Whether in local level planning emphasis should be on developing local area, local markets, or on developing social and economic infrastructure or some combination of the two;
- Whether, the micro-plan will be a closed-ended plan or an open-ended plan *(through focus group discussion key-informant interview, key-performant interview and wherever necessary, through scoring and ranking);*
- Whether, the plan will be a sectoral plan (say a social sector plan for health-education-housing or health immunization-nutrition or a livelihood plan for off-farm livelihoods etc.) or an integrated plan for improving the social, economic, natural resources, political and financial assets of the community (*through review of secondary data, group discussion, semi-structured key-informant interview, semi structured key performant interview and wherever necessary, through scoring and ranking*); and
- Whether, the time horizon of the plan will be a long term, short term or medium term (*through review of secondary data, group discussion, semi-structured key-informant interview, semi-structured key performant interview and wherever necessary through scoring and ranking*) plan.

The planning process has also to *inter alia* determine the :

- composition of the multi-disciplinary team of planning facilitators, avoiding biases such as *professional bias, gender bias and people bias;*
- kind of participation that the facilitator is attempting at harnessing. There are eight kinds of participation, viz., passive participation, participation by furnishing information, participation by consultation, participation for material incentives, functional participation, interactive participation, participation by self-mobilization, participation by contribution and partipulation (participation by manipulation). Fig. 3.5 is an illustration of the kinds of participation. Ideally for micro-level planning, the facilitators should be seeking interactive-participation, that is, participation where people participate in joint analysis, providing multiple perspectives, preparing action plan, form and strengthen local organizations/institutions and for empowerment;
- entry point for the planning process (*through review of secondary data, group discussion, semi-structured key-informant interview, semi-structured key performant interview, night meeting and wherever necessary, through scoring and ranking*);
- time to start the micro-level plan avoiding time bias and seasonal bias (*through review of secondary data, group discussion, semi-structured key-informant interview, semi-structured key performer interview*); and
- outline of a corrective mechanism and a feedback loop, to feed monitoring and evaluation data into the planning process for mid-way corrections and enhancing the quality of planning and its execution.

Step-5 : Community's Dream : Determining the Community's Perspective

The understanding the community's perspective is fundamental to facilitating a good micro-plan. What changes does the community see as signalling their development, which must be reached in the foreseeable future : good governance, increased freedom, increased political participation, enhanced social, capital, sustainable livelihoods, modernization of agriculture, higher levels of household income or whatever. There can be sectoral dreams (read perspective) as well like social development ("health for all" or "free and compulsory education for all children"). There are several methods, which can be used to develop community's perspective. *Dream Mapping, Futuristic Transects and Semi-Structured Interviews come in handy. Facilitation of the dream map may require a current mapping first and then moving on to draw the future scenario. The current map may be a study of the secondary data or an existing map.*

Step-6 : Situation Analysis

PLA is a system which, when applied to a community or an area where a community is located, produces in most cases all the required data. Reference is invited to Figure 3.6 (which again is a subset of Figure 3.6, involving steps 6 to 8a). There are five kinds of analyses that are possible, viz.:

- Analysis of Space through *Social Mapping, Resource Mapping, Infra-Structure Mapping, Natural Resource Mapping, Census Mapping, Literacy Mapping, Health Mapping, Livestock Mapping, Asset Mapping, Well-Being Mapping, Semi-structured interview (SSI) and so on.*
- Analysis of Time through *Historical Transect, Time Line, Oral History, Then-and-Now Social Mapping, Then-and-Now Resource Mapping, Then-and-Now Infrastructure Mapping, Then-and-Now Natural Resource Mapping, Then-and-Now Census Mapping, Then-and Now Literacy Mapping, Then-and Now Health Mapping, Then-and-Now Livestock Mapping, Then-and-Now Asset Mapping, Then-and-Now Well-Being Mapping etc. Seasonality Diagrams and Participatory Calendars (such as Food Calendar, Employment Calendar etc.) Ergograph and Daily Routines are also analysis of time in the short run.*
- Analysis of Relationships through *Venn Diagramming, Relational Matrices, Mapping and SSI.*

- Analysis of Institutions through *Venn Diagramming, Scoring-Ranking and Matrix-Ranking, Matrix Scoring*
- Analysis of Preferences through *Scoring-Ranking and Matrix-Ranking, Matrix Scoring, Forced Choice, Pairwise Ranking.*

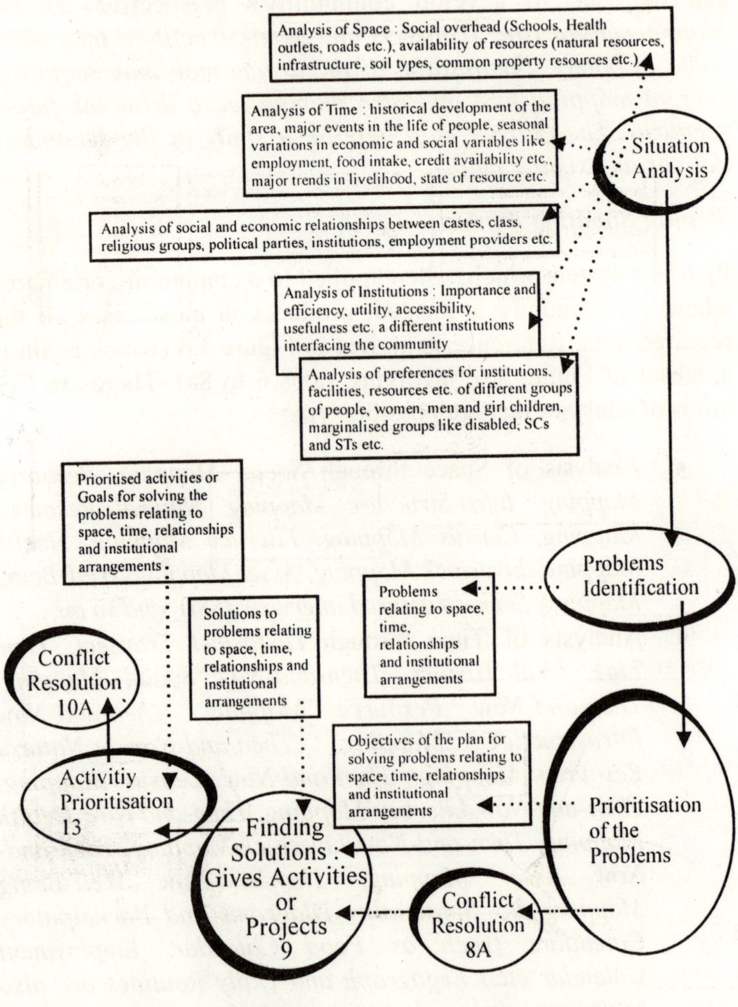

Fig. 3.6 : Phase of Low Level of Facilitation Warranted

Step-7 : Potential Problem Identification

The situation analysis will pave the way for the community's potential identification and problem identification against the backdrop of the community's potential. Problem identification is a

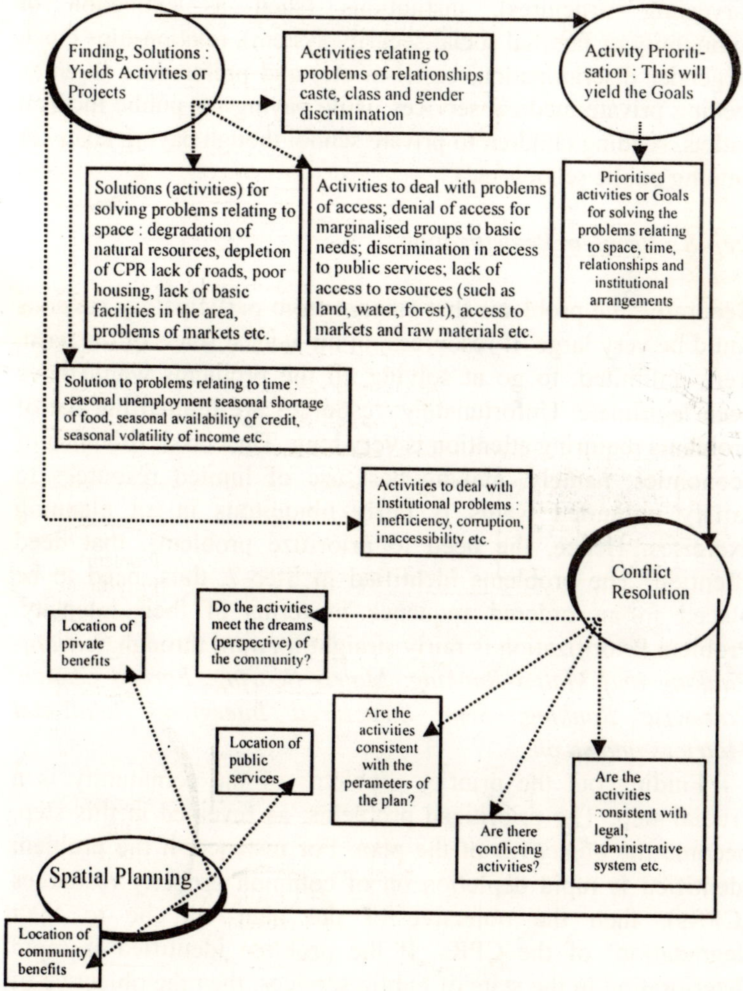

Fig. 3.7 : Phase of high Facilitation and Moving to box three of Johari's Window

step, which is co-terminus with the situation analysis. The same tools and techniques apply. Hence, it is important to separate the problems relating to space (such as lack of access roads; or "unfreedom" as Sen calls it), time (seasonal unemployment, long run degradation of moral values, break down of traditional water harvesting structures), institutions (such as extinction of community or familial social security system), relationships (such as gender discrimination, casteism etc) and preferences (such as seeking private medical services while paying for public medical outlets, sending children to private school though paying taxes for running public schools etc).

Step-8 : Problem Prioritization

Generally, the problems that emerge from participatory sessions could be very large. If resources, in the widest sense of the term, were unlimited, to go at solving all the problems would have been legitimate. Unfortunately, resources are limited but list of problems requiring attention is very long. The classic dilemma of economics, namely, making best use of limited resources to satisfy unlimited wants is fairly ubiquitous in all planning exercises. Hence, the need to prioritize problems, that need attention. The problems identified in Step-7, thus, need to be placed in an ordered sequence in terms of their intensity. Problem Prioritization is fairly straight forward through *Scoring-Ranking and Matrix-Ranking, Matrix Scoring, Forced Choice, Pair-wise Ranking, Semi Structured Interview, Relational Matrices and so on.*

Finding out the priority problems of the community is a crucial step. The prioritized problems, as revealed in this step, become the *objectives* of the plan. For instance, if the problem identified is rapid depletion on of common property resources (CPRs), then the objective of the plan will be to 'halt degradation' of the CPRs. If the problem identified is rapid deterioration in the state of public services, then the objective of the plan will be to 'improve the quality of public services', and so on.

Step-9 : Conflict Resolution

In most cases the community is not homogeneous. The heterogeneity of communities generates varied interest groups. In most cases, these interest groups will have some common problems and some problems, which are unique to some of the groups. With limited resources, it may not be possible to meet the plethora of needs articulated by diverse groups and priority indicated. There may arise a need to resolve the conflict. *Problem-Problem Matrix, Cause and Effect Matrix or by Voting may be useful for the purpose.* Voting should be a last resort and the minority view has to be taken cognizance of.

A secondary source of conflict can emerge when the priority problems do not meet with the perspectives of the community. That is, there is a mismatch between the community's dream and the problems prioritized. It may be necessary to go back to the community's dream map and facilitate a comparison. Either the community's dream has to be modified or the community has to re-examine the problem priorities and come to a solution. It is possible that solving the problems alone may not automatically lead to realization of the community's dream. There may be a need to add objectives which go beyond solving the problems of the community. If that is the case, then the community may add objectives in addition to what may be generated by the problem solving exercise.

Step-10 : Finding Solutions

Once the list of problems is arrived at, solutions to those problems have to be located. There can be two sources of solutions. One the community will come up with its solutions, which may be based on indigenous knowledge (tacit knowledge), indigenous technology, traditional wisdom and practices. In terms of *Johari's Window,* this is based on Box-2 (They Know-We Do Not Know). Secondly, the facilitators may have to supply the community with knowledge which outsiders have such as technical knowledge, that is fill in Box-3 of *Johari's Window* (We Know-They Do Not Know) and help the community make an informed choice, generate alternative solutions and take a final decision. The solutions must meet the needs of physical planning, temporal planning and spatial planning. That is, the community must say "What they want" (say 2 vocational training centres); when they want it" (say in years 2 of the plan period) and "where they want" say one on the Panchayat Land adjoining the Gram Panchayat Office and the other in the SC colony of the village. This will enable the community to make an informed choice. There are several ways to arrive at solutions. *Semi-Structured Interview, Card Sorting Method and Card Matching Method and Problem Activity Matrix* are some of the methods, which have been used with good results. A Problem Activity Tree can graphically produce a good picture of how each problem is sought to be tackled.

Step-11 : Activity Prioritization

Once the activities have been identified, there may be need to have the activities prioritized. This can be for two reasons. If the micro-planning process is to generate a Closed-Ended Plan, then there may be a need to eliminate those activities, which lie beyond the ambit of the exercise. *Card Sorting Method or Sector Activity Matrix* can be used. If alternatively, resources are limited, activities may be prioritized using any of the ranking and scoring methods, and a list of activities in descending order of priorities may be drawn up, on the expressed understanding that activities will be taken up according to their rank in the list of priorities.

The list of prioritized activities gives the goals of the micro-level plan.

Step-12 : Conflict Resolution

As in case of the prioritization of the problems, the list of prioritized activities can also lead to conflicts, for a variety of reasons. These conflicts may have to be resolved. One method of resolving the conflict is the use of *Problem Activity Matrix*. Those activities, which directly and indirectly solve the maximum number of problems are chosen. A *Functional Linkage Matrix* can also be used. Activities, which reinforce the maximum number of other activities, have a higher priority. Some facilitators of micro-level planning, therefore, like to call conflict resolution as the second stage of prioritization.

Step-13 : Spatial Planning

The final step in the tactical planning phase is the spatial planning. Each of the activities has to be located in the space. For instance, if a series of water harvesting structures is to be constructed, the exact locations of the structures have to be decided. Similarly, for other activities there is a need to find the exact location where they will be grounded. Generally, there will be three kinds of activities. Activities giving individual benefit to households (such as support for housing to a widow-headed households) for giving individual benefits, a "well-being grouping map" may be used and each household marked. Then locate/mark especially the households which will receive the benefits. For activities or benefits accruing community owned assets (say a pond), a natural resource map may be used and the location of the new pond marked. If activities which are in the nature of public good, are to be provided, use may be made of a infrastructure map (for locating, for example, a school or a Public Health Centre) and mark the location of the new school or Primary Health Centre on the infrastructure. Activities accruing benefits to community owned assets and activities which are in the nature of public goods, the best course is to use mapping of various kinds.

The Use of Participatory Methods in the Second Stage of Micro-Level Plan : The Stage of Action Planning

Step-14 : Determining Allocation of the Project.

Once the activities are finalized, it is necessary to allocate the activities across sectors. Normally, the activities that emerge out of a participatory micro-level plan are many. While some of the activities get eliminated at the conflict resolution stage, the possibilities are that there will be many activities, which do not fit into either the scope of the planning exercise or cannot be accommodated within the available resources. If an open-ended or integrated plan is developed, then the chances of generating a long list of desired and prioritized activities are very high. In all cases, for success of planning, it would be important that as many of the activities identified by the community get implemented as possible.

For this purpose all activities have to be classified as falling into one of the seven sectors outlined below (reference is invited to Figure 3.8) :

People Sector	Bank Sector	Government Sector	Donor Sector	PRI Sector	Combined Sector	Residual Sector
Activity-1p	Activity-1b	Activity-1g	Activity-1d	Activity-1pi	Activity-1c	Activity-1r
Activity-2p	Activity-2b	Activity-2g	Activity-2d	Activity-2pi	Activity-2c	Activity-2r
Activity-3p	Activity-3b	Activity-3g	Activity-3d	Activity-3pi	Activity-3c	Activity-3r
Activity-4p	Activity-4b	Activity-4g	Activity-4d	Activity-4pi	Activity-4c	Activity-4r
Activity-5p	Activity-5b	Activity-5g	Activity-5d	Activity-5pi	Activity-5c	Activity-5r
Activity-6p	Activity-6b	Activity-6g	Activity-6d	Activity-6pi	Activity-6c	Activity-6r

Note : p stands for people's sector; b for bank sector, g for government sector, d for donor sector, pi for PRI sector, c for combined sector and r for residual sector.

Fig. 3.8 : Activity-Sector Classification Matrix

(a) People's Sector
(b) Bank Sector
(c) Government Sector
(d) Donor Sector
(e) PRI Sector
(f) Combined Sector
(g) Residual Sector

The people's sector will have those activities which people themselves can carry out without external support. Such activities could be maintenance of village ponds, upkeep of community forest, social fencing of a common property, etc.

The Bank sector will consist of those activities for which there is a possibility of havings credit/financing from commercial banks or the Regional Rural Banks. These activities could be setting up of commercial ventures like an oil mill or a flourmill. It could also include activities for which government subsidy, credit and beneficiary contribution, all are required, like housing support under Indira Awas Yojana for weaker sections of society.

Within the Government Sector would be included activities for which outright grant (such as widow pension) is available and activities which can be undertaken only out of government finance such as laying down of roads. This sector could also include activities that can be undertaken under MP Local Area Development Fund and MLA Local Area Development Fund.

The Donor Sector will include activities for which funding is available from donor agencies. For example funds available from CARE India for supplementary nutrition under the ICDS Programme. This sector will include activities, which could also be undertaken by the non-governmental organizations.

The PRI Sector will include activities which can be covered by the Panchayati Raj Institutions, such as street lighting. It is true that the PRIs have little leeway and resources, but these institutions being the third tier of governance, have a major role to play in not merely funding/executing activities but also in advocacy work to which we shall revert later.

The combined sector will have activities, which will require the inputs from the people, the banks, the government, donor agencies and PRIs. An integrated Watershed Treatment Plan will fall under this category.

Activities, which cannot be included in any of the sectors, should be placed in the Residual Sector. This sector will have the richness to generate ideas for policy work or include activities, which either lie beyond the territorial area for which the micro-level plan is being prepared or encompasses more than one micro-level planning areas, which can be dealt within another level of planning. For example, if a micro-level plan is being prepared for a Panchayat in India and activities have been generated (such as a building a dam across a river for medium irrigation project, they may not be dealt with in micro-plan of a Panchyat) which involves several Panchayats. Such activities will be referred to those involved in higher level of planning such as Intermediate Panchayat Level or Block level Planning.

Implementation of the micro-level plan becomes easy when activities are so classified. Implementation of the people's sector can be the entry point activities and then the work of persuading, influencing and obtaining approval of the other development players could follow. In some cases, where schemes already exist, such as with Bank Sector and the welfare activities covered by the Government sector, these could constitute the second step activities and involve in most cases finding margin money, connecting the community with the powers that be and advocacy work.

		First Year	Second Year	Third Year	Fourth Year	Fifth Year
People's Sector Activities	Must Do	Activity 1p	Activity 2p	Activity 3p	Activity 4p	Activity 5p
	Should Do	Activity 1p	Activity 2p	Activity 3p	Activity 4p	Activity 5p
	Could Do	Activity 1p	Activity 2p	Activity 3p	Activity 4p	Activity 5p
Bank Sector Activities	Must Do	Activity 1b	Activity 2b	Activity 3b	Activity 4b	Activity 5b
	Should Do	Activity 1b	Activity 2b	Activity 3b	Activity 4b	Activity 5b
	Could Do	Activity 1b	Activity 2b	Activity 3b	Activity 4b	Activity 5b
Government Sector Activities	Must Do	Activity 1g	Activity 2g	Activity 3g	Activity 4g	Activity 5g
	Should Do	Activity 1g	Activity 2g	Activity 3g	Activity 4g	Activity 5g
	Could Do	Activity 1g	Activity 2g	Activity 3g	Activity 4g	Activity 5g
Donor Sector Activities	Must Do	Activity 1d	Activity 2d	Activity 3d	Activity 4d	Activity 5d
	Should Do	Activity 1d	Activity 2d	Activity 3d	Activity 4d	Activity 5d
	Could Do	Activity 1d	Activity 2d	Activity 3d	Activity 4d	Activity 5d
PRI Sector Activities	Must Do	Activity 1pi	Activity 2pi	Activity 3pi	Activity 4pi	Activity 5pi
	Should Do	Activity 1pi	Activity 2pi	Activity 3pi	Activity 4pi	Activity 5pi
	Could Do	Activity 1pi	Activity 2pi	Activity 3pi	Activity 4pi	Activity 5pi
Combined Sector Activities	Must Do	Activity 1c	Activity 2c	Activity 3c	Activity 4c	Activity 5c
	Should Do	Activity 1c	Activity 2c	Activity 3c	Activity 4c	Activity 5c
	Could Do	Activity 1c	Activity 2c	Activity 3c	Activity 4c	Activity 5c
Residual Sector Activities	Must Do	Activity 1r	Activity 2r	Activity 3r	Activity 4r	Activity 5r
	Should Do	Activity 1r	Activity 2r	Activity 3r	Activity 4r	Activity 5r
	Could Do	Activity 1r	Activity 2r	Activity 3r	Activity 4r	Activity 5r
		1st year	**2nd year**	**3rd year**	**4th year**	**5th year**
TOTAL	Total Must*					
	Total Should**					
	Total Could***					
	Grand Total#					

Notes : * Add up all the "must" activities of the year. ** Add up all the "should" activities of the year. *** Add up all the "could" activities of the year. # Add the total of the must, should and could do activities. p stands for people's sector; b for bank sector, g for government sector, d for donor sector, pi for PRI sector, c for combined sector and r for residual sector. The numerical stands for the year of implementation.

Fig. 3.9 : MSC Analysis – Time Matrix

Step-15 : Injecting the Time Element

Once the activities are allocated across sectors, it would be necessary to divide the activities according to a time period. Normally, a micro-level plan for three to five years should be adequate. That is, activities which would be done in period-1 (year-1, month-1 or week-1 as the case may be) are clubbed in period-1. Those activities which would be undertaken in period-2, should be classified separately. And so on. The exercise at injecting time element into a micro-plan, generates sequencing of activities easily. It would then also be necessary to have a hard look once again to the activities and divide them into "must" and "could do" categories. A *MSC-Time Matrix* of the kind shown in figure 3.9 can be developed.

Step-16 : Determining Appropriateness for Marginalized Groups

It often happens that after considerable efforts, when a micro-level plan is prepared, the marginalized groups are left out. The benefits flow to those who are more vocal and those who can represent their interest forcefully. Hence, it is imperative to make it doubly sure that the activities do benefit the marginalized groups. To check this a *Project Benefit Matrix* may be worked out with the community. Have all the projects written as elements of the first row and all the marginalized groups as the elements of the first column. Then ask the question, project-wise whether the project helps the marginalized groups catalogued in the first column. If the project helps, mark a right mark and if it does not, put a cross mark. Continue till the exercise is completed with all the projects. This is particularly critical in the Indian context where stratification of society is high and despite best efforts, it often happens that the marginalized group get lost in the planning process. This step will at least act as a reminder for the facilitators and the community, that they owe it to the "silent minority" that their concerns are reflected in the final micro-level plan. Reference is invited to Figure 3.10.

	Activity 1	Activity 2	Activity 3	....	Activity n-1	Activity n
Widows	3	3	5	5	3	5
Female Headed Households	✓			✓	✓	✓
People are differently abled		✓	✓		✓	
Scheduled Castes	✓		✓	✓	✓	
Scheduled Tribes	✓	✓	✓	✓		
Especially Disadvantaged Groups (Scavengers etc.)				✓		✓

Note : A tick mark indicates the benefit of the activity to the relevant group. A cross mark indicates non-applicability of the activity to the relevant group.

Fig. 3.10 : Project Benefit Matrix

Step-17 : Budgeting

The issue of budgeting often occupies a great deal of time and energy of the micro-level planning process. The budgeting should follow the same pattern as the sectors. Since there are seven sectors, seven budgets have to be prepared and then aggregated. Thus budgets for the People's Sector, Bank Sector, Government Sector, Donor Sector, PRI Sector, Combined Sector and the Residual Sector have to be prepared.

In preparing the budgets for the people's sector, the estimates have to be made by the people. For the bank sector, people should make their own estimate but take into account the unit costs often specified by the banks or by NABARD (in India). For the Government Sector, PRI Sector and Combined Sector, estimates have to be made by the people by being cognizant of the cost estimates specified by the Government. For instance, for constructing school building there are approved construction rates for brickwork, for floor work, for fixtures, etc. The community will also prepare the budget for the Donor Sector and the residual Sector. Since in case of the these sectors, donors and other agencies have to be found and persuaded, the estimates have to be realistic as far as possible, avoiding both over-financing and under-financing. One good way to facilitate the process is to obtain data of what outlays these actors have approved of similar projects in the past.

	Quantity of Raw Materials Required	Equip-ment	Infrastructure Required	Information Required	Person-Hours of Labour Required	Money Required	Risks Involved
Activity 1p							
Activity 2p							
Activity 3p							
Activity 4p							
Activity 5p							
Activity 6p							
Activity							
Activity N-1p							
Activity Np							
Grand Total for the year							

Note : 'p' stands for people's sector. For other sectors, 'p' will be substituted by 'g' or 'b' for government and bank sector respectively or whatever as the case may be.

Fig. 3.11 : Year-wise Sector-wise Budget Table

Once sectoral budgets are completed, the budgets can be aggregated to obtain a total picture. A suggested model is given in Fig. 3.11.

The grand totals of the Year-wise Sector-wise totals (last row of the above table) when aggregated for all the years will generate the sector-wise grand total for the plan period.

The sector-wise grand totals for the plan period for all the sectors when aggregated will generate the total budget for the plan for the whole plan period.

Step-18 : Monitoring and Evaluation

Finally comes monitoring and evaluation. Monitoring and evaluation are both the final and crucial stage because it is the stage that links cyclically with the first stage. A participatory monitoring and evaluation system acts like the "eyes and ears" of the "micro-level plan", as it were, and provides a mechanism to take corrective action, in-built into the micro-level planning system. For instance, bottlenecks would have to be cleared if there are delays in the achievement of goals, goals which seem impossible to achieve may require rescheduling, which could lead to modification of the plan. Unforeseen changes in the resource and constraints situation, unexpected adverse impacts or other stochastic conditions would have to be taken into account, which could also warrant modification of the plan wherever necessary.

Attitudes and Application of PLA

Even at the cost of suffering the stricture of being repetitive, we wish to reiterate what we said in Chapter 2 earlier about attitudes and behaviour in relation to PLA.

Imparting knowledge about PLA is not likely to be a greater problem than what one would encounter with regard to training in any other tool/technique. The real crunch will be imparting the right kind of orientation to the different actors in the application of the PLA techniques, which will be difficult. There are two problems that are basic to it, which can be best summarised in terms of two sketches. The first one relates to reorienting the understanding of the various actors in micro-level planning about the intelligence and knowledge base of the common man. There is a widespread non-understanding that the common man is very intelligent, and the storehouse of communal knowledge about what is good for the community is beyond question. The success of participatory planning will require that the orientation of all the actors in local planning from the Gram Panchayat level to the Zilla Parishad or District level functionaries (both officials and elected), changes from one of imparting to the people what they perceive as the people's problems and what solutions they can offer, to one of listening to the people and paying heed to their advise and ideas. The orientation has to change from the "lecturing mode" to the "learning mode". It is only then that the use of participatory micro-level planning would succeed and, indeed, local level plans *per se,* and programmes and schemes for operationalising local level plans under ground conditions, would have a sustainable foundation.

The second problem would be to inculcate in the actors involved in local level planning, the ability to empathise with the common man. The actors in micro-level planning have not only to accept that the common man deserves to be respected for his intelligence and knowledge, but they (actors in local level planning) should imbibe an ability to look at the problem areas from a common man's perspective. For instance, when the local level planner is involved in understanding the extent of poverty in the local area economy, the criterion for judging poverty should be a criterion which local people perceive as correctly reflecting the extent of poverty in the area under reference. That is, those involved in local level planning and the potential users have to be trained to avoid the pitfall of the extension worker who is reluctant to use communal wisdom and local knowledge.

These are difficult things to do and they become almost intractable problems, when it comes to such bureaucrats and government functionaries who exude a feeling of having "arrived". Affecting attitudinal changes in these functionaries is important but under the given circumstances is a somewhat difficult proposition. It has, nevertheless, to be achieved. The solution to the problem of "people in charge" not willing to change attitudes (which die hard with flux of time) lies in more, and more persuasive training, greater insistence on people's participation and not throwing in the towel.

Notes

1. The Constitution (Seventy Third Amendment) Act 1993. It was passed by the Parliament as the Constitution (Seventy Third Amendment) Act 1993 and it received the assent of the President of India on 20th April, 1993. See *Extraordinary Gazette of India,* No. 69, New Delhi, dated April 20, 1993/Chaitra 30, 1915.
2. See for details Beebe, James. (1987) : "Rapid Appraisal: The Evolution of the Concept and the Definition of Issues" in Khon Kaen University, 1987, *Proceedings of the 1985 International Conference on Rapid Rural*

Appraisal, Khon Kaen, Thailand: Rural Systems Research and Farm Systems Research Project; and Thesis, Joachim and Grady, Heather M. (1991) : *Participatory Rapid Appraisal for Community Development* (London: International Institute for Environment and Development, and Save the Children Fund).

3. Jamieson, Neils. (1985) : "The Paradigmatic Significance of Rapid Rural Appraisal", paper read at the Conference on Rapid Rural Appraisal, September 2-5, Khon Kaen, Thailand.
4. Thesis, Joachim and Grady, Heather M. (1991): *loc. cit.*
5. *Ibid.*
6. See Mukherjee Amitava, (1993) : "Micro-Level Planning and Participatory Rural Appraisal Techniques: Similarities, Potential and Training Needs", *The Administrator,* Vol. XXXVIII, No.1, 1993, pp. 41-60.
7. Mukherjee, Amitava (1991) : *Methodology and Data Base for Decentralized Planning* (New Delhi: Heritage Publishers), Vol. 3, Part C, Chapter-3.

4

Micro-Level Planning for Rural Development in Participatory Framework : The Hard Systems Approach

– AMITAVA MUKHERJEE

INTRODUCTION

In chapter 3 we have discussed the application of PLA/PLA in developing a micro-level plan, using a soft-systems approach. (In this chapter PRA and PLA have been used inter-changeably.) That is, no problem is assumed. The situation is analysed, problems, if they occur, are identified and then planning is undertaken. In case of a "hard systems approach" a problem is known or taken to exist and hence a micro-level plan is developed. In this chapter we will deal with the application of PLA/PLA in the hard-systems approach to micro-level planning.

In order to do justice to the tasks at hand, we must look first at the steps in Hard Systems Approach to Micro-Level Planning, but since micro-level plans have different space specificities, it is not possible to have one outline of a methodology. Based on our experience we give below a suggested methodology which has steps that closely approximate the steps that could be common to most methodologies.

Pre-Planning Stage

Step-1: Assessing Environment for Micro-Level Planning, that is :

- an assessment of administrative and organizational environment for Micro-Level Planning;

- an assessment of financial environment;
- an assessment of planning environment; and
- assessing the environment for people's participation.

Step-2: Assessing local level planning parameters.
Step-3: Determination local level planning approach.
Step-4: Determination local level planning process.
Step-5: Finding implications for steps of local level planning.
Step-6: Reconciliation.

Planning Stage

Step-7: Setting goals and determining objectives.
Step-8: Preparatory Stage.
Step-9: Reconnaissance Stage.
Step-10: Main Field Study.

Strategic Planning Phase

Step-11: Current Area Analysis, which includes aggregate area analysis, inter-area analysis, intra-area analysis, natural resource analysis, gender analysis and market centre studies.
Step-12: Simulation of future scenario, with regard to population, labour force, poverty, consumption, local level area income, agriculture and so on.
Step-13: Problem prioritization.
Step-14: Formulation of strategies.
Step-15: Project identification.
Step-16: Assessment of projects and strategies.

Tactical Planning Phase

Step-17: Project prioritization.
Step-18: Action planning.

Post-Planning Phase

Step-19: Implementation, Monitoring and Evaluation

PLA being a very flexible set of methods and many new ones emerge during actual working in the field, it may be impossible to say exactly in which of these steps would PLA methods be applicable. It will vary from case to case and which method will be appropriate will or can only come out at the time of applying the method at the grassroots level. However, based on our experience with micro-level planning, the relevance of PLA techniques and the applicability of PLA may be briefly illustrated below in respect of some of the steps mentioned above :

PART-I : PRE-PLANNING STAGE

Step-1

Assessing environment for local-level planning has four elements, viz., administrative and organizational environment, assessment of financial environment, assessment of planning environment, and finally, environment for people's participation in local level planning.

An assessment of environment for people's participation will indicate in broad terms the extent of applicability of PLA tools. In every case where the environment for people's participation is well articulated, the scope of applying PLA tools will be so much more extensive.[1] And wherever the institutional arrangement for Micro-Level Planning is also based on local-level participation, such as the Panchayati Raj Institutions, the use of PLA would be easier and appropriate. For instance, in West-Bengal where micro-level planning is entrusted to the care of the Panchayats, a lot of data generation is through methods akin to PLA like group discussions at the Muhalla level. (A *Muhalla* is a locality in a village). Folklores, diagrams, mapping and group discussions are powerful methods in ensuring people's participation.

Step-2

Assessing local level planning parameters encompasses, but is not restricted to, ascertaining: **one**, what major private sector interests, such as mining, lumbering and plantations operate in the local area being planned for; **second**, the principal markets, major commodities and import economic influences which are operative in the local level economy; **third**, the extent and classes of natural resources available in the local area being planned for, and finally, an assessment of what objective criterion is seen by the people as yardsticks to decide for or against their support of local level planning.

Obviously, existing PLA techniques applicable in this step will be several and still more could be improvised in the process of executing this step. Review of secondary data, construction of diagrams, analysis through group discussions, direct observation and semi-structured interviews could be utilized to ascertain what private sector interests operate in the local area economy. The principal markets, major commodities and important economic influences could be located through mapping, Venn diagram and ranking or scoring. The extent and class of resources available at the local level could be seen through a transect, resource mapping and such other methods. Primary resource mapping such as the one shown in figure 4.1 can be used to elicit information on land, water, and tree resources, land use, land and soil types, cropping patterns, land and water management, productivity, watersheds, degraded lands, treatment plants, etc.. Similarly, modified preference ranking, direct matrix ranking, simple ranking and scoring are methods most suited for assessing what objective criteria are seen by the people as yardsticks for supporting or otherwise, micro-level planning. The extent and quality of the operationalisation of the different techniques will depend upon the time at the disposal, and the ingenuity, of the local level planning as well.

Steps-3 and 4

Determining the planning process and the planning approach is largely an exercise at arriving at certain decisions appertaining to:

(i) direction of local level planning from projects to strategies or from strategies to projects;
(ii) availability of and nature of data for planning purposes;

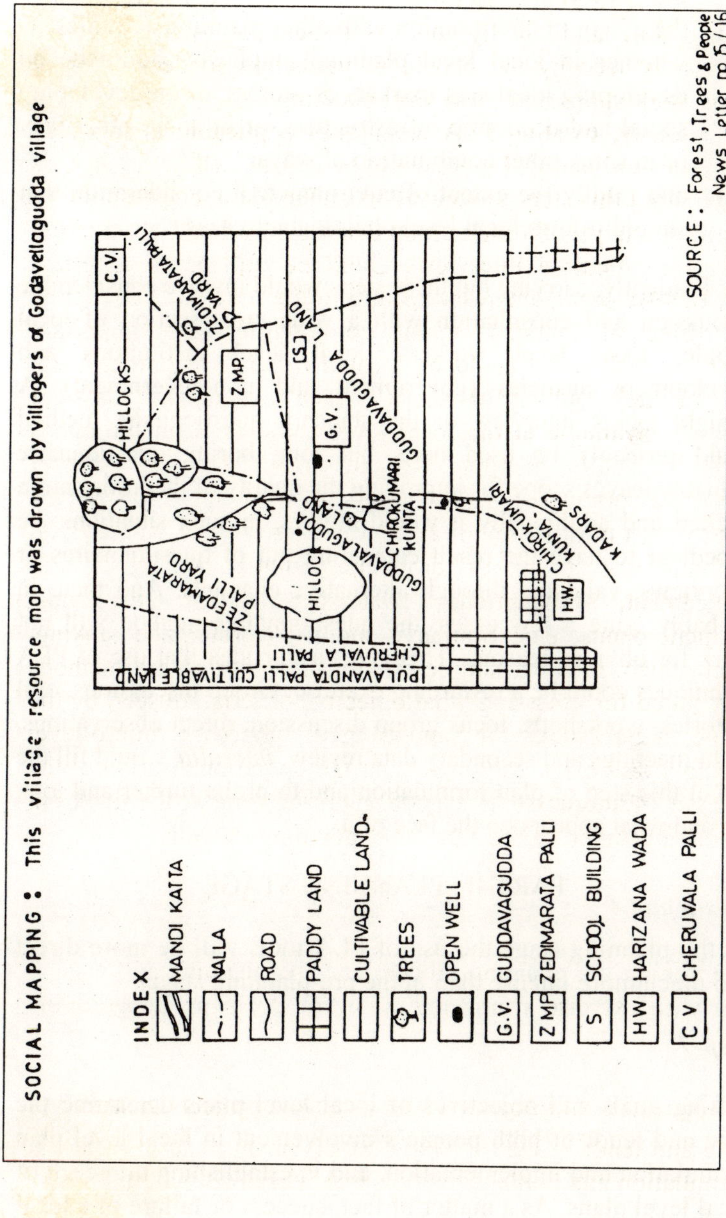

Fig. 4.1 :Social Mapping : This village resource map was drawn by villagers of Godavellagudda village

(iii) nature of planning itself as to whether it will be nested plan or a combined plan;
(iv) the extent of coordination with other planning activities;
(v) whether in local level planning emphasis should be on developing local area markets or sectors, or on developing social and economic infrastructure, or in some other way or in some other combination of ways;
(vi) and finally the extent of environmental consideration that should inform local level planning activities.[2]

Evidently, carrying out these steps would involve considerable discussion and consultation with a wide cross-section of local people, local level workers, local level institutions and development agencies (government and non-government). A straight jacket interview or the standard questionnaire method could probably be used here, but long boring questionnaire arguably leaves scope for improving the quality of the information elicited and additionally it would always, in such situations, be expedient to have the result emanating out of questionnaires or interviews, validated through alternative channels. And then, in probably quite a few cases, the questionnaires method will not work for obvious reasons. This gives a fair idea that use of PLA techniques could be a rewarding exercise. Group discussions, oral histories, workshops, focus group discussion, direct observations, night meetings and secondary data review, *interalia,* would fill the bill at this step of plan formulation and to probe further and look beyond what appears on the face of it.

PART-II : PLANNING STAGE

At the planning stage the use of PLA tools will be more direct and much more intense than in the pre-planning stage.

Step-7

Setting goals and objectives of local level plans determine the tone and tenor of both people's involvement in local level plan formulation and implementation, and in establishing the reach of local level plans. As a matter of fact, success or failure of a local level planning exercise depends much on what and how goals and objectives of a plan are set forth.

Here resort to tools like historical profile, time trend analysis, social mapping, seasonal calendar, mobility map, maps, folklore, flow/casual diagrams, oral histories[3], direct ranking matrix, wealth ranking and group discussions of all varieties will be particularly rewarding.[4] For instance, social mapping presents information on village layout, infrastructure, population, chronic health cases, handicapped, malnourished children, family planning cases, vaccinations, widows, destitute and so on. Reference is invited to Figure 4.2. Then again in setting goals and objectives, it is essential

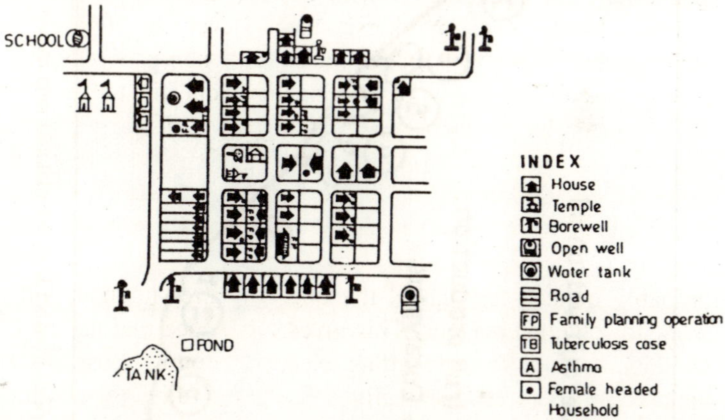

Fig. 4.2 : Social Mapping : This map was drawn by villagers o Ramenahally village.

Source : Forest, Trees & People Newsletter No. 15/16.

to identify the major problems of the area. A geographical transect and a historical transect are effective tools in this regard[5]. Since geographical transects are observatory walks, undertaken by walking through the area, with a group of villagers, either following a particular course, cross country or covering the area in a combing or sweeping motion, they generate valuable data on: natural resources, topography, indigenous technology, soils and vegetation, farming PLActices, problems and opportunities that are cross-checked with resource mapping and modelling. Figure 4.3 illustrates a typical transect of Manjakandriana Region

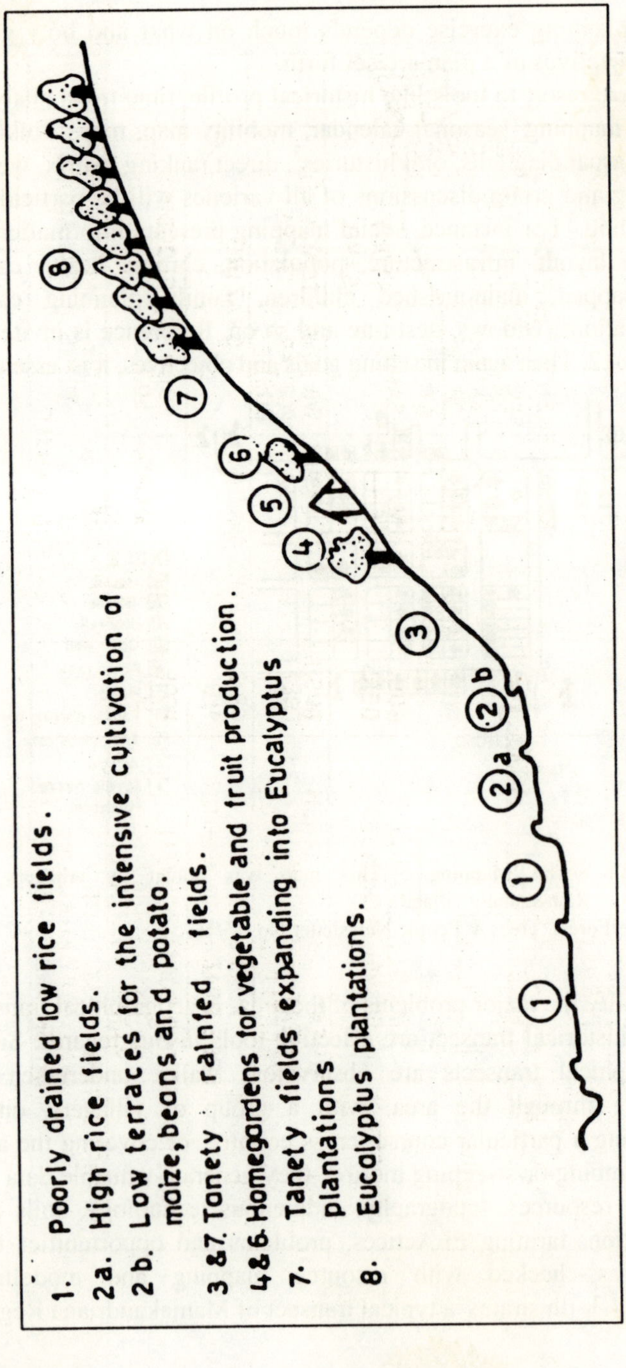

Fig. 4.3 : Typical transect from Manjakandriana region

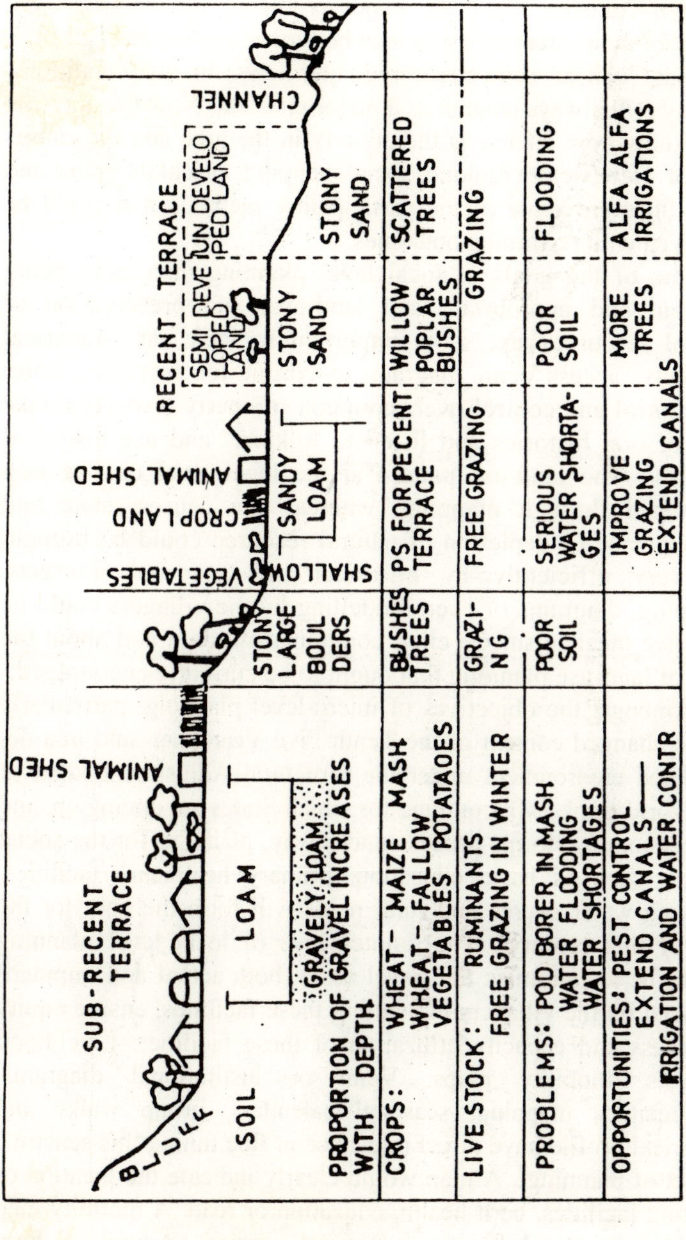

Source : Forest. Trees & People Newsletter No.15/16.

Fig. 4.4 :Geographical Transects : This is a transect of a village in northern Pakistan

of Madagascar whereas Figure 4.4 is a transect of a village in northern Pakistan. Once the major problems are identified, the extent of their intensity could then be further probed through PLA methods such as semi-structured interviews. In our conditions, poverty will always emerge as a major problem. Now the question is to know how intense is the poverty in the area and the causes thereof. Here wealth ranking, social mapping, casual diagrams and trend lines are some of the participatory methods that could be deployed with rewarding outcomes.

One of the goals of local level planning invariably being efficient and appropriate and land-use, and preservation of natural resource base, it is important to look at historical transects; access Venn diagrams to exhibit, for instance, water use control and control over common property resources; take note of oral histories and listen to folklore[6] and use historical profiles[7]. The land-use pattern at the local level can be best developed through mapping, whereas the causes, state and consequence of depletion of natural resource could be brought out very efficiently by historical transects and transects. Mapping, diagrams or even modelling by the villagers could be effective mechanisms to elicit communal wisdom and about the kind of land-use planning that ought to be currently encouraged.

Amongst the objectives of micro-level planning, particularly in the changed context of the Tenth Five Year Plan and in a de-regulated environment under the Structural Adjustment Loan of the World Bank-IMF combine for which States are queing up, and the economic reforms process under way, planning for the social sectors such as basic education, primary healthcare facilities, drinking water source and rural roads will form the core for the rest of this century[8]. The quintessence of local level planning would be to minimise the travel costs (both actual and imputed) incurred by the villagers in availing these facilities, ensure equity in access and capacity utilization of these facilities. Livelihood analysis, mobility maps, Venn or institutional diagrams, participatory mapping, seasonal calendars, group walks and historical profile have direct relevance in fine tuning this sensitive aspect of planning[9]. A map would clearly indicate the location of existing facilities, be it health, education or road. A mobility map would indicate where people generally travel to avail of these facilities, generating in the process the distance traversed and time expended for these purposes. A Venn or institutional diagram would indicate what role the local level institutions play in communal life and to what extent that are used, precipitating thereby insights into the possibilities of improving delivery of the services by tackling problems of maintenance, implementation and upkeep of existing functions vis-à-vis establishing new facilities in each sector. Such moves would not only reflect communal will having a wider base of support but also increase economic use of increasingly scarce financial resources.

Almost everywhere, one of the objectives of planning at the local as at other levels is to increase productivity in agriculture, particularly food crops, where the role of participatory methods cannot be overemphasized. Given the fact that in the face of ecological and environmental degradation, and paucity of financial resources, as also for other factors, the use of low external input sustainable agriculture (LEISA) seems to be a key answer to our problem of low productivity in agriculture, where indigenous technology and indigenous knowledge constitute the critical elements. Even the World Development report of the World Bank for 1992 explicitly recognised this fact. There is hardly any alternative method for understanding indigenous technology, which is better suited to local level planning than participatory methods. Oral histories, folklores, diagrams and transects depicting changes in productivity levels for the better or worse, concurrently with disuse of indigenous knowledge and technology are a few of the participatory methods that could be put to good use. For instance, a historical transect can be used to generate data of the area being planned for, at different points in time to give evolutionary trends in land-use, vegetation, erosion, population and the like. In Figure 4.5, a historical transect for livestock, trees, water and crops, drawn by villagers of Ardanaryapura village is presented. Naturally, issues relating to food security also become import. RRA has been used several years back in assessing food (in)security position in Sudan and it has recently been used also in the context of assessing the impact of structural adjustment programme on food security in Zimbabwe[10]. PLA has also been used in India to assess the impact of structural adjustment programme on food-security[11].

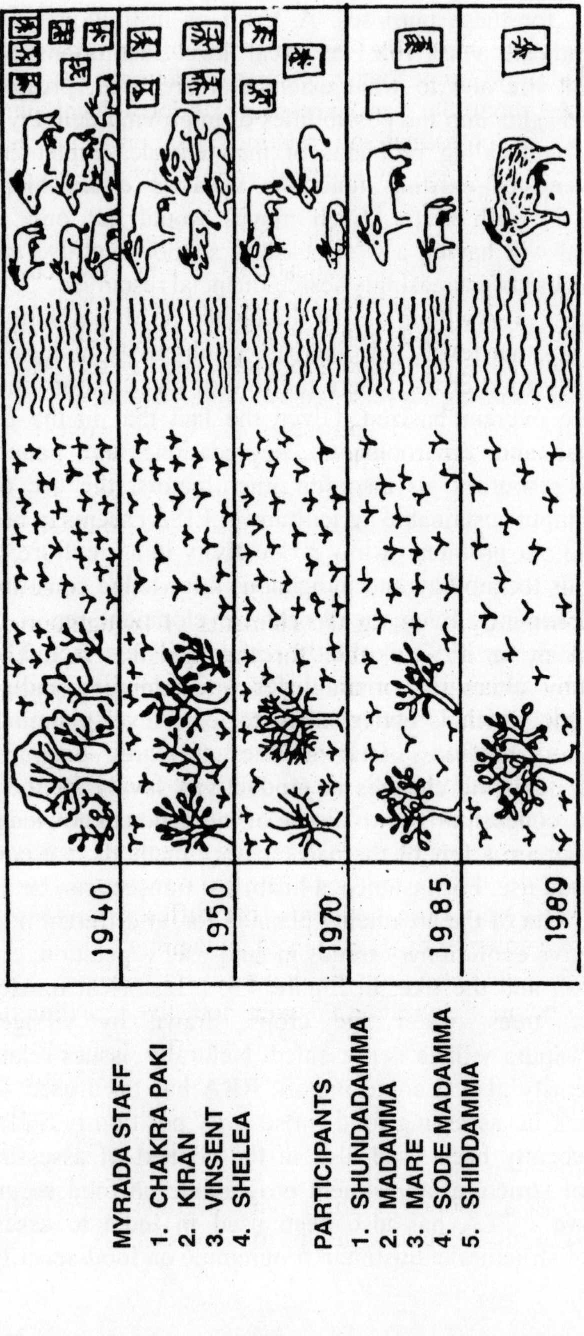

Fig. 4.5 : Historical Transects of Ardanarypura Village
Source : Forest, Trees & People Newsletter No.15/16

Step-8

Preparation may be briefly taken as preparing for reconnaissance and includes working out a consensus among the planning participants about the various aspects of local level planning, collection of information relating to projects recently implemented, writing an overall area description and an assessment of further data needs.

Apparently, though PLA can have several alternative uses, here one would wish to indicate its utility, particularly in working out a consensus. One of the principal tenets of PRA is triangulation. This can be suitably borrowed or modified to work out a consensus at the preparation stage among the actors in a micro-level planning exercise. Of the factors frequently cited for failure of local level plans is lack of cohesion and complementarily amongst the various actors in the game, born out of either the actors pursuing their respective path as a matter of course or of adhering to what the 'boss' has mandated without committing themselves to the cause. This can be largely circumvented by building a consensus among the actors in local level planning, by adopting the elements of triangulation from PLA and make it applicable for the purpose. A schematic illustration of triangulation used in PLA to build up consensus is best provided by the drawing of Figure 4.6.

Vital information, quickly and at a lower cost, about projects recently implemented, with causes of success or failure, would come out of group walks and semi-structured interviews; maps indicating location of projects would add a spatial dimension to the investigation; and either simple or matrix ranking could provide valuable clues about how the different projects were useful to the community as perceived by them.

All this quite apart, even writing an overall description of the local area being planned for becomes both lively, authentic and informative by maps (social, natural resource, farm etc.), Venn diagrams, historical transects of especially vulnerable areas identified by the local people, and sustainability analysis matrix[12]. A set of social maps could provide valuable information about the location of vulnerable groups, and when overlaid over a resource map, provide a graphic description of the access of the vulnerable groups to resources.

Steps-9 and 10

Reconnaissance is for having a quick understanding of the different dynamics of the area, where the participatory methods can be used quickly obtaining basic information about the area, and even for the design and execution of formal survey(s) or more in-depth investigations. Thus the immediate purpose is to help concentrate attention of subsequent formal surveys that may use different statistical methods, like random sampling and attempt at a quantification of critical aspects of rural life or the production system. The need is both to have a "feel" for the local area and to discover important, even if tentative, organizing concepts upon which to base further probing. For instance, the local level planner may wish to map agro-ecological zones, develop a working typology of the cultivators of the area being planned for and have a glimpse of how the common men feel about the trials and tribulations. If not for anything else, use of participatory methods to conduct an informal "survey" would act as guidepost, for ensuring that the questionnaire to be subsequently fielded is drafted to be understandable, sensitive and relevant for local issues and problems.

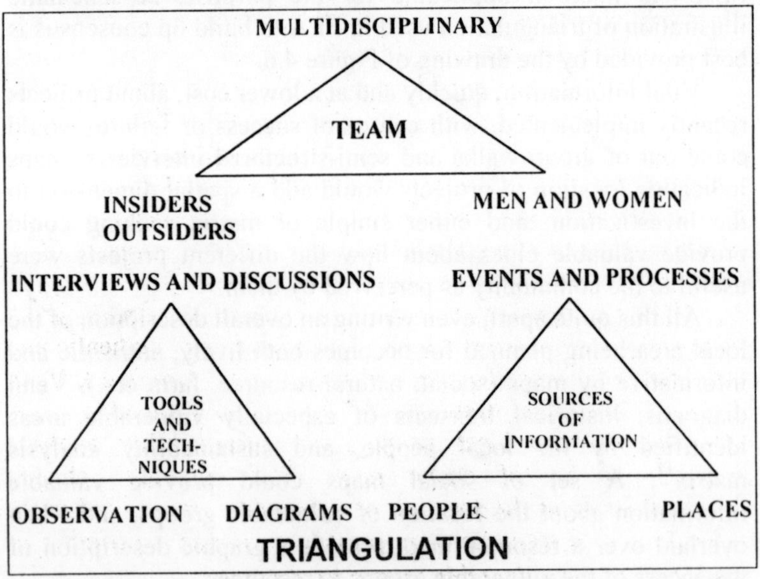

Fig. 4.6 : Schematic Illustration of Triangulation used in PLA
Source : Forest, Trees & People Newsletter No. 15/16

Steps-11 and 12

Reconnaissance and Main Field Study also consists, in the main, of taking stock of government organization and policies, and secondary and primary data (in terms of quality and quantity) and to fill in the data gaps to the extent possible[13]. In these steps PLActically all known tools of PLA will be relevant, in some form or the other, especially so for finding out leadership pattern and participation, utilization of extension services, dietary habits, incidence of tenancy, use and utility of wood obtained from different species of trees for building, fencing and fuel, preparation of land use maps and natural resource position and management[14]. The data generated through PLA techniques will be important as supplemental information or qualitative data, to reinforce and validate (contradict?) a whole lot of official data that may already be in existence.

One aspect on which data generated through PLA will have a wide applicability is data on poverty, to supplement official data on poverty. Wealth ranking has been found extremely suitable in doing so, particularly with regard to identifying not only the poor but the poorest of the poor[15]. As a matter of fact the poor and the poorest of the poor identified through PLA quite often are very much different from the poorest of the poor identified on the touchstone of quantitative figure of income and/or calorie intake, the primary reason being the perception of poverty of the common man is fundamentally different from the conception of poor imposed from above by either the State or the arms of the State. For instance, in a village named Phanar in Garhwal Himalayas, inaccessible except on food, the concept of poverty is related to the number of meals that a household can afford per day, whatever the means of livelihood and irrespective of the social hierarchy. In other cases, such as in Boksa Basti in Nagal Jwalapur in Dehradun district (a fully tribal village) Uttaranchal, the concept of household poverty as revealed by PLA is related to the number of livestock that each household has. In another village, in the district of Midnapore it was revealed through PLA by the villagers that poverty was related to the head of the household: a widow-headed household is considered the poorest; a women-headed household is poor but not amongst the poorest; other households headed by able-bodied men are poor[16].

As an illustration, one wonders if there is another aspect of local level planning where maps could be better used than at this stage. The variety of maps that PLA can uniquely offer would serve the purposes of micro-level planning from the right perspective: resources maps of catchments, villages, forests, fields, farms and home gardens; social maps of village habitats; health maps indicating health and welfare status of each family; topical maps, soil and water availability map, and impact and action monitoring maps. Each of these maps provide graphical information about usage of water and agricultural inputs or soil degradation and so forth, from the people's perspective and, therefore, has the potential to increase the efficiency of micro-level planning[17].

Steps-13 to 18

These steps relate to prioritization of problems, formulating strategies and identification of projects, and then the whole of the tactical planning stage. In these steps the involvement of the common man has to be both much more intensive and extensive than anywhere else in the system, for a full incorporation of collective wisdom and to reflect communal needs and aspirations. PLA potentially has a dual role in this respect: one, act as a vehicle for eliciting communal perceptions in each of the issues having to do with micro-level planning, and two, impart to the community a sense of belonging that they are an integral part of the whole exercise of local level development. These are vital. A good example of how this works is provided by the use of PLA in the development of an early curriculum for basic education is as depicted in Figure 4.7.

The range of PLA tools that can be applied is considerable. Wealth ranking, check-list, rapid nutrition assessment, all the diagrammatic techniques, historical profile and transect are some of the tools that would come in handy[18]. Seasonal diagrams can be used for obtaining seasonal patterns of rainfall, employment, income and expenditure, debt, credit requirements of the community, food and nutrition, diseases, fodder, milk production, marketing and such other data. The seasonal diagram

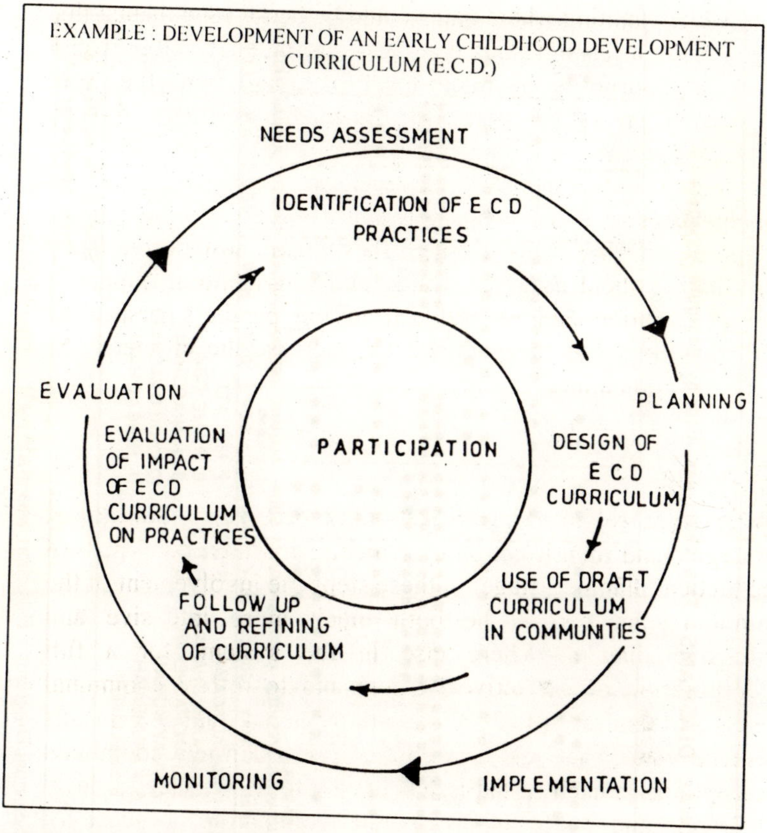

Fig. 4.7 : PLA and the Project Cycle
Source : Forest, Trees & People Newsletter No. 15/16

at Figure 4.8, made by villagers of Basapura, illustrates these points very precisely. The issues of sustainability of relatively large projects can be investigated quite well through "rural rides", as was done by William Corbett as early as in the 19th century[19]. We maintain that sustainability of rural development projects can be ensured reasonably well if they are chosen and owned up by the people. In this, on the face of it, PLA methods would be efficient.

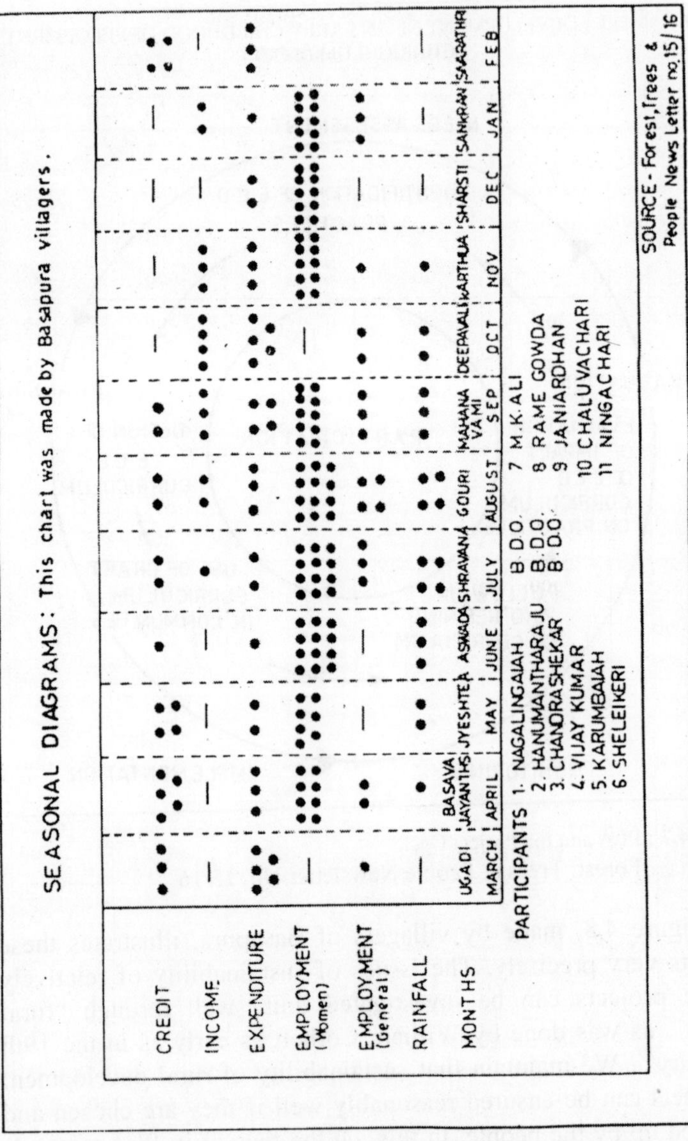

Fig. 4.8 : Seasonal Diagrams : This chart was made by Basapura Villagers.

Village – Rajawala
Block – Sahaspur
Nyaya Panchayat – Bhauwala
District – Dehradun

	Food Grains	Cerelas	Sugar	Milk	Clothing
1960	o o	ooo ooo ooo	o o o	ooo ooo ooo	o o o
1970	oo o o	ooo oo oo	oo o o	ooo oo oo	oo oo oo
1980	oo oo oo	oo oo o	oo oo oo	ooo oo oo	oo oo oo
1990	ooo ooo oo	oo oo o	ooo ooo oo	ooo oo oo	ooo oo oo
1991	ooo ooo oo	o o	ooo ooo oo	ooo ooo oo	ooo ooo oo
1993 (May)	ooo oo oo	o	ooo ooo ooo	ooo ooo ooo	ooo ooo ooo

Participants : (1) Harsh Bardhan Dimri
(2) Sultan Singh
(3) Gita Ram
(4) Deveshwari Devi

Fig. 4.9 : Rapid Food Assessment

Village - Rajawala
Block - Sahaspur
Nyaya Panchayat - Bhauwala
District - Dehradun

LARGE FARMERS

	Natural Manure	Chemical Fertiliser
1970	ooo ooo ooo	o o
1980	ooo ooo ooo	ooo ooo ooo
1990	oo oo o	oooo oooo ooo
1991	oo oo oo	ooo ooo ooo
1992	oo oo oo	ooo ooo ooo
1993 (May)	ooo oo oo	ooo oo oo

Participants : (1) Sultan Singh
(2) Kripal Singh
(3) Rajpal Singh
(4) Murli Dhar

Fig. 4.10 : Rapid Fertiliser Consumption Assessment

	COBBLER	TAMARIND	LEAF PLATE	CUSTARD APPLE	BRICK MAKING	FIRE WOOD	PONGEMEA
TIME CONSU	O O O	O O O	O O O	O O O	O O O O O	O O O O	O O
PROFITS	O O O O O	O O O O	O O O	O O O O O	O O O O	O O	O
LABOUR	O	O O	O	O	O O O O	O	O
BANK LOAN	O O	—	—	—	—	—	—
HARD WORK	O O	O O	O O	O O O	O O O O	O O O O	O O

STAFF: ELIAS
SURESH
PADMOVATH

PARTICIPANTS: P. LAKSHMINARAYANA
KRISHNAPPA
GANGULAMANA
GANGOJAMANA

Source : Forest, Trees & People Nws Letter No. 15/16

Fig. 4.11 : Matrix Ranking in Godavellagudda Village done by the Village Women after First Selecting their own criteria

Step-17 is assessment of projects and strategies, for which a very effective method could be scoring or ranking of the projects or strategies as perceived by the people. For instance, we carried out a Rapid Consumption Assessment and a Rapid Fertilizer Assessment in 21 villages in Dehradun to ascertain the impact of structural adjustment programme on food security and fertilizer off-take[20]. The results were dramatic as exemplified in Figures 4.9 and 4.10. The local level planner can use matrix ranking for working out a gradation list in respect of such items as crops; varieties, types and breeds of livestock; trees; fodders; supplementary income generating activities and the like. These could then form the basis for working out the plan priorities. An example of ranking of non-agricultural livelihoods by women of village Godavellagudda, after first selecting their own criteria, is at Figure 4.11.

We ought to refrain from the temptation of elaborating on the use of PLA tools in the various steps of planning at the local level. Because the process and methodology of planning at the local level exhibit wide variations (and that is its beauty) according as political will to shed power increase or decrease, the desired speed of response to meet local needs and availability of resources (not only financial) vary, and hence the use of PLA would vary a good deal. We have only provided some illustrations of the probable use of PLA tools and their unexplored potential in areas of concern for local level planning. Suffice it to say that PLA has been found useful, both in developing and developed country situations, in areas such as forestry, fuelwood, social and agro-forestry, extension, planning for formal surveys; health, nutrition and primary health care; FSR surveys; irrigation; village development plans; project identification and preparation; gender analysis and planning and evaluations. These are the sectors that are within the domain of micro-level planning, which indicate that many of the methods in PLA have been (implicitly) tested for potential use in local level plans. This is cause for cheer.

Use of diagrams and participatory methods for monitoring and evaluation cannot be over-emphasized[21]. Figures 4.12a to 4.12e provide a classic illustration monitoring of the project for Sal Forest regeneration in Jamboni Range, West Bengal. Even a foreigner, Bergman, who knew none of Indian languages, and who came to India to evaluate a social forestry project in village

Lathur in Tamilnadu, was successful in using matrix scoring in the evaluation of the project[22].

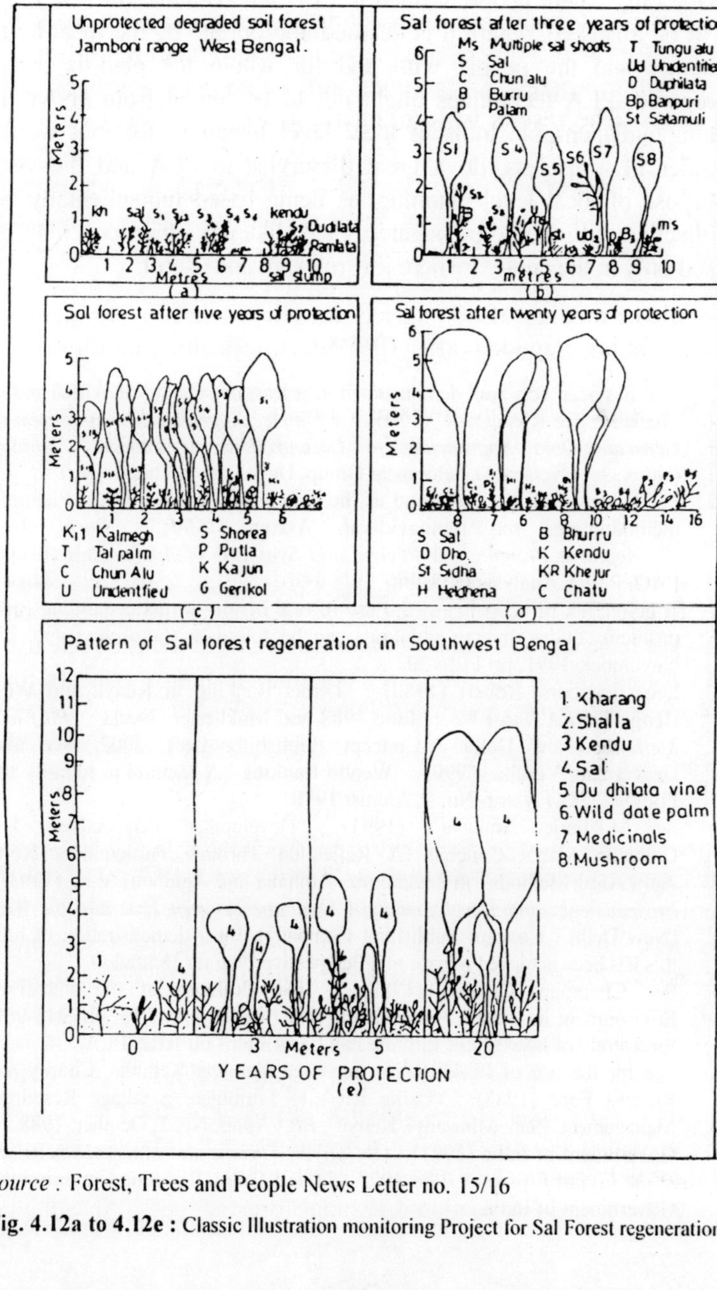

Source : Forest, Trees and People News Letter no. 15/16

Fig. 4.12a to 4.12e : Classic Illustration monitoring Project for Sal Forest regeneration

We would also, however, wish to guard ourselves against being misunderstood, as is most likely the case. Use of PLA should be made only where people trained in PLA are available (or else PLA will be misused), where it is deemed appropriate by the local level planner and the people with and for whom the plan is being prepared. PLA techniques ought not to be forced from above as being indispensable tools in local level planning, for that would render PLA useless, do a great disservice to PLA and the very purpose of local level planning, as being based fundamentally on collective will, would be negated. PLA, like any other tool, may be used only in the context where it is relevant and useful.

Notes

1. This has been very well demonstrated in at least one country in Africa and in Thailand. See Klepper, R. (1980) : *A Simple Diagnostic Survey System to Generate Data Appropriate to Decentralized Agricultural Planning* (Norwich : Overseas Development Group, University of East Anglia).
2. For evidence of these in some of the better known Local Level Planning methodologies see Bendavid-val, Avrom (1990) : *Rural Area Development Planning: A Review and Synthesis of Approaches* (Rome: FAO, Policy Analysis Division).
3. A collection of accounts of the use of oral history in understanding rural problems under diverse situations can be found in *Panoscope,* No. 27, November, 1991, pp.11 to 20.
4. See Chambers, Robert (1988) : "Direct Ranking in Kenya and West Bengal", *RRA Notes* No.1, June 1988 and Mukherjee, Neela : *100 Field Methods* (New Delhi : Concept Publishing Co.), 2002. See also Groverman, Verona (1990) : "Wealth Ranking : A Method to Identify the Poorest", *RRA Notes,* No. 9, August 1990.
5. See Mukherjee Amitava : (1993) : "Development Perspective : The Common Man's Concern (A Reflection Through Participatory Rural ApPLAisal Methods" in Mukherjee, Amitava and Agnihotri V.K. (1993) : *Environment and Development: A Dialogue between East and the West* (New Delhi : Concept Publishing Company), for a demonstration of how this has been achieved in case of a Perspective Plan for Dehradun.
6. See Chapman, Graham (1983) : "The Folklore of the Perceived Environment in Bihar", *Environment and Planning,* Vol.15, pp. 945-968, for a study of how useful folklore can be as a tool for RRA/PLA.
7. See for the use of PLA/RRA in resource planning Kabutha, Charity and Richard Ford (1988) : "Using RRA to Formulate a village Resources Management Plan, Mbusanyi, Kenya", *RRA Notes,* No. 2, October, 1988.
8. Government of India (1991) : *Objectives, Thrusts and Macro-Dimensions of the Eighth Five Year Plan 1992-97* (New Delhi: Planning Commission), Government of India.

9. Mascarenhas, James and P.D. Prem Kumar (1991) has given a very good account of how to use mapping in planning of projects and finding out socio-economic conditions in an Indian situation. "Participatory Mapping and Modelling User's Notes", *PLA Notes,* No.12, pp. 9-20.
10. See Maxwell, Simon (1989) : "Rapid Food Security Assessment: A Pilot Exercise in Sudan", *PLA Notes,* No. 5, pp. 15-21, and Government of Zimbabwe (1991). *Structural Adjustment and Communal Agriculture in Zimbabwe. Case Studies from Mangwende and Chivi Communal Areas: A Report of a Rapid Rural ApPLAisal* (London: IIED, and FSR Unit, Ministry of Land, Agriculture and Rural Settlement, Harare, Zimbabwe).
11. See Mukherjee, Amitava (1994) : *Structural Adjustment Programme and Food Security* (Aldershot: Avebury). See particularly Chapter 8.
12. See Craig, Ian (1988) : "Sustainability Analysis in North East Thailand", *PLA Notes,* No. 3, pp. 15-18.
13. Honadle, George. (1982) : "Rapid Reconnaissance for Development Administration: Mapping and Modelling Organization Landscape", *World Development,* Vol.10, No. 8.
14. See Devavaram, John *et al.* (eds.) : *Participatory Rural ApPLAisal: Proceedings of the February 1991 Bangalore PLA Trainers Workshop,* (London: IIED and Bangalore (MYRADA), pp. 102-111.
15. See Groverman, Verona (1990) : "Wealth Ranking: A Method to Identify The Poorest", *RRA Notes,* No. 9, pp. 4-9, and Sarkar, Anup 91991). "Wealth Ranking in Mahilong, Bihar" in Mascarenhas, James *et al.* (eds.): *Participatory Rural ApPLAisal Proceedings of the February 1991 Bangalore Workshop* (London: IIED and Bangalore (MYRADA), pp. 123-124. See also Chandramauli, K. (1991): "Passing the Pen Approach: Identifying the Poorest of the Poor Families: *PLA Notes,* No. 14, pp. 29-32. See PLAmualratna, Anthony. (1985): *Village Concepts of Poverty in the North East of Thailand: An Example of Focus Group Research* (Honolulu: Population Institute, East West Centre).
16. Mukherjee, Neela (1993) : *Participatory Rural ApPLAisal Concepts, Methods and Applications* (New Delhi: Concept Publishing Co.).
17. See Mascarenhas, James *et al.* (1991) : "PLA In India: Review and Future Direction", in Mascarenhas, James *et al.* (eds.) : *Participatory Rural ApPLAisal Concepts Proceedings of the February 1991 Bangalore PLA Trainers Workshop* (London: International Institute for Environment and Development and MYRADA: Bangalore), pp. 10-48.
18. See Hubbard, Michael, Robert Leurs and Andrew Nickson (1989) : "Using Rapid Rural ApPLAisal for Project Identification: Report on a Training Exercise in Jamaare Local Government Area, Buchi State, Northern Nigeria", *RRA Notes,* No. 6.
19. Pretty, Jules (1989) : "The Rural Rides of William Cobbett: RRA and Sustainable Agriculture in 1820s", *RRA Notes,* No. 6.
20. Mukherjee, Amitava (1994) : *Structural Adjustment Programme and Food Security* (Aldershot, England: Avebury).
21. F.A.O. (1990) : *Community's Tool Box* (Rome: FAO) Community Forestry Field Manual No. 2.
22. Paul Bergman (1993): "Telling the Wood from the Trees", in *India – U.K. Association News Letter,* Issue VIII, January, 1993.

5

Creation and Maintenance of Alternative Data Bases through Participatory Rural Appraisal for Rural Development Planning

— AMITAVA MUKHERJEE

INTRODUCTION

The Constitution (Seventy-third Amendment Act) as approved by Parliament enjoins, *inter alia,* as under:

243-G. "Subject to the provisions of this Constitution, the Legislature of a State may, environment by law, endow the panchayats with such powers and authority as may be necessary to enable them to function as institutions of self-government and such law may contain provisions for the devolution of powers and responsibilities upon panchayats at the appropriate level, subject to such conditions as may be specified therein, with respect to:

(a) the preparation of plans for economic development and social justice;
(b) the implementation of schemes of economic development and social justice as may be entrusted to them including those in relation to the matters listed in the Eleventh Schedule.

243-G. "The Legislature of a State may, by law:

(a) authorize a Panchayat to levy, collect and appropriate such taxes, duties, tolls and fees in accordance with such procedure and subject to such limits;

(b) assign to a panchayat such taxes, duties, tolls and fees levied and collected by the State Government for such purposes and subject to such conditions and limits;

(c) provide for making such grants-in-aid to the panchayats from the Consolidated Fund of the State; and

(d) provide for the constitution of such funds for crediting all moneys received, respectively, by or on behalf of the panchayat and also for the withdrawal of such moneys therefore as may be specified in the law."[1]

The subjects to be covered in terms of the Eleventh Schedule added to the Constitution, as referred to in article 243-G are:

(i) agriculture, including agricultural extension;

(ii) land improvement, implementation of land reforms, land consolidation and soil conservation;

(iii) minor irrigation, water management and watershed development;

(iv) animal husbandry, dairying and poultry;

(v) fisheries;

(vi) social forestry and farm forestry;

(vii) minor forest produce;

(viii) small scale industries, including food processing industries;

(ix) khadi, village and cottage industries;

(x) rural housing;

(xi) drinking water;

(xii) fuel and fodder;

(xiii) roads, culverts, bridges, ferries, waterways and other means of communication;

(xiv) rural electrification, including distribution of electricity;

(xv) non-conventional energy sources;

(xvi) poverty alleviation programmes;

(xvii) education, including primary and secondary schools;

(xviii) technical training and vocational education;

(xix) adult and non-formal education;

(xx) libraries;

(xxi) cultural activities;

(xxii) markets and fairs;

(xxiii) health and sanitation, including hospitals, primary health centres and dispensaries;

(xxiv) family welfare;

(xxv) women and child development;

(xxvi) social welfare, including welfare of the handicapped and mentally retarded;

(xxvii) welfare of the weaker sections and, in particular, of the Scheduled Castes and Scheduled Tribes;

(xxviii) public distribution system; and

(xxix) maintenance of community assets.

The above provisions of the Seventy-third Constitution Amendment Act delineates some of the areas in which the panchayats will operate in their socio-economic functions. The general tone and tenor of the Seventy-third Constitution Amendment Act 1993 leaves considerable scope for state variations. For instance, powers of the Gram Sabhas under Article 243-A: representation of Chairpersons of lower level PRIs in higher level PRI in terms of Article 243-C; the manner of election of Chairpersons in panchayats at the village level under Article 243-C (5); manner of reservation of posts of Chairpersons for Scheduled Castes and Scheduled Tribes and women in terms of Article 243-D (4); powers of the panchayats under Article 243-G and areas which will come under Article 243-H, have all been left open in the Constitution, providing considerable scope for the state governments to exercise discretion. It is, therefore, expected that the final framework, powers and jurisdiction of the Gram Panchayats shall be consistently disuniform across the states. Indeed, the panchayats may not function at all where the states do not frame necessary rules or the Legislature does not legislate the necessary Acts for the purposes of giving effect to all the provisions of the Seventy-third Constitution Amendment Act 1993. The whole exercise will in that case be in futility, except perhaps the fact that elections to the panchayats shall be held mandatorily at intervals prescribed by the Constitution. It may be mentioned that some amount of legislation will come about, atleast in respect of the mandatory provisions of the Seventy-third Constitution Amendment Act.

In pointing the contours of database for giving effect to the provisions of the Seventy-third Constitution Amendment Act, one has to take account of these broad realities. In the worst case scenario of the panchayats being unable to function for want of supplementary legislation and/or rules (the Indian Statute Book is replete with laws which could not be implemented in the absence of rules/States laws necessary for giving effect to the law), then there is no need to generate a database. In the other limiting case when the supporting legislations are so broad based as to empower the panchayats to their fullest extent, the database will have to be fairly exhaustive and, in the first instance, would be expensive in terms of the resources required to put the database together. We assume the best case scenario where the state would legislate and devolve powers of self-governance and development to the Panchayati Raj Institutions at both the district and sub-district levels.

FUNCTIONS OF THE PANCHAYATS

The kind and extent of database are dependent upon the functions of the panchayats. Based on the above assumption and on a reading of the provisions of Articles 243 to 243-O of the Constitution, the functions of the panchayats will primarily relate to :

(i) assessing the resource base of the economy, raising of resources and auditing resource use;

(ii) prepare plans for economic development and social justice, implementation of schemes for economic development and social justice, expending resources raised; and

(iii) govern at the appropriate level as democratically elected governments at the district and sub-district tiers.

The data needs of the panchayat will naturally revolve around the aforesaid three basic functions. While matters of self-governance may be dealt with separately, we propose to concentrate here on matters appertaining to the economic and developmental functioning of the panchayats.

PLANNING FUNCTIONS AT THE LOCAL LEVEL

Planning at Panchayat Level

The Seventy-third Amendment requires each Gram Panchayat, in consultation with Gram Sabha, to prepare area plans (and not merely recommend programmes and schemes to the hierarchy of officials or bodies – a role to which they have been reduced or condemned presently). The village plan is, therefore, a must, and is the cornerstone of the arch of local level planning. And the Panchayati Raj Institutions are the statutory area institutions through which the bricks of local level planning have to be developed and collated upto the district level. Agricultural Extension Officers, BDOs, DRDAs and such other functionaries are to be the arms of the PRIs – and have an indirect place in the planning process.[2]

The village area plan will have at least five dimensions :

One, designing of actions and interventions necessary to enable all the workforce in the village (including women) to first maximise their earnings and employment from their existing avenues or sources of work and employment, given their abilities, inclinations and skills, and to facilitate the fullest use of productive resources, tools and techniques, have to be the first things on the agenda of the village area plan.

Two, universalisation of elementary education, literacy, primary healthcare, sanitation, drinking water, housing for the poor, etc. to improve the quality of life of all inhabitants are to be areas of major concern. Hence, actions and interventions necessary for achieving these ends will have to be identified.

An extended aspect of improvement of quality of life will be promotion of food security (which includes eliminating malnutrition of every description and lowering infant mortality rate) by stepping upto the maximum extent feasible, local production of foodgrains, pulses and oilseeds; and by rejuvenating, protecting and conserving common property resources, forests and micro-environments (that supply upto 33 per cent of food consumed by the rural poor).[3] Almost concurrently, the panchayats have to minimize dependence on the Centrally or State operated (wayward and undependable) public distribution system which in any case will probably wane away in the wave of the current macro-economic policies being vigorously pursued by the government. Fodder and feed production to meet local needs of animals for encouraging growth in livestock will be an integral part of this exercise because collection of these and the time and energy spent for this activity will have a distinct bearing on the food security question.

Three, actions and interventions needed to augment

(a) local energy supply to meet as much of the local energy demands as can feasibly be met;
(b) extension and improvement of communication, information and trading (village *haats*, etc.) network;
(c) storage and processing facilities sustainable at the local level; and
(d) a systematic plan for land-use, water-use, labour-use, animals-resource use, pasture and forest resource development has to be clearly identified.

Four, the panchayats would need a strategy and action plan for raising of local resources, including material, labour, commodities and financial, to the fullest feasible extent and redeployment of resources available from Centrally or State sponsored schemes in accordance with the needs of the local plan (all its components outlined in points one to three above) in conjunction with local resources.

Five, prioritization and phasing of various actions and interventions envisaged in several areas, covered under points one to three above, with reference to resources availability, operational feasibility and determining implementation responsibilities between the panchayats, cooperatives, households and other available instruments at the village level, panchayat level, or outside the panchayat level, as the case may be.

Planning at District and Intermediate Levels

The planning tasks for the panchayats at the block and district levels will have a somewhat different orientation, and would basically be four:

One, they have to analyze and assimilate the area plans of the Gram Panchayats and visualize supporting actions and interventions, investment and technical backstopping, as may be warranted so as to enable the Gram Panchayats (or a combination of Gram Panchayats) to achieve the fruition of their plans. These will constitute the core of the area plans at the block or district level.

Two, they have to prepare area plans (relevant to their needs and resources) akin to those prepared by Gram Panchayats, in the block and in the district. Actions and interventions etc., required to enable the town and municipal panchayats to fulfil their plans, have to be worked out, in order that, *inter alia,* the provisions of the Seventy-fourth Constitution Amendment Act 1993 are also smoothly operationalised.

Three, panchayats at the district and block levels will need to visualize and establish complementarities between points one and two above, and share that with the Gram and Town Panchayats.

Four, Panchayats at the district and block levels have to visualize actions and interventions necessary beyond points one and two above to generate development impulses and raise the development level of the district or the block, as the case may be, to the fullest level achieved in any other district in the state (or if outside the state) in key respects, such as primary education, particularly female literacy, access to basic health facilities, lower infant mortality rate, higher agricultural productivity, maximum food security, employment generation and attainment of other components of the minimum needs programme.

This at first sight may look like a seemingly overexhaustive process, but such a detailed approach is necessary to overcome the weaknesses of the present process, namely, a "top-down approach", unconcerned about raising productivity and quality of life of the common man, planned by "targetitis", excessively sectoral in application, with heavy orientation towards financial outlay, minimal effort at optimization of local resource use and/or raising of local resources; inadequate care, use and management of primary resources of labour, land, water, vegetation and livestock, to mention only a few.

We wish to reiterate that the panchayats will be required to raise their own resources, by and large, and levy such of the taxes and levies as may be decided by the State Finance Commissions. This then enjoined by implication, that panchayats must assess the taxable capacity of the people falling under their territorial jurisdiction, have a thorough grasp of natural/environmental resources of their area income levels of the people and so on. A database for the panchayats, therefore, would also be required to subserve these needs.

This then is the broad canvas against which to work out the database. Clearly there would be a different database for each level of Panchayati Raj Institutions. We may briefly describe the database for the different tiers of Panchayati Raj Institutions as follows:

DATA REQUIREMENT OF VILLAGE LEVEL FOR THE MICRO-LEVEL PLANNING[4]

The requirements must be classified into five broad categories :

A. Infrastructure Details (data on basic amenities),
B. Demographic Details (census data on population, livestock),
C. Agro-Economic Details (census data on irrigation, agriculture, forestry, land-use, etc.),
D. Environment Details, and
E. Gender Details.

Let us examine the individual elements in each of these five broad categories.

A. *Infrastructure Details*

1. *Health*

(i) Village health guide available (Yes/No)?

(a) If yes, number of compounders
(b) Number of midwives/nurses

(ii) Distance of the village from nearest

(a) Primary health centre (PHC)
(b) Additional PHCs
(c) Sub-centres
(d) Medical shop
(e) Ayurvedic dispensary
(f) Homoeopathic dispensary
(g) Unani System of Medicine
(h) Others

(iii) Personnel (number)

(iv) Number of private nursing homes

(v) Number of practising doctors for each of the following types:

(a) Allopathic
(b) Ayurvedic
(c) Homoeopathic
(d) Unani
(e) Others

(vi) Past epidemic details (last 3 years) for each type of epidemic diseases:

	Epidemic Types	*Population Affected*	*Area Affected*
(a) Cholera			
(b) Jaundice			
(c) Dysentery and diarrhoea etc.			

(d) Other epidemics that may be peculiar to the area

2. Education

(i) Educational institutions (number)

	For Boys	*For Girls*	*Co-educational*
(a) Anganwadi (Pre-primary)			
(b) Primary School			
(c) Middle School			
(d) Secondary School			

(ii) Primary School Building

The details to be kept for each type are:
(a) Number of buildings
(b) Number of classes
(c) Number of rooms

The following are the suggested broad category of buildings:

(a) Kuccha
(b) Pucca
(c) Kuccha with asbestos roof
(d) Kuccha with tiled roof
(e) Pucca with slab roof
(f) Pucca with asbestos roof
(g) Others (specify)

(iii) Secondary School Building. The details to be kept for each type are:

(a) Number of buildings
(b) Number of classes
(c) Number of rooms

The suggested broad category of buildings:

(a) Kuccha
(b) Pucca
(c) Kuccha with asbestos roof
(d) Kuccha with tiled roof
(e) Pucca with slab roof
(f) Pucca with asbestos roof
(g) Others (specify)

(iv) Library facilities (number)

(a) Library with reading room
(b) Library without reading room

(v) Number of school going children in the age group of 5-14 years

(a) Boys
(b) Girls

3. *Drinking water*

(i) Number of sources and population benefited by each of the sources with a break-up of the SCs and STs and total.
The various sources are:

(a) Ordinary wells
(b) Hand pumps
(c) Piped water supply, with number of domestic connections
(d) Piped water supply, with number of standposts
(e) Other sources

(ii) Any hamlet without sources of potable water and its population, with break up of SCs, STs and total.
(iii) Other data
(iv) History of past drinking water scarcity (last 5 years)

(v) Whether affected by scarcity (yes/no)? If yes,
  (a) If possible, quality of drinking water with reference to
    - Fluoresces
    - Iron
    - Guinea worms
    - Salinity
    - Other causes

  (b) Distance of the nearest sources of drinking water

4. Transport

(i) Approach roads (yes/ no)? If yes,
  (a) All weather road with type of road (length)
  (b) Fair weather road with type of road (length)

  The various types of road are :
  (a) Black top
  (b) Metal road
  (c) Murran road
  (d) Earthen soil road
  (e) Bridle Path

(ii) Distance from nearest (shortest distance by existing roads)
  (a) National Highway
  (b) State Highway
  (c) Major District Road
  (d) Other District Road
  (e) Classified Village Road
  (f) Panchayat Samiti Road
  (g) Panchayat Road

(iii) Bus connections available (yes/no)?
  (a) If yes, whether available throughout the year?
  (b) If seasonal, during which month or months?

The months to be indicated in discrete group such as:
  Between 0-2 months
  Between 2-4 months
  Between 4-6 months

Between 6-8 months
Between 8-10 months

(iv) Railway connections available (yes/no)?

5. *Communication*

(i) Distance of the village from the nearest
 (a) Branch Office
 (b) Sub-Post Office
 (c) Post Office
 (d) Telegraph Office

(ii) Telephone facility available (yes/no)?

6. *Employment*

(i) Number of people employed for each category of workers
 (a) Agricultural labourers
 (b) Marginal farmers
 (c) Small farmers
 (d) In livestock, forestry and fishing
 (e) Inter farmers
 (f) Rural artisans
 (g) Carpenters, blacksmiths, weavers, potters
 (h) In household industry
 (i) In manufacture other than household industry
 (j) In quarrying
 (k) In construction
 (l) In trade and commerce
 (m) Transport, storage and communication
 (n) Employees
  - Central Government
  - State Government
  - Local Bodies
  - Public Sector
  - Private Sector
 (o) Other categories

(ii) Employment (number) of
  (a) Women
  (b) Schedule Tribes
  (c) Schedule Castes
  (d) Backward Castes
  (e) Handicapped
  (f) Others

(iii) Number of unemployed people (total)
  (a) Number of uneducated unemployed
  (b) Number of educated unemployed (having below school final education)
  (c) Number of educated unemployed (with above school final education)

(iv) Number of people employed for each category of workers

Details to be covered are:

(a) Number with respect to

- Nature of employment, such as wage employment, self-employed through government programmes, etc.
- Category belonging to SC/ST
- Period of the year when employed, if seasonal
- Period of employment in months

7. *Power*

(i) Is the Village electrified? Yes/no.
(ii) If yes in (i)
  (a) Consumption sectors (connections) and load committed
  (i) Domestic
  (ii) Commercial
  (iii) Agricultural
  (iv) Others
  (b) Distance from the nearest sub-station
(iii) Is there a Solar Plant (yes/no)? If yes:

Type, ownership, number and capacity of each of the following types :

	Community	*Private*	*Total*
(a) Solar generator			
(b) Solar water pump			
(c) Solar heater			

(iv) Whether windmill exists (yes/no)?
If yes, ownership, purpose and number of each of the following :

	Community	*Private*	*Total*
(a) Power (with capacity)			
(b) Irrigation			
(c) Drinking water (with capacity)			

(v) Does a Bio-gas Plant exist
(yes/no)? If yes, number and installed capacity as under:

	Community	*Private*	*Purpose (Power cooking)*	*Installed Capacity*
- Human Waste				
- Animal Waste				
- Vegetable Waste				
- Other Waste				

8. *Housing*

Basic data

(i) Number of families with houses
(ii) Number of families with house sites but not houses
(iii) Number of families without houses and without even house sites
(iv) Number of pucca houses (brick walls and RCC/RBC roofs)
(v) Number of kuccha houses (brick walls and tin/asbestos roof)
(vi) Number of thatched houses

9. *Industries*

(i) Cottage Industries

(a) Number of category-wise
(b) Total investment
(c) Number of people employed (males/females separately)

(ii) Industrial Co-operative Societies
(a) Number of category-wise
(b) Number of members
(c) Number of borrowing members
(d) Number of defaulters
(e) Amount outstanding
(f) Amount overdue
(g) Number of employed (males/females separately)

The various categories of Industrial Cooperatives could be categorized as :
(a) Primary weavers co-operative society
(b) Primary coir society
(c) Mats and mattings society
(d) Husk co-operative society
(e) Handicraft society
(f) Handloom society
(g) Others
Other data

(iii) Number of people who benefited under government schemes

10. Economic Services

(i) Number of each of the Agricultural Services Centres, wherever existing:
(a) Implements centres
(b) Repair centres
(c) Servicing centres
(d) Implements, repair, service centres
(e) Implements, repair centres
(f) Repair, Service centres

(ii) Number of depots
(a) Government seeds depots
(b) Government fertilizer depots
(c) Government pesticide depots
(d) Government seed, fertilizer and pesticide depots
(e) Government seed, fertilizer depots

(f) Government seed, pesticide depots
(g) Government fertilizer, pesticide depots
(h) Private seed depots
(i) Private fertilizer depots
(j) Private pesticide depots
(k) Private seed, fertilizer, pesticide depots
(l) Private seed, fertilizer depots
(m) Private seed, pesticide depots
(n) Private fertilizer, pesticide depots

(iii) Godowns

(iv) Mandis

(v) Animal Husbandry: Number of
(a) Livestock units
(b) Pig farms
(c) Poultries
(d) Rabbit farms
(e) Milk collection centres
(f) Cattlefeed outlets
(g) Broiler farms
(h) Artificial Insemination centres
(i) Veterinary dispensaries
(j) Veterinary stock centre
(k) Cold storage
- Potatoes
- Fish and sea food
- Milk
(l) Go-sevaks
(m) Other data

(vi) Other details
(a) Poultry production and sale
(b) Milk production and sale
(c) Meat production

11. Public Distribution System

(i) Number of fair price shops:
(a) Selling rice
(b) Selling wheat
(c) Selling sugar
(d) Selling kerosene

(e) Selling rice and wheat
(f) Selling rice and sugar
(g) Selling wheat and kerosene
(h) Selling wheat and sugar
(i) Selling wheat and kerosene
(j) Selling rice, wheat and sugar
(k) Selling rice, wheat and kerosene
(l) Selling rice, sugar and kerosene
(m) Selling wheat, sugar and kerosene
(n) Selling rice, wheat, sugar and kerosene

12. Pisciculture

(i) Number of tanks
(ii) Number of tanks covered under pisciculture with area
(iii) Fish hatcheries
(iv) Availability of fish feed (yes/no)?
(v) Availability of fish manure (yes/no)?
(vi) Availability of fish seed (yes/no)?
(vii) Other data
    (a) Production of fish
    (b) Sale of fish
    (c) Number of beneficiaries of pisciculture schemes

13. Co-operative Credit and Other Societies

(i) Details for each type of cooperative societies such as the following:
    (a) Number of societies
    (b) Number of members
    (c) Number of borrowing members
    (d) Number of defaulters
    (e) Amount outstanding
    (f) Amount overdue
    (g) Number of employees (males/female separately)

The following are the various types:
- Agricultural Credit Cooperative
- Fishermen's Cooperatives

- Large area multi-purpose societies
- Milk Cooperatives

(ii) Where the co-operative societies do not exist in the village
   (a) Distance from the nearest co-operative
   (b) Number of members of the village
   (c) Amount outstanding

14. Miscellaneous Facilities

(i) Recreation and Cultural Centres
   (a) Playgrounds
   (b) Community gardens
   (c) Community centres
   (d) Community TV
   (e) Reading room/library
   (f) Child Welfare Centres
   (g) Women Welfare Centres

B. Demographic Details

1. Population (number)

(a) Current census
(b) Males
(c) Females
(d) Males, females in the age group 0 to less than 5
(e) Males, females in the age group 5 to less than 14
(f) SC population
(g) ST population
(h) Migrant population
(i) Literates
(j) Total number of families
(k) Number of families below poverty line
(l) Number of SC families below poverty line
(m) Number of ST families below poverty line
(n) Number of farmers families
(o) Number of small farmers families
(p) Number of large farmers families
(q) Number of births since last census till 1st of March
(r) Number of deaths since last census till 1st of March

(s) Number of infant deaths in the age group of 0-1 years
(t) Number of people with disabilities
(u) Kinds of disabilities found in the village (locomotor, visual, mental etc.)

2. *Livestock and Poultry*

(i) Number of
  (a) Cows
  (b) Buffaloes
  (c) Sheep
  (d) Goats
  (e) Horses and ponies
  (f) Mules
  (g) Donkeys
  (h) Pigs
  (i) Camels
  (j) Rabbits
  (k) Poultry

C. Agro-Economic Details

1. *Land Classification (in hectares, otherwise specified)*

(i) For general details there would be separate heads for government and private lands
(a) Total Area (sq. kms.)
(b) Area under Forest
  - for social forestry
  - social
  - rural fuel
  - village wood lots
  - Reserve
  - DPF
  - UPPF
(c) Area under non-agricultural uses
(d) Barren and uncultivable land
(e) Permanent pastures and grazing lands
(f) Land under miscellaneous tree groups

(g) Cultivable waste
(h) Fallow lands
(i) Current fallow
(j) Net area sown
(k) Area sown more than once
(l) Total cropped area
(m) Irrigated area
- Minor
- Flow
- Lift
- Medium
- Major

(n) Cropped area
Mean yield during
- Kharif
- Rabi
- Summer

(o) Land Holdings (Number and Area)
- Holdings less than 1 hectare
- Holdings 1-2 hectares
- Holdings 2-4 hectares
- Owned holdings
- Leased holdings

(p) Land kept reserved
(q) Patches of wasteland
- Below one hectare
- Between two and four hectares
- Above four hectares

(r) Area under fodder
(s) Area available for fodder

(2) Irrigation general details

(a) Total area irrigated during kharif, rabi, summer (hectares)
(b) Gross area irrigated (hectares)
(c) Net irrigated area (hectares)
(d) Annual rainfall (cm)
(e) Normal rainfall (cm)

(3) Other Data

(i) Crop-wise details for each type of crops

(a) Total area cultivated (hectares)

- Paddy
- Wheat
- Ragi
- Maize
- Groundnut
- Oilseeds
- Pulses
- Others

(b) Average yield

- Paddy
- Wheat
- Ragi
- Maize
- Groundnut
- Oilseeds
- Pulses
- Others

(ii) Price Crop-wise

(a) Paddy

- Market
- Support
- Procurement

(b) Wheat

- Market
- Support
- Procurement

(c) Ragi

- Market
- Support
- Procurement

(d) Maize

- Market
- Support

- Procurement

(e) Groundnut
- Market
- Support
- Procurement

(f) Oilseeds
- Market
- Support
- Procurement

(g) Pulses
- Market
- Support
- Procurement

(h) Others
- Market
- Support
- Procurement

(iii) Cost of cultivation of such types of crops (per hectare)

(a) Paddy
(b) Wheat
(c) Ragi
(d) Maize
(e) Groundnut
(f) Oilseeds
(g) Pulses
(h) Others

Irrigation Schemes Details

(i) Major/medium/minor (flow)/minor (lift)/energized wells/all wells; with information about potential created and used
(a) in use
(b) with water distribution system

(ii) Ownership
(a) Government
(b) Public sector
(c) Private sector

(iii) Sources used in schemes (number)

(a) Rivers

(b) Streams

(c) Tanks

(d) Underground water

(e) Potential created during kharif, rabi and summer

(f) Area covered during kharif, rabi and summer

5. *Income*

(i) Monetary Value of Consumed Forest and Common Property (CPR) Resource Products

Sl. No.	*Item Consumed*	*Quantity*	*Rate (Rs)*	*Money Value (Rs)*
(a)	Minor forest produce			
	Mahua flower	Qts	Qt	
	Mahua seed	Qts	Qt	
(b)	House construction Material **			
	Bamboo clums	Clum		
	Khair poles	Pole		
	Teak poles	Pole		
(c)	Fuelwood ***	Qts	Qt	
(d)	Grazing fodder @	Qts	Qt	
(e)	Agricultural Implements @@	Trees	Trees	
(f)	Wild tubers and bulbs as household vegetables	Qts	2/Manday/ Household (hh)	

Note : ** Two teak poles, 8 Khair poles and 200 clums of bamboo are used in the construction of one house. On average 200 clums of bamboo are used for constructing a fence. The average life of a house may be 10 years and that of a fence, four years. It may be assumed that house construction and fencing are uniformly distributed over each household's life cycle.

Contd. ...

(ii) Village Income *Contribution in Rs.*
(if possible)

(a) Primary Sector
Agriculture
Industry
Forestry
Direct monetary income
Sale of minor forest produce (MFP)
Sale of minor CPR products
Monetised income through self-consumption
Self-consumption of MFP
Self-consumption of minor CPR products
House construction material
Fuelwood
Grazing and fodder
Agricultural equipment
Wild tubers and bulbs
Sale of products from forests and common property resources products (CPRP)
Monetised income through self-consumption of CPRP
Construction material
Fuelwood
Grazing and fodder
Agricultural implements
Wild tubers and bulbs

(b) Secondary Sector
Manufacturing

(c) Tertiary Sector
Casual Labour
Labour in the forest department
Labour in other departments
Labour in agricultural fields

*** This may be based on the stated average daily consumption per household during the winter months and during the other 10 months.

@ Total fodder consumption/day/cattle may be assumed to be 8 kg.

@@ On an average, one plough has a life span of 7 years and is made out of one tree. It may be assumed that plough construction is uniformly distributed over time.

(d) Others Services
Carpentry
Vaidya
Shopkeeper
Tailor
Blacksmith
Cobbler
Goldsmith
Others

(e) Total

(iii) Month-wise distribution of mandays spent for different income earning activities (if possible)

Activities	*Agriculture Dept.*	*Forest Dept.*	*Irrigation Dept.*	*Other Farmer's Field*	*CPR NTFP Collection*						*Total*
					Mahua Flower	*Mahua seed*	*Kendu leaves*	*Sag seed*	*Fruits*	*Animal Hunting*	*Forestry activities*
Months											
January											
February											
March											
April											
May											
June											
July											
August											
September											
October											
November											
December											
Total											

(iv) Return on Labour for NTFP Collection and CPR Collection

Activities	*Mahua flower*	*Mahua seed*	*Kendu leaves*	*Sag seed*	*Fruits*	*Animal Hunting*	*Fish*
(a) Total collection Period (days)							
(b) Hrs/day of collection							
(c) Total hrs. of collection							

(d) Total mandays of collection
(8 hrs/day)
(e) Quantity collected in one day (kgs)
(f) Total collection in one season
(g) Total hrs for drying, processing
(h) Mandays for drying, processing
(i) Reduction in weight due to moisture and other losses by wt. of flower (moisture loss)
(j) Reduction in weight due to moisture and other losses by wt. of leaves (moisture loss)
(k) Reduction in weight due to moisture and other losses (Dry seed wt. is 10 per cent of fresh wt.)
(l) Net wt. after losses (kgs)
(m) Procurement price per kg.
(n) Return per person per season (Rs)
(o) Return per manday (Rs)

D. *Environmental Details*

1. *Environmental Resource Data*

(i) Environmental Resource Availability Classification *

Resource Available	*Abundantly Available*	*Moderately Available*	*Marginally Available*

(a) Forest

- Social
- Rural fuel
- Village wood lots
- Village forest
- Reserve
- Others

(b) Water

(i) From natural resources

(ii) From artificial sources

(c) Minerals

(d) Land/Soil

- Non-agricultural uses
- Barren and uncultivable land
- Permanent pastures and grazing lands
- Land under miscellaneous tree groups
- Cultivable waste
- Fallow lands
- Land kept reserved
- Patches of wasteland
- Below 1 hectare
- Between 2 and 4 hectares
- Above 4 hectares
- Area under fodder
- Area available for fodder

(e) Micro-environment

- Home gardens (also known as homestead, or household kitchen backyard or dooryard gardens)
- Vegetable and horticultural patches (protected with wells, etc.)
- River banks and riverine strips
- Levees and natural terraces
- Valley bottoms
- Wet and dry water courses
  : rainstreams (dividing and braiding, etc.)
  : dry river beds (nallas, wadis, luggas, etc.)
  : drainage lines
- Alluvial pans
- Artificial terraces
- Silt trap fields (depositional fields, gully fields, etc.
- Raised fields and ditches or ponds (especially in wetlands)
- Water harvesting in its many forms
- Hedges and windbreaks

- Clumps, groves or lines of trees or bushes
- Pockets of fertile soil (termitaria, former livestock pens, etc.)
- Sheltered corners or strips, by aspect of slope, configuration, etc.
- Plots protected from livestock
- Flood recession zones
- Small flood plains
- Springs and patches of high groundwater and seepage
- Strips and pockets of impeded drainage
- Lake basins
- Ponds, including fishponds
- Animal wallows (for example for buffaloes)

(f) Air

(g) Others (Specify)

Note : * Availability in relation to the development/economic needs of the people of the area.

*(ii) Environmental Resource Suitability Classification ***

	Basic Suitability	
	Suitable (Y/N)	*Unsuitable (Y/N)*
(a) Forest		
- Social		
- Rural fuel		
- Village wood lots		
- Village forest		
- Reserve		
- Others		
(b) Water		
(i) From natural resources		
(ii) From artificial sources		
(c) Minerals		

(d) Land/Soil

- Non-agricultural uses
- Barren and uncultivable land
- Permanent pastures and grazing lands
- Land under miscellaneous tree groups
- Cultivable waste
- Fallow lands
- Land kept reserved
- Patches of wasteland
- Below 1 hectare
- Between 2 and 4 hectares
- Above 4 hectares
- Area under fodder
- Area available for fodder

(e) Micro-environment

- Home gardens (also known as homestead, or household, kitchen, backyard or dooryard gardens)
- Vegetable and horticultural patches (protected, with wells, etc.)
- River banks and riverine strips
- Levees and natural terraces
- Valley bottoms
- Wet and dry water courses
  : rainstreams (dividing and braiding, etc.)
  : dry river beds (nallas, wadis, luggas, etc.)
  : drainage lines
- Alluvial pans
- Artificial terraces
- Silt trap fields (depositional fields, gully fields, etc.
- Raised fields and ditches or ponds (especially in wetlands)
- Water harvesting in its many forms
- Hedges and windbreaks
- Clumps, groves or lines of trees or bushes
- Pockets of fertile soil (termitaria, former livestock pens, etc.)
- Sheltered corners or strips, by aspect of slope, configuration, etc.
- Plots protected from livestock

- Flood recession zones
- Small flood plains
- Springs and patches of high groundwater and seepage
- Strips and pockets of impeded drainage
- Lake basins
- Ponds, including fishponds
- Animal wallows (for example for buffaloes)

(f) Air

(g) CPR

(h) Others (Specify)

Note : ** Suitability in relation to the economic activity or needs of the people of the area and its development.

(iii) Order Suitability of Environmental Resource *

	Order of Suitability		
	Highly Suitable	*Suitable Moderately Suitable*	*Marginally*

(a) Forest
- Social
- Rural fuel
- Village wood lots
- Village forest
- Reserve
- Others

(b) Water
(i) From natural fesources
(ii) From artificial sources

(c) Minerals

(d) Land/Soil
- Non-agricultural uses
- Barren and uncultivable land
- Permanent pastures and grazing lands

- Land under miscellaneous tree groups
- Cultivable waste
- Fallow lands
- Land kept reserved
- Patches of wasteland
- Below 1 hectare
- Between 2 and 4 hectares
- Above 4 hectares
- Area under fodder
- Area available for fodder

(e) Micro-environment

- Home gardens (also known as homestead, or household, kitchen, backyard or dooryard gardens)
- Vegetable and horticultural patches (protected with wells, etc.)
- River banks and riverine strips
- Levees and natural terraces
- Valley bottoms
- Wet and dry water courses

  : rainstreams (dividing and braiding, etc.)
  : dry river beds (nallas, wadis, luggas, etc.)
  : drainage lines

- Alluvial pans
- Artificial terraces
- Silt trap fields (depositional fields, gully fields, etc.
- Raised fields and ditches or ponds (especially in wetlands)
- Water harvesting in its many forms
- Hedges and windbreaks
- Clumps, groves or lines of trees or bushes
- Pockets of fertile soil (termitaria, former livestock pens, etc.)
- Sheltered corners or strips, by aspect of slope, configuration, etc.
- Plots protected from livestock
- Flood recession zones

- Small flood plains
- Springs and patches of high groundwater and seepage
- Strips and pockets of impeded drainage
- Lake basins
- Ponds, including fishponds
- Animal wallows (for example for buffaloes)

(f) Air

(g) CPR

(h) Others (Specify)

Note :* Suitability in relation to the economic activity or needs of the people of the area and its development.

(iv) Status of Suitability of Environmental Resource *

	Status of Suitability	Current Unsuitable (Y/N)	Permanently Unsuitable (Y/N)
(a) Forest			
- Social			
- Rural fuel			
- Village wood lots			
- Village forest			
- Reserve			
- Others			
(b) Water			
(i) From natural resources			
(ii) From artificial sources			
(c) Minerals			
(d) Land/Soil			
- Non-agricultural uses			
- Barren and uncultivable land			
- Permanent pastures and grazing lands			

Note : * Suitability in relation to the economic activity or needs of the people of the area and its development.

- Land under miscellaneous tree groups
- Cultivable waste
- Fallow lands
- Land kept reserved
- Patches of wasteland
- Below 1 hectare
- Between 2 and 4 hectares
- Above 4 hectares
- Area under fodder
- Area available for fodder

(e) Micro-environment
- Home gardens (also known as homestead, or household, kitchen, backyard or dooryard gardens)
- Vegetable and horticultural patches (protected with wells, etc.)
- River banks and riverine strips
- Levees and natural terraces
- Valley bottoms
- Wet and dry water courses
  : rainstreams (dividing and braiding, etc.)
  : dry river beds (nallas, wadis, luggas, etc.)
  : drainage lines

- Alluvial pans
- Artificial terraces
- Silt trap fields (depositional fields, gully fields, etc.
- Raised fields and ditches or ponds (especially in wetlands)
- Water harvesting in its many forms
- Hedges and windbreaks
- Clumps, groves or lines of trees or bushes
- Pockets of fertile soil (termitaria, former livestock pens, etc.)
- Sheltered corners or strips, by aspect of slope, configuration, etc.
- Plots protected from livestock
- Flood recession zones
- Small flood plains
- Springs and patches of high groundwater and seepage

- Strips and pockets of impeded drainage
- Lake basins
- Ponds, including fishponds
- Animal wallows (for example for buffaloes)

(f) Air

(g) CPR

(h) Others (Specify)

(v) Limiters of Suitability of Environmental Resource

	Limiters of Suitability*	
	For Temporarily Unsuitable Resources(Y/N)	*For Permanently Unsuitable Resources(Y/N)*
(a) Forest		
- Social		
- Rural fuel		
- Village wood lots		
- Village forest		
- Reserve		
- Others		
(b) Water		
(i) From natural resources		
(ii) From artificial sources		
(c) Minerals		
(d) Land/Soil		
- Non-agricultural uses		
- Barren and uncultivable land		
- Permanent pastures and grazing lands		

- Land under miscellaneous tree groups
- Cultivable waste
- Fallow lands
- Land kept reserved
- Patches of wasteland
- Below 1 hectare
- Between 2 and 4 hectares
- Above 4 hectares
- Area under fodder
- Area available for fodder

(e) Micro-environment

- Home gardens (also known as homestead, or household, kitchen, backyard or dooryard gardens)
- Vegetable and horticultural patches (protected, with wells, etc.)
- River banks and riverine strips
- Levees and natural terraces
- Valley bottoms
- Wet and dry water courses

    - rainstreams (dividing and braiding, etc.)
    - dry river beds (nallas, wadis, luggas, etc.)
    - drainage lines

- Alluvial pans
- Artificial terraces
- Silt trap fields (depositional fields, gully fields, etc.
- Raised fields and ditches or ponds (especially in wetlands)
- Water harvesting in its many forms
- Hedges and windbreaks
- Clumps, groves or lines of trees or bushes
- Pockets of fertile soil (termitaria, former livestock pens, etc.)
- Sheltered corners or strips, by aspect of slope, configuration, etc.
- Plots protected from livestock

- Flood recession zones
- Small flood plains
- Springs and patches of high groundwater and seepage
- Strips and pockets of impeded drainage
- Lake basins
- Ponds, including fishponds
- Animal wallows (for example for buffaloes)

(f) Air

(g) CPR

(h) Others (Specify)

Note : * Record here the characteristic of the resources that limit it suitability in use for development. Use more space and/or separate paper as may be necessary.

(vi) Opportunities for Improving Environmental Resource

	Better Management Practices		
	Suitable Production Methods	*Conservation Methods*	*Others (Specify)*
(a) Forest			
- Social			
- Rural fuel			
- Village wood lots			
- Village forest			
- Reserve			
- Others			
(b) Water			
(i) From natural resources			
(ii) From artificial sources			
(c) Minerals			

(d) Land/Soil

- Non-agricultural uses
- Barren and uncultivable land
- Permanent pastures and grazing lands
- Land under miscellaneous tree groups
- Cultivable waste
- Fallow lands
- Land kept reserved
- Patches of wasteland
- Below 1 hectare
- Between 2 and 4 hectares
- Above 4 hectares
- Other margins
- Area under fodder
- Area available for fodder

(e) Micro-environment

- Home gardens (also known as homestead, or household, kitchen, backyard or dooryard gardens)
- Vegetable and horticultural patches (protected with wells, etc.)
- River banks and riverine strips
- Levees and natural terraces
- Valley bottoms
- Wet and dry water courses

  : rainstreams (dividing and braiding, etc.)
  : dry river beds (nallas, wadis, luggas, etc.)
  : drainage lines

- Alluvial pans
- Artificial terraces
- Silt trap fields (depositional fields, gully fields, etc.
- Raised fields and ditches or ponds (especially in wetlands)
- Water harvesting in its many forms
- Hedges and windbreaks

- Clumps, groves or lines of trees or bushes
- Pockets of fertile soil (termitaria, former livestock pens, etc.)
- Sheltered corners or strips, by aspect of slope, configuration, etc.
- Plots protected from livestock
- Flood recession zones
- Small flood plains
- Springs and patches of high groundwater and seepage
- Strips and pockets of impeded drainage
- Lake basins
- Ponds, including fishponds
- Animal wallows (for example for buffaloes)

(f) CPR

(g) Others (Specify)

(vii) Environmental Resource Depletability Classification

(a) Depletable Maintainable Resources *	- Fishing ponds/ water-bodies - Fuelwood forest - Fodder forest - Grazing lands - Forests - Others (Specify)
(b) Depletable: Maintainable Non-Renewable **	- Soil - CPR - Others (Specify)
(c) Non Depletable ***	- Solar energy - Hydro energy - Wind power

Note : * Resources that renew themselves; can be maintained with proper management practices; or resources which after depletion will renew themselves if left undisturbed for a specified period of time.

** Resources susceptible to depletion but can be maintained with proper care/practice. If depleted these resource are lost for ever.

*** Resources unaffected by overuse or overexploitation.

Contd. ...

- Rivers/streams
- Sea water
- Others (Specify)

(d) Non-Maintainable and Non-Renewable *
- Minerals
- Oil
- Others (Specify)

(viii) *Major Environmental Resources and Sector Matrices*** *(Separately for each resource such as Forest, Arable Land, Water, Air, CPR, etc.)*

Sector	*Status*	*Uses*	*Problems*	*Opportunities*	*Sector Summary* ***
(a) Agriculture					
(b) Small Scale Manufacturing					
(c) Crafts					
(d) Trade					
(e) Private Services					
(f) Others (Specify)					
(g) Resources **** Summary					

E. Gender Details

1. Data on Gender Analysis

(i) Male-Female Composition (various categories of work)

Note : * Resources once used are gone for ever, but their use can be prolonged by proper use.

** An environmental resource is deemed to be major in either case when it is very crucial for a sector and is available or when though it is very crucial it is not available/unsuitable.

*** This column is for summarizing the most important problems and opportunities arising from each sector's interaction with natural resource in question.

**** This row is for summarizing the most important aspects of the status, uses, problems and opportunities associated with each resource, on account of its interface with the local economy.

	Male (%)	*Female (%)*
(a) Wage Salary *		
(b) Casual Labour *		
(c) Self-employed *		
(d) Unpaid Family Work **		
(e) Expanded Domestic Work **		
(f) Conventional Domestic Work **		

(ii) Women's Work Patterns by Economic Status (Percentage of Women's Time)

	Wage Agriculture	*Own Agriculture*	*Domestic*
(a) Landless Wage Labour			
(b) Marginal Farmer/Entrepreneur			
(c) Marginal Farmer			
(d) Small/Medium Farmer Entrepreneur			
(e) Small/Medium Farmer			
(f) Large Farmer/Entrepreneur			
(g) Large Farmer			
(h) Landlord/Entrepreneur			
(i) Landlord			

(iii) Occupation Status of Women's Work (Outside Home)

	High	*Low*
(a) Landless Labourers		
(b) Marginal Farmers		
(c) Small Farmers		
(d) Medium Farmers		
(e) Large Farmers		

(iv) Occupation Status of Women's Work (Inside Home)

	High	*Low*
(a) Landless Labourers		
(b) Marginal Farmers		
(c) Small Farmers		
(d) Medium Farmers		
(e) Large Farmers		

Note : * These relate to work outside the home.
** These relate to work inside the household.

(v) Women's Status within Household (in Female-headed Households)

	Highest	*High*	*Medium*	*Low*
(a) Extent of decision-making				
(b) Proportion of Household income contributed by women				
(c) Strength of inside/outside dichotomy				
(d) Household economic status				

(vi) Women's Status within Household (in Widow-headed Households)

	Highest	*High*	*Medium*	*Low*
(a) Extent of decision-making				
(b) Proportion of Household income contributed by women				
(c) Strength of inside/outside dichotomy				
(d) Household economic status				

(vii) Women's Status within Household (in Landless Households)

	Highest	*High*	*Medium*	*Low*
(a) Extent of decision-making				
(b) Proportion of Household income contributed by women				

(c) Strength of inside/outside dichotomy
(d) Household economic status

(viii) Women's Status within Household (in Small and Marginal Farmer Households)

	Highest	*High*	*Medium*	*Low*
(a) Extent of decision-making				
(b) Proportion of Household income contributed by women				
(c) Strength of inside/outside dichotomy				
(d) Household economic status				

(ix) Women's Status within Household (in Medium and Large Farmer Households)

	Highest	*High*	*Medium*	*Low*
(a) Extent of decision-making				
(b) Proportion of household income contributed by women				
(c) Strength of inside/outside dichotomy				
(d) Household economic status				

2. *Female Wages (Percentage of Male Wages)*

(a) Agriculture
(b) Allied activities

(c) Plantation
(d) Service sector
(e) Others (Specify)

3. *Female Literacy (Percentage of Male Literacy)*

4. *Malnutrition in Female Children*

	Normal	*Mild*	*Moderate*	*Severe*
(a) Infants				
(i) Male				
(ii) Female				
(b) Toddlers				
(iii) Male				
(iv) Female				
(c) Pre-School Going				
(v) Male				
(vi) Female				

5. *Guide of Malnutrition (0 to 5 years)*

	Normal	*Mild*	*Moderate*	*Severe*
(i) Male				
(ii) Female				

6. *Age-Specific Female/Male Death Ratios*

(a) 0-5
(b) 5-9
(c) 10-14
(d) 15-19
(e) 20-24
(f) 25-29
(g) 30-39
(h) 40-49

(i) 50-59
(j) 60-69

7. *Infant Mortality Rate by Mother's Education*

Educational Level

(a) Literate
(b) Primary and above
(c) Literate below primary
(d) Illiterate

DATA REQUIREMENT AT BLOCK LEVEL FOR PLANNING

The requirements must be classified into the following details :

(a) Infrastructure details (data on basic amenities)
(b) Demographic details (census data on population, livestock)
(c) Agro-economic details (census data on irrigation, agriculture, forestry, land=use, etc.)
(d) Environmental details
(e) Gender details

A. *Infrastructure Details*

1. *Health*

(i) Health Institutions (above PHCs)
(a) Number
(b) Type
(c) Ownership
(d) Number of doctors
(e) Number of nurses
(f) Operation facility available (y/n)? etc.
(g) The types are:
- Community health centres
- Dispensaries including TB centres

- Maternity and family welfare
- Ayurvedic
- Homoeopathic
- Unani
- Allopathic
- Others

The ownership details are:

- Government
- Local Bodies
- Others

(ii) Number of mobile vans available

2. Education

(i) Educational Institutes (number)

(a) College with +2 Science
(b) College with +2 Commerce
(c) College with +2 Arts
(d) College with +2 Science and Commerce
(e) College with +2 Science and Arts
(f) College with +2 Arts and Commerce
(g) College with +2 Science, Arts and Commerce
(h) College Science
(i) College Commerce
(j) College Arts
(k) College Science and Commerce
(l) College Science and Arts
(m) College Arts and Commerce
(n) College Science, Commerce and Arts

3. Transport

(i) Railway Station (number)
(ii) Length of roads with type of road surface for each
(a) National highways and number
(b) State highways and number
(c) MDR and number
(d) ODR and number
(e) CVR and number

(f) Panchayat Samiti road
(g) Panchayat road
(h) Waterways

The various types are:
(a) Black top
(b) Metal road
(c) Murran road
(d) Earthen soil road

4. Communication

(i) Telephone Exchanges with number of lines

5. Employment

(i) Vocational Guidance and Counselling
 (a) Number of centres
 (b) Persons assisted

6. Housing (Slum Details)

(i) Number of towns
(ii) Number of towns having slums
(iii) Slums details for each of the slum areas
 (a) Slum area
 (b) Slum population
 (c) Population rehabilitated so far

7. Economic Services

(i) Co-operative Societies
The following to be collected for each types
(a) Number type-wise
(b) Number of members
(c) Number of borrowing members
(d) Number of defaulters
(e) Amount outstanding
(f) Amount overdue

(g) Primary Land Mortgage Banks
(h) Irrigation societies and others
(i) Other type (specify) not collect at village level

(ii) Institutional Finance and Banking
(a) Number of Commercial Banks and Rural Banks
(b) Number of Commercial Banks and Scheduled Banks
(c) Amount lent for agricultural purposes
(d) Amount lent for industrial purposes
(e) Amount lent for other purposes
(f) Credit deposit ratio of latest date

(iii) Financial Institutions other than Banks (No.)

(iv) Animal Husbandry
(a) Number of slaughter houses
(b) Meat processing units
(c) Feed missing plants
(d) Others (specify)

8. *Judicial and Administrative Service*

(i) Number of Police Stations located in the block
(ii) Number of Outposts located in the block
(iii) Population covered
(iv) Number of Magistrate Courts
(v) Number of Munsif Courts

9. *Miscellaneous Facilities*

(a) Capacity of Bal Bhawan/Creches
(b) Strength of Bal Bhawan/Creches

B. Demographic Details

The demographic details are to be collected at village level and consolidated at the corresponding block level.

C. Agro-Economic Details

The agro-economic details are to be collected at village level and consolidated at the corresponding block level from panchayat level data.

D. Environmental and Gender Details

The environmental and gender details are to be collected at village level and consolidated at the corresponding block level from panchayat level data.

DATA REQUIREMENT AT DISTRICT LEVEL FOR PLANNING

The data requirements for district level planning may be classified (as in case of block and village planning) into the following details :

(a) Infrastructure details (data on basic amenities)
(b) Demographic details (census data on population, livestock)
(c) Agro-economic details (census data on irrigation agriculture, forestry, land=use, etc.)
(d) Environmental details
(e) Gender details

A. Infrastructure Details

1. Health

(i) Hospital (number) with specialization for each type
   (a) Government
   (b) Local Bodies
   (c) Others
(ii) Personnel (number)
   (a) Doctors
   (b) Surgeons
   (c) Neuro Surgeons
   (d) Orthopedic Surgery
   (e) Gynaecology, etc.
   (f) ENT specialists
   (g) Nurses/midwives
   (h) Laboratory technicians
   (i) X-ray radiologists, etc.
(iii) Number of surgery wards in different hospitals with:
   (a) Number of beds
   (b) Number of medical wards
(iv) Availability of blood bank? (y/n)

2. *Education*

   (i) Educational Institutes (number and seat capacity)

	Govt.	*Govt. Aided*	*Govt. Unaided*
(a) Engineering			
(b) Medical			
(c) Polytechnics and Diploma Institutions			
(d) Arts and Crafts			
(e) Teachers Training			
(f) Music			
(g) Dance			
(h) Other Fine Arts			
(i) P.G. Colleges			
(j) Universities			

3. *Drinking Water*

   (i) Urban Water Supply
      (a) Population benefited
      (b) Population to be covered

   (ii) Number of DWS Projects
      (a) Completed
      (b) Ongoing

4. *Transport*

   (i) Railway Lines
      (a) Length of broad gauge lines
      (b) Length of metre gauge lines
      (c) Length of narrow gauge lines
      (d) Length of electrified lines

   (ii) Means of Transport
      (a) Waterways
      (b) Airways
      (c) Airports (number)
      (d) Roadways

   (iii) Ports and Harbours
      (a) Major ports
      (b) Minor ports
      (c) Fishing harbours with trawler berthing capacity
      (d) Fishing jetties with trawler berthing capacity

5. *Communication*
   (i) Number of telegraph offices
   (ii) Number of telephone exchanges

6. *Employment*
   (i) Number of employment exchanges
   (ii) Number of job seekers registered as on 31 December of previous year (category-wise)
      (a) Non-matrics
      (b) Matrics
      (c) Intermediates
      (d) Arts Graduates
      (e) Science Graduates
      (f) Commerce Graduates
      (g) Medical Graduates
      (h) Engineering Graduates with description
      (i) Diploma holders with description
      (j) Certificate holders with description
   (iii) SEEUY
      (a) Applications received
      (b) Approved by district committee
      (c) Sanctioned
      (d) Rejected
      (e) Pending
      (f) Amount disbursed
   (iv) Training (ITI)
      (a) No. of centres
      (b) Trades
      (c) Capacity
      (d) Non-trained
      (e) Number of employee
   (v) Number of migrant labour (category-wise) if possible.

7. *Industries*
   (i) Large Scale Industries (for each category)
      (a) Total investment
      (b) Number of employed
      (c) Functional units
      (d) Sick units

(e) Total number of units

(ii) Medium Scale Industries (for each category)

(a) Total Investment
(b) Number of employed
(c) Functional units
(d) Sick units
(e) Total number of units

8. *Economic Services*

(i) Apex Co-operative Societies (for each type such as District Co-operative, and Apex marketing societies)

(a) Number type-wise
(b) Number of members
(c) Number of borrowing members
(d) Number of defaulters
(e) Amount outstanding
(f) Amount overdue
(g) Number of employed (males/females separately)

(ii) Number of members of societies for each of the following type:

(a) Milk society
(b) Handloom society
(c) Fisheries
(d) Handicraft
(e) Others (specify)
(f) District land development society
(g) Milk supply unions
(h) Central Co-op., if not covered at block level

(iii) Animal Husbandry: District Milk Co-operative Union details

(a) Collection from milk centres
(b) Sale
(c) Number of employed (males/females separately)

(iv) District Co-operative Society Details

(a) Collection
(b) Sale

(c) Number of employed (males/females separately)

(v) District Handloom Co-operative Society Details
  (a) Procurement
  (b) Sale
  (c) Number of employed (males/females separately)

9. *Miscellaneous Facilities*
  (i) Recreation and Cultural Centres
    (a) Stadiums
    (b) Museums
    (c) Zoo
    (d) Art Galleries

B. Demographic Details

The demographic details are to be collected at village level and consolidated for the district as a whole.

C. Agro-Economic Details

The agro-economic details are to be collected at village and block levels with respect to basic and other data and consolidated for the district level.

D. Environmental and Gender Details

The environmental and gender details are to be collected at the village level and consolidated at the corresponding block level from the village level data. They would be in terms of percentage of village where the particular kind, state etc. of environmental resource available.

PEOPLE'S PERCEPTION AND PEOPLE'S WISDOM[5]

These data bases together would provide a formidable wealth of information for local level planning. However, it would be apparent from the foregoing that though valuable data will be collected, there will still be three important gaps that would remain to be filled in the quantitative data. These are:

(i) There would be little data or information about the problems as perceived by the people, which the local level planning at different tiers need to tackle. Felt needs of the people do not get appropriately reflective from the data mentioned above. Different actors involved in the task of planning, implementation and monitoring will perceive the problems faced by the common people from different perspectives, and it is possible that neither of these perspectives would mirror a true and fair account of what the people perceive as their real problems. Incorporation of people's perception of their own problems remains a critical element.

(ii) Even if the problems are correctly perceived by the actors involved in development and by the planners at the local level, there still remains the distant possibility of solutions to such problems as thought of by the different actors engaged in the "art of development" being different from what the people think as most appropriate. There is no debate on the issue that for plans, programmes and projects to be successful and schemes or projects to be sustainable, each of the schemes or projects identified to answer the problems faced by the common man, must be backed by the collective wisdom of the community and have "collective will" behind it.

(iii) The "hard data" may suffer, to some extent, the infirmities associated with collection, collation and processing of data by people who are not actual users. Such data needs cross-checking and supplementation. Since problems of such data have been dealt with, in detail, in Chapter 1, it is not pursued here any further.

These gaps can be tackled at various plans and through different methods. One such set of methods is provided by Participatory Rural Appraisal (PRA).

It is, therefore, necessary to have participatory data (that is data collected through PRA) which will provide a means to respond to the foregoing dimensions.

PARTICIPATORY DATA

It may appear at first site that collecting participatory data will be somewhat more difficult for the households of villages that will have to be covered; but on deeper inspection, it will be apparent that the task is simpler. On an average the number of villages under a panchayat are not many and indeed the maximum number of villages under a panchayat on an average are (at present) 30, in only one state and they are far less in others.

For collecting participatory data of the kind we are talking about, each village should prepare several diagrams or maps which would reflect a true and fair account of their economy and its problems. The genetic definitions of these diagrams or maps are provided in Chapter-1 but for ease in reading they are summarized as follows[6] :

(a) Diagrams

Diagrammatic models can be defined as simple, schematic devices which present information in a readily understandable visual form. Their usefulness is two-fold. First, the act of constructing the diagrams is in itself an analytical procedure and helps the constructors to think through the dynamics they are trying to put down on paper. Second, the diagrams become a means of creating communication and discussion between different people. They may be constructing the diagram together or one person may be attempting to use the diagram to inform others of how they see an issue. Such communication may be between different disciplines, or people with different sectoral responsibilities, or between farmers and development specialists or among farmers themselves.

Agro-eco-system can be analysed in terms of four basic patterns: space, time, flows and decisions. Each pattern can, in turn, be represented by diagrams. For example, spatial patterns can be represented by maps and transects, temporal patterns by graphical trends and calendars, pie charts, trend lines flow by flow diagrams of various kinds, and decisions by decision trees and venn diagrams. The diagrams most commonly used are outlined below.

(b) Maps

Maps are the most familiar of diagrams. They may exist already and are an important component of the secondary data review, but for the purposes of PRA they need to be simplified. Farmers can then use them to inform the development specialists of the location of the different parts of the farm, and their relationship to basic resources, such as water, and to the major land forms of the area. The maps drawn in the field are sketch maps, which are bold and simple in design.

(c) Transects

Transects have probably greater practical utility than maps, primarily in focusing attention on the different zones or micro-environments in a watershed, village or farm. Their primary purpose should be to identify the locations of the major problems and opportunities in the agro-eco-systems. They have a particularly important role in overcoming the "roadside bias" that is common in field visits. The act of constructing a transect forces the team to carry out a thorough traverse of the village or other location. Like maps they need to be simple and idealized. Although they have some location similarity with botanical or soil survey transects they are very different in form and purpose.

(d) Seasonal Calendars

Seasonal Calendars are simply extended versions of the crop calendars which have long been used in FSR. All the major changes that occur within the rural year are represented including those concerned with climate, cropping patterns, livestock (sources of foilage and key events such as calving, sales, migration) and labour demand; changes in prices may also be included.

Where data is not available, the patterns can be constructed on the basis of questioning and discussion; for example, a qualitative estimate of labour demand can be obtained by asking: "Which is the peak month?", "What is done?", "Which is the next peak?" and so on.

There should also be room on the calendar to include the types of problems and constraints (agricultural and others) and point out opportunity; for example, when new crops could be grown.

Eighteen month calendars, in which the last six months, repeat the last six, are useful in fully revealing the seasonal patterns. Sometimes, it is more useful to start the calendar with the beginning of a season, rather than the beginning of the year.

(e) Other Diagrams dealing with Time Trends

Longer term changes in the agro-eco-systems can be represented through diagrams such as historical profiles and graphical time trends. One additional diagram which deals with both spatial and temporal patterns is the transect through-time or historical transect. Interesting changes in land=use can be revealed. In one example, it was the persistence of farmers in their production of tree crops, despite repeated setbacks, which stayed over as a clear feature of the system.

(f) Decision Trees

Decision trees are a valuable aid to understand farmers' strategies for managing their resources and the reasons why they take up or give up particular technologies. Produced as part of the most-interview analysis they can help identify the key factors or important conditions that influence the farmers. Any cut-off points for the farmer's decisions can be marked on the branching points.

(g) Venn Diagram

A related aspect of decision-making, however, is the role of institutional relationships. Simple Venn diagrams can be produced to analyse these relationships and to identify areas for improvement. They consist of touching or overlapping circles of various sizes, each circle representing an individual or institution, the size of the circle indicating its importance, and the overlap indicating the degree of contact or overlap in decision-making.

As a first step it is recommended that:

(a) a historical transect;
(b) a transect;
(c) a social map;
(d) a census map;
(e) a health map;
(f) wealth ranking in the village;
(g) mobility map;
(h) a resource map; and
(i) a venn diagram may be prepared for each village by the panchayats.

Examples of the different diagrams and maps are at Figures 5.1 to 5.9.

The diagrams and maps will be much more accurate and will have a much better appreciation at the village and the panchayat levels, where familiarity with "lifeless numbers" is somewhat remote. These diagrams, prepared by the villagers themselves, would have embodied in them community's knowledge, understanding and wisdom about their capabilities, resources, strengths, weaknesses, problems and the probable solutions. Panchayati Raj Institutions which would take fiscal and developmental decisions on information generated by these diagrams backed by quantitative data, of the kind we discussed earlier, would be much nearer to realistic decision-making than they would have been had they acted upon only quantitative data.

It is our further proposal that these diagrams be displayed at the Panchayat Bhawan or Panchayat office where people can see for themselves a picture of their area and its economy. And changes in them be affected at prescribed intervals to show the progress or retrogression. These would then partake the nature of monitoring and evaluation tools.

PARTICIPATORY METHODS IN GOVERNMENT

Since participatory data collection is a distinct break from the conventional data generation, people are reluctant to accept it; men inherently resist change. The question likely to be asked is:

has participatory data generation been resorted to by institutions (other than the NGOs) responsible for developmental activities? The answer is in the affirmative and it would be worthwhile recording some of the salient features of the experience.

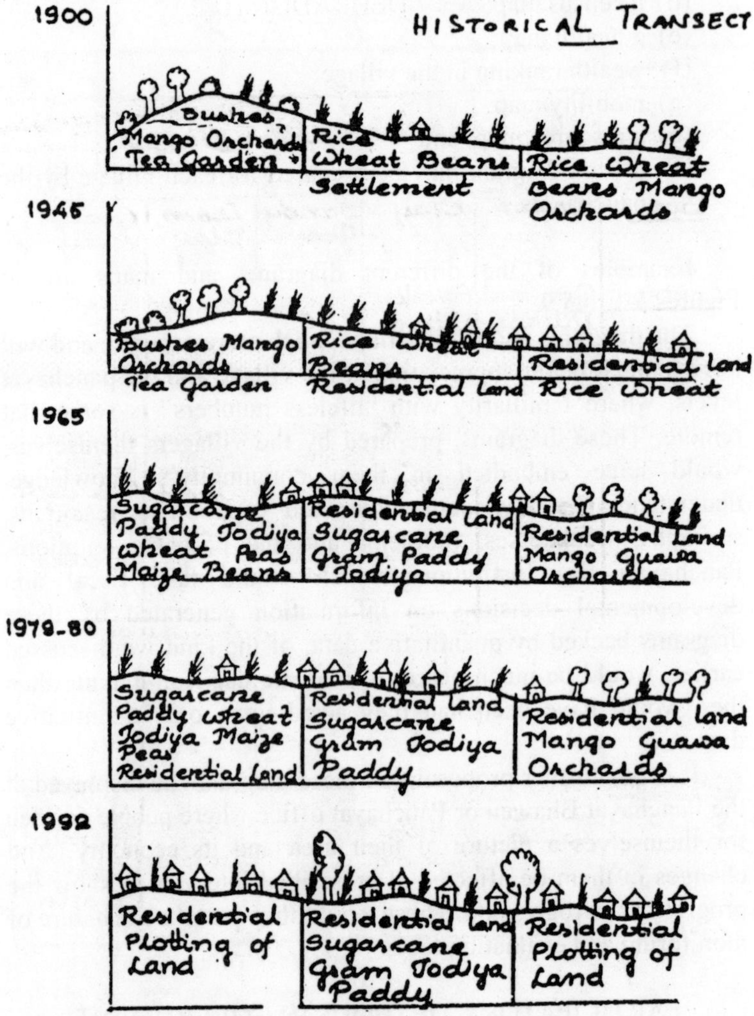

Fig. 5.1 : Transect through time illustration Land Use Trend in Harrawala Village in Block Doiwala

VILLAGE : HARRAWALA

BLOCK : DOIWALA

DISTRICT : DEHRADUN (U.P.)

SOIL	Loam	Clay	Sandy Gravel	Loam Clay	Gravel Clay
LANDUSE	Farmland Village	Farmland Village	Grazing Farmland Village	Farmland	Farmland Village
CROP & VEGETATION	Paddy Maize Wheat Todiya Peas	Oilseed Sugar-cane	Todiya Maize Sugar-cane Paddy Beans	Paddy Maize Wheat Todiya	Sugar-cane Paddy Todiya Beans
PROBLEMS	Erosion	Drought Pests	Drought Pests Low fertility of Soil	Drought Pests	Erosion
OPPORTUNITIES	Soil Conser-vation.	Water transport Rainfed farming	Rainfed farming	Constsu-ction of Canals	Flood recession farming Soil Erosion

Fig. 5.2 : Transect

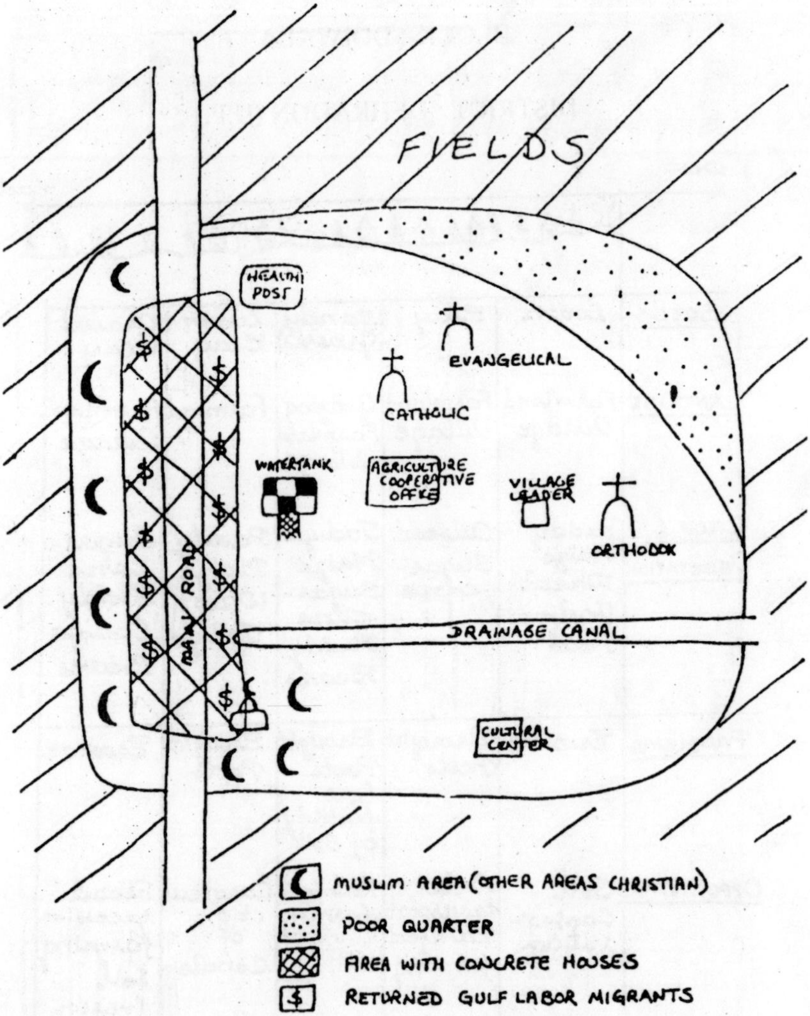

Fig. 5.3 : Social Map of a Village in Upper Egypt

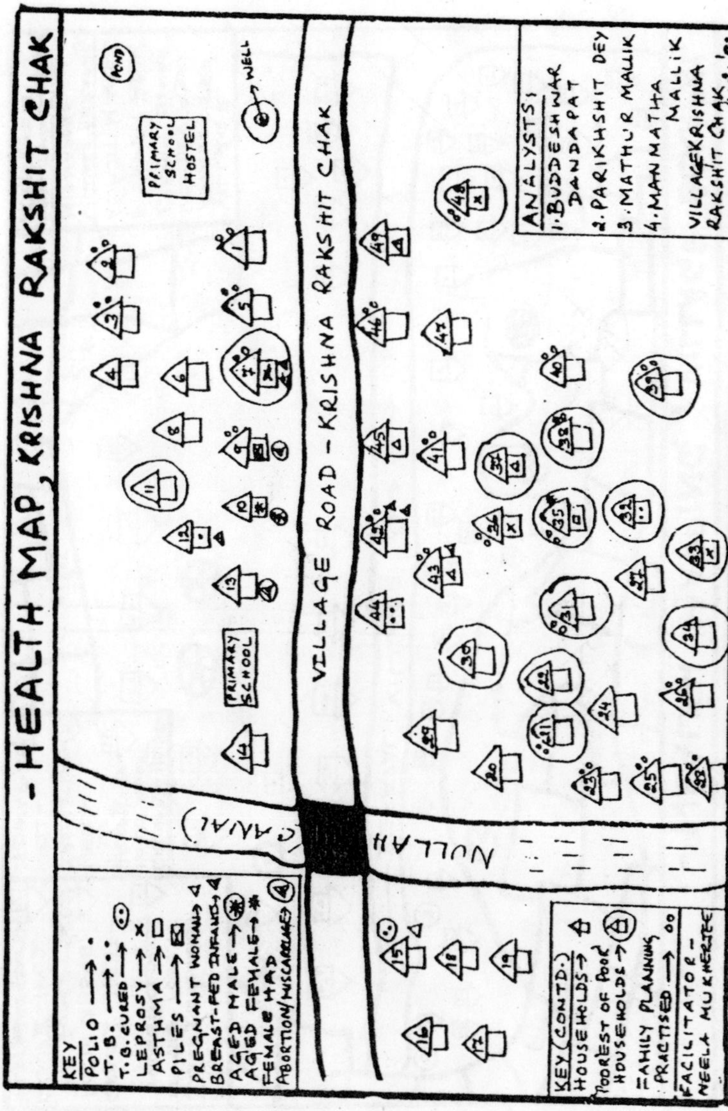

Fig. 5.4 : Health Map, Krishna Rakshit Chak

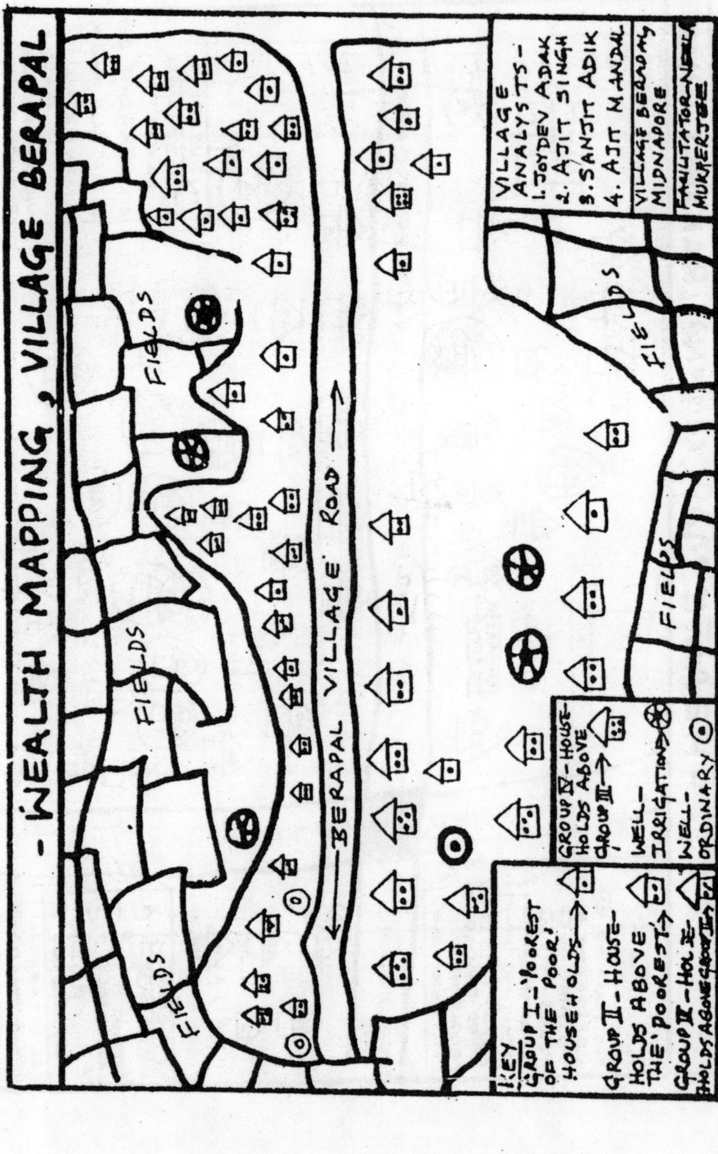

Fig. 5.5 : Wealth Mapping, Village Berapal

Fig. 5.6 : Wellbeing Grouping, Village Kalsigeriya

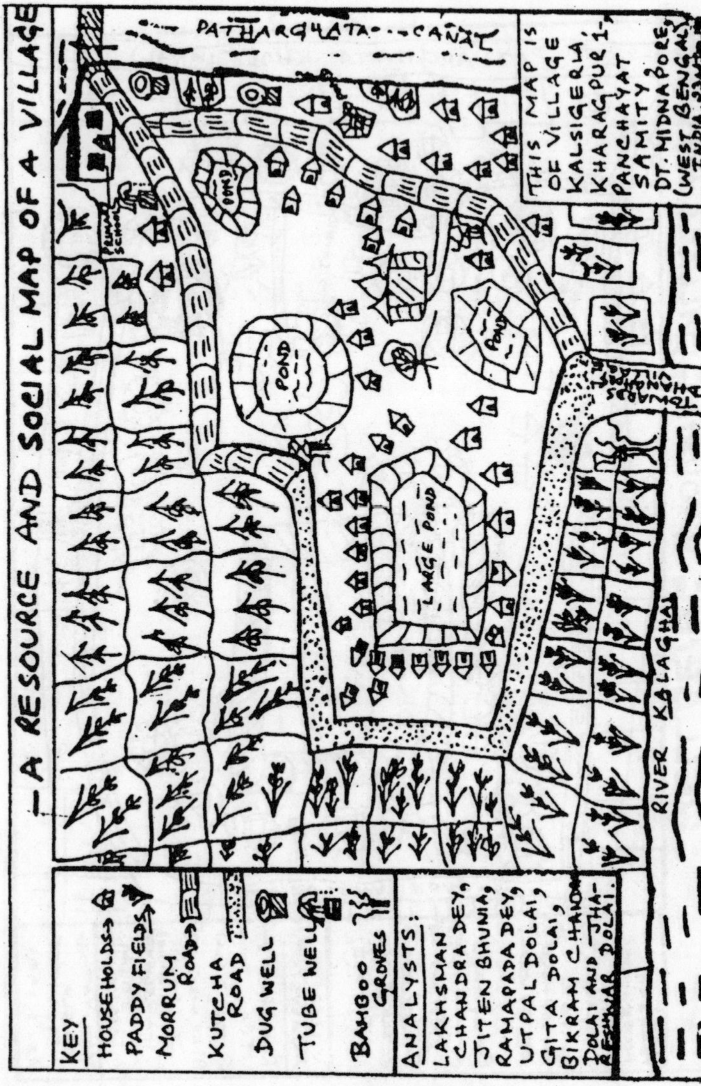

Fig. 5.7 :A Resource and Social Map of a Village

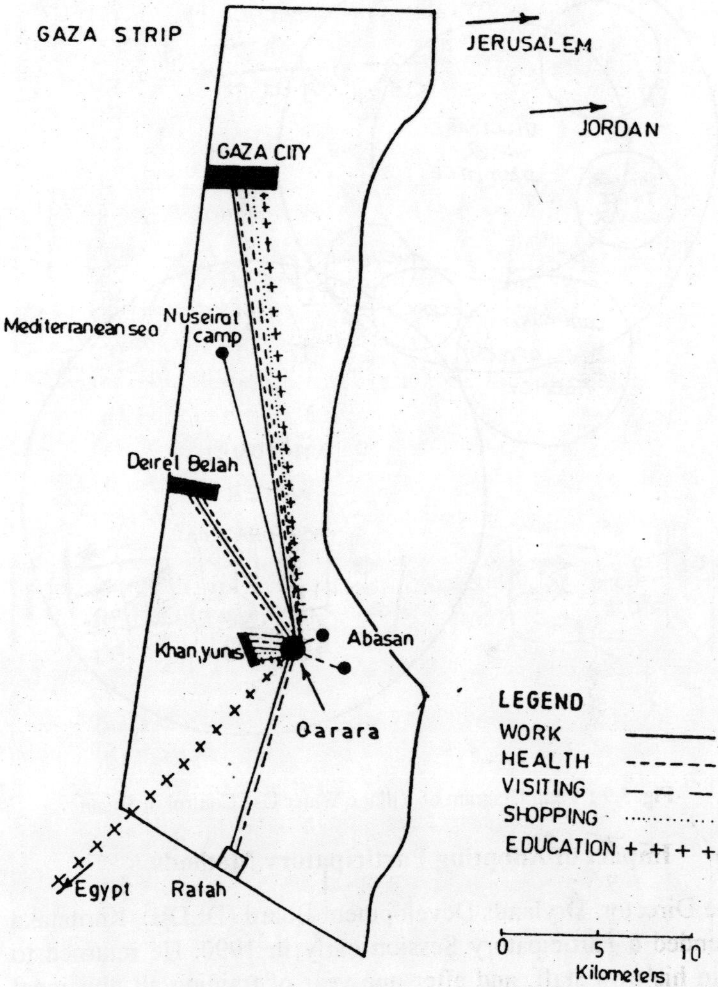

Fig. 5.8 : Mobility Map of Women from Qarara Area Gaza

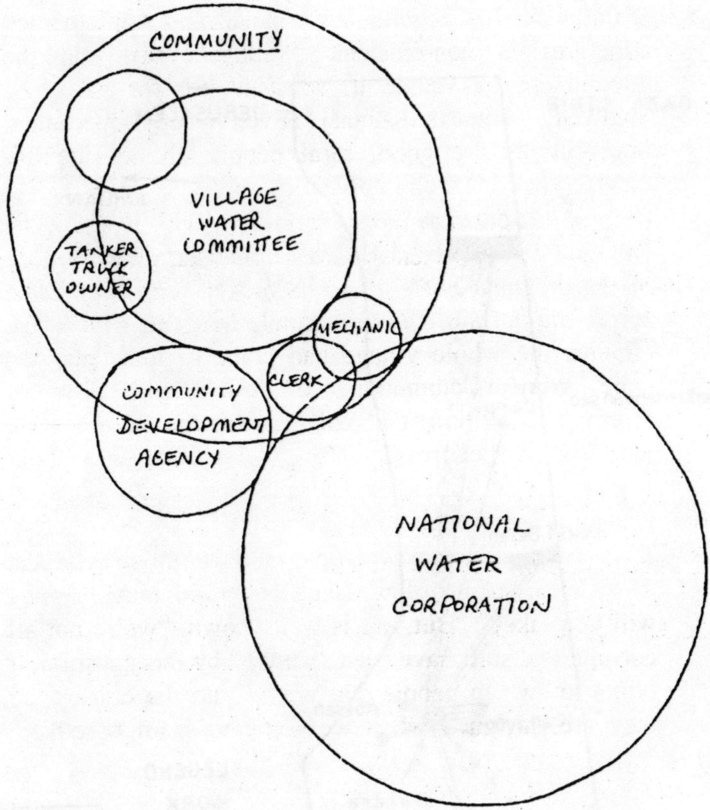

Fig. 5.9 : Venn Diagram of Village Water Use Control in Sudan

(a) Impact of Adopting Participatory Methods

The Director, Drylands Development Board (DLDB), Karnataka attended a Participatory Session early in 1990. He returned to train his own staff, and after one year of training all divisional level staff, he said: "In one year, our bureaucracy has become sensitive ... Participatory methods have totally changed our attitudes to the planning process".[7] Government participants of the workshop drew attention to several problems in their work, some of which were highlighted by the participatory process:

- It is difficult to meet targets with current planning and implementation methods.
- Maintenance of government planned and implemented structures is non-existent: "Villagers say that the government has made it, so it is not for us to be involved" (Somesh Kumar).[8] Even when government interventions are good, rural people do not identify themselves with such interventions.
- People have lost interest in government works. The Director, Development Board, Karnataka, told the story of the pregnant buffalo and its broken leg. They came across the buffalo whilst walking a transect; within five minutes the whole village had come to look and had gone away. Commenting on this rapid flow of information within the village and the comparative indifference expressed by the villagers about government technologies, he said "How can this happen when our technologies do not spread?"
- Villagers have low expectations of government officials. The first question often asked is: "How much money will you take?" "But," as is well known, "we're not all corrupt, and staff have been shattered by this question. It is not known to people that we will not be corrupt, so they are intrigued when we come to learn together." Many government workers are doing good work and simply need support.
- Attention was drawn to the impact upon cross-disciplinary working within the Drought Prone Areas programme of Andhra Pradesh. Before the participatory sessions began, the participants from each of the different departments sat separately, but by the end of the participatory sessions exercise they were sitting in a mixed team, their moral was high, they were now willing to be with the villagers and exhibited considerable respect for people's wisdom. A further impact on internal institutional working has occurred after high level officials have been in the field and seen for themselves the working of participatory methods. They are then less inclined to send instructions from

State HQ about what should be done at the village or taluka levels. However, this has also been noted that if the most senior officers present were not supportive of, or exhibited an understanding of participatory methods, then the whole participatory exercise would be jeopardized.

(b) Components of Government Participatory Methods

The emphasis by government trainers has been principally upon changing attitudes. As A.K. Monnappa, also of the DLDB, Karnataka, put it: "We went to a village and sat on the ground, refusing chairs, and we got so much information from the people that we realized this new attitude was the key to opening the door.[9] The objective is to build self-confidence first, adding methods later.

This has been made explicit by calling the attitude change component "Learning to Unlearn". In this, the emphasis is upon what has been learnt. Participants are told not to expect people to come to them, rather they must search out villagers; all sessions are mandatory; all sleep together in the village – drivers, senior and junior officials; no badges of office are permitted – these are considered barriers. The night half is crucial in demonstrating to villagers that the government is committed; it also has a demonstrative effect upon junior officials when senior officials refuse mattresses or special comforts. "In one case, 40 staff stayed in a Harijan colony, staying-up to one o'clock at night, talking – we realized it was a short way to the people"[10] (A.K. Monnappa). The current training is low-cost and on-the-job, making it more effective and efficient.

Participants were divided into small groups to discuss the issue of institutionalizing participatory methods in government. A summary of these "buzz" sessions follows in the form of answers to three questions:

(i) Which methods are most useful to governments?

As with all participatory methods, all methods were seen to be potentially valuable, with the choice varying according to objective rather than type of institution. There were some reservations over the ability or the capacity of the PRA team drawn from the government to use social mapping or wealth ranking, but it was pointed out that the departments were already using these methods (for example, in Gujarat). The one method strongly emphasized was the night halt, and its value lies in proving commitment and provoking attitude change. Night camps have been one of the methods used in West Bengal to identify the tenants during the early land-reforms movement in the state, which has been successful.

(ii) What are the pressure points that can be identified to encourage adoption?

The responses received were as varied as they could, and were something like the following:

- Exercises must be task-oriented – "fewer barriers remain in those fully involved" (Somesh Kumar).
- Ensure that participants attend the whole of the training course, because those who miss introductory sessions or turn up only for the debriefing often remain unconvinced.
- Identify departments that can work with people or are autonomous. Start cautiously.
- Approach training institutes, though training must remain low-cost and on-the-job, so as to relate immediately to work.
- Convince donors and bankers of the value of participatory methods.
- Develop personal rapport with the government officials (and vice versa for government with NGO officials).
- Encourage more flexible reporting procedures.
- Night halt is essential, with those engaged in the exercise not permitted to bring extra gears.
- The NGOs must be less hostile to the government

- Government could use NGOs and VOs to conduct monitoring and evaluation of the government projects.
- Conduct training for elected representatives.
- Offer more field exposure for civil servants (in Uttar Pradesh, the Chief Secretary had reportedly issued an instruction some time back that all IAS officers, with more than a certain length of service, spend one day a month staying overnight in a village).
- Facilitate government to government extension. The government staff, who are convinced about the utility of participatory methods, are the best teachers and convincers.

(iii) What are the constraints to adoption of participatory methods on a large scale?

The response received were :

- Current targeting and reporting procedures.
- Rigidity of working practices.
- Need supportive leadership. It is ESSENTIAL to convince the top person first, or else no progress would be possible.
- Current working practices are compartmentalized, and there is poor coordination, particularly horizontal co-ordination.
- Training is centralized; PRA is not on training curricula. The current emphasis in training activities at different levels is upon statistical approaches and training decisions are not made at district level.
- Political interference.
- Frequent transfers of trained personnel.
- The government has to establish new relationships with villagers, given that the past history of relations has been bad.

- Attitude of some NGOs, often hostile to government, is a big constraint. It may be noted that some NGOs can be just as bad as the government (for example, centrally placed with no internal participation).
- Attempts at meeting people's priorities through a top-down approach could create conflicts. For example, S. Devaraj recalled the case of a participatory method applied to watershed coming up with the need for 165 IRDP loans, which conflicted with an allocation of 100 IRDP loans for the whole block.

CONCLUSIONS

In sum, it seems that the task at hand in the realm of database creation, as in several other spheres, is arduous and difficult, but it has to be created through both conventional methods and PRA methods, and once so created it will be quite simple to update it particularly so, the portions emanating out of Participatory Rural Appraisal methods and use it as a solid basis for decision-making. Those who are oppressed by a sense of difficulty of this process should console themselves by the saying of the ancient Greeks. "It is not the easy thing, but it is the difficult thing that is beautiful. And there is no short-cut."

Notes

1. *The Gazette of India Extraordinary*, Part II, Section 1, dated 20 April, 1993.
2. Indications about these were provided by L.C. Jain in a personal communication to me vide his letter dated 26 April, 1993, bearing number IDS/284/105.
3. N.S. Jodha
4. The Report of the Committee of the Study Group on Information Gap, Planning Commission, New Delhi, 1989 had suggested some of the data needs in a different context.
5. See Robert Chambers: *Rural Appraisal: Rapid, Relaxed and Participatory* (Sussex: I.D.S., Discussion Paper), No. 311, October 1992 for a discussion of the evolution of this concept. And see Neela Mukherjee: *Participatory Rural Appraisal: Concept and Applications*, Concept Publishing

Company, New Delhi, 1993 for application of these methods in the Indian context.

6. See Jennifer, A. McCracken, Jules N. Pretty and Gordon Conway: *An Introduction to Rapid Rural Appraisal for Agricultural Development*, International Institute for Environment and Development, London 1988.
7. Wild Life Institute : *PRA and Eco-Development Course Handbook*, Wild Life Institute, Dehradun 1992.
8. Somesh Kumar: "Anantapur Experiment in PRA Training", *PRA Notes No. 13*, pp. 112-117.
9. Wild Life Institute: *Loc. cit.*
10. *Ibid.*

6

Applications in Africa

Rapid Rural Appraisal for Local Level Planning Wollo Province (Ethiopia)

– IRENE GUIJT and IAN SCOONES

INTRODUCTION

The Upper Mile and Cheleka Catchment – Disaster Prevention Programme is a collaborative effort between the Ethiopian Red Cross Society and the Ministries of Agriculture and Health. The UMCC-DPP is located in Wollo Province in the Ethiopian highlands, and was created to develop disaster response strategies with a broader scope than standard Red Cross activities. The village level work is carried out in Kalu and Ambassel Awrajas (districts) by Development Agents (DAs) with the assistance of sub-district (woreda) and district level experts.

OBJECTIVES AND ACTIVITIES

The overall objectives as set by the participants were:

- to know how to use RRA tools for systematic data collection and village development planning;
- to be able to act as trainers of RRA; and
- to involve the community in planning and implementation in Ancharo and Amemo Project Areas (PAs).

In order to achieve these objectives, the following activities were formulated:

- to investigate the two PAs using the range of RRA tools;
- to discuss development options, possible solutions and identify projects and production niches in the two PAs;

- to investigate administrative and management problems in planning and implementation of daily work;
- to devise work plans that incorporate RRA activities; and
- to assess issues of resource allocation, natural resource management, decentralization and land ownership under the New Economic Policy of the Ethiopian government.

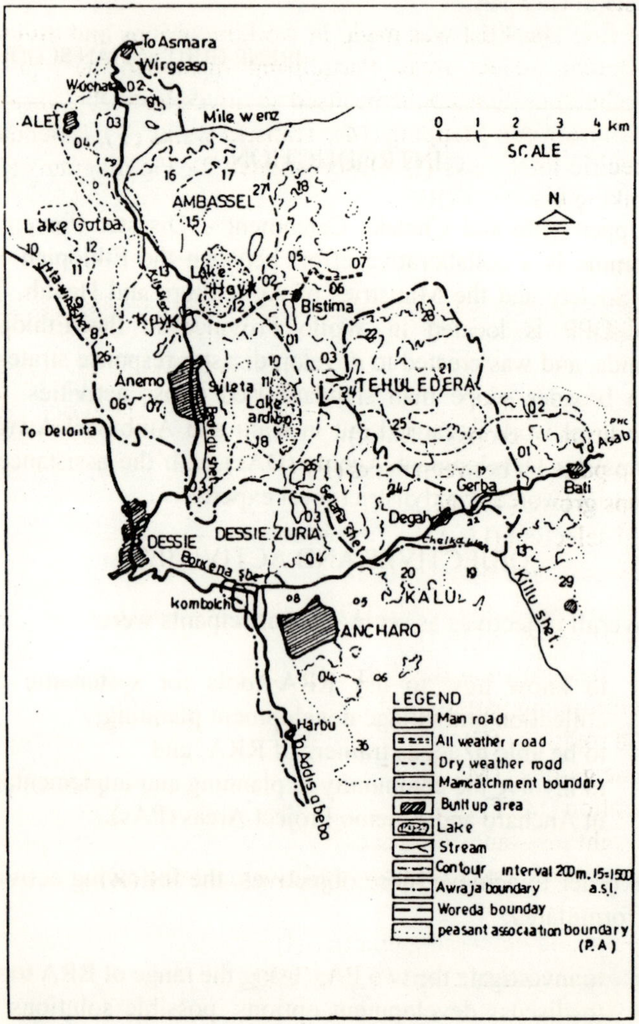

Fig. 6.1 : Location of Anchard and Amemo Peasant Associations

PREPARATION FOR THE FIELDWORK

In preparation of the first period of fieldwork, a common checklist was made by both the Amemo and the Ancharo groups. Due to the general objectives of the RRA exercise, the first checklist includes a wide range of topics. After this, continual refining of problems and opportunities led to formation of new checklists in each PA.

The first checklist was made in working groups and divided into different subject areas. Participants discussed the type of RRA techniques that could be used to investigate the various issues. These were: Mapping (M), Transect walks (T), Calendars (C), Specific interviews (I), Observations (O), Pie diagrams (P), and Ranking exercises (R).

Checklist-1

Agriculture

Rainfall patterns (C)
Condition of crops (T.M.O.)
Crop patterns between years (P)
Crops grown (T.C.M.)
Seed selection (I.R.)
Crop pests and diseases (C)
Local ways to control crop pests and diseases (I)
Major legume crops (R)
Varieties grown in Belg season (C, R)
Intercropping patterns (M,C)
Crop rotations (C)
Home gardens (M)
Irrigation (M, T)
Drought resistance of crops (R)
Selection of grain crops for quality or quantity (R)
Fertilizer use (I)
Storage and processing practice (I)
Cash versus other crops (T, M, C, R)

Health and Nutrition

Nutrition patterns (C, P)
Sources of food in times of scarcity (P)
Nutrition related diseases (C)
Nutritional value of different crops (R)
Health issues (C, O, I)
Child health (C, O, I)
Family planning (I)

Livestock

Grazing condition (T, M, C)
Livestock fodder sources (T, M, P, C)
Fodder quality of crops (R)
Production of livestock (C, I)

Natural Resources

Land ownership (T, M)
Competition between farm, grazing and forest land (M, T, P)
Water supplies for people, animals and agriculture (M, T)
Fuel sources (M, T, P)
Tree planting (M, T, R)

Soil and Water Conservation

Erosion problems (T, M)
Historical changes (I)
SWC measures (T, M, R)
Soil fertility (M, T)
Soil types (M, T)

Marketing

Market (M)
Marketing (C)
Transport (M, R)
Prices (C)

Labour

Men and women (C)

Others

Income generation activities (P, R)
Daily work of women (P)
Migration of peasants (C)

The report on Ancharo PA provides an analysis of the important issues in agriculture, livestock, natural resources, health, nutrition and income generation. The report attempts to highlight the key problems faced by the people of Ancharo and the local opportunities for development. The report concludes with a series of Best Bets — outlined plans for facing the problems of the area. The report has been written jointly by all the participants in the RRA exercise. They were:

Participants

Balcha Alemu	Development agent
Tegenen Awegechu	ERCS, Dessie
Amadeselassie Fanta	Animal husbandry expert
Elizabeth Mekonnen	Home economics expert
Endalemaw Belay	Development agent
Mesfin Kiflu	Development agent
Wondmagagen Kassa	DA supervisor
Seid Mohammed Ali	Peasant Association leader
Alebachew Begashaw	Plant protection expert
Alemayehu Geberehiwot	Development agent
Marlies Rothweiler – Spohn	Agronomists, UMCC-DPP
Mayumi Katsube	Monitoring, UMCC-DPP
Ian Ssoones	Trainer, IIED

FIELDWORK PROGRAMME

During the 5 days of field investigations, a total of 121 people were interviewed, of which 86 per cent were men. Interviews were carried out mostly in the two main village cities, but also among people resident in Ancharo town and those living in scattered settlements.

Activity/Topic	People Interviewed
Day 1	
Transect 1	2 men
Transect 2	4 men
Map	5 men
Day 2	
Natural resources	2 men
Livestock	13 men
Nutrition and health	3 men; 7 women
Crops, rainfall	5 men
Day 3	
Irrigation	3 men
Home gardens	3 men
Crop varieties	2 men
Livestock ownership	3 men; 2 women
Income sources	2 men; 2 women
Soil and water conservation	5 men
Livestock production	5 men
Economic history	2 men
Nutrition and health	2 men; 3 women
Day 4	
Tree planting	2 men
Gully control	7 men
Income sources	6 men; 1 woman
Home gardens	3 men
Irrigation	2 men
Livestock fodder	3 men
Agriculture/fertilizer use	8 men
Day 5	
Income sources/home gardens	7 men; 1 woman
Beekeeping	1 woman
New crops, fertilizer, pests	5 men

Checklist-2

Following the second day of fieldwork, a revised checklist was drawn up. This focused on the questions for the second phase of the field investigations.

Background

- Economic history of Ancharo
- Changes in natural resource-base over time

Health, Nutrition, Income

- Are there really no major disease problems? Actual situation from local perceptions.
- Areas of production potential in PA for fruit and vegetables.
- Comparison of income sources in village 1, 2 and Ancharo town.
- Why is the health post not functioning?
- Is labour or water source the major constraint for home garden development?
- Labour calendars for men and women.
- Food scarcity patterns between years.
- Cotton supply for weavers: constraints and options for improving trading links.

Natural Resources

- How and when the closures used? Cut and carry systems for grass; use of products? Are products equitably distributed?
- Soil and water conservation measures: costs and benefits from the peasants' perceptive.
- Planting of trees at homes: do people have the confidence to start?

Livestock

- Hay purchase options for livestock owners.
- Hiring of grazing land.
- Goat and sheep mortality: is it really as high as 50 per cent?
- Lack of oxen: proportions of households with 0, 1, 2, > 2?

- Fallow land use: options for planting legume trees and shrubs.

Agriculture

- Irrigation potentials and constraints.
- Changes over time of crop types and varieties.
- Preferences for different varieties.
- Reasons for fallow land: lack of oxen; ex-PC land; fertility declines.

Ancharo 01 Peasant Association is located around 8 km north-east of Combolcha. It borders Bosana 05 PA to the north, Beke 04 PA to the east, Kalida 02 PA to the south and Rufo 08 PA to the west.

The PA is divided into two agro-climatic zones. The moist weyna dega represents 75 per cent of the area and the dry weyna dega represents 25 per cent. The altitude ranges from 1800 m to 2300 m.

The crops grown in the area include sorghum, teff, legumes and oil seed crops. Sixty per cent of the area is used for farmland, only 13 per cent is for grazing and 21 per cent is used for forest land. The forest land includes the forest known as Abu Lea. The remaining land use includes 2 per cent for villages and 4 per cent that is unusable (see Figure 6.2).

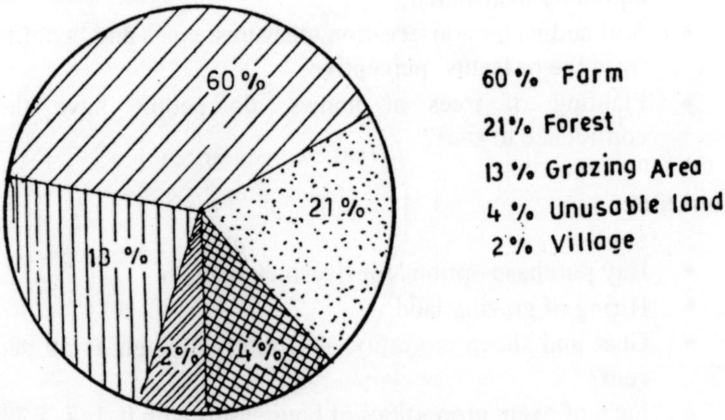

Fig. 6.2 : Land Use in Ancharo
Source : Data from D.A. Office & N Ancharo

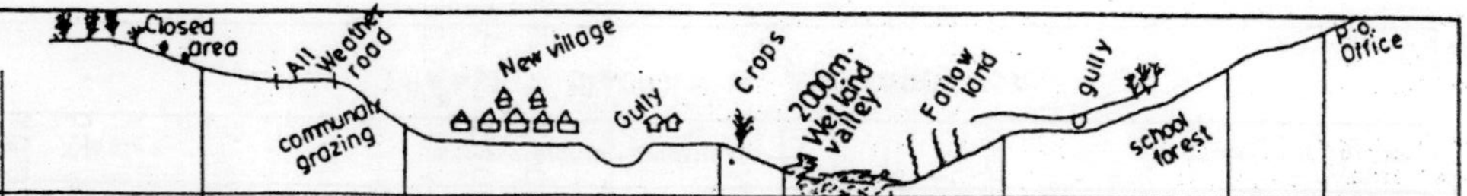

Soil	Sandy Rocky	Sandy Loam	Loamy Sand	G.L	Alluvial Soil	sandy Loam	Sandy	Rocky	
Tree	Trees + Jun P.P Olea Eucalypths						Eucalyptus of trees + Shurbs	Coffee chatt Gessho	
Land Ownership	State Forest Land	Communal land	Village land	Private land	Private land	Private land	School land	Private land	Town land
Crops			Sourgum Maize H bean	Sourgum Teef H-bean	Teef				
Crop Pests			Afids Stock borrer ball worm Striga hermotica	S.bor w s	Shoot fly				
Live stock		All Live stock Morning & Even-ing	Goat Sheep Chicken		Cattle	Cttle			
Grazing land		Communal Grazing Evening & Morning	Individual Grazing		Individual Grazing	Individual Grazing			
Erosion Problem	* *	*	* * * *		*	*	* * * *	* *	*

Fig. 6.3 : Transect diagram in Ancharo PA

Anchorrs
North East

Land use	Hill side Closur + Grazing	Arable land former Village	Grazing land Arable	Arable land	Village	Arable land	Grazing land
Vegetation Crops	Trees + shrubs	Crops, trees teff barley	grass land Fallow	Crops Cant. beans, peas, wheat, sorghum, maize, noog, mustard repeseed, sesame, grass, peas. etc.		Crops	grass land
Shrubs, trees Grasses	Juni perus olea Euphordia Euco-lyptus acacia	Eucalyptus Hyparrhenia	curissa cynodon	opuntia phorbia acacia cordia Hyparrhenia			Erded cynodon pennisetum
Soils	Stony	sandy loam	stony	loam		clay	clay
Treatment	Clousre	stone bunds (not maintained	s t one bunds				
Water		ground water flow	flow		spring		river
Live stock	small ruminants	small cattle	ruminants - - - - -			small cattle	ruminants - - - -
Problems	Erosion lack of soil cover	decreasing fertility	erosion over grazing	Decreasing striga	fertility lack of trees	root rot water bgging	live stock para site
Opportunities	Closure		srowse plants	irrigation		irrigation	irrigation

TRÂNSECT DIAGRAM IN ANCHARO P.A.

Fig. 6.4 : Transect Diagram in Ancharo P.A.

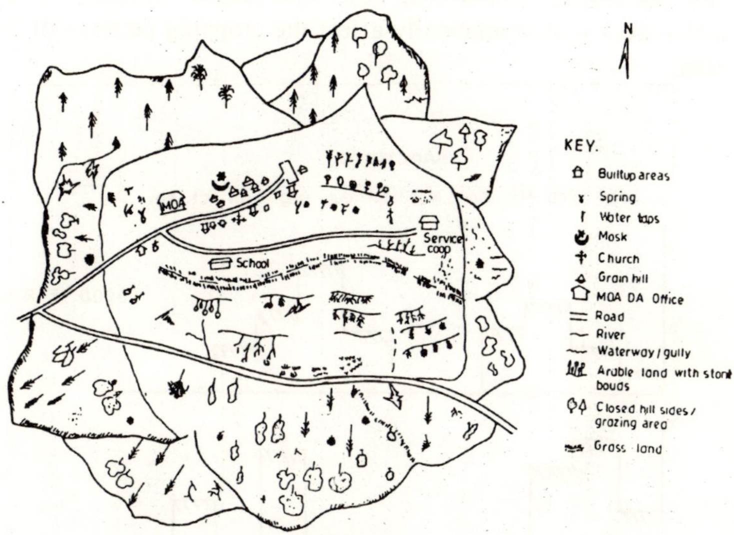

Fig. 6.5 : Map of Ancharo (01) PA

In the PA there are two planned villages established over the last 2-3 years; one is called Sida Ager and the other is called Gerbi. The total population of the PA is 558 households.

Transect 1 (see Figure 6.3 and 6.4): At the highest point in the eastern part of the PA, the Abu Lea state forest closure can be found. At the foot of the hill is the road to 04 PA and below this the viliage of Sida Ager. Near the village are found major gullies. Below the village is the marsh land and beyond this a mixture of fallow land and crops. Up the hill towards Ancharo town is found the school forest which is little used and beyond this the DA centre.

Further details of the area are found in the map of Ancharo PA (see Figure 6.5).

Rainfall Distribution

If the rainfall is normal, the Belg season will be from February to March and the Meher season will be during July and August (see Figure 6.6). However, rainfall distribution often varies. In an abnormal year (e.g. 1990), the belg season will give more rain and the meher season will have mid-season droughts. These differences will dramatically affect the cropping patterns of the area.

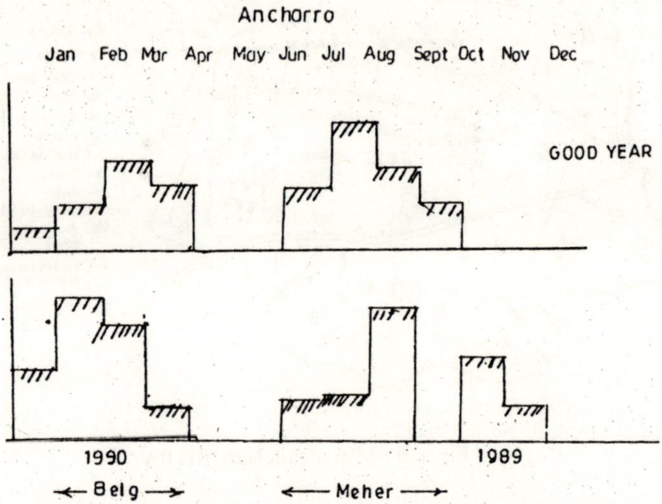

Fig. 6.6 : Rainfall pattern in Ancharo

Agricultural Production and Protection

Sorghum, teff, barley, wheat, legumes and oil crops grow in the area. These are affected by stalk borer, African bollworm and aphids. People have tried to control these using pesticides supplied by UMCC-DPP. The peasants around Ancharo use cow dung, some plant residues and a little chemical fertilizer (supplied by UMCC-DPP). But peasants cannot get fertilizer at the right time, as they do not have the money to buy it.

Livestock

In Ancharo there are cattle, goats, sheep and equines. But there is a serious shortage of grazing land, and livestock is affected by diseases and parasites. In order to overcome the fodder shortage the peasants feed the animals residues from teff, sorghum and legume.

Natural Resources

Eucalyptus, juniper, weira and acacia are planted in the area, especially on the closure sites. Due to the mountainous landscape there is serious erosion. To face the problem the people have planted trees and have dug terraces and bunds.

Nutrition, Health, Income

In Ancharo, nutrition is dependent on the crops grown locally. There are no vegetables, so the peasants cannot get a balanced diet. In the area there is influenza and diarrhoea, there is a clinic that attempts to solve these problems.

The peasants try to get additional income from weaving, poultry keeping, animal sales, beekeeping and wage labour.

HISTORY OF ANCHARO

In the past, the farmers depended on crop production and there were sufficient oxen for ploughing. The market price for livestock was very low with one cow fetching only 1-20 birr. In the past, there was more or less sufficient land for all the farmers. Some farmers had more land (4 ha or more) and often had the best land in the valley. In previous times the richer ones used to help the poor in difficult.

The soils have always been poor on the hillsides, but in the past there was enough land. The types of crops grown have remained the same, although more are grown for cash now. As it is no longer possible to survive only by farming, more people are becoming weavers.

Before the revolution the land was administered by the imperial government and the lord's representatives came to collect taxes in kind, e.g. honey, grains, livestock products and labour. However, there was no big landowner in the area.

Ancharo used to be an important market town and trading point. It was the end point of the coffee trade route from Jimma. This trade was controlled by merchants in Ancharo, but stopped after the revolution. The main market has transferred to Combolcha which is accessible for trucks. Most merchants left for other towns.

In the past, the natural resources of the area were plentiful. There were large natural forests on the hills. These were rich in wildlife (lions, gureza). There were also large areas of grassland between the fields and there was no fodder shortage.

AGRICULTURAL PRODUCTION

Farmers have very limited cropping land in Ancharo. The average holding is estimated to be about 1 ha, but many have less. Cropping land is often distributed in different areas with some in the highland and some in the lowland. Land is of very different agricultural quality, with the low lying wetland having high irrigation potential and rich soils, while the highland soils are poor and barren. Home garden areas in the new village sites are limited and are mostly without water supply. Of all areas, the wetland area that dissects the PA represents the major 'production niche' for intensification of agriculture (see below). However, opportunities do exist for agricultural improvement in other areas also.

Cropping Patterns (see Figure 6.7)

The major crops in order of production output and farmers' priority are shown below :

1. Sorghum
2. Teff
3. Legumes
4. Barley/Wheat/Adja

The combination of crops in any one year depends on the rainfall conditions. When rainfall is low or irregular, the cropping pattern will change. For example, more teff will be planted when there is insufficient rainfall at the time appropriate for sorghum planting (as in 1990). Shifts in proportions of crops are shown in Figure 6.8 according to different rainfall conditions.

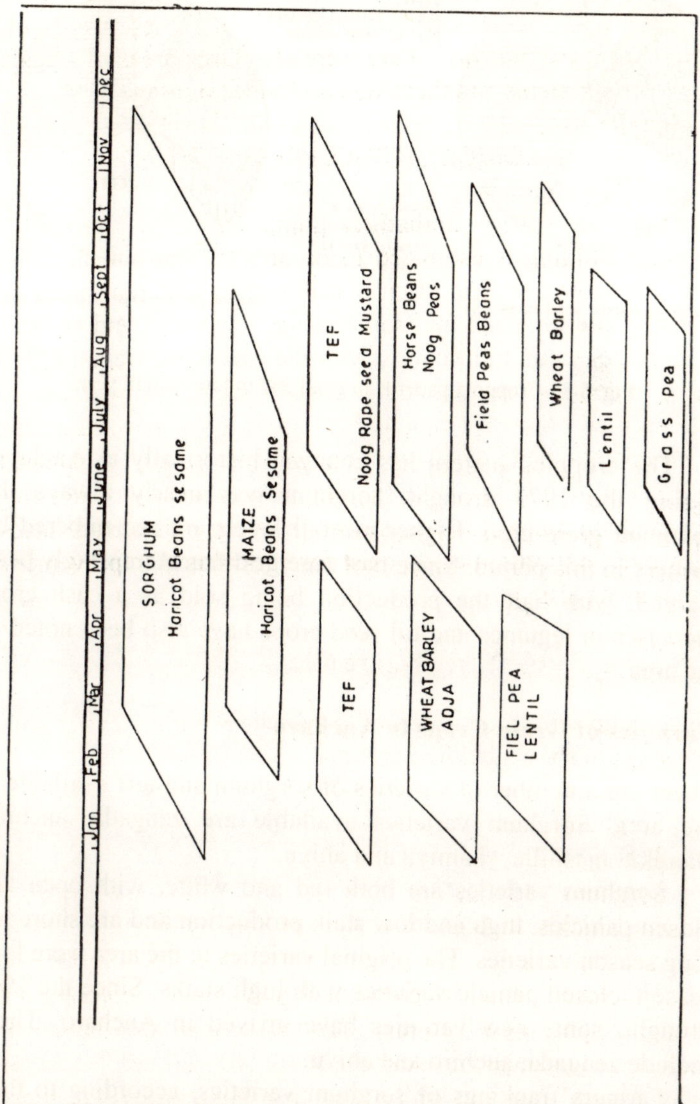

Fig. 6.7 : Seasonal calendar of crops

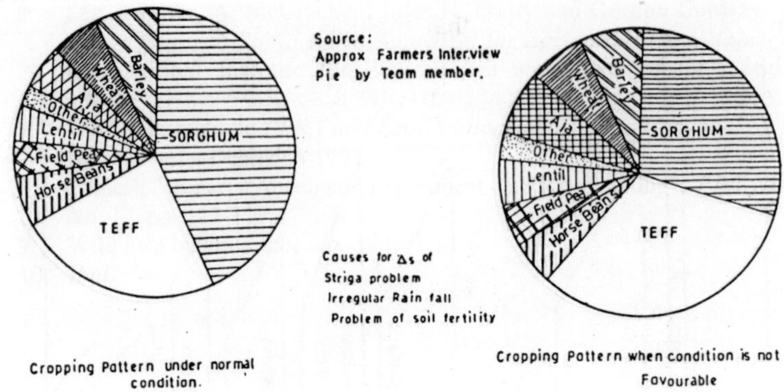

Fig. 6.8 : Cropping patterns in good and in low rainfall years

The cropping pattern has changed historically in Ancharo. Before the 1973 drought, sorghum was nearly always the dominant grain crop. Higher rainfall levels are remembered by farmers in this period. Since that time, teff has increasingly been planted, with half the production being sold as a cash crop. Increases in legumes and oil seed crops have also been noted in the area.

Varieties of Grain Crops in Ancharo

There are a number of varieties of sorghum and teff available in the area. Sorghum varieties available are zengada, anchiro, cherekit, mashilla, chamiyu and ahiyu.

Sorghum varieties are both red and white, with open and closed panicles, high and low stalk production and are short and long season varieties. The original varieties in the area were long season, closed panicle varieties with high stalks. Since the 1985 drought, some new varieties have arrived in Ancharo. These include zengada, anchiro and ahiyu.

Farmers' rankings of sorghum varieties, according to their own criteria, are shown below. The farmers ranked zengada or nech mashilla first in an overall assessment, but as the tables show, the qualities of different varieties are not totally consistent in the perceptions of the different farmers interviewed. An 'ideal' variety for the area might combine the bird-resistant qualities of anchiro and the high production rates of zengada or nech mashilla. Qualities that include early maturation are also favoured under conditions of unreliable rainfall experienced in recent years. Short season varieties also allow early Belg season crop planting.

Teff Varieties

bungen nech
bungen kay
inat nech
inat kay

Red and white varieties of local teff are known in the area. Nech teff is favoured for low lying areas, while kay teff is planted in the highland area. Bungen teff varieties are suitable in all areas. Some new varieties have been introduced. The farmers ranked three varieties of teff found in the area. Overall, they preferred nech teff for its high market value and good taste for injera (a local food).

Ranking of Sorghum Varieties (1)

Criteria	Charakit	Aengada	Ahayo	Anchiro	Nechmash
High production	4	2	3	5	1
Pest resistant	3	2	3	1	3
Drought resistant	1	2	3	3	3
Early maturing	32	4	5	1	
Taste	4	2	3	3	1
Use as forage	4	2	3	4	1
Use in housing	5	2	3	4	1

Conclusion : nech mashilla is first.

Ranking of Sorghum Varieties (2)

Criteria	Zengada	Anchiro	Chevelit	Mashilla	Chamiyu	Ahiyu
Early variety	6	5	2	3	1	4
High production	1	3	4	5	6	2
High market price	2	4	6	1	3	5
Drought resistant	2	1	3	4	5	6
Pest resistant	3	1	2	5	6	4
Resistance to disease	1	2	3	6	5	4
Amount sown	1	2	5	4	6	3
Overall preference	1	1	5	3	4	6

Ranking of Teff Varieties

Criteria	Nech	Bungen	Kay
High production	2	3	1
High sale price	1	3	2
Early maturing	3	1	2
Taste	1	3	2
Drought resistant	2	1	2

Conclusion : Nech teff is the best one.

Major Crop Pests

Farmers identified the major pests and diseases that caused damage in the field and the store as:

Insect pests

Stalk borer
Bollworm
Aphids
Grasshopper
Shootfly
Weevils

Diseases

Rust
Powdery mildew
Smut
Root rot

Plant Parasites

Striga

Local control of pests and diseases is limited to crop rotation and weeding (for striga). Underground storage sites are chosen in order to limit weevil damage. Endod, rate (plant types) and berberi (pepper) are added to crops stored underground to reduce damage. Pesticides are applied by most farmers. These are supplied free of charge by MoA with UMCC-DPP project support.

The seasonal incidence of crop pests and diseases are shown in Figure 6.9 as per information provided by local farmers.

Crop Rotations and Intercropping

The farmers practise traditional crop rotation and intercropping (see Figure 6.10). This varies according to climatic conditions. An example of crop rotation practised:

Year 1 – Sorghum
Year 2 – Teff
Year 3 – Sorghum

Rotations make limited use of the Belg season rain. Flexible planting with a variety of crops does not appear to be widely practised. Examples of intercropping practised are: sorghum with haricot bean, sesame seed and maize teff with nuch oil seed.

Options for increasing the range of crops within crop rotations and intercropping mixtures were discussed. However, farmers in the areas have little experience with the whole range of potential cash crops. Exposure through demonstration plots on farmers' fields could be helpful in this.

Soil Fertility

The types of soil in Ancharo are clay, sandy clay and clay loam. Much of the land on the hill slopes is of poor quality (see transect diagram). It is eroded, rocky, thin and of low fertility. Consequently, the farmers apply natural fertilizers (manure) and practise crop rotation in order to improve and/or maintain the soil fertility. While the farmers know the benefits of crop rotation and intercropping (see above), they do not know the most appropriate ways. Improved methods should be explored with the farmers.

Chemical fertilizers (Di-Ammonium Phosphate and Urea) have been supplied free by the project in the past. The farmers experimented with fertilizers for three years and had noted their beneficial effects on crop production in most field sites. However, they cannot afford them, even on long term credit arrangement with the Service Cooperative. This appeared to be the opinion of all farmers interviewed. For this reason, alternative methods of fertility management must be sought and appropriate crop varieties that require less fertilizer input must be introduced.

Home Gardens

In Ancharo, home garden activity is only carried out during the rainy season due to the shortage of water in the area. Villagers plant extra sorghum and a few peppers in their gardens. There are limited opportunities for vegetable production.

However, one farmer has developed his garden extensively in the Sida Ager villagisation area. His name is Abdi Said and he is able to make use of water running from a spring above his house. He grows a range of different vegetables including pepper, sugarcane, lettuce, onion, garlic and cabbage.

The team investigated with another group of farmers their preferences for different types of vegetables (see below). The farmers ranked a range of vegetables according to criteria of cash sale, importance for food preparation, early ripening, consumption/taste, low bird attach and drought resistance. The farmers ranked the pepper highest for its importance in food preparation and its good taste. There is a high demand for home garden vegetable production in both villages in Ancharo, but without effective water supplies it will be impossible.

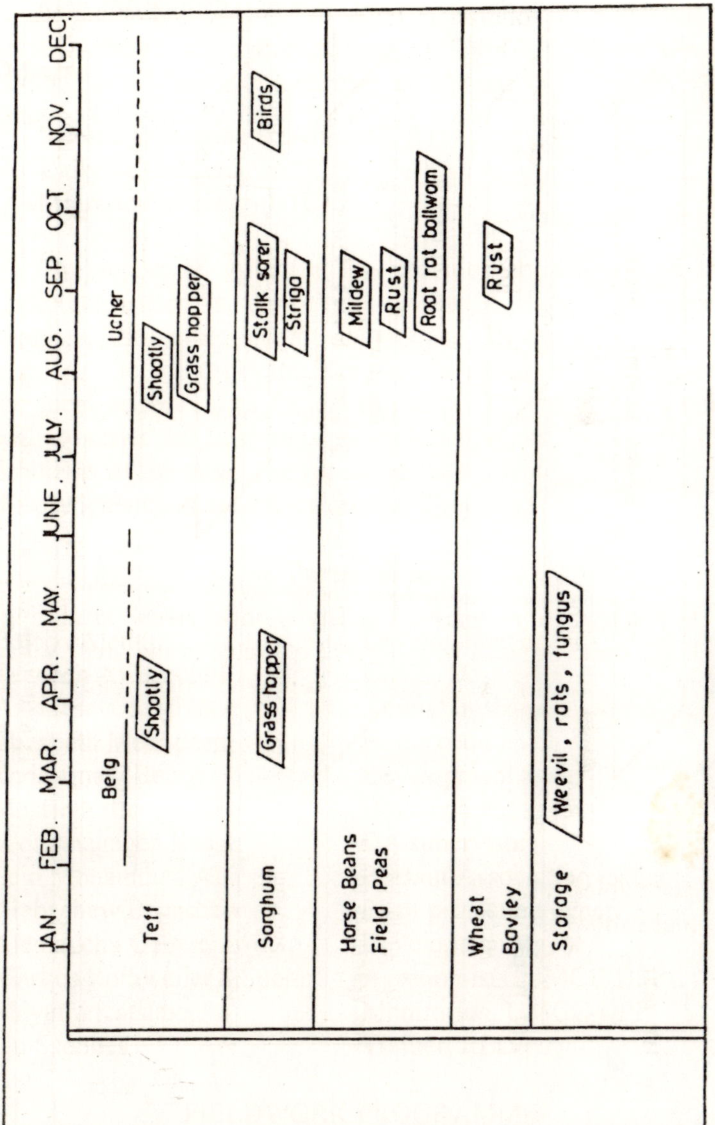

Fig. 6.9 : Seasonal calendar of pests and diseases

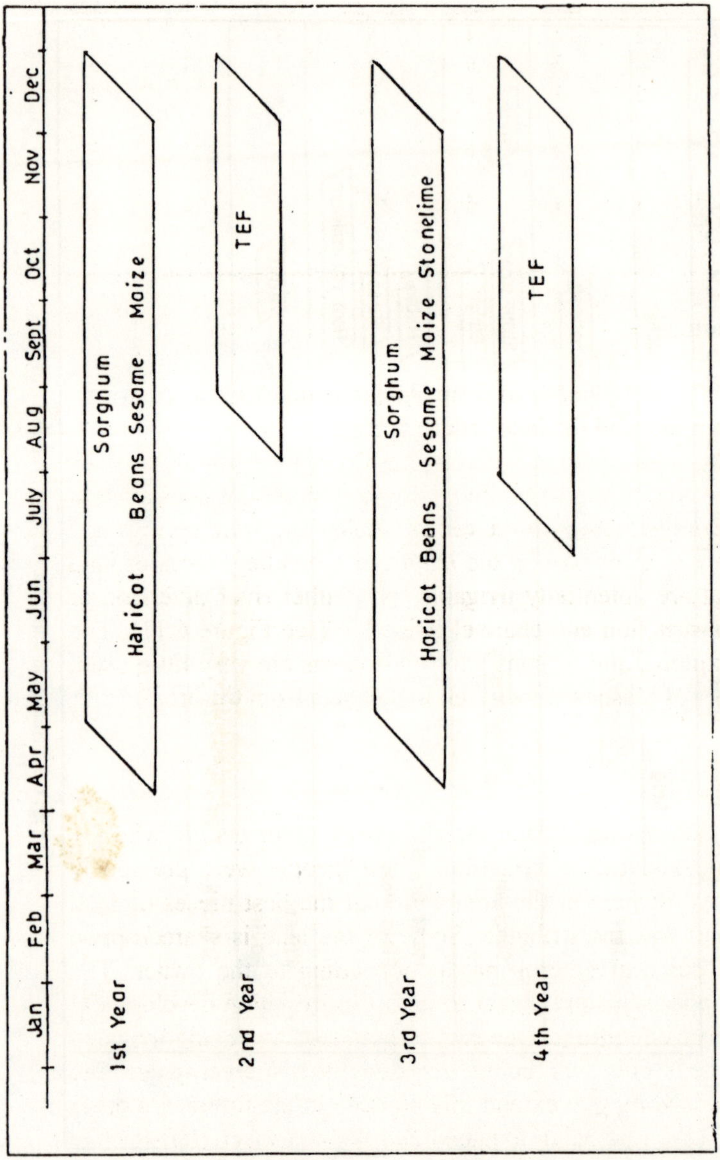

Fig. 6.10 : Crop rotation in Ancharo (4 years)
Source : From Approx Farmers' Interview

Ranking of Vegetables

	Onion	Garlic	Tomato	Pumpkin	Pepper	Cabbage	Potato
Cash sale	2	2	4	5	3	5	1
Food prep.	2	2	6	5	1	4	3
Early ripen.	3	3	5	6	2	1	4
Amount consum.	2	2	6	4	1	5	3
Low bird attach.	1	1	5	3	4	2	1
Resists drought	1	1	3	3	3	3	2

Irrigation

Irrigation is not widely used in Ancharo due to two reasons : water shortage and the land tenure system.

In Ancharo, there is no river that flows throughout the year. Spring sources are also limited. However, potential does exist in the waterlogged areas in the central valley and from springs and temporary streams. Along the length of the valley, areas of land exist that are potentially irrigable with either river diversion or pond construction and channel irrigation (see Figure 6.11). The group explored the reasons why these areas are very little used. A number of reasons were given by farmers from the areas.

Land Tenure System

The irrigable plots of land are owned by older people who are reluctant to invest in irrigation. These people were previously larger land owners in the area and kept the best pieces of land when land was redistributed. Some of the land is sharecropped with 50 per cent of crop production going to the owner. The sharecropper is also reluctant to invest in irrigation development under these conditions. One plot of land that was being irrigated was visited. This was being irrigated by a sharecropper. The farmer was hoping to extend this practice in the future. On other plots no land was being irrigated and the areas were left for hay production.

Ex-Producers' Cooperative (PC) Land

An area near Gerbi village, that is potentially irrigable, was not fully utilized this year. Ex-PC members indicated their hope to develop the land for vegetable and sugarcane (see Best Bets).

PA Committee Land

A portion of irrigable land is held by the PA. This is only used for hay production.

The potentials for irrigation were explored with the assistance of a MoA zonal office irrigation engineer (see Best Bets).

Problems and opportunities

The problems identified in the agriculture sector in Ancharo are summarised as follows :

- irregular rainfall,
- shortage of arable land,
- pest and diseases,
- low soil fertility, and
- lack of experience in cash crop production.

A number of recommendations can be made to help solve these problems :

- introduction of new crop varieties that can cope with irregular rainfall and require low fertilizer inputs,
- promotion of Belg season planting,
- practice of improved crop rotation and intercropping,
- timely control of pests,
- use of natural and chemical fertilizers (with appropriate financing mechanisms),
- application of soil conservation measures (see section of natural resources),
- investigation of the possibility to expand irrigation, and
- encouragement of horticultural production.

LIVESTOCK RESOURCES IN ANCHARO

The majority of people in Ancharo are primarily engaged in agricultural activities, growing crops such as sorghum, teff, barley and legumes. Due to the restricted area of grazing land, people rear few animals.

Cattle are the dominant types of domestic animals in the area. Oxen are important for ploughing and cows provide milk. Donkeys are used for transport. In the area, the dominant disease affecting livestock is black lag. Many livestock are also affected by internal and external parasites. The mortality rate of sheep and goats born in the area is an average of 25 per cent, although it may reach 50 per cent.

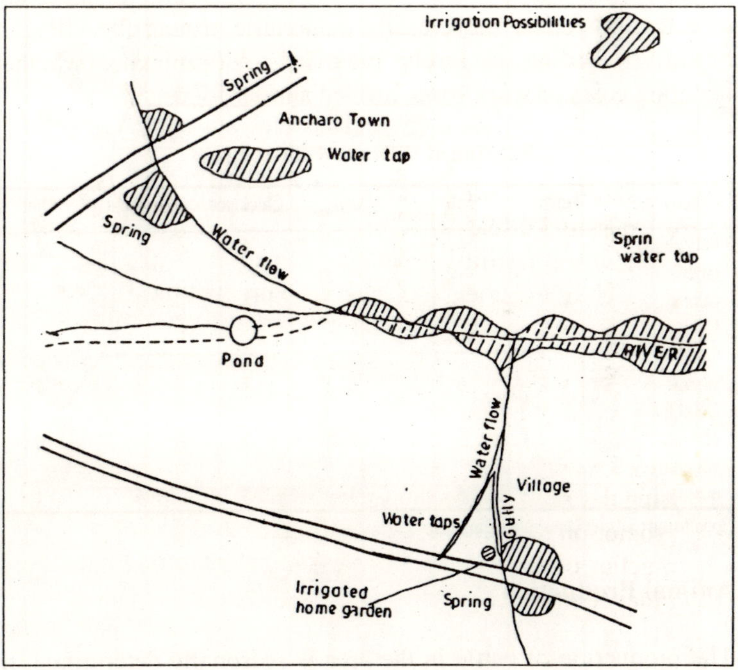

Fig. 6.11 : Possible irrigation sites in Ancharo

Fodder Situation

People informed us that there is a major shortage of animal forage. In the event of drought, cattle can feed on tree leaves (e.g. wanza, weira). Normally, cattle are fed on crop residues from teff, pea, horse bean, chick pea, sorghum and, in a small quantity, hay. A comparative ranking of fodder types was made (see below). The peasants thought that teff resudues were the best. In addition to crop residues, the peasants use different types of weeds as animal forage. The main one is the local oats variety called asendabo, clover (wajma), weshamelas and chewchewe.

Cattle are not allowed to migrate to other areas, even during times of drought. The people from neighbouring PAs, where there is more grazing land, do not allow movement of animals. Some farmers rent their fallow land to people with livestock for grazing. Others who have fields in the wetland valley can cut hay which can be sold to those with many cattle. Goats and sheep are able to find fodder more easily than cattle around the villages. Selective feeding is rarely practised. All animals, whether lactating cows or work oxen, are fed similar food.

Ranking of Different Fodder Types

Criteria	Teff	Pea	Bean	Chick pea	Sorghum	Hay
Palatability	1	6	5	4	3	2
High calorie Content	1	6	4	5	3	2
Good for storage	1	6	5	4	3	2
Good for equines	-	3	1	2	-	4
Fattening quality	2	5	4	3	6	1

Conclusion : teff residues ranked highest.

Animal Production

The production of cattle in the area is seasonally determined. In the wet season when green grass is available, they obtain 1 litre of cow milk. In the dry season, the yield available for human consumption may be only half a litre. Goats usually kid twice a year, but mortality may be high. From the local hens the peasants obtain 140-200 eggs per year.

People have tried improved poultry breeds, but they have had many problems with fatal diseases. They also require more food than the local breeds. The peasants indicated that they were ready to try again, if good advice was given.

Improved cattle breeds are not considered an opportunity locally due to the fodder shortage. People commented that improved breeds were not very suitable under local conditions.

Livestock Income

Peasants use livestock as a means of raising cash income. This varies seasonally (see Figure 6.12). In December and January, animals are sold in order to pay government taxes and marriage payments. Between April and June, sheep and goats are sold in order to get supplementary food supplies or to purchase clothes.

Prices of livestock vary according to supply, physical health and condition of the animal and the type of animal. The prices also vary seasonally. Price ranges are the following:

Sheep	35-95	birr
Goat	25-100	birr
Ox	400-900	birr
Cow	250-500	birr
Donkey	60-180	birr

Oxen Shortages

Although peasants depend on crop planting for the majority of their income (see Figure 6.14), many of them do not have sufficient oxen to plough the land (see Figure 6.13). Thirty nine per cent of peasants have no oxen and a further 34 per cent have only one. Those with few oxen can borrow from friends, but their crop yields are lower according to the group interviewed.

With low crop yields and little chance of earning income, peasants find it difficult to purchase more animals. The numbers have grown slowly since the last drought (1984-85), when many died. The lack of grazing land and fodder supplies make the situation very difficult.

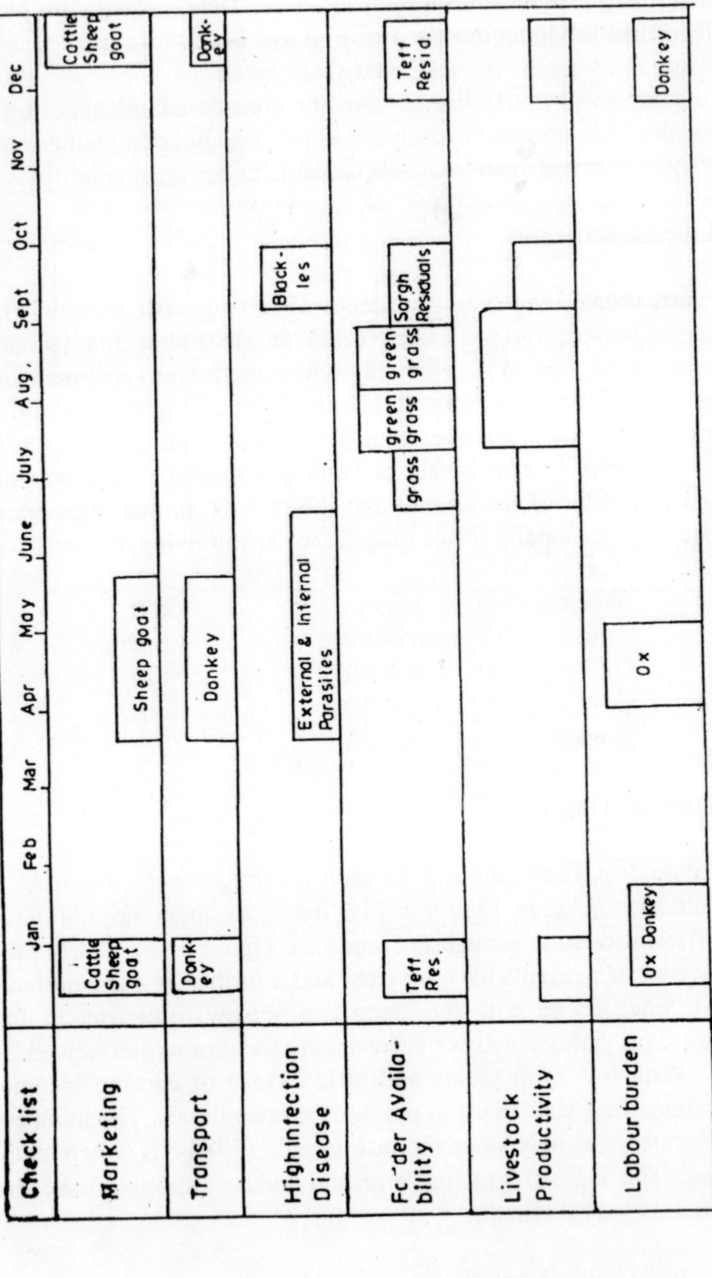

Fig. 6.12 : Seasonal calendar of livestock

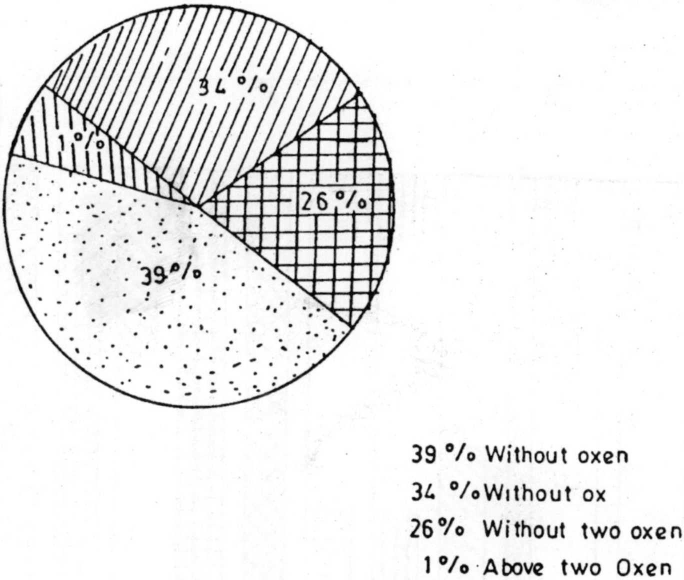

Fig. 6.13 : Percentage of people owning oxen

Beekeeping

Some peasants keep bees near their homes in traditional hives. These provide honey for selling or home use (see Figure 6.14). The bee keepers have problems as the bees find it difficult to find food in the new villagisation sites. Many bees leave the hive to seek food in the forest land. A further problem is the effect of pesticide applications to the cropping land and the areas near the villages, which has killed many bees in the area.

Problems and Opportunities

To improve animal disease problems, the following steps must be taken: Supply of veterinary medicines and improved sanitation of the houses where cattle live.

To solve the problems of fodder shortage, it is necessary to undertake: planting of legumes in fallow lands; demonstrate forage crops for intercropping; cut and carry systems from the forest lands and forage storage mechanisms – silage.

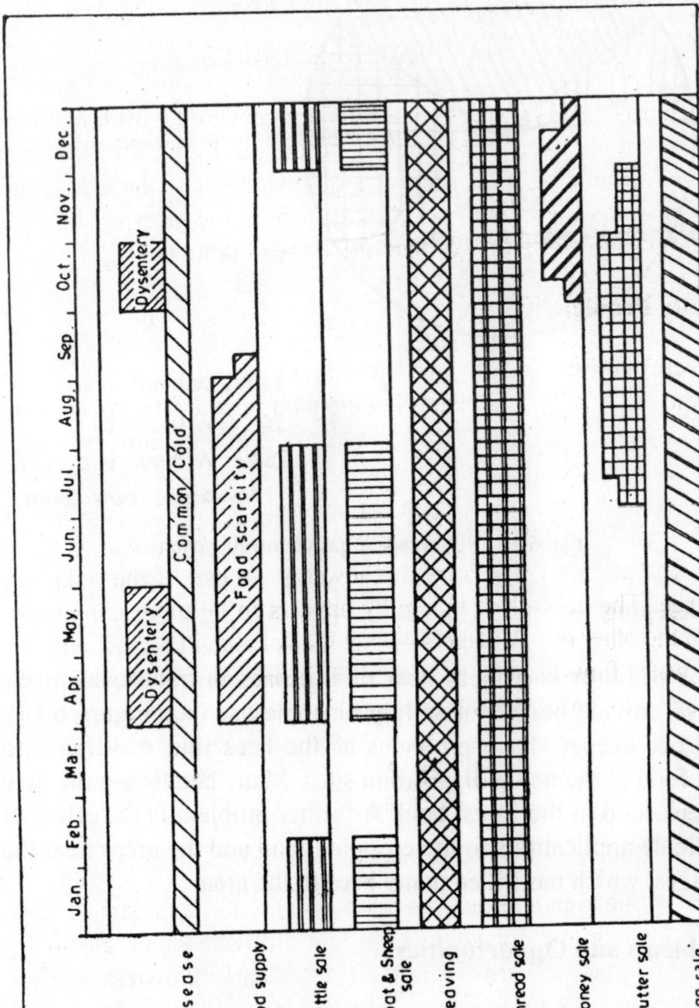

Fig. 6.14 : Seasonal Calendar of disease, Food Supply and Incomes Sources

To raise the low productivity:

- Improved breeds of hens,
- Distribution of improved bee-hives.

NATURAL RESOURCES

Ancharo 01 PA is largely in a hilly area covered with forest land. The famous Abu Lea natural forest is found in this area. However, there is a shortage of arable land due to the topography and soil erosion in the area. Consequently, the priority should be given to soil and water conservation (see Figure 6.5).

Gully Problem

Several gullies exist in the PA. The main gullies in the PA are found in the arable land and in one main village site. As is shown in the map, the first gully not only reduces the cultivation land but also affects the landholding of the private home gardens in the village. If sufficient materials and technical support are provided, the gully could be controlled.

The second gully is located towards the end of the Sida Ager village. The control of this gully appears to be more complicated than the other one. Villagers cannot block the gully as this will shift the water flow to another channel affecting another portion of the village. The only option is to move the village to a more appropriate site. The problem is so serious that the village will be completely flooded during heavy rains. The gully also threatens the road.

Erosion on Farmland

Most of the area is prone to erosion, so the farmers have to leave their land fallow for some time and cultivate other plots. The distribution of soil erosion in the PA is clearly shown on the map and transect diagrams.

Tree Plantation

The extent of tree planting on the hillside closures using FFW is very encouraging. Some farmers were concerned that they were not benefiting from the projects of hillside closure. The new policy on natural resources is still unclear about how this land will be used in the future. At this time it is the PA leaders with the DA who distribute the grass (cut and carry system) and the thinnings from tree cutting. Some farmers complained that this was not done fairly, while others were happy with the arrangement.

The farmers were not able to plant trees in their home gardens or farmlands because of the fear that they would be moved from their place at any time. Under the new economic policy this is prohibited and the farmer now has secure rights to land and the trees on it. Farmers told us that they were hopeful about planting trees in the future, but they would wait until next year when management support should be given to the farmers to encourage them to plant trees in the home gardens or fields.

Seedling Support

It was gathered from the discussions that seedlings provided by the MoA give results and show a high survival rate. Previously, a private farmer produced and sold seedlings to the villagers, but this practice has disappeared as the man, living in Ancharo town, is now old. Now that farmers are willing to plant trees in their home gardens and fields, it is recommended that seedlings should be distributed to private farmers. Interviews have shown that the demand is high.

The advantages and disadvantages of different tree species, found in the famed Abu Lea forest, are shown below. This is based on interviews with farmers in the area.

Tree type	Positive aspects	Negative aspects
Eucalyptus	House, furniture,	High transpiration
Globulus	Medicine, tool,	Dominates other plants
	fuel, fast growing	- same -
Eucalyptus	- same -	
Camaldulensis		Slow growing
Juniperus	House, furniture,	
Proceras	Fuel, high duration	Has spines
Local Acacia	Fuel, fence, feed	Slow growing
Olea	Tool, incense, feed	
Africana	Fuel, furniture	Take more space on the hill
Bushes & shrubs	Fuel, feed, fence, fast growing	

Soil Conservation Methods

Soil and water conservation is a priority in the area because of the severe soil erosion. The possible soil and water conservation methods were discussed with farmers who ranked them according to a range of criteria.

Problems

- Erosion of farm land,
- The widening of gullies and their competing with farmland,
- Land-use conflicts between farmland, grazing areas and forests, and
- Fuel wood problems.

Opportunities

Conservation with gabions has been started in one gully in Sida Ager village to protect the road. This should be continued to fill the gully. Villagers should also be encouraged to plant the sides of the gully with bamboo, sesbania, sisal, etc.

To alleviate the conflict between different uses of land, more effective management of the forest land should be encouraged to allow more products to be used.

The fuel wood problem can be tackled by encouraging planting of trees on private land or home gardens and farmland. Sufficient seedling support and extension are needed to enable the farmers to plant trees.

Ranking of Soil and Water Conservation Measures

Criteria	Tree planting	Stone bunds	Soil bunds	Check Dam	Tree Planting on farmland
Labour cost and time	4	2	3	1	5
Material cost	2	3	4	1	5
Controls erosion	4	1	2	5	3
Changes climate	1	-	-	-	2
Improves soil fertility on farmland	4	2	3	5	1

NUTRITION, HEALTH AND INCOME SOURCES

In order to improve the living standard of the community, it is important first to improve the health, the nutrition condition and to raise the awareness of the society. The nutrition and income sources of the peasants were observed using the methods and techniques of RRA.

The main crops of the area are already mentioned in the agriculture section. Their daily diet consists of an average of three meals a day which are prepared with sorghum injera, with different types of legumes (wott). Only in the rainy season do people get some vegetables. People's daily diet shows nutritional deficiencies in protein and vitamin-rich foods.

People regularly sell animal products in the market and they consume very little themselves. Eggs from poultry keeping area are sold in the market. Milk is mostly sold, but milk obtained during butter-making is consumed at home.

There is seasonal variation in the quantity of food eaten. In the dry season, there is a scarcity of food, so farmers try to have other activities, besides their farming, to raise some income. They sell animal products, sell livestock, participate in FFW or weaving activities (see Figure 6.14).

Labour patterns and income sources were investigated in detail in both villages (see Figures 6.15 and 6.16), with special discussions with the weavers. The greatest income source of these villages is farming, while other activities such as wage labour, livestock and weaving contribute lesser amounts. Opportunities for encouraging income generating sources were investigated with a ranking exercise of different income sources in Gerbi village.

Home Improvement

The sanitary condition of the houses and compounds was observed to be very poor. Women were interviewed, who suggested that they had a lot of work to do. Besides the daily activities of women which are preparing food, fetching water, collecting firewood, child care, they also participate in FFW activities and in the field (see Figure 6.15).

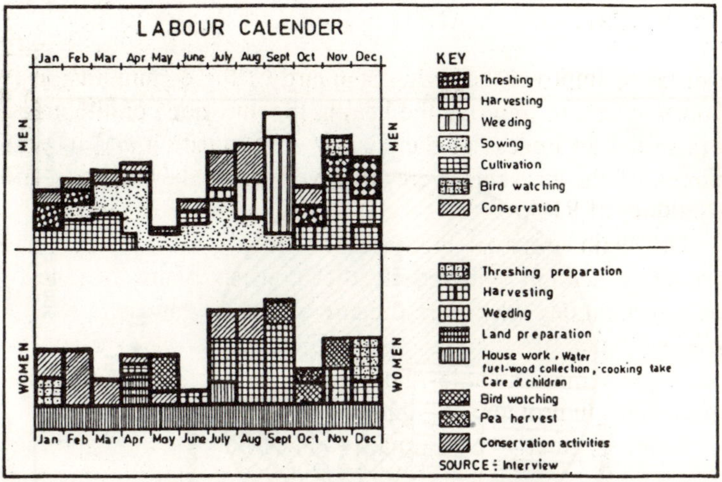

Fig. 6.15 : Labour calendar of men and women

Ranking of Income Earning Opportunities

Type of activity	Good	Bad
1. Weaving	Regular income	Scarcity of material
2. Animal sale	Continuous production if you have many cattle	If few animals, daily production is low
3. Beekeeping	No investment needed, You cannot own a bee they always move, Lack of feed around new villages, Seasonal production	Pesticides reduce bee population.
4. Poultry	Cost of feeding Supply of improved chicks Disease: all can die	
5. Thread making	or be eaten by birds and cats No demand for local thread Cannot produce more; time consuming, low returns	

Source : Six Farmers Group Discussion

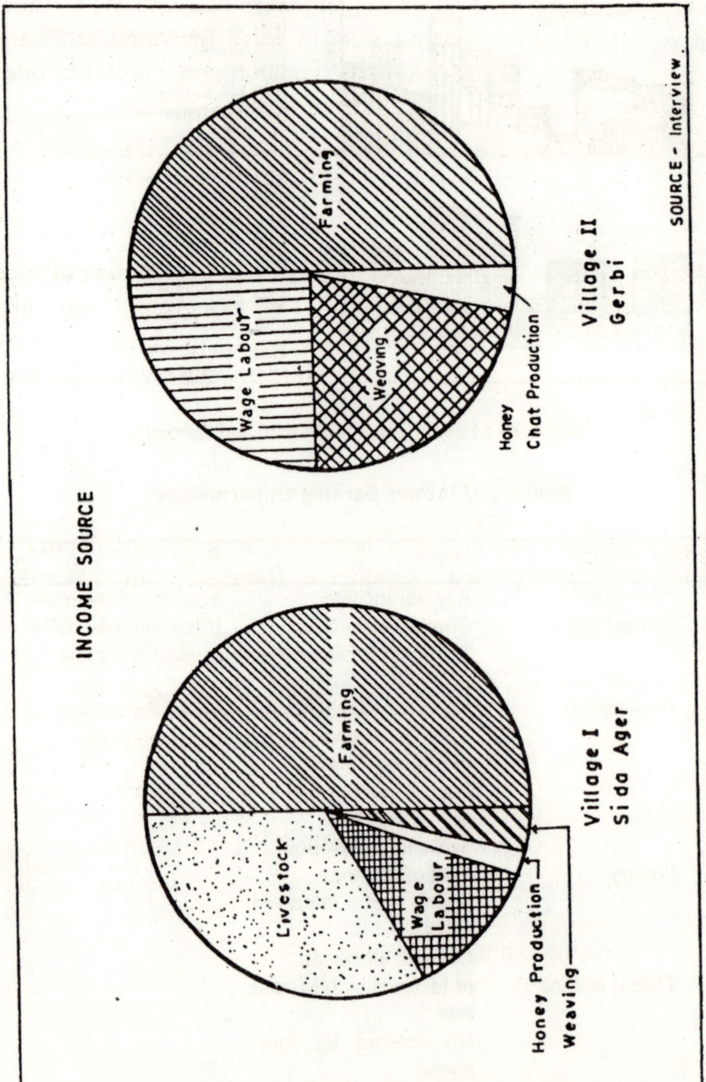

Fig. 6.16 : Income sources in Sida Ager and Gerbi

Improved houses in Sida Ager village were visited and four family heads were interviewed. Both men and women mentioned possible ways of improving the homes. They mentioned that improved stoves, shelves and chairs were of great use to them. The improved stoves enable them to solve fuelwood problems, as they consume 50 per cent less compared to the previous ones. They also enable them to keep the children from being burnt and allow them to maintain good sanitary conditions in the house.

Mother and Child Care

Mothers go to the Ancharo clinic for post- and pre-natal care. They breast-feed their children for 2-3 years and give supplementary food at the age of two. There are some symptoms of nutritional deficiency disease in children. They vaccinate their children, especially during the last two years.

Family Planning

Breast-feeding is used as the method of child spacing. Religious beliefs prohibit them from using other forms of family planning.

Health

There is a general lack of awareness of the health situation among the villagers. In general, both men and women do not think there is any serious health problem, except common cold. However, some women mentioned that they kept losing weight and they did not know the reason. Many children have swollen bellies, eye infections and running noses. Skin infection has been observed among both adults and children. Dysentery is apparent during April, May and September.

There is a health post in the PA. Due to drug shortages, the health post cannot serve the villagers properly. Therefore, the villagers go to Ancharo health station when they have problems. The community health attendant (CHA) said that he requested the health station staff to provide him with the essential drugs, but his request had not been fulfilled for months.

The CHA's activities in this PA needs to be activated and the higher level health institutions should give proper support. For the short term, the health centre could provide drugs to the health post. The long term solution for the constant supply of drugs has to be worked out by MoA.

PROBLEMS AND OPPORTUNITIES

During workshop analysis of the findings, lists of problems and opportunities relating to agriculture, livestock, natural resources, health, nutrition and income were drawn up by the RRA team.

Problems

Agriculture

Irregular rainfall
Shortages of arable land
Decreasing fertility
Waterlogging in lowland
Striga in sorghum
Lack of experience with cash crops including vegetables

Livestock

Forage shortage
Overgrazing
Lack of oxen
Low productivity of stock
Internal and external parasites; black leg

Natural Resources

Gully erosion between villages
Erosion on farmland
Uncertainty over ownership of trees
Competition between closed areas and farm land
Lack of fuel

Health, Nutrition, Income

Nutritional diseases
Poor sanitary condition of houses
Lack of awareness of health situation
Food scarcity – lack of Belg crops
No vegetables and fruits

Opportunities

Agriculture

Coping with uncertain rainfall patterns:

- crop varieties for variable rainfall,
- changes in cropping practices (e.g. planting early), and
- Belg season planting.

Intensification and diversification:

- irrigation in wetland areas – drainage and residual moisture use, pond construction and irrigation;
- encourage dry season irrigated vegetable plots;
- increase input use: high yielding varieties, fertilizers etc.,
- demonstration of cash crops,
- improve seed supply for improved varieties and new crops,
- crop rotation with different crops (nuch, oil seeds, haricot beans), and
- intercropping with legumes.

Fertility Management

- crop rotation
- seed dressing
- research on striga

Livestock

Fodder shortage:

- browse tree/shrub planting on degraded land
- forage seeds: trial demonstration plot, seed distribution to contact farmers
- fodder storage (e.g. silage production)
- cut and carry systems from fields

Livestock productivity:

- improved breeds, especially poultry
- tethered controlled grazing for animals

Natural Resources

Erosion control:

- check dam construction with gabion in village
- stone bunds on farmland
- tree planting on farmland

Fuel shortages:

- tree planting around homes (but beware of impact of eucalyptus on vegetable gardens)
- improved clay stoves

Ownership of natural resources:

- new economic policy and firm rights of ownership of trees on home sites and farmland,
- management agreements for closed areas to allow use and distribution of tree and grass products to Peasant Association.

Health, Nutrition and Income

Alternative income generating activities beyond those already observed –

including training and market identification,

Education and extension on health issues, and

Home gardens for fruit and vegetable production.

Checklist-3

Preliminary Best Bets

Following the development of the problems and opportunities list in the workshop, a further checklist was drawn up, outlining specific issues to be investigated for identifying the Best Bets for the development of Ancharo PA.

What new *income generating activities* are possible? What exist now? What potentials for extending?

Home garden development: Trade-offs between vegetables and trees (especially eucalyptus).

New varieties of crops: Farmers' attitudes and experience; what production niches are there within the existing system?

Fodder crops: What options for intercropping? What options for planting browse plants on fallow land?

Irrigation development: Pond construction, waterway development. Where in the PA? Who benefits? Constraints of land ownership? What crop and vegetable types (frost resistant)? Health implications of pond/irrigation development? What expert advice is needed?

Tree planting: Are people confident enough to invest in tree planting? Uncertainty over future status of closed area use and options for management plans?

Gully reclamation: What sites? Who benefits? Secondary impacts? Incentive requirements (e.g. Food for Work)?

Best Bets

A total of eleven best bets for the development of Ancharo PA were outlined in the final stage of the RRA process :

1. *What? Tree Planting*

Why? In order to meet the fuelwood demand and the material needs for construction.

Where? On and around the individual farmlands and homesteads.

How? 1. Extension advice to encourage individual initiative.

1. Seedling supply for the individual farmers by MoA.

When? From next Belg season onwards.
Who? DAs supported by other MoA staff.

Assumptions: This can only succeed if the land holdings are constant and the farmers are assured of their land and trees' ownership under the new economic policy.

2. *What? Gully Control*

Why? In the case of heavy rainfall, there is a major possibility that the gully will expand and destroy the nearby farmland.

Where? The gully down from Abu Lea forest (village Sida Ager).

How? Construction of gabion in the upper and lower part of the first gully (see Figure 6.4). Plantation of gully with bamboo, sisal etc.

Costs: Gabion – to be provided by the project.
Stones – to be collected locally.
Labour – to be provided by the villagers with FFW assistance.
Experts: Advice needed from awraja office.
When? Before the start of the next Belg season.

3. *What? Ensuring a supply of high quality thread to Ancharo weavers.*

Why? Weaving is an important source of income for both villages, but the profit margin on gabi making is low. With higher quality thread, the returns to weaving could be increased.

Where? In both villages of Ancharo, particularly Gerbi.

Who benefits? The weavers of the two villages (approximately 50 households).

How? Negotiation between an official of MoA zonal office with the Domestic Distribution Corporation to ensure a regular supply of higher quality thread to the Ancharo Service Cooperative. At present, the Ancharo weavers are not able to purchase such thread as they are not registered as weavers. Thread available in the open market is both expensive and of poor quality. The Service Cooperative (SC) bought thread in the past, but again it was of poor quality. SC officials estimate that the demand from Ancharo and surrounding PAs' would be significant.

Cost? None.

4. *What? To train a group of people in embroidery.*

Why? Increasing the added value of products made by Ancharo weavers, by encouraging embroidery.

How? Train a group in embroidery skills and investigate market outlets for embroidered products.

Who? Training to be carried out at Combolcha Rural Technology Centre.

Market investigations to be carried out by the Home Economics team.

Follow-up in Ancharo by the DA and Home economics expert.

Costs : Training course and materials – UMCC-DPP.

5. *What? Supply of small-scale spinning machines.*

Why? To improve the quality and reduce the cost of the thread available to Ancharo weavers; to increase the range of income earning opportunities in the villages.

Where? In Gerbi village.

How? (i) Investigate the purchase of appropriate spinning machines for small-scale production (locally manufactured or imported).

(ii) Train a group of women in their use.

Who? UMCC – to investigate supply of appropriate spinning machines in collaboration with Home Economics expert, Combolcha.

Combolcha Rural Technology Centre for training of women.

Regional and awraja Home Economics experts and in follow-up in Ancharo.

Costs: Purchase of spinning machines
Training of women
Time : 1 year

6. *What? Vegetable garden development around the drinking water supply of Gerbi village.*

Why? To encourage the production of vegetables in Ancharo to improve nutrition and income sources.

Where? Approximately 1-2 ha below the Gerbi village drinking water supply overflow.

How? Survey of area by irrigation expert.

Supply of vegetable seeds to farmers.

Extension support by DA.

Who benefits? The owners of the land around the drinking water supply (approximately 6-10 farmers).

Costs? Limited/ none

- DA for discussions with concerned farmers.
- Irrigation expert for assistance with design of irrigation system (canal and pond silting).
- Agronomist (awraja) for advice on appropriate (frost resistant) vegetables.

When? Immediately.

7. *What? Fodder species trial field*

Why? In Ancharo PA there is a severe shortage of forage and grazing land . Only 13 per cent of the land is for grazing.

Where? Site selected by DA in consultation with demonstration farmers. 0.25 ha of land will be required in total, possibly at several different sites.

Who benefits? Ultimately all livestock owners.

How? Choice of site.

Establishment of fodder species.

Training of farmers.

Who? DA and awraja livestock expert.

- Demonstration farm's costs.

- Costs of seed supply.

Time: Over 5 years

Constraints: The availability of land may be limited. For this reason the area for the trial field may be limited.

8. *What? Improved poultry breeds*

Why? In Ancharo the productivity of poultry is very low and income derived is small. Improving poultry production should result in nutritional and income benefits for the peasants.

Where? Ancharo PA – interested households.

How? Provision of 1-2 hens to a number of peasants.

- Extension support from DA and awraja expert on feeding, sanitary care etc.
- Veterinary support from MoA.

Costs: Costs of supply of hens.

Constraints : Self-financing of improved breed purchase is currently unlikely in part because of previous failures (due to disease, costs of feed, predation). There is a need to investigate credit mechanisms for the purchase of improved breeds.

9. *What? Supply of Kenya top-bar beehives*

Why? Beekeeping is one of the important income generating activities in Ancharo. With the traditional beehive there is a great difficulty in collecting the honey. Bees tend to abandon traditional beehives regularly.

How? Supply of beehives to selected farmers.

- Extensions support on use of new hive.
- Advice on provision of appropriate fodder around the home.

Who?

- UMCC-DPP/MoA for purchase and supply of appropriate hives.
- Awraja expert and DA for extension support.

Costs : Costs of hive supply (up to 50) – to be supplied/subsidized by UMCC-DPP. Farmers are currently not in a position to purchase improved hives outright. They need convincing of their worth. Options for local manufacture of improved hives could be investigated.

Constraints : Honey production is constrained currently by lack of food around the new villagisation sites. There is a need for careful management of appropriate sources of food to ensure reasonable returns. The impact of pesticide applications on bee populations needs to be investigated.

10. What? Changes in agricultural production system

1. Supply of new varieties of seeds.
2. Application of new techniques of intercropping and crop rotation.
3. Preparation of pesticides for emergency cases.
4. Investigation of use of chemical fertilizers.

Why? Since farmers only have a small plot of land which has low soil fertility, it is necessary to take all measures to improve the crop production.

Where? The whole PA of Ancharo.

How? 1. Supplying seeds of new varieties, pesticides and introducing appropriate crop rotation and intercropping techniques during Belg season.

2. Training of farmers on general agricultural techniques through extension work.

Costs : For purchase of new seed varieties and pesticides, for establishing a demonstration field, for operational costs such as transportation, per diem etc.

Expert : The DA and experts from the Awraja office are needed.

11. What? Irrigation from the river diversion, and spring and pond development.

Why? Due to the drought, the peasants have suffered a lot. In order to cope with this, irrigation can help. In the case of a home garden, irrigation can help generate income and prevent food scarcity. It will also give the peasants some knowledge about how to garden.

When? Can start at any time.

Who benefits? Peasants that have land in the irrigable area.

Cost : Food for work.

Who responsible?

- Experts from Awraja and regional offices.
- DA
- Peasants to provide labour.

Constraints : There is an indication that the land to be irrigated is owned by weak and/or old people, which might make it difficult to work on irrigation.

7

Applications in Africa : Rapid Rural Appraisal in Amemo PA, Ambassel, Awraja

– IRENE GUIJT and IAN SCOONES

INTRODUCTION

The report on Amemo PA provides some insights into the important issues in agriculture, livestock, natural resources, health, nutrition and income generation. The report attempts to highlight the key problems faced by the PA members and gives suggestions for directions of development. The report concludes with a series of Best Bets – outlined plans to face the problems of the area. The report has been written jointly by all the participants in the RRA exercise.

Participants

Fanaye Nega	Development agent
Fetence Tenow	Development agent
Gebre Reda	Sub-district level supervisor
Girma Makonen	D.A. supervisor sub-district level
Helmut Spohn	Agronomist, UMCC-DPP
Mamo Tsegaye	Project coordinator, UMCC-DPP
Mohammed Ahmed	Peasant Association leader
Said Ali	Development agent
Tadewos Ero	Extension expert, Zonal Office
Yimer Kebede	Development agent

LH 6

Zelaem Getu	Agronomist, District Office
Irene Guijit	Trainer, IIED

Fieldwork Programme

The fieldwork took place over five days, with discussion and analysis in between. A total of 134 people were interviewed of whom about 30 per cent were women. Both individual and group discussions were held with inhabitants from all the settlement areas and the scattered houses.

Activity Topic	People interviewed
Day 1	
Transect 1	1 man
Transect 1	4 men, 1 woman
Map	4 men, 3 women
Day 2	
Livestock	10 men, 3 women
Health/Nutrition	7 men, 11 women
Agriculture	4 men, 1 woman
Natural resources	4 men
Day 3	
Livestock	2 men, 1 woman
Health/Nutrition	2 men, 8 women
Agriculture	8 men, 2 women
Natural resources	2 men
Income generation	6 men, 5 women
Day 4	
Livestock	1 man, 1 woman
Agriculture	8 men
Income	1 man, 2 women
Fuel (wood)	1 man, 1 woman
Day 5	Assessment of best bets in a group discussion with 17 men and 2 women from Amemo PA.

Checklist-2

Checklists were made and reformulated to guide the interviewing and to fill in the gaps of knowledge. For Amemo, two main checklists were used. The first checklist was used before the fieldwork started (see Introduction). The second subgroup prepared specific questions for their interviews beforehand, based on the checklist.

Agriculture

- Interest for developing irrigation potential: from the river and from the springs

- Use of cash crops and preferences for cash crops
- Familiarity with horticultural activities
- Vegetable preferences
- Forage intercropping: experience with and/or interest in
- Grain varieties

Livestock

- Ranking of livestock preference (why cattle are preferred)
- Ranking of sources of fodder

Fuel (wood)

- What sources of fuel are used (dung, different vegetation)?
- Have sources of fuel changed over time?
- Which sources are preferred?
- Why has sesbania disappeared from the area?
- Are improved stoves used at all?
- Attitude towards fuel situation and hillside closures
- Use of Hitecha nursery

Non-agricultural Income Generation Activities

- Different types of activities (including handicrafts)
- Historical comparison of activities
- Work calendar of men and women
- Calendar of income sources

INTRODUCTION TO AMEMO PA

This report is the result of a Rapid Rural Appraisal (RRA) exercise carried out in the Ethiopian Red Cross Upper Mille and Cheleka Catchment – Disaster Prevention Programme (UMCC-DPP) in Wollo Province. One of the 72 Peasant Associations (PAs) in Wollo is Amemo, PA No. 08. Amemo PA borders on PA 09 in the north, PA 01 in the south, PA 04 in the east and PA 07 in the west (see Figure 7.1). Through the middle of the PA runs the main road from Dessie, 25 km in the south, to Kayk, 8 km in the north.

BEST BETS / CRITERIA	LIVESTOCK	POULTRY BREEDS	BEE KEEPING	WEAVING SUPPLY	EMBROIDERY	GULLY CONTROL	TREE PLANTING FARMS & nomes	IRRIGATION RIVER DIVERSION	IRRIGATON SPRING & PONDS	AGRICULTURAL SEEDS	SPINNING MACHINE	VEG. GARDENS
Cost	L	L/M	L/M	0	M	H	L	M	H	M	H	L
Time (until first benefits)	3 Y	2-3 Y	6M-1Y	2 M	3-6M	1Y	5Y	1-2 Y	1-2Y	5Y	1Y	5M
Technical Difficulty	L	M	6M-1Y	L	L	L	L	L	L	L	M	L
Need for F.F.W	L	-	-	-	-	M	L	L	M/H	L	-	-
Experts Needed	✓	✓	✓	✓	✓	✓	-	✓	✓	✓	✓	✓
Benefits amount of people	H±70%	H-100%	L-10%	L±5%	L-H 20%	H 60%	H-100%	L-10%	L-M	H-100/	L-M 20/	L-20%
Bureaucratic requirements	H	H	H	H	H	H	L	M	M	M	H	L
Social Problems	L/M	L	L	L	M	L	H	H	H	L	M	L
Negative Impact	L	L	-	-	-	-	L/M	-	-	-	-	-
Impact on Major Problem of P.A	H	M	L/M	L/M	L/M	H	H	H	H	H	L/M	H

SYMBOL : L: Low; M: Medium; Y: Year (s); m: month(s); ✓: Necessary; -: none; H: High

Fig. 7.1 : Matrix for Assessment of Best bets for Ancharo P.A.

The area of Amemo totals about 800 ha, and the population is about 700 households, totalling 3264 people. There are three settlement areas, of which two are the result of recent villagisation; Amemo village, Hitecha village, and the town Sulula. Scattered houses lie on both sides of the valley. Amemo PA lies between 2000 to 2700 metres above sea level, and its climatic zone is weyan dega. The main type of soil is clay. The main crops grown in the Amemo area are teff, sorghum, maize, sheat and pulses. Cattle, equines, sheep and goats are the most common domestic animals. Within the Peasant Association, there are a number of natural springs and one permanent river, the Gelana river, which flows from the southern part of the PA to the north.

Its natural resources such as springs, rivers and the villagization area attracted a number of organizations and individuals. Most of the organizations started to settle within the PA, and complete with the limited farmland, grazing land and forested land. The farmers complain about this use of their PA land for regional organizations. To minimize the problems resulting from the shortage of land, it is advisable to grow different cash crops. If the inhabitants are well oriented, and if the extension activities focus on modern animal husbandry and modern agricultural practices, it is possible to overcome the problems in Amemo Peasant Association.

Land is mainly used for farming and forestry (see Figure 7.2). Two transects were walked in the PA for a first orientation of the location of natural resources (see Figures 7.3 and 7.4). Transect 1 was walked diagonally through the valley from the northwest to the southeast. The second transect was walked from west to east and cut the first transect at the river Gelana. On both transects, the presence of the hillside closures high up on the hills is noticeable. Agriculture dominates the rest of the slopes. Housing becomes more concentrated around the road from Dessie to Hayk, and cuts through the middle of the transects.

AGRICULTURE

In Amemo PA, the main source of income and food is agriculture, making it the backbone of the PA. The agricultural system and practices in this area are traditional. Therefore, the productivity of their farmland is very low. Many farmers know this problem and have tried new methods, such as improved seeds and fertilizers to increase their yields. They continue to show interest to adapt to other new methods.

There is a serious shortage of arable land, each family only having 0.5 ha to use. Therefore, competition between farming land, grazing land, forested (closed) areas and land occupied by government institutions is high.

Cropping Pattern

At Amemo, the major cultivated crops (ranked by occurrence) are:

1. Teff (*erigrostis abbysinica*)
2. zengada (a highland sorghum variety)
3. maize
4. wheat
5. adja (emmer wheat)
6. berberi (chilli)
7. horse beans and field beans
8. grasspea
9. nuch (niger seed) and linseed
10. coffee and chat (local chewing leaf)
11. a few vegetables (onion, garlic, carrot, potato)

The diagrams show the preference of crops during a calendar year, and the preference for the Belg and Meher seasons (see Figures 7.5, 7.6, 7.7 and 7.8).

Ranking of Grain Crop Preference

Criteria	Teff adja	Zeng adja	Wheat adja	Maize	Pulses
Low labour	5	4	2	4	1
Drought tolerant	1	2	3	4	5
Fast maturing	3	5	4	1*	2
High market value	1	3	2	3	4
High food value	5+	1	1	1	2
Overall preference	1	2	4	3	4

* Refers to local use of crops in milky stage.

\+ Because it is a cash crop, people rarely eat it themselves and for them it has no nutritional value.

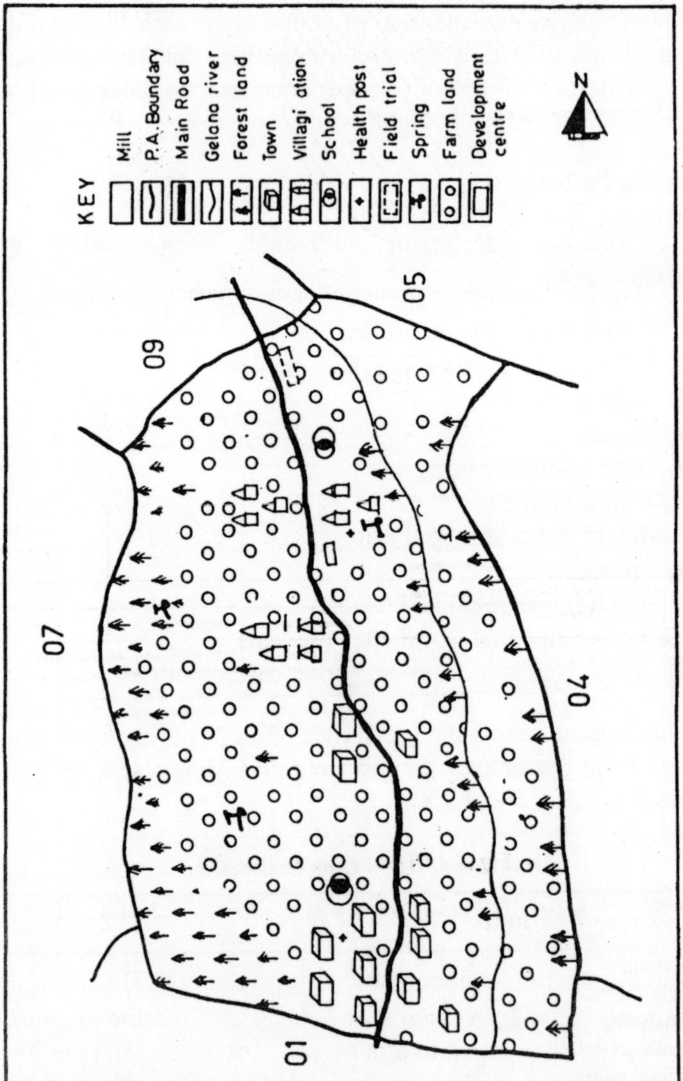

Fig. 7.2 : Map of Amemo Peasant Association

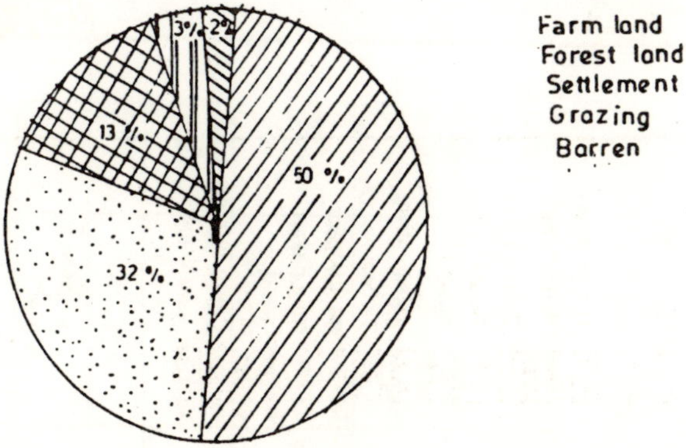

Fig. 7.3 : Land-use distribution of Amemo Peasant Association

TRANSECT OF AMEMO P.A.

Land use	Natural & Planted Forest closed site	Farm land Scattered Houses(East grazing)	Farm land Village, Garden ROad	Farm land river
Soil	Red & Rocky	Sandy clay	Black Clay	Black clay
Soil treatment		Soil & stone bund	Soil & stone bund	stone bund
Trees	Juniperus Olea Eclcu Bushesh	Eucalyptus	Eucalyptus	Eucalyptus & acacia
Wild animals	Ape + Hayna			
Village		Scattered houses	Villagization	
Crops		Sorghum Teff Barley wheat Maize	Teff, Wheat, Horse peas Rough, peas Oil seed Gullo	The same as Column III
Pest, & Disease		Grasshupper stalk Sorw Apids Root rotes	The same as Column III	The same as Column III
Water	Spring		Spring	River
Live Stock		Cattle, Sheep, Goat, Mule Poultar & Donkey house	The same as Column III	The same as Column III

Fig. 7.4 : Transect of Amemo P.A.

Influence of Climate

Normally, the rain is about 1100 mm (measure at Hayk station). This year* the rainy season started very late and the amount of rain was little compared to other years. As a result, more teff was planted this year than is otherwise the case. The lower rainfall will result in lower yields mainly for sorghum, maize and pulses.

---

* Refers to the year when this plan was made (Editor's note).

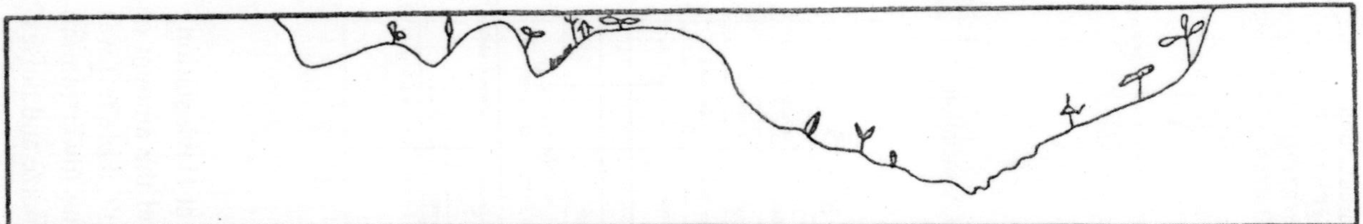

AREA	WOKALABA	LAKOLE	ROAD/AMEMO	Road/Amemo	Gelana River	KORI	KORIBER
Veg : Olea Acacia Eucalyptus Juniperus	Acacix Eucalyp-tus	Eucalyptus Acacia	Eucalyptus Acacia	Acacia few Eucalyptus	Acacia	Acacia Eucalyptus Eucalyptus Euphorbia	Closed Juni perus Acacia Eucalyptus Olea Euphorbia
Crops: Teff Barley	Terraced Teff Pulses Barley Zengada chatt	Few Teff Zergada	Teff Pulses Zen-gada Barbri	Teff Zengada Pluses Berbri	Grazing par-tly Swampy	Teff wheat Zenga-da oil crops pluses berberi chad coffee orange	Grass
Soils: Degraded shallow sandy loam stony	Shallow sandy loam loam sand stony	Degraded shallow stony	Shallow Sandy loamy sand stony	Deep clay ver-tisol some stone	Clay stony	M Deep clay ver Vertisol stony	Shallow sandy Stony
Disease + Pests	Root rot snow mildew shoot fly	< <	< <	< <	< <	< <	
Weeds: Striga other +++	+ + + + + +	–	+ + + + + +	+ + +	=	+ + + +	=
Erosion +++	+ +	+ + +	+ + +	+	–	+ +	

Fig. 7.5 : Transect of Amemo P.A.

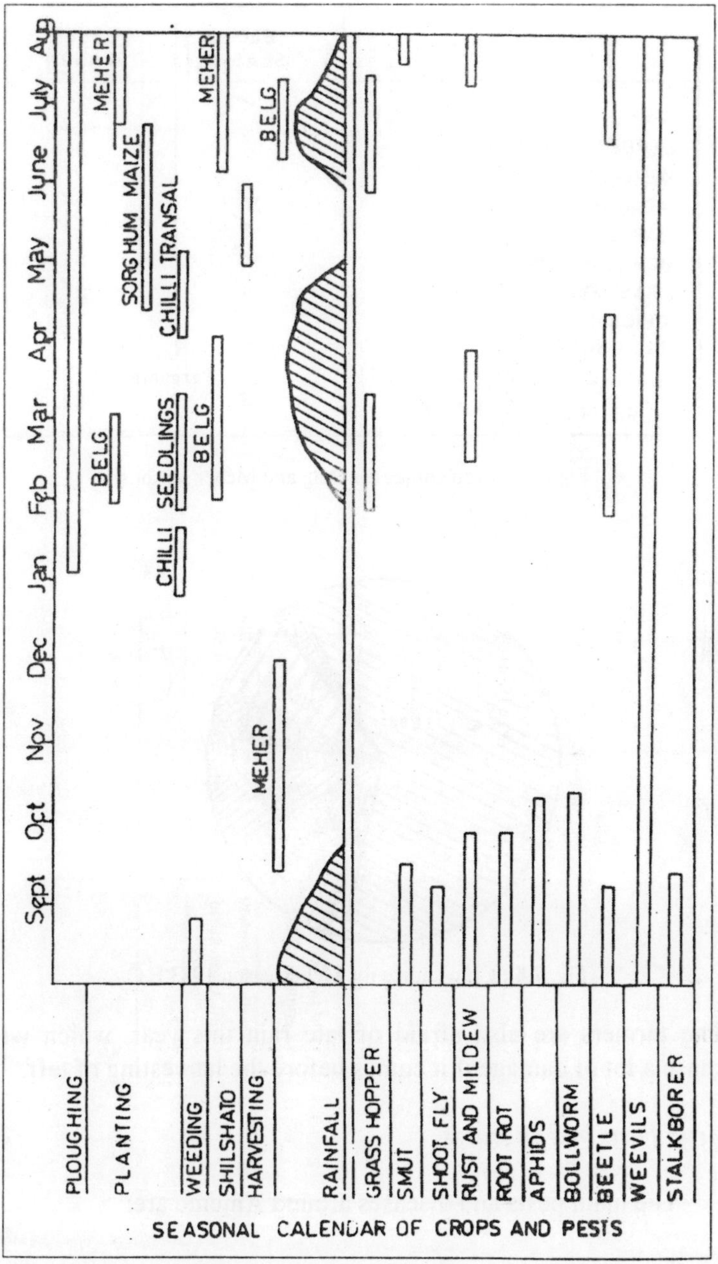

Fig. 7.6 : Seasonal calendar of crops and pests

CROPS	BELG SEASON	MEHER SEASON
TEFF	✓	✓
BERBERI (chilli papper)		✓
WHEAT		✓
ADJA (Local grain)	✓	✓
BARLEY	✓	✓
HORSE BEANS	✓	✓
GRASS PEA	✓	✓
CHICK PEA	✓	✓
OIL CROPS	✓	✓
CASH CROPS (Induding chat)	Perennials	
VEGETBLES AND SPICES	✓	✓

Fig. 7.7 : Crop choice for Belg and Meher seasons

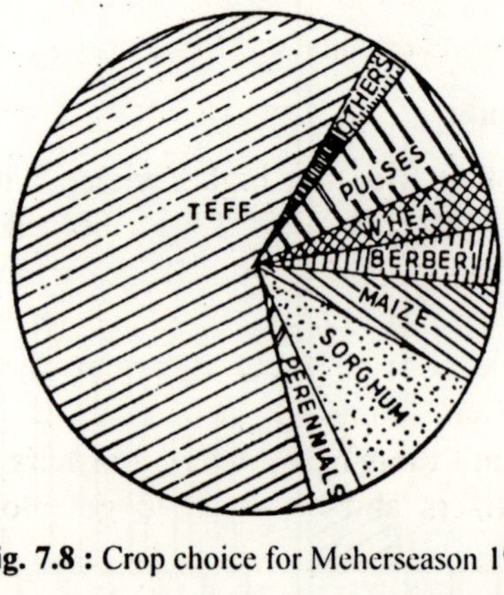

Fig. 7.8 : Crop choice for Meherseason 1983 E.C.

The farmers are also afraid of late rain this year, which will cause a lot of damage if it comes before the harvesting of teff.

Crop Pests and Diseases

The main pests and diseases around Amemo are:

1. grasshopper

2. stalk borer
3. rust and powdery mildew
4. smut
5. teff shoot fly
6. aphids
7. rootrot
8. storage pests: weevils and rats

This year infestation was much lower than normal due to the lower rains. The farmers do not practise local ways to control pests and diseases. One farmer said he prayed to prevent pest damage.

Intercropping

There is very little intercropping. However, systematic crop rotation is practised, with cereals following legumes. On fertile land, teff sometimes follows sorghum or maize. The most drought-tolerant crops in Amemo area are teff and sorghum. Some oil crops are grown in borders around the fields but shortage of land prohibits expansion of this crop.

Use of External Inputs

Farmers assured us that they got higher yields with improved seeds of maize, wheat and teff. They showed interest in improved seeds of other crops, even for unfamiliar crops.

When they were members of the now disbanded producers' cooperatives, the farmers applied chemical fertilizers. All farmers use manure and some use ash on the fields close to their homes, or around their homesteads. Farmers are familiar with chemical fertilizers and are keen to get more chemical fertilizers.

Irrigation

Only very few farmers use irrigation from the springs to irrigate horticultural crops. Most vegetables are grown under rainfed conditions, e.g. berberi, onion, carrot and potato. There is an interest to expand the land under irrigation, but technical help and seeds are necessary inputs.

Cash Crops and Home Consumption

The most important perennial cash crop is chat. Approximately two-thirds of the production is sold in Dessie and Hayk. At the moment, very little coffee is being planted. It will be very difficult to expand the coffee plantations due to the limited garden land around the homes in the villagization areas. See the table below for more informations :

Labour Demand – Use of Crops

Rank	Crop	% for market	% for home consumption
1.	teff	100	Only when others not available
2.	berberi	50	50
3.	zengada/maize	–	100
4.	wheat	–	100
	barley	–	100
	adja	100	–
5.	chick pea	33	66
6.	guava	50	50
	horse bean	50	50
	pea	–	100
	lentils	50	50
7.	oil crops	50	50

Conclusions : Labour input is not considered important, the yield is more important for choosing a certain crop.

Agricultural Management Practices

The recommended seed rate of the different crops depends on the fertility of the land. The farmers take special care to use clean seed for planting, by using local sieves. Most crops are weeded twice to three per season at the right time. In fields planted with horse beans, weeding had been minimal, however. The weeds were harvested and used as fodder.

Storage

Sorghum is stored in underground pits. Other crops are stored in special baskets and clay vessels inside the houses. The main storage problems for these types of storage are weevils, rodents and mould. To decrease or avoid weevil infestation, farmers store the sorghum after a new crescent arises. Storage before this time will cause high weevil infestation.

Demonstration Plots

The farmers find the demonstration plots very useful to learn about the application of fertilizer, new agricultural practices and the use of new improved seeds.

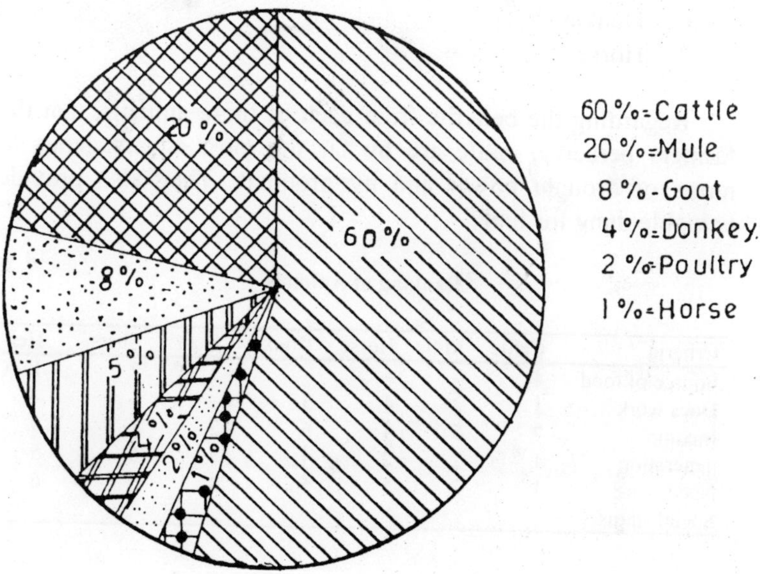

Fig. 7.9 : Presence of animals in Amemo P.A.

Main Problems

The main agricultural problems listed by the farmers interviewed are: shortage of farming and grazing land, shortage of rain (especially this year), diseases and pests (but less this year) and the lack of technical knowledge.

LIVESTOCK

During the RRA fieldwork, the livestock situation was investigated. The following types of domestic animals are present in Amemo PA: cattle, mules, horses, donkeys, sheep, goats and hens. The rank according to number owned is given in Figure 7.9 and the order of importance is given below:

1. Cattle
2. Chicken
3. Goat
4. Sheep
5. Mule
6. Donkey
7. Horse

Regarding the benefits from each of these animals, that the farmers perceive, cattle are by far the most advantageous in terms of drought power and by=products. They also provide valuable dung for fuel.

Ranking of Animals

Criteria	Cattle	Mule	Horse	Donkey	Goat	Sheep	Hen
Source of food	4	–	–	–	3	2	1
Does work	1	2	4	3	–	–	–
Income generation	7	5	4	6	2	1	3
Needs care	1	2	2	4	7	6	5
Social status	1	2	5	5	4	3	6

Livestock Diseases

There are several diseases which afflict the animals.

Type of animal	Disease	Local treatment
Sheep/goat	Diarrhoea wounds	Cutting and burning
Horse/mule/donkey	Gedehabi	Cutting
Cattle	Gugubso	Cutting
Chicken	Fengil	Local alcohol

Besides their own local treatments, sick animals are taken to the veterinary clinics in Hayk. However, the expenses are sometimes too high for them to pay.

Fodder

The animals are fed on grass, weeds, crop residues and tree leaves. There is a major problem with the provision of fodder. There is virtually no grazing land, except for small strips along fields and around the homes. Almost all fodder has to be collected and brought to the animals who are kept in and around the houses. There are some small stretches of grazing land around the Geland river, but these can only be used by the farmers whose fields end at the river. Hillside closure areas are used for the collection of fodder grasses. However, no other plant may be used for this purpose. During the month of November, the people are allowed to use the closure areas under a cut-and-carry system.

Opportunities to Solve Problems with Fodder

The solutions suggested by community members include the selling of animals so reduce the numbers requiring fodder, to increase the amount of land to be used for grazing purposes and to increase the use of the hillside closures. They expressed interest in new breeds. However, their social status is measured by the number of cattle they own. Although the improved breeds will provide as many benefits with fewer animals, the social status will also be affected by owning fewer animals. Furthermore, improved breeds need good quality fodder and until that situation has improved, it is not advisable to start with the introduction of improved breeds. The focus should be on the introduction of forage crops that do not complete with other crops.

NATURAL RESOURCES

Soil Types

Amemo PA has many different types of soils, as can be seen on the transects. Included are clay, sandy white coloured soil, red coloured soil, humus, etc. However, the main soil types are clay and sandy loam (see Figure 7.10). Near the river, soils are dark clays and less rocky than the areas higher up on the hills.

Before the Ethiopian revolution all the hills were owned by individual (private) peasants. Due to this individual ownership and the lack of knowledge about soil conservation, the forest was cut and burnt. This resulted in an increase of the erodability of the soil and erosivity of the rains. Soil fertility was also decreased by repeated ploughing on the hillsides.

After the revolution (1974), the hillside plantations were protected by closing the forest and through extension campaigns by the Ministry of Agriculture. With the provision of food for work (FFW), the people constructed terraces and checkdams. All these measures helped to stop the erosion from the hillside areas (see Figure 7.11).

Erosion

Although erosion has decreased, there is still some ongoing sheet erosion from the fields. More severe is the problem of the gullies that start at the river and are developing uphill in the farmers' fields. In Figure 7.12, the existence of terraces and checkdams can be seen.

Tree Plantation

Of the total area of the PA, 32 per cent is covered with forests. The hillsides are covered by planted and natural forests. There is also a nursery of 0.5 ha. In the nursery, seedlings are prepared for plantation throughout the PA. Three-quarters are assigned to hillside plantation and one-quarter to be planted by the people on their own land. The main trees in the nursery are: juniperus, eucalyptus, globulus, acacia and olea. In the order of importance the ranking by the people is :

1. Eucalyptus
2. Acacia
3. Juniperus

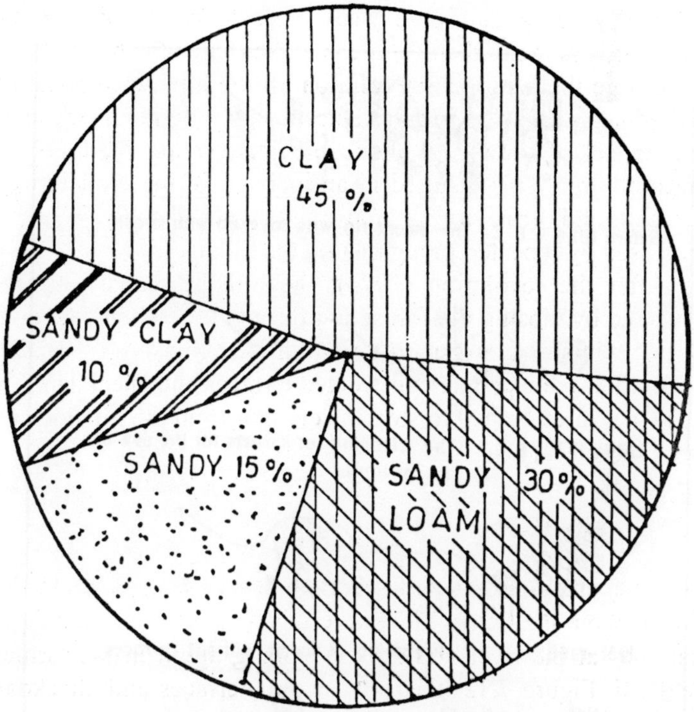

Fig. 7.10 : Major soil types in Amemo

Eucalyptus, because it regenerates naturally, cutting is not forbidden by law, it grows fast and makes good construction wood. People like Acacia because it makes good charcoal, but they are forbidden to cut this and other trees if it grows on public land.

The Hitecha Nursery

In 1981, there was some sesbania in the nursery for planting on the land of the producer's cooperative members. However, the cooperative has now been disbanded and the sesbania trees on cooperative land have been cut down. Some farmers say sesbania roots interfere with ploughing if they are planted along the edges of fields. The views of the farmers concerning sesbania were very different but generally not positive, despite the fact that it can provide good fodder.

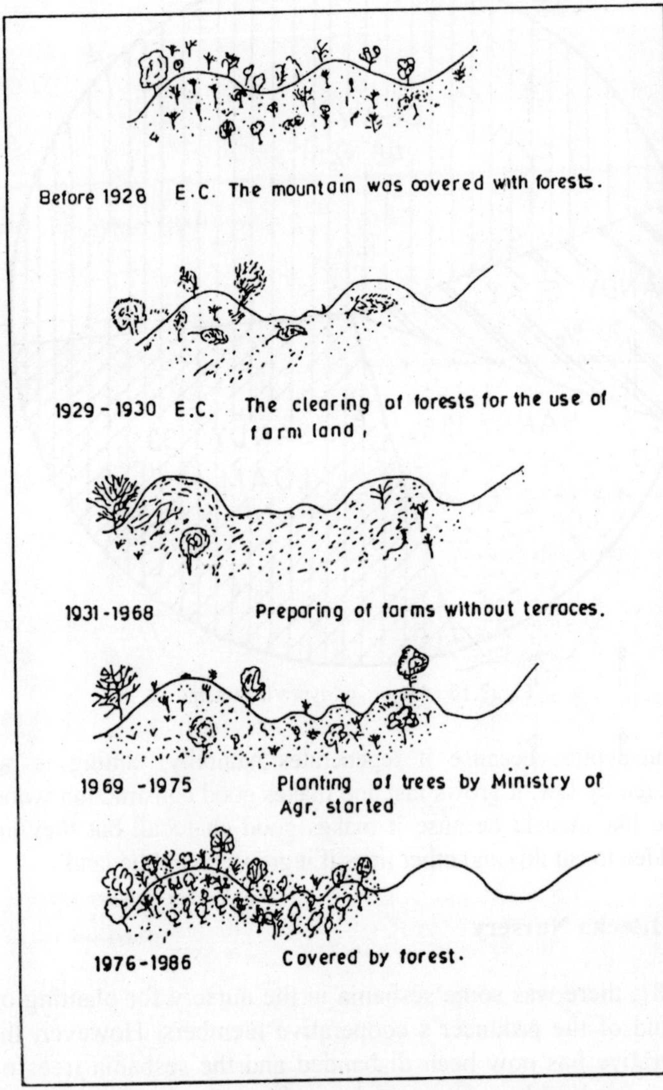

Fig. 7.11 : History of Abalfo; Geta mountains (wole-Agar) (as told by a 72 years old community member)

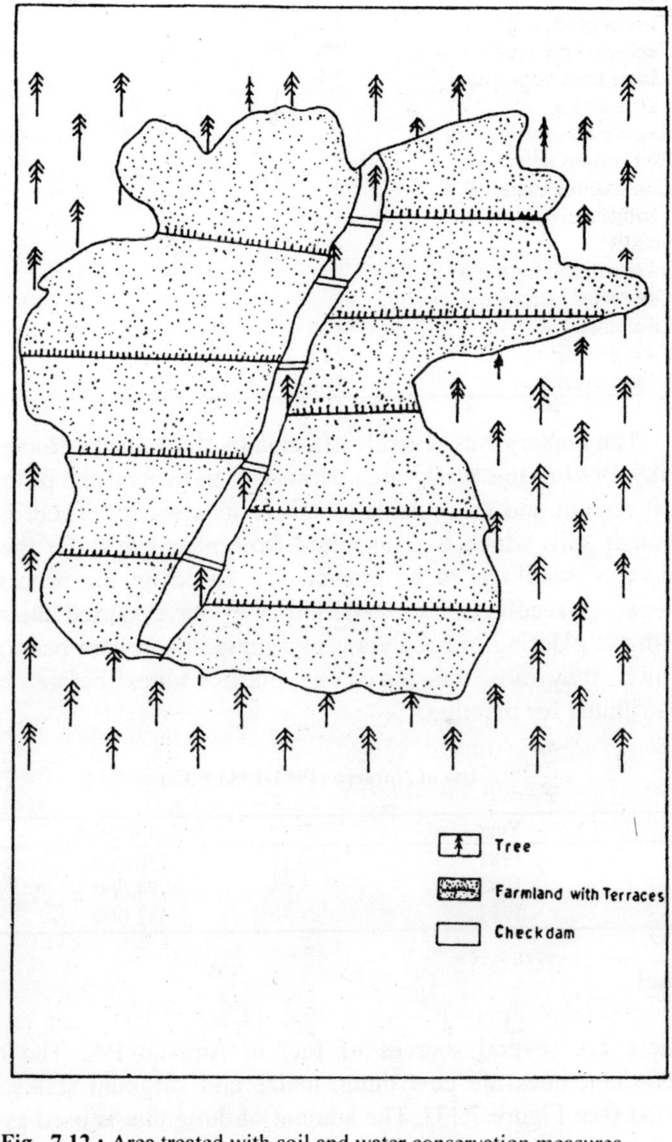

Fig . 7.12 : Area treated with soil and water conservation measures

Ranking of Importance of Trees in Amemo

Criteria	Eucalyptus	Juniperus	Acacia	Olea
Timber production	2	1	-	3
Fuelwood production	3	4	1	2
Makes farm implements	2	-	-	1
Fast growing	1	3	2	3
Regenerates easily	1	-	2	3
Soil conservation	4	3	1	2
Construction material	2	1	3	-
Termite resistant	3	1	4	2
Fodder	-	-	1	2
Increases soil fertility	-	3	1	2
Completes with crops	1	2	3	4
Local medicine	1	-	-	2
Fencing	2	3	1	4
Drought resistant	4	3	1	2

The nursery was severely affected by the security problem of 1989/1990 in the Wollo area. However, in general the problems still remain and it is unable to utilize its capacity. There is not enough soil, which is transported from near Hayk, for the full quota of seedlings to be planted. To speed up the process of preparing seedlings for plantation, they have started this year with the planting of eucalyptus and juniperus in bare beds, after which they are transferred to plastic tubes before being distributed for planting.

Use of Nursery (1981-1983 E.C.)

Year	No. of seedlings
1981	250,000
1982	74,000
1983	332,000

Fuel

There are several sources of fuel in Amemo PA. The most important ones are cow dung, maize and sorghum stalks, and wood (see Figure 7.13). The amount of dung that is used as fuel has decreased due to the inability of farmers to keep many cattle. This is a result of the shortage of grazing land and of alternative fodder sources. If people had the choice they would prefer using wood. However, there is a severe shortage of wood for fuel, which started when the state took over ownership of the forest lands and closed the hills from public use.

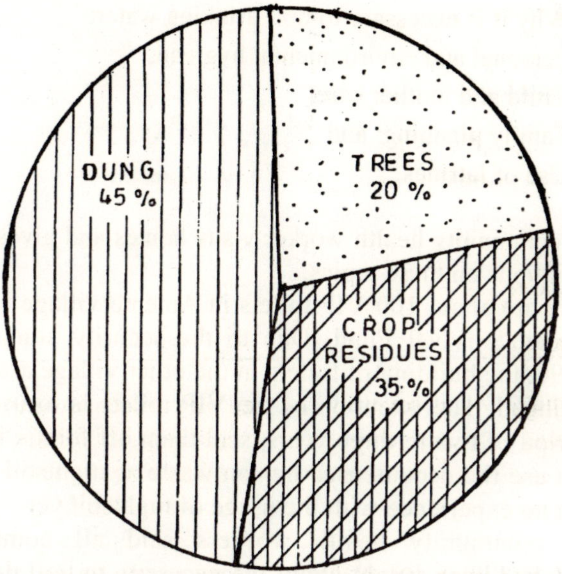

Fig. 7.13 : Fuel sources in Amemo P.A. 1983 E.C.

Generally, there is a problem to get enough fuelwood from different sources. The problem of shortage of land needs to be taken into consideration to solve this problem. Solutions suggested by the people in Amemo PA are:

1. Study the land-use plan again;
2. Some part of the hillside closure areas should be given to private peasants to manage and plant with private plantations; and
3. More seedlings for plantation by the people in their own areas should be available from the nursery.

HEALTH AND NUTRITION

Health Services

There are two health centres in Amemo PA. There is a health post in Amemo village and a health clinic in Sulula (in the south of the PA). The health centres give basic health educations on such topics as:

- Why it is necessary to boil drinking water;
- Personal and environmental hygiene;
- Child and mother care;
- Family planning; and
- Use of latrines.

The community health worker visits homes and gives group demonstrations on these topics.

There are about 100 VIP toilets in Amemo village built by the Belgian Survival Fund. Due to the security situation in 1989/1990, the building of toilets in the other village areas was not continued. The intention of the VIP toilets is to use them for a period of two to three years, seal them off for six months and then use the decomposed human waste as nightsoil. There has been no experience with the usage of nightsoil yet.

The community health workers said all community members had been taught about the necessity to boil drinking water. However, during the interviewing, no woman said she discontinued with boiling water for drinking purposes, either because there is no time, or not enough water containers or the fuelwood to do this. The women strain the water from the springs through a piece of cloth into the water storage pots.

Although it was difficult to get information on specific diseases, there are some general diseases common in the Amemo communities. Eye diseases are very common and many children were seen to have this. Influenza and the common cold are found at all times, as are diarrhoea and vomiting. Bilharzia was said to be a common disease by several PA members. However, Gelana river is a fast-flowing stream, and reports about the incidence of Biharzia in Lake Hayk, to where Gelana river flows, are not consistent. The period when the degree of disease increases is between April and September (see figure 7.14).

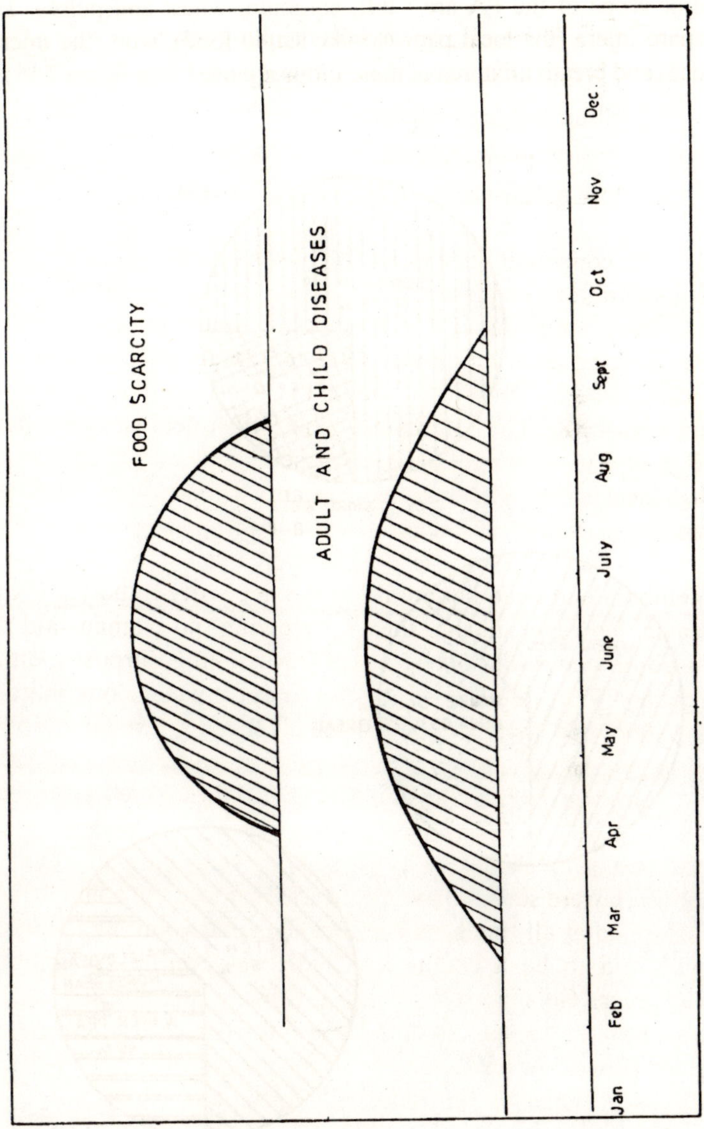

Fig. 7.14 : Food scarcity period and increased occurrence of disease

Nutrition

Major crops of the PA are : teff, sorghum, wheat and pulses. To prepare injera (the local pancake-like staple food), wott (the injera sauce) and bread; mixtures of these crops are used (see figure 7.15).

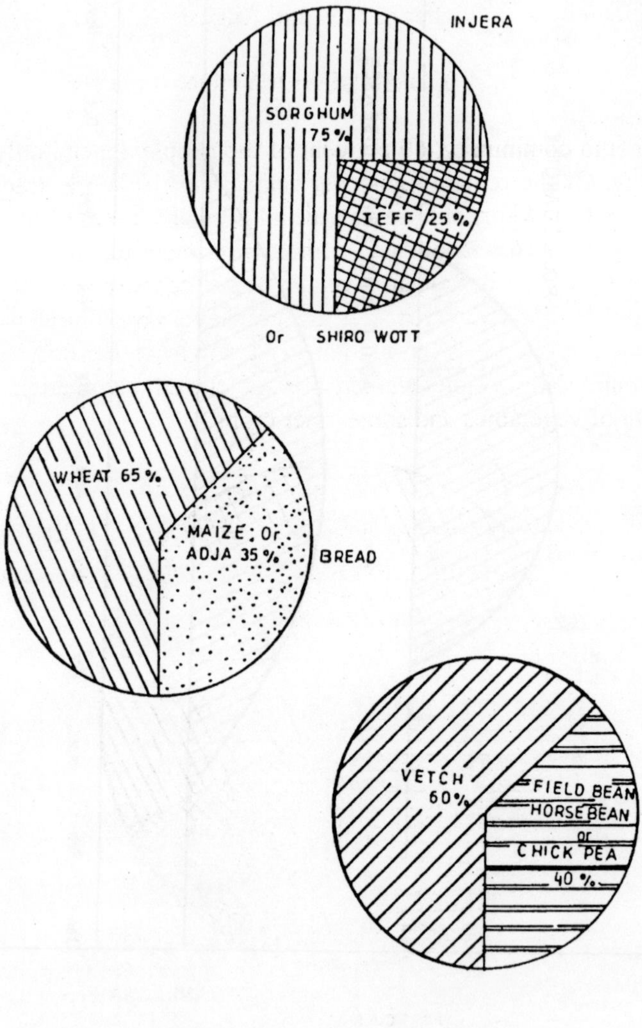

Fig. 7.15 : Preparation of daily foods

Injera: sorghum 75 per cent, teff 25 per cent.

Bread: wheat 65 per cent, maize or adja 35 per cent.

Wott: vetch 60 per cent, field bean/horse bean/chick pea 40 per cent.

Of the vegetables, potato, onion and pepper are well known by the people for their diets. However, the lack of irrigation makes it difficult for people to grow other nutritious vegetables. Food scarcities are higher in May and August.

INCOME GENERATION

In Amemo community, 60 per cent of the people depend only on farming. Of the remaining 40 per cent, Food for Work, trading, handicrafts and horticulture provide additional sources of income (see Figure 7.16). About one-fifth of the men are involved in trading throughout the year. Roughly 40 per cent are periodically engaged in trading, when they do not have agricultural work. The men trade in different industrial goods and crops. Only about one-tenth of the women are sometimes involved in the trading of vegetables and some other crops.

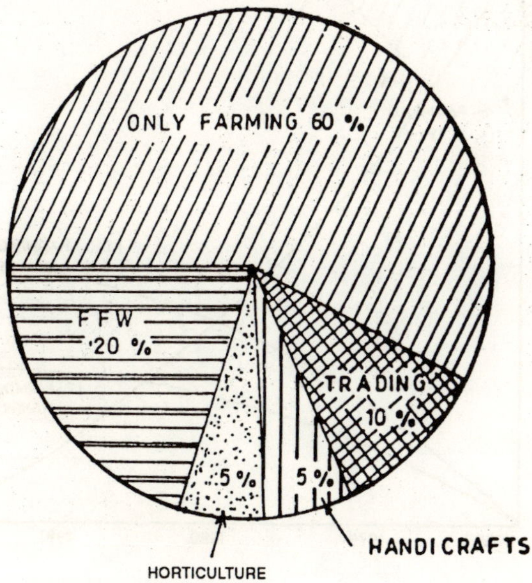

Fig. 7.16 : Income generation in Amemo

In a comparison of living standards between 1985 and 1989, it became clear that those households involved in both farming and trading were better off than those dependent solely on farming (see Figure 7.17). Handicrafts ensured a reasonable standard of life in the PA.

Cash crops are not grown on a large scale. Most of the teff crop is sold in the market, as are the surplus of all other major crops (see Figure 7.18). Of the few vegetables grown in Amemo PA, pepper and onion have a high market value. Carrot and potato are less interesting for marketing. Chat and coffee, both of which are perennial, have the highest market values in the nearby markets.

Very few households receive extra income from (hand) crafts: pottery, metal-work, weaving. For example, pottery, for which the resources are available in the PA, is practised by 6 of the approximately 700 households. Clothing, cooking utensils and agricultural tools can be provided in the area through these households.

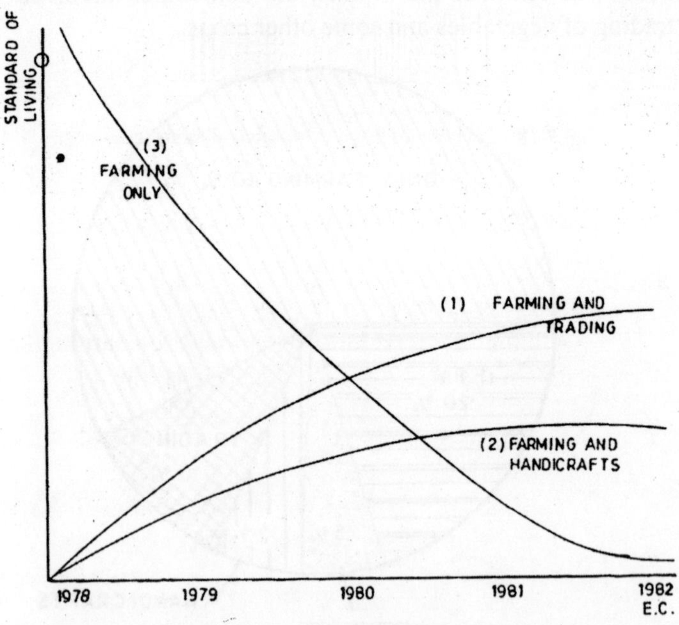

Fig. 7.17 : Comparison of living standard (1978-1982 E.C.)

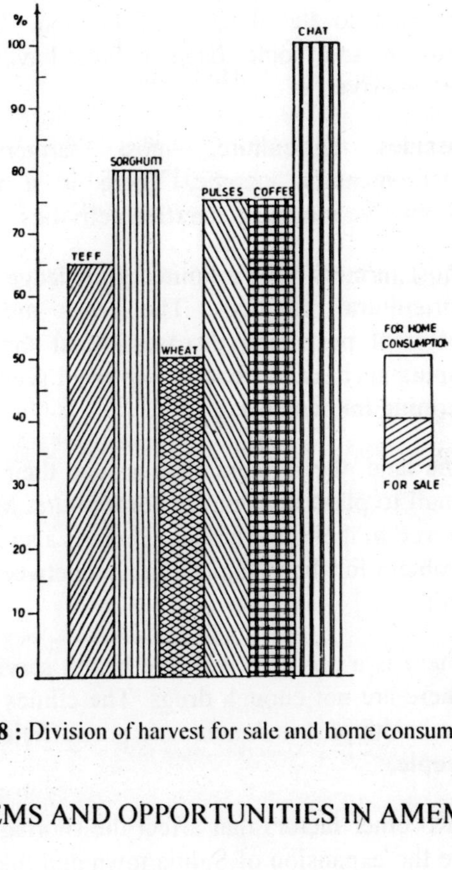

Fig. 7.18 : Division of harvest for sale and home consumption

PROBLEMS AND OPPORTUNITIES IN AMEMO PA

Problems

1. All the farmers have a shortage of farmland. As a result, the agricultural production is low.

2. There is a shortage of grazing land which creates difficulties for the feeding of the many domestic animals that the farmers have. Due to this, there is little or no income from livestock activities.

3. Because it is illegal to use any trees from the hillside closure sites, all households have serious problems with fuelwood. This problem is made worse because there is no private tree planting.

4. Due to the topography of the PA, the slopes are exposed to the dangers of erosion. There is sheet erosion and some large gullies have formed near Gelana river.

5. Besides agriculture, most farmers have no supplementary income. There is a problem with alternative income generation activities.

6. Most farmers have a limited knowledge about modern agricultural practices. The crops are attacked by different pests and diseases. Most farmers have no inputs such as fertilizers, improved seeds and modern farming implements.

7. The land, the farmers have around their homes, is too small to plant trees or for horticulture. Many have just moved to their new homes. There is also a water supply problem for the villagisation area between Amemo and Sulula.

8. There is a problem with the health service in the PA. There are not enough drugs. The clinics in Sulula and the health post in Amemo are not sufficient to serve the people.

9. Two other factors that affect the shortage of farmland are the expansion of Sulula town and the land that has been given to the adult education campaign and the seedling nursery (which is not being used to the maximum capacity).

10. The problem with the livestock diseases cannot be completely helped because there is not enough medicine from the woreda and awraja levels.

11. Wild animals are a problem in the area. The crops and domestic animals are attacked by apes and hyenas who live in the hillside closures.

FINDINGS

This report gives an introduction about agriculture, soil and water conservation, livestock, health and nutrition, and income generation in Amemo PA. By using different RRA techniques, the major problems of PA 08 were investigated, and some best bets were formulated. On the last day of fieldwork, a small group discussion with about 20 villagers was held to ask for their ideas about problems and solutions in their PA. The villagers agreed with the basic analysis and that all the best bets were good options. However, they mentioned additional problems that had not been discovered in the PA during the fieldwork.

1. There are different centres in the PA that serve larger areas, such as Hitecha nursery, the school, demonstration plots, the adult literacy campaign. These areas are used to train farmers from other PAs also. This has increased the shortage of land. The villagers thought it was necessary to get some compensation from the neighbouring PAs for the land that others were also benefiting from.
2. The villagers again raised the issue of the hillside closures. The fuelwood problem is partly a result of these closure areas. They are not allowed to cut any of the trees that are now growing on the mountains. They want the land-use system of the closures to be changed so that some areas can be owned and managed by farmers.
3. The villagers say there is enough water around Hitecha. This water is used by all the people living near Hitecha. However, it is very dirty and it stimulates the introduction of different kinds of diseases so that people around Hitecha face a great problem. They would like some materials and technical advice so that they can construct a pipe and use it.
4. There is one health post in PA 08 but there is not enough medicines. This makes it difficult for some diseases to be cured. The villagers would like to supply

of medicines to be increased, so that more medicines of different kinds are made available for different diseases.

BEST BETS FOR AMEMO PA

By joining the nine best bets that had already been formulated by the RRA team, and which the villagers confirmed, with the new problems and solutions, a total of eleven best bets were formulated. They are described in some more detail below :

Tree Planting

What? Increase the tree-planting by individual farmers, probably of Eucalyptus and Acacia species.

Why? Trees can help solve the following problems: shortage of fuelwood, of construction wood and of farm implements. The farmers expressed a preference for these two trees. Eucalyptus is fast-growing and regenerates naturally. Acacia is also good for fodder, makes good quality charcoal, gives protection because of its thorns and is drought resistant.

How? 1. By distributing more seedlings to the private farmers from the nursery than is done. More usually goes to hillside closures.

1. By giving technical and management advice.
2. By paying Food for Work.

Where? The seedlings come from the Hitecha nursery and are to be planted along gullies, in the valley and in the homesteads.

Who? The DAs and farmers are responsible for the work. The entire community will benefit from this.

Improved Stoves

What? Introduce improved stoves in Amemo, where they were constructed with the wrong type of clay before.

Why? To decrease fuelwood demand in traditional fireplaces.

Where? Every household in Amemo PA.

How? Technical – Home economic experts shall select model households and prepare model stoves. They will also train the women.

Financial – Training material and costs of the experts to be covered by the project. Building material and labour to be met by the community members themselves.

When? Starting from now, contact can be made with the home economists.

Who? The whole PA has indirect benefits from a reduction in the demand for fuelwood. The households involved have direct benefit.

The project and the Ministry of Agriculture is responsible for the planning and financing. The Home Economics experts and the DA are responsible for implementing it. All the individual households are responsible for maintaining them.

Cash Crop Production

What? The production of haricot beans, oil seeds (linseed and nuch) and of fruit trees (guava and gesho) can be encouraged.

Why? These crops can be used for income generation because they have a high market value and demand. They can also be used for local food consumption.

How? Find voluntary farmers.

Decide on exact crops to introduce.

Distribute improved seeds and seedlings.

Give technical and management advice.

Where? In the fields and around the homes of interested farmers, and wherever water for extra irrigation is available.

When? Can be started during the first Meher season.

Who? The DAs and farmers are responsible.

All interested farmers will benefit.

Beekeeping

What? The keeping of bees can be intensified.

Why? The honey can be sold in the market and can also be consumed at home.

The bees can help with the pollinisation of crops and trees.

How? Introduce improved beehives.

Give technical and management advice.

Introduce improved oil seeds and other flowering trees.

Where? Near the hillside closures, around homesteads and near riverbanks.

When? After decision on what kinds of beehives are available and effective, and then continuing throughout the year.

Who? The animal resource experts and the farmers.

Participating farmers.

Irrigation Development

What? The development of irrigation from the springs and the Gelana river for horticultural purposes.

Why? To decrease the land shortage problem and to develop alternative sources of income by producing vegetables and fruits.

To obtain different sources of food.

Where? The springs near Sulula town, Hitecha and near the Service Cooperative. The Gelana river diversion site is not yet determined, but the west bank of the Gelana river will probably be irrigated.

How? Technically – For both the use of the springs and the river, an organizational structure to use irrigation has to be established (the setting up of water users' groups).

- Springs: protection of the springs that are not yet protected, followed by the creation of distribution systems.
- River diversion: a careful survey of the river to identify potential areas for diversion, choosing the technically easiest location for the first diversion. Technical follow-up for both areas is the provision of seeds and technical assistance.

Financially – The community will provide labour and locally available construction materials. The costs of the experts involved, different hand tools, gabions, cement and seeds will be provided by the project.

When? Investigation can start this dry season.

Who? The farmers with potential irrigable land will benefit directly.

The PA is responsible for the organizational structure that has to be established. The project is responsible for the technical survey and construction activities. The DAs and the PA members are responsible for implementation and maintenance of the irrigation systems.

Bamboo and Sisal

What? The intensification of bamboo and sisal plantation.

Why? To increase income generation activities.

To control soil erosion and stabilize check-dams.

To provide a source of materials for local use (bamboo: furniture, fencing, utensils; sisal: rope).

Where? Bamboo in gullies where check-dams were constructed, near Hitecha spring and along the Gelana river. Sisal can be planted along the check-dams.

How? Technically – The sisal and bamboo planting materials need to be collected and multiplied in the nursery. Labour needs to be organized for the planting.

Financially – The project will pay for the costs of the experts that need to be consulted. The PA will provide the labour.

When? The coming rainy season (Belg).

Who? The community members that will do the planting will benefit from their work.

The DA, experts and farmers are responsible for the implementation. The farmers will be responsible for the maintenance and use of the products.

Drinking Water

What? To supply clean drinking water to village No. 2.

Why? The women in village No. 2 need to walk 1 km with the heavy water jugs on their backs.

Where? The water will be diverted from Hitecha spring and will run along the main road to the village No. 2.

How? When developing the spring for irrigation purposes, a tube for drinking water can be installed.

Financially, this project will be expensive and will require a special budget allocation.

When? This depends on if and when the budget planning allows for this particular expenditure.

Who? Technically – Awraja experts need to check the capacity of the springs and to make a budget and a design. The PA members can provide labour.

Improved Use of the Nursery

What? The use of the nursery at Hitecha must be improved so that it is using its full capacity to benefit the people in Amemo PA.

Why? There is a shortage of seedlings to plant around the homesteads, and a need to try out different kinds of trees. Besides this, the nursery is known to function below its full capacity.

Where? Hitecha nursery.

How? Discussions should be started at the awraja and woreda levels to see how the use of the nursery can be improved. Further investigation within the PA is needed to determine what kind of trees they would like to have in the nursery. Together with the agronomists, decisions can then be made about any new types of trees to include in the nursery.

When? Discussions at the awraja and woreda levels can start as soon as possible.

Who? The person responsible to initiate discussion about the nursery must be fairly senior in the UMCC-DPP. The awraja staff is responsible for changing the decisions about the use of the nursery. The DA and the nursery supervisor are responsible for determining what will be grown.

Intercropping with Forage

What? The cropping patterns, as it now is, can be changed to include the intercropping of more fodder crops.

Why? There is a shortage of fodder and grazing land. To avoid having to buy fodder from elsewhere, the possibilities of growing it should first be explored.

Where? The first experiments should be done on a small-scale with interested farmers in the PA.

How? First identification of contract farmers.

Decisions about what type of intercropping to try.

Trials with different forage intercropping possibilities.

Extension to other interested farmers.

When? Identification of contract farmers can get started now. Trials will start at the beginning of the Meher season.

Who? The DA is responsible for identifying contact farmers. Experts about fodder crops will need to give advice.

Planting Fodder Crops in the Community

What? Introduction of drought-resistant fodder plants around homes.

Why? To make the best possible use of the little available space in the PA and to solve the problem of the shortage of grazing land.

Where? In the homesteads of interested farmers.

How? Identification of interested farmers.

Identification of possible plants and the best location for trying them out.

When? Discussion with interested farmers can start now. Planting can then start at the beginning of next Meher season.

Who? The DA is responsible for identifying interested farmers. He will help the farmers decide on what to plant and where to plant it. Experts from the awraja level can advise on the type of plants possible.

Health Post

What? Improving the supply of medicines and the service of the health posts in the PA.

Why? The health posts are not working to their full capacity. The choice of medicines and the supply is not good.

Where? The health posts/clinics in Amemo PA.

How? Further discussion with PA members and the community health agents is needed to identify exactly what the problems are. It would be advisable to include MoA staff from the woreda or awraja level in the process.

When? Discussions can start now.

CRITERIA \ BEST BETS	Improved Nursery	Closed stove	Tree Planting	Fodder Planting	Irrigation	Cash Crops	Legume intercropping	Bamboo & sisal	Bee-keeping	Health Post	Drinking water
COST	L	L	L	L	H	L	L	L	H		H
Tree	Y	m	Y	m	spring river	Y	Y	Y	Y		Y
Technical Defficulty	L	L	–	L	M	L	L M	L	H		H / M
Need for E.F.W.	✓	–	–	–	✓	–	–	–	–		✓
Experts Needed	✓	✓	–	✓	✓	✓	✓	✓	✓		✓
Benefits (no. of people)	H	H	H	M / H	L(25%)	L	L	M	L		M 30%
Bureaucratic requirements	M	L	H	L	L	L	–	–	H		H
Social problems.	L	L	–	L M	H	L	L M	L	L		L
Negative Impact.	–	L	–	L(?)	L(?)	–	L	–	M		–
Impact on Major Problem of P.L.	H	H	H	H	H	H	H	L / M	L / M		H

SYMBOLS: L : Low Y: Year(s) ✓ Necessory (?) Not enough Information Available yet.
M : Medium m: month(s) –: none
H : High

Fig. 7.19 : Matrix for assessment of best bets for Amemo PA

Who? The DA and the MoA staff are responsible for discussing with the farmers. Final responsibility for improving the service should be planned by MoA.

Following the formulation of these best bets, an initial assessment of their technical, financial, bureaucratic and social feasibility was made. The results are summarized in the matrix given in figure 7.19.

8

Applications in India: Vikasnagar*
(Officers of the Indian Administrative Service, 1991 Batch)

– AMITAVA MUKHERJEE

INTRODUCTION

The Block Vikasnagar : Its People and their Perceptions

Nestled cosily between the gigantic Himalayas and the dwarfish Shiwaliks and bordered by the perennial Yamuna in north and west, the Vikasnagar block of Dehradun district (See Fig. 8.1) presents a smooth transition from hilly areas to the Doon Valley. Criss-crossed by tributaries of Asan and Yamuna, dissected by the power channel of the Yamuna Hydel-power project, the block is rich in natural resources like water, flora and fauna.

The Vikasnagar block (See Fig. 8.2) is only ten years old. Its earlier name, 'Chorpur', meaning the land of thieves, has been changed to Vikasnagar, meaning the land of development. But the people feel that change in name has hardly changed their life and living standards. Agriculture is their mainstay of livelihood. A Muslim farmer echoed the views of many farmers of the block when he said that irrigation was the main bottleneck to higher levels of assured agricultural production. The level of per capita income in the block is low, with the female wage rates lower than the corresponding wage rates for men. There is large-scale unemployment, though some of it is being mitigated by the work in the Yamuna project which has been going on for the past thirty years.

---

* This is a Block Plan for the people of Vikasnagar, District Dehradun, India, prepared in terms of people's perceptions and aspirations. Thirteen participants, all officers of the Indian Administrative Service, took part in this exercise. They are: Anil Malik, Sandeep Garg, Ashok Khemka, Shantwanu, B. Srinivas, A. Jaythilak, Ms. Ishita Roy, Jan-e-Alam, Satyabrata Sahu, Ms. Anu Agarwal, Madhu Sudan Padhi, Manoj Sharma and Veer A. Raghav. The Staff Associate monitoring the project was Professor Neela Mukherjee.

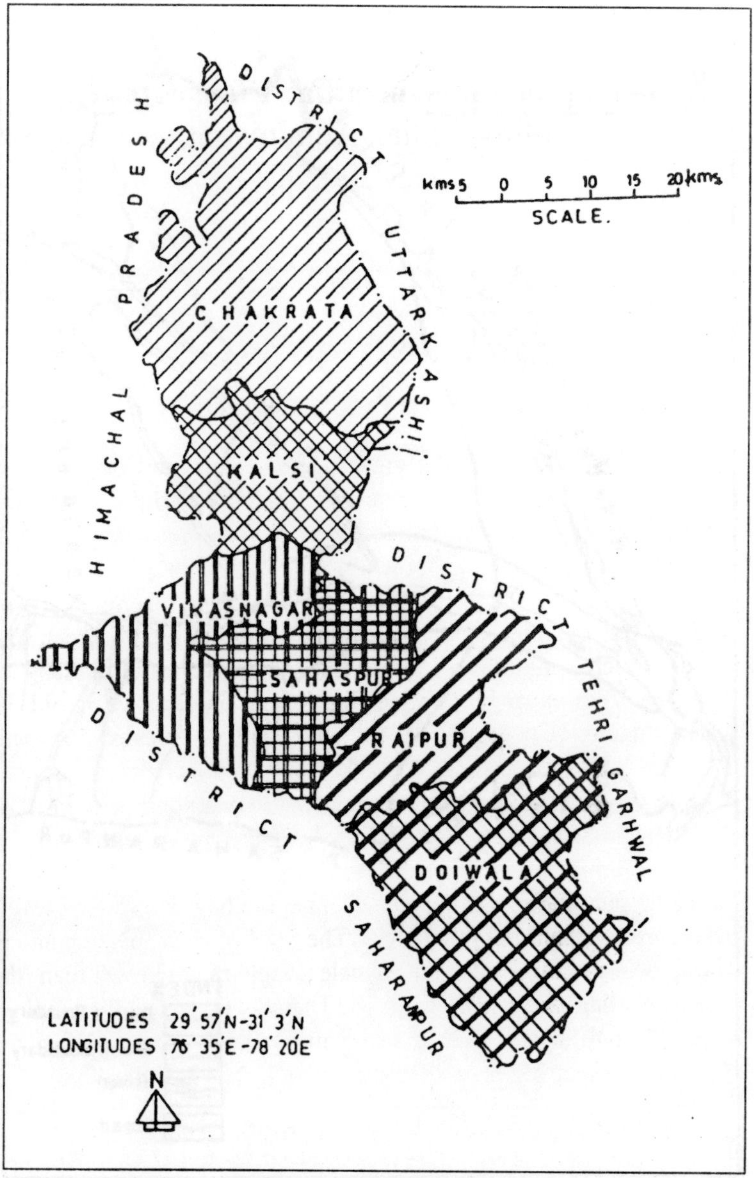

Fig. 8.1 : District Dehradun

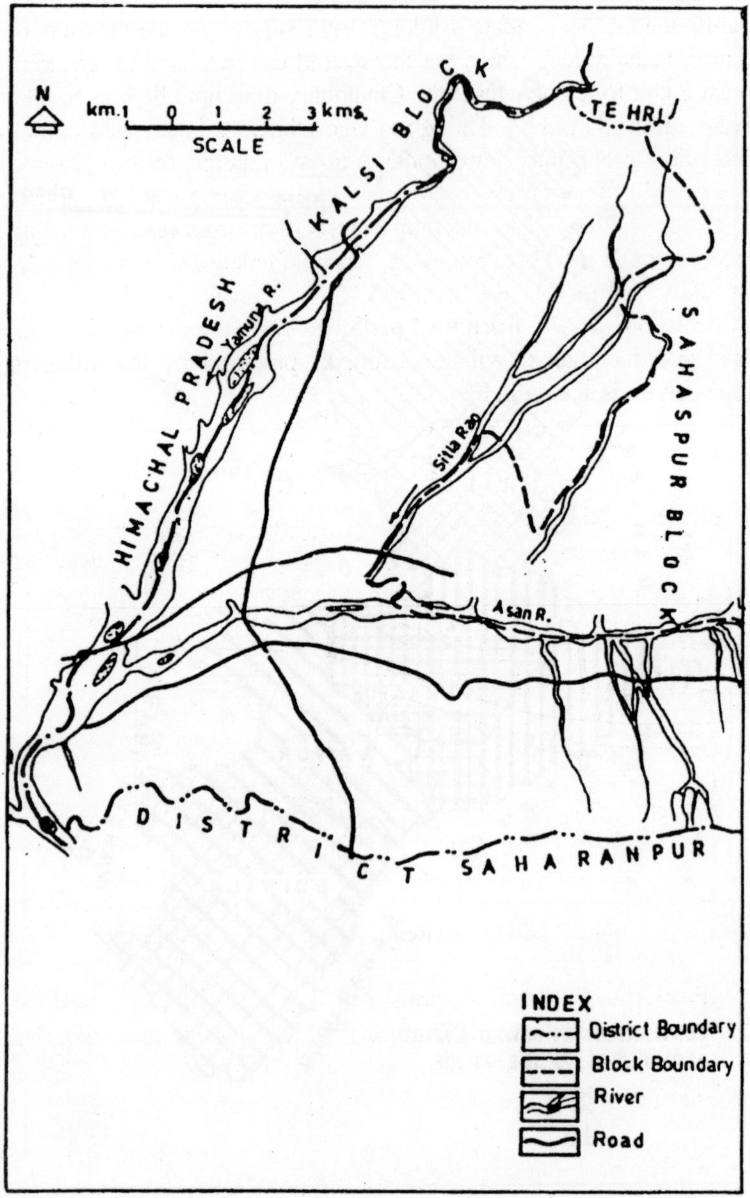

Fig. 8.2 : Block Vikasnagar

Most of the villages suffer from diseases caused by poor sanitation and inadequate drinking water supply. As the villagers of Timli, located deep inside the forest, told us, "we have to go to at least 2 km. to fetch water if the Chaudhary does not allow us to take water from his pipes". Though village Dhakrani in the same block has many group interviews, indirect questionnaires, semi-structured interviews, focus group discussions, participatory rural appraisal methods (PRA) like mapping transect, priority ranking, utility matrix, social and resource maps, seasonal calendars, gender issues in daily routine of the people etc. were used to elicit direct information based on people's participation. An example of social and resource map of village Timli, as prepared by the villagers themselves, is shown in Fig. 8.3.

Fig. 8.3 : Social and Resource Map of Timli Village

Participatory Rural Appraisal (PRA) methods were used by us for this block-level planning. PRA was used to avoid the problems associated with long and costly formal surveys. These problems include the following :

- the problem of collecting too much data,
- the problem of collecting irrelevant data,
- the problem of producing inappropriate results, and
- the problem of low involvement of the local people.

PRA has an in-built mechanism to encourage participation of local people in the process of development by involving local people in research and design of socio-economic endeavours so as to lead to increasing commitment and empowerment of the common masses.

The principles of PRA can be briefly outlined as (see Chapter 1 for details):

Increased involvement of the local people throughout the stay in the villages through personal interviews, group interviews, focus-group discussions, mapping, transect, etc.

Learning from the common people, using local terminologies, so that the repository of local knowledge and wisdom is optimally utilized for treating the issues at hand.

Ensuring involvement of people in the entire process from different backgrounds and with different areas of local expertise so as to make the PRA inter-disciplinary in character through visual methods such as social/resource mapping, transect walks, seasonal calendar, preference ranking and scoring, construction of diagrams, etc.

The villagers also described the rainfall patterns, the crops sown, the water sources, the labour demand and the labour migration which are indicated in the seasonal calendar (See Fig. 8.4).

Analysis of Seasonal Calendar

Rainfall is maximum in July and August and there is some winter rainfall in January and February.

Kharif crops include rice, maize, millet, etc., while vegetables are grown in winter. Wheat and pulses are grown in rabi season.

Labour demand is maximum during July and August and also during November and December.

There is no water problem in the rainy season but the problem is acute during summer months.

There is no labour migration from rural to urban areas from July to January, but during non-agricultural season people do migrate to nearby towns.

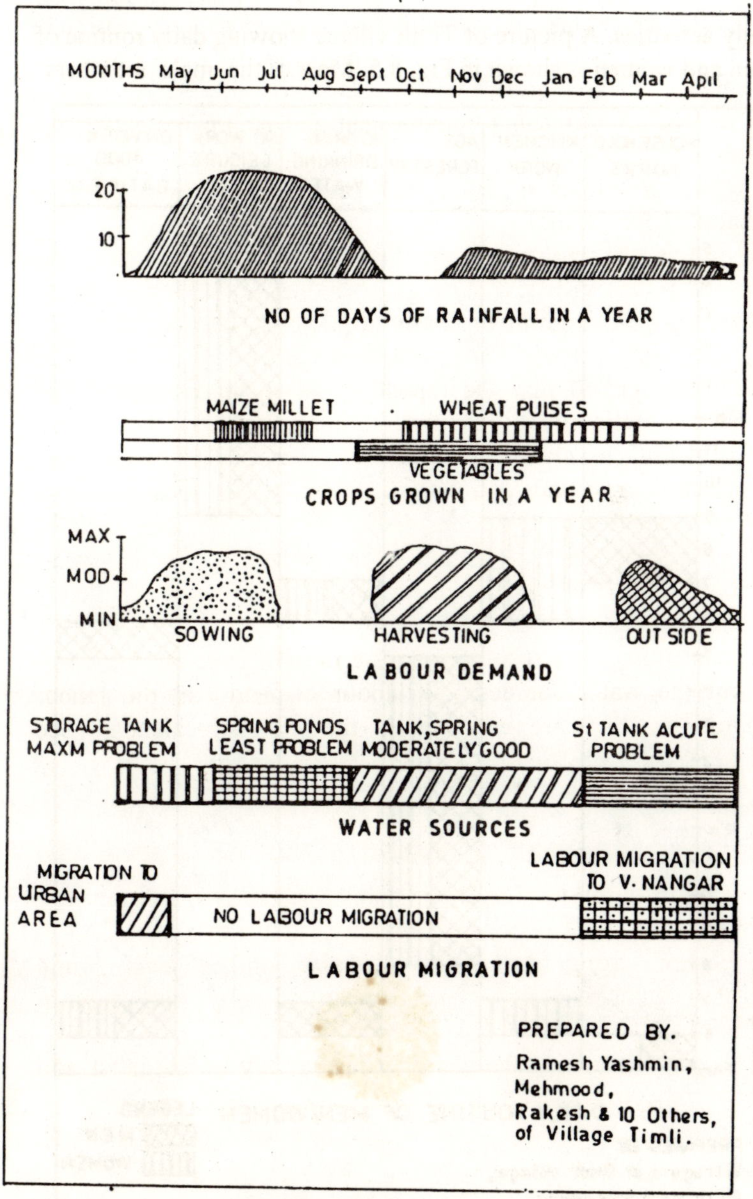

Fig. 8.4 : Seasonal Calendar

We talked to menfolk and womenfolk in separate groups during our stay in the villages of Vikasnagar block about their daily activities. A picture of Timli village showing daily routine of men and women is shown in Fig. 8.5. Most of the male members

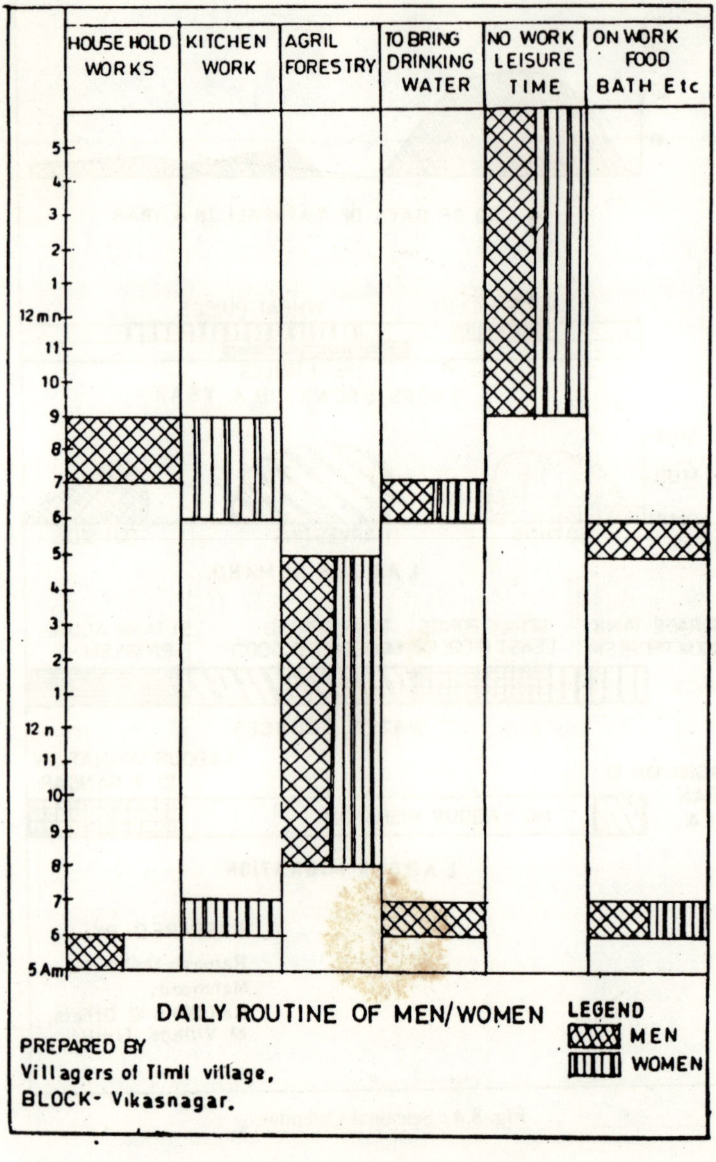

Fig. 8.5 : Daily Routine of Men/Women

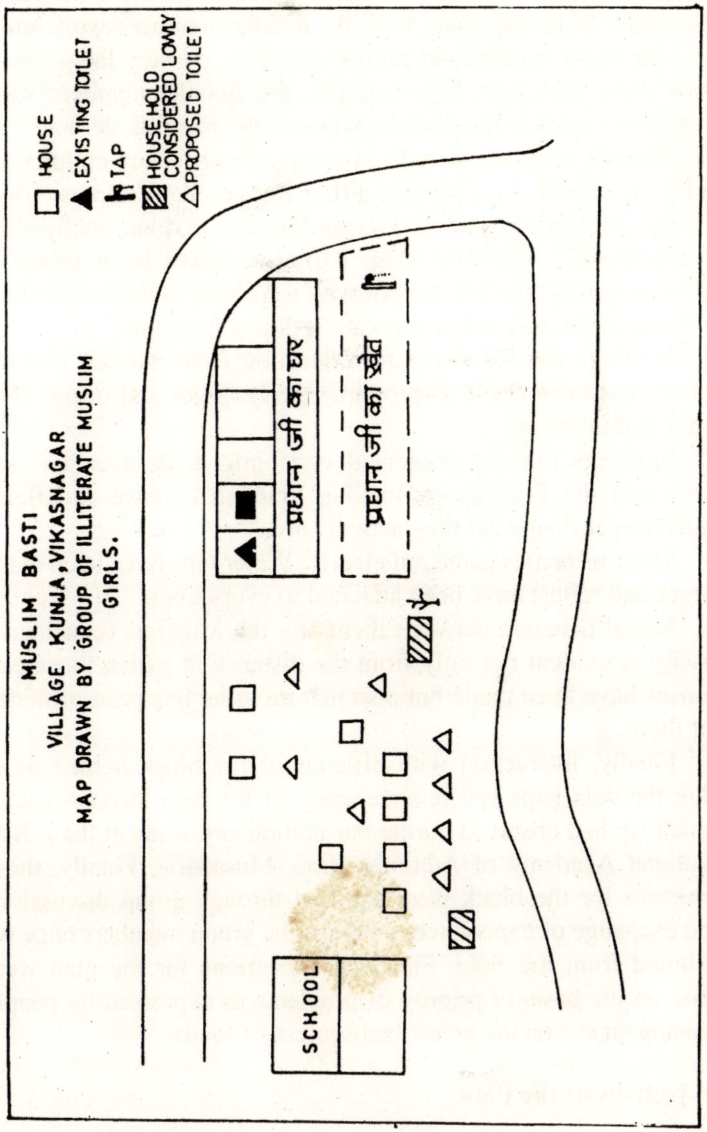

Fig. 8.6 : Muslim Basti village Kunja, Vikasnagar map drawn by group of Illiterate Muslim

spend their daytime in agricultural fields whereas the womenfolk engage themselves in household chores. Some women go to forests to collect fuel for their kitchen and fodder for their cattle. We learn from the chart that the female members work more than the male members in general and they are very laborious in their daily activities. For example, the female members work four hours extra in the kitchen, whereas the menfolk do not.

Though there are schools in most villages, many children do not go to school. As a Muslim girl of Kunja village told us, "How I wish I could go to school! Though I have eyes, I am totally blind to the world". The map (Fig. 8.6) was drawn by a group of illiterate young Muslim women who were very enthusiastic about it. Some interesting inferences can be drawn from this:

It brings out the desire for education from the fact that the school has been made disproportionately larger and nearer than what it actually is.

It brings out the perceived economic disparities between them and the Pradhan by making Pradhan's house and fields much larger than what they actually are.

Their priorities came out clearly. Water taps have been made larger and toilets have been attached to every home.

Social distance between them and the Muslims (considered lowly) is evident not only from the distance at which those two houses have been made but also that no toilet has been provided for them.

Finally, interaction with officials of the block helped us to plug the data gaps and remove many of the data inconsistencies which we had observed during our preliminary study at the L.B.S. National Academy of Administration, Mussoorie. Finally, these priorities for the block were clarified through group discussions and exchange of experiences amongst the group members once we returned from the field. Financial allocations for the plan were done on the basis of priority of problems as expressed by people keeping an eye on the prescribed sources of funds.

Objectives of the Plan

Based on people's perception and the available resources of the block, the following objectives have been decided upon for the formulation of the block plan :

To reduce the infant mortality rate by a frontal attack on the problems of bad sanitation and inadequate drinking water supply.

To raise the overall status of the women through a multi-sectoral approach.

To stress the importance of primary education among the people by various motivational campaigns.

To design a suitable scheme to arrest the degradation of forests through plantations at various places and to restore ecological balance.

To increase the income of the farmers by improving agricultural production and other allied activities like animal husbandry and horticulture.

To set up a processing industry for providing wage employment to the local people.

To provide suitable all-weather roads and communications to all the villages.

SOURCES OF FINANCE

The finance available for block Vikasnagar, including district and state sector plans, institutional and bank credit, income of gram sabhas, U.P. State Finance Corporation, Housing Board Finance and Central Government contributions, is Rs. 21.76 crores. The details of the flow of finances from different sources are as follows :

Source		% age in total outlay
1.	District Sector Plan	23.5
2.	State Sector Plan	21.11
3.	Central Contribution	2.94
4.	Contribution from Gram Sabhas	0.02
5.	Institutional Finance (Block Credit Plan)	39.02
6.	U.P.S.F.C. Credit	13.13
7.	Housing Board Credit	0.28
		100.00

Therefore, 47.57 per cent of the total outlay is available as grant, amount to Rs. 10.35 crores, while the remaining 52.43 per cent of the outlay is available on loan from the financial institutions, amount to Rs. 11.4 crores.

Other Means of Finance Generation

A cooperative body, called the Vikasnagar Industrial Development Cooperative (V.I.D.C.), is proposed to be set up to finance viable, income generating, agro-processing units in

Vikasnagar. It is proposed that the people of the block would contribute towards the equity capital of the cooperative. No problem is envisaged for contribution from the people for setting up of such a cooperative because the cooperative would be used to finance agro-processing units to be set up in future in the region. This would not only provide wage employment to the people of the block, but would also increase their income level due to better prices provided for their farm produce.

The capital structure of the cooperative is proposed as follows:

Equity (9%)		Rs. 50 lakhs
(5,000 households from the block contributing at an average of Rs.1000 per family).		
Loan from the State Govt.	(35%)	Rs. 194 lakhs
Loan from N.C.D.C.*	(56%)	Rs. 311 lakhs
Total capital		Rs. 555 lakhs

The capital of Rs. 5.55 crores of Vikasnagar Industrial Development Cooperative would be used to contribute towards the equity capital of viable, agro-processing based units in the block of Vikasnagar, so that the people of Vikasnagar benefit not only in terms of income generation, but also as an alternative marketing unit for their farm produce and providing wage employment to them.

DRINKING WATER

"Water, Water everywhere
not a drop to drink."

Nothing better than the lines quoted above could sum up the problem of safe drinking water in Vikasnagar development block. Water is a basic necessity for existence. Non-availability of safe drinking water gives rise to a large number of problems ranging from high incidence of various water-borne diseases and high mortality rate to intolerable drudgery for womenfolk of the area.

* National Cooperative Development Corporation

Though the data base maintained by both the block development office and Centre for Micro Planning and Regional Studies in the L.B.S. National Academy of Administration, Mussoorie, claims that every village in the block has been supplied with at least one source of safe drinking water, the naked reality is that half the population of the block is still compelled to depend on water from ponds, canals and rain water storage tanks. In some areas, the water source is so far away that women spend three hours each in mornings and evenings for fetching water. Hence, provision of safe drinking water to all the people overrides all other development concerns and the popular excuse of lack of funds or the resource crunch, etc. cannot be an excuse at all for not providing a safe source of drinking water to the people. To arrive at a reasonably accurate idea of the magnitude of the problem eight villages in the block were selected on a random basis for an intensive study of the problem of drinking water in the block. It was found that four out of the eight villages studied did not have a source of safe drinking water.

However, the difficult and rocky terrain of the area under study poses serious difficulties in this task. It is not that the government has not made efforts to alleviate the problem in the past but the government plans have not succeeded in many villages due to various reasons.

For planning of drinking water in the block, the following five alternatives were studied:

- Hand pumps,
- Water supply through taps and pipe lines,
- Water storage tanks to tap rain water,
- Tubewells, and
- Wells.

The ground water table in the block varies from 50 feet to 350 feet. Except for five villages where the water level is more than 300 feet, the rest of the 30 villages are proposed to be installed with India Mark II hand pumps. These hand pumps, sturdy and efficient as they are, have been very successful wherever these have been installed. One hand pump will cost Rs. 35000 and given that one hand pump is required for a population of 250.

Following a modified criteria, four hand pumps need to be provided in each of the 25 villages identified as problem villages.

Financial Allocation

The total number of hand pumps proposed to be installed is 100. Therefore, the total requirement of funds is Rs. 35 lakhs (at the rate of Rs. 35,000 per hand pump).

For the rest five problem villages, we propose that tubewells be set up. This will cost us Rs. 20 lakhs as each tubewell with a capacity of 20 horse power will cost Rs. 4 lakhs.

Funds requirements will be as follows:

1. Hand pumps India Mark	100 Nos.	Rs. 35 lakhs
2. Tubewells	5 Nos.	Rs. 20 lakhs
		Rs. 55 lakhs

Maintenance of these drinking water facilities is of paramount importance. We have seen how many of such schemes fail due to poor maintenance.

It is proposed that one person from each village be selected or nominated by the GS and trained for maintenance. Each village GS will also be supplied with a maintenance kit for repairs of hand pumps and tubewells. The duration of this training will be 15 days.

The training expenses are envisaged to be Rs. 1000 per person

Total Rs. 30,000

(A) Toolskit for hand pumps
25 kits @ Rs. 600 per person = 15,000

(B) Toolskit for tubewells
5 kits @ Rs.1000 per person = 5,000

Total A+B	=	20,000
		55.00
		0.30
		0.20
Total funds required		55.50 lakhs

A total of Rs. 55.5 lakhs are required to take care of the problem of drinking water.

Before ending this note, it needs to be impressed upon the villagers that the facilities as planned above should be used only for drinking water purposes. Overuse of these facilities shall lead to more frequent breakdowns and faster wear and tear.

Water for other uses such as washing clothes, toilet, bathing, cattle, etc. needs to be drawn from other sources. For these purposes, it is proposed to construct a water harvesting storage tank in each village.

Each tank of the size of 30 x 30 x 5 mts shall cost		Rs.40,000 each
60 such tanks will cost 40,000 x 60	=	24.0 lakhs
Add		55.5 lakhs
Total funds requirements for this plan		79.5 lakhs

Conclusion

This plan, if properly implemented, will improve the health status of the population of the deficient areas. Diarrhoea which is a major cause of infant deaths can be controlled through provision of potable water. Above all, the awareness among the villagers about the use of safe drinking water will go a long way in ensuring a better quality of life.

HEALTH, FAMILY WELFARE AND SANITATION

The best indicator of the health status of any area is the Infant Mortality Rate (I.M.R.) which is 98/1000 for Vikasnagar block. It is a long way from the target of 60/1000 set out in the National Health Policy. Unless the health situation improves, the physical quality of life will remain low leading to poor human capital formation. Hence, it is imperative that the health scenario takes a change for the better through need-based block-level health planning and people's participation.

In view of the low socio-cultural status of the females in the block, their access to awareness and utilization of health services remain very poor. So, the gender issues involved in the health sector would also be taken into consideration while preparing the health plan.

In this chapter we would,

(a) prioritize the major health problems of Vikasnagar, based on Participatory Rural Appraisal methods used in three sample villages in the block, and
(b) use the villagers' suggestions and priorities in preparing a health plan for the block.

Statistical Outline of Health in Vikasnagar Block Data Base

Population		97,771*	
Number of households		18,179*	
I M R		98 / 1000	
M M R		4-5 / 1000	
Number of Allopathic Institutions			Beds
(a) Govt. Allopathic Dispensaries	3	- Katapatar	4
		- Kolisahaspur	4
		- Vikasnagar	4
(b) P H C	3	- Herbertpur	4
		- Rudrapur	4
		- Paschimnala	4
(c) Women's Hospital	1	- Vikasnagar	4
(d) P P C	1	- Vikasnagar	10
Number of Ayurvedic Dispensaries	3	- Langa	4
		- Horawala	4
		- Herbertpur	4
Number of Homoeopathic Dispensaries	1	- Sambhawala	0
Number of Maternity, Child & F.P sub centers	21		
Number of Doctors			
Allopathic	10		
Ayurvedic	8		
Homoeopathic	1		
Number of Nurses (Gen. Nursing)	1		
Number of Health Visitors	3		
Number of Health Supervisors	3		
Number of A.N.M.S	21		
Number of Male Health Workers	8		
Number of Non-Medical Assts.	2		

Source : Dr. R.C.S. Sayana, Deputy C M O, Dehradun.
* Census 1991 figures.

Methodology

A health PRA is an application of the methodology of Participatory Rural Appraisal to learn from rural people about issues related to health. Since the rural people are the victims of poor health conditions in villages, it is they who can tell us about their experiences and perceptions. It is only through direct participation that one learns about the health status of rural people, the kinds of illness, their linkages, sources, origin, treatment and other aspects. Hence, direct participation has the potential in improving the efficiency of health services. It can also make the process of planning truly need based.

Sampling

During our visit to the block headquarters, we were told by the medical officer that all the villages in Vikasnagar experienced frequent epidemics of water-borne diseases. She mentioned that the three most recent incidents were in the villages of Dhakrani, Kathapathar and Dhakrani Colony of which the latter two were relatively smaller villages. Hence, these three villages were chosen as the sample.

Prioritization of Problems as perceived by the Villagers

In Dhakrani village, with a population of 5323, a group of Gujjar women sat with us and prepared a health facility map of the village (Ref. Fig. 8.7). After the map was drawn, the discussions proved to be quite enlightening. Only houses of Gujjar families were represented in the map, though houses of other families existed in the village. The first facilities to be drawn on the map were the five private allopathic medical doctors who cater to the felt needs as far as minor ailments and injuries are concerned. Later, it came to light that one of the medical practitioners was only a lab analyst practising as a quack. Then the sub-centre was drawn. The discussions showed that the villagers were dissatisfied with the doctors and the sub-centre since comprehensive care was not given. They were sore at the fact that they could not afford the costs of long-term hospitalisation. It was at this point that one of the women mentioned, "It would have been so nice if we did not fall prey to diseases in the first place." The villagers unanimously agreed with this proposition and said that the root cause of all health problems is "gandagi" which was all pervasive. They also said that they used their courtyards for defecation. Our observation showed that drinking water was available in the village through the pipes and yet diarrhoea was common.

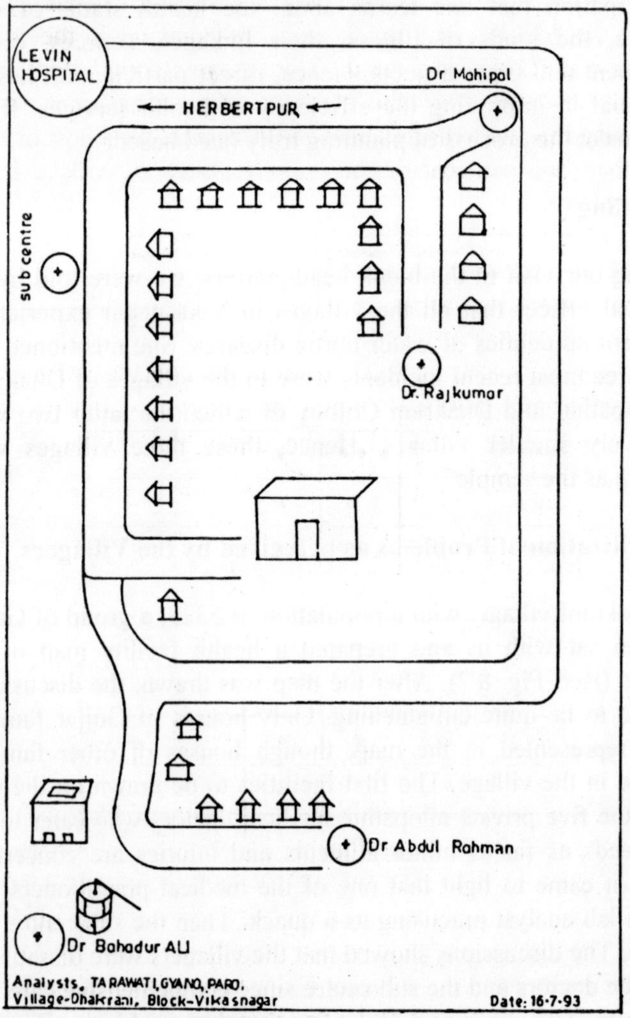

Fig. 8.7 : Village Map of Health Facilities

In the same village, another group of women prepared a seasonal matrix on diseases causing infant mortality (See Fig. 8.8). The five major diseases identified were diarrhoea, jaundice, measles, malaria and pneumonia and their incidences were marked with grains. All the diseases show a definite seasonal pattern. Diarrhoea and "jaundice" are the most common during the summer months and the women attributed it to lack of water. Jaundice could be due to Hepatitis A infection in view of this disclosure. Measles and pneumonia are common in the winter months and malaria in autumn. The villagers complained of the mosquito menace from the stagnant water after rains. While discussing this, the villagers blamed the excreta for a host of flies. Less than one per cent of the households of the village had a sanitary latrine.

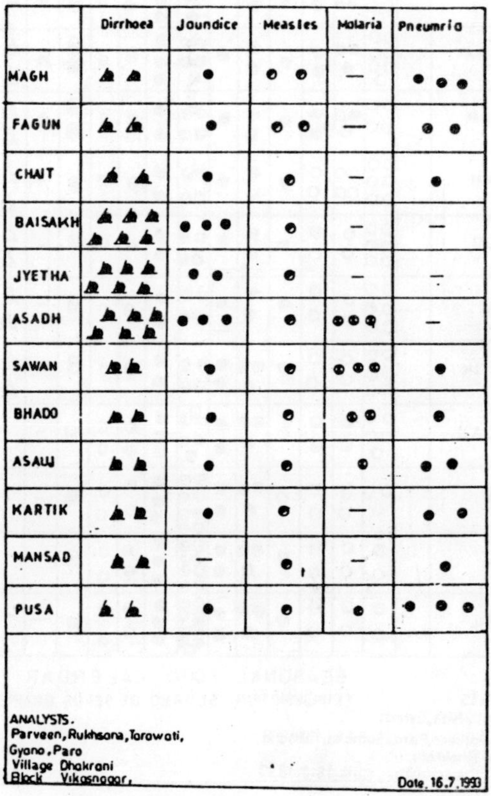

Fig. 8.8 : Seasonal Calendar of Diseases causing Infant Mortality (Scoring by Seeds)

In Dhakrani, the women made a seasonal food calendar for adults using grains (See Fig. 8.9). In all the food items, there is not only discrimination against the females but also a definite seasonal pattern (except in maize which is preferred in winter over wheat). Pulses are consumed more in winter because they produce "heat in summer." Vegetables are also eaten more in winter (like spinach, cauliflower, peas, etc.) due to greater availability. Mangoes are consumed in summer and in other months bananas are resorted to. Lassi is popular in summer.

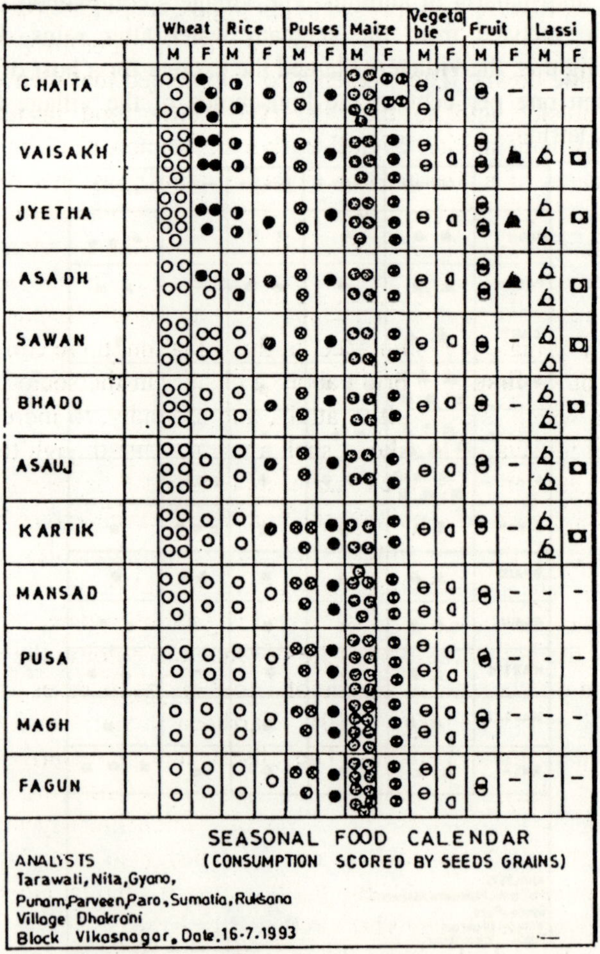

Fig. 8.9 : Seasonal Food Calendar (Consumption scored by Seeds Grains)

The seasonal food calendar reveals sex discrimination in terms of food consumption. When we asked the women about food discrimination, they denied it vehemently even after the map was made. They said it was natural for the male to eat more and the question of discrimination did not arise. They have internalised the cultural norm of male supremacy to such an extent that they do not feel wronged. But further discussion brought out the comment that young males should be very healthy in order to command a healthy dowry. Dowry was rampant, they said, and they did not mind suppressing the growth of a female child to postpone puberty in order to delay the inevitable dowry. The women also commented that men worked hard outside and so they deserved better food in terms of quantity and quality. Significantly, the women also mentioned that status of a pregnant or lactating mother was not different from that of an ordinary woman. The sex discrimination flowed not out of any ignorance on the part of the women (as is evidenced by the frequent references to qualitative nature of certain foods), but is a product of the overall socio-cultural pattern of male predominance. In this situation, there can be two ways out – firstly, to bring about a change in the socio-cultural milieu which is difficult to attain, and secondly, to increase the size of the available cake in such a manner that though the male gets a bigger slice, the female shall at least be provided the minimum need of required nutrition. From the calendars and the interviews, the low intake of fruits and vegetables is very glaring. The implications for planning would be to concentrate on homestead based fruit plants and vegetable gardens.

In the neighbouring village of Dhakrani colony, the women made a matrix scoring a scale of 1 to 8 on the diseases affecting the villagers (Ref. Fig. 8.10). Diarrhoea, malaria and anemia showed a higher ranking. The observations on diarrhoea and malaria tallied with those in Dhakrani village. The word used for anemia by the villagers was "sookhi" which literally means to "shrivel up". They looked anemia. They also complained of work infestations which is a major cause of anemia. No sanitary latrine was visible anywhere in this village too.

In short, the health problems of the block can be prioritized as follows :

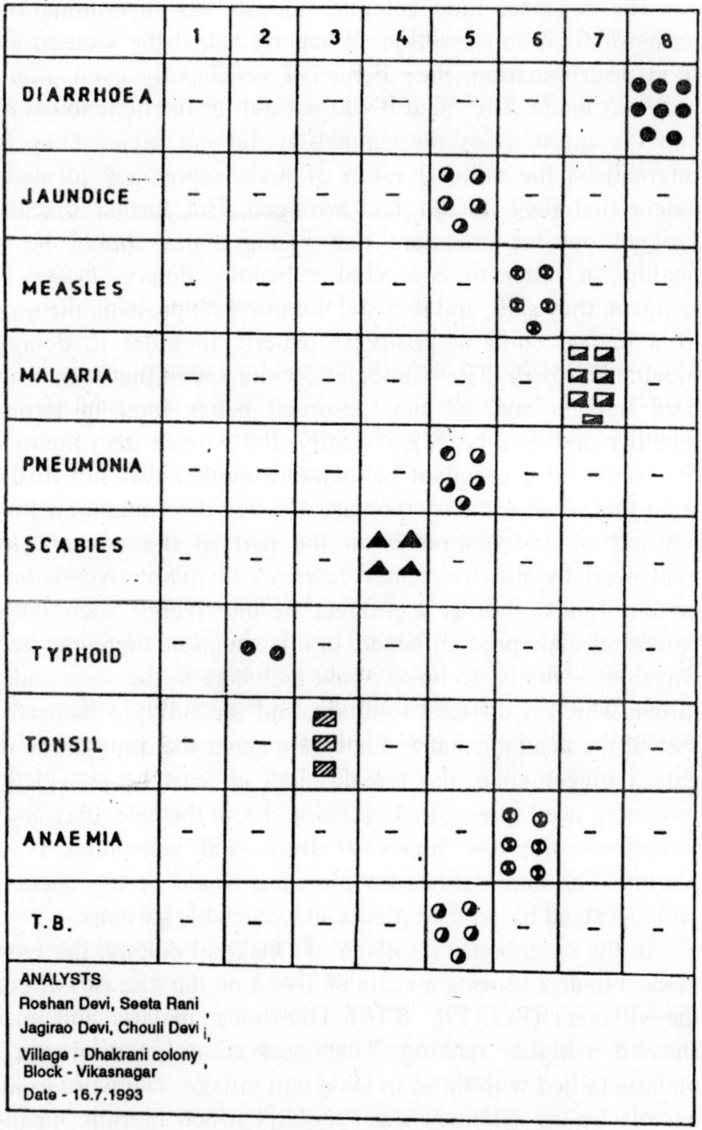

Fig. 8.10 : Incidence of Diseases (Scoring by Seeds)

1. Water-borne infections, water-washed diseases, water-based infections and water-related infections coupled with non-existent sanitation facilities.

2. Malnutrition-Protein Calorie Malnutrition and Fluid Electrolyte Malnutrition.
3. Vaccine – preventable diseases.
4. Acute respiratory infections including pneumonia.

The Plan

The stated objectives of the National Health Policy (N.H.P.) are not reflected in actual practice. The sectoral priorities implemented in the N.H.P. can be gauged from the distribution of public expenditure between curative and preventive services. About 55 per cent of the public expenditure on health services in India is spent on curative health care and medical education, while the share of public health services which are more relevant to rural health needs is just one-third of the total expenditure. Hence, in this plan for the block it is proposed to rectify the imbalance by concentrating wholly on preventive and promotive aspects of health. The P.H.Cs have not justified their existence in terms of health education, environmental sanitation, etc. Studies have shown that P.H.Cs have "flopped totally" and hence a novel attack on the diseases is proposed.

The inferences drawn from the PRA exercises indicate that the provision of drinking water alone cannot control water-borne diseases unless coupled with proper environmental sanitation. Clean drinking water and safe sanitation are not only basic to health and well-being but also have the biggest impact in altering the disease profile in a block like Vikasnagar. Universal access to safe drinking water and universal access to sanitary means of excreta disposal were two goals of the International Drinking Water Supply and Sanitation Decade. Therefore, it is felt that emphasis on sanitation would have maximum returns. In Vikasnagar, less than one per cent of the rural population has access to a sanitary latrine.

Goals can be achieved in many ways but if the achievements are to be self-sustaining, there must be active, willing and informed people's participation. All development plans must be responsive to people's felt needs and genuine aspirations. Mobilization of many organisations like NGOs on a massive scale to create popular awareness of demand for and participation in this plan will create its own momentum. It must be noted that the health plan should closely follow the implementation of the plan of education and drinking water. Experiments have shown time and again in the health sector that supply need not necessarily create its own demand. Unless the people are educated and aware of the need to make use of the services, there is bound to be massive underutilisation and misutilisation.

After the implementation of the plan for drinking water and the Information Education Communication approach in the education plan, the momentum will be used to drive home the fact that lack of environmental sanitation is the major cause of mortality and morbidity and in keeping with the people's priorities, sanitation should be given the pride of place.

There are 18,179 households in the block, of which 14,000 households do not have access to a sanitary latrine. Of this, 4,000 belong to the Scheduled Castes and Scheduled Tribes. The plan is to have 100 per cent coverage in sanitary latrines for the entire block. The Technical Advisory Group of the Government of India, UNICEF on rural sanitation has recommended the pour-flush water seal leached double pit latrine which needs only 1.5 to 2 litres of water for flushing. The cost of this latrine is Rs. 3,400 including the enclosing walls and the ceiling. Work will be taken up for an SC / ST household if it is ready to contribute to the cost of the latrine by way of labour contribution alone. In other words, the beneficiary belonging to the SC/ST category would have a stake of about Rs. 600 per latrine. The households belonging to categories other than SC/ST would have a higher stake of Rs. 2,000 per latrine, with government subsidy of Rs. 1,400 per latrine. The difference of Rs. 1,400 could be had on credit from banks. There would be continuing conscientisation among the villagers for adopting, using and maintaining the latrines they themselves have helped construct. Since the latrine would have a proper enclosure and ceiling, the privacy of the rural women can be ensured.

Before the thrust on sanitation, there would be an intensive health education campaign using audio-visual techniques emphasizing appropriate sanitation practices, the ways to break the sanitation barrier, ORT, growth monitoring, immunization, breast feeding, food supplementation and family planning.

The glaring drawback in the existing curative services is the paucity of drugs in the healthcare institutions. This drawback is sought to be removed by allocating Rs. 3.3 lakhs for the supply of medicines. Besides, allocation is also made for the upgradation of the homoeopathic dispensary and for the repairs of diagnostic and therapeutic instruments of the eleven existing healthcare units.

Vegetable kits worth Rs. 200 would be distributed to the female heads of 10,000 households to enable them to maintain homestead vegetable gardens which would yield nutritive sources of food.

Family Welfare

There will not be any separate family planning drive during the next one year. As a result of the plan, it is expected that the IMR will drop. There has never been a significant and sustained fall in birth rates which has not been preceded by a significant and sustained fall in child death rates.

Funding for the Plan	*Amount in lakhs*
1. Sanitation	
14,000 households	252
(further 140 lakhs are required as loan)	
2. Vegetable Kits	
10,000 households @ Rs. 200	20
3. Repair of 11 existing healthcare units	
(excluding homeopathic unit)	
11* 10,000	1.1
4. Upgradation of Homoeopathic Dispensary	0.1
5. Medicines for 33 healthcare institutions	
33* 10000	3.3
Total Funds for the Plan	276.5

Note : A further amount of Rs. 140 lakhs is required as loan for construction of rural latrines.

Conclusion

A novel approach of tackling the problem of high mortality and morbidity by concentrating on its single largest cause – water-borne diseases is attempted.

Preventive and promotive aspects of health are strengthened at the cost of curative aspects.

The approach is multi-disciplinary.

Involvement of NGOs, international agencies like UNDP, UNICEF and W.H.O. would be made use of.

An attempt is made to extend sanitation facilities to all households without any access to them.

Appropriate, cost-competitive technology has been emphasized.

Community participation is the basis of the formulation and implementation of the plan.

The discrimination faced by the women is sought to be mitigated.

EDUCATION

Introduction

The importance of education in our development process is unchallenged. It has often been dubbed as the panacea for problems relating to adoption of family planning techniques, health and sanitation, superstitions, women's exploitation, bonded labour, etc.

An attempt was made by this group to analyse the existing situation in the education sector in Vikasnagar block through the data collected from various sources and through empirical observations. On the basis of this, a plan for improving the education scenario in the block has been proposed.

Some Empirical Observations

Besides the data obtained from secondary sources, the group as small sub-groups of two, visited 15 odd villages in the block where they interacted with the people (through unstructured interviews and several PRA methods).

Many Children do not Go to School

Since the village visit started in the morning itself, coinciding with school timings, we were amazed to find many children in their homes and when asked why they didn't go to school, the answers were :

"Just like that" – showing total indifference to education.

"He keeps running away from school even though we bought him a new bag. He is very naughty!" It is naughtiness or is it some problem which he faces in school ....?

"We have eight children; husband died, how can we afford it."

Some of the villages visited like Kunja, Garant, Thakrani had almost 50 per cent Muslim population. It was observed that this phenomenon was more prevalent in case of Muslim families.

Awareness regarding importance of education was high.

It was encouraging to note that most people were aware of its importance and also sent their children to schools. In the Hindu and Harijan *bastis* of village Garant some students were travelling all the way up to Herbertpur for High School education.

While interacting with a group of totally illiterate, married Muslim women, it was found that they were highly desirous of education and remorseful that they could not go to school. In fact, it has been highlighted in the map (attached) drawn by the young ladies themselves where they have made a disproportionately big school. These girls could not open the pen, did not know their age but were very vocal about their problems and desires.

Less Faith in Government Schools

In casual conversation with the villagers, it was found that they were quite pessimistic about government schools mainly because:

Teachers hardly come,

They teach mechanically, and

Roof leakages etc.

Most held private schools in high esteem which they feel bring better results.

Gender Issues

Though no significant difference was found in the enrolment patterns of boys and girls, the drop-out rate was much higher for females (exact figures for the block could not be obtained). This was more in case of Muslim families, where most girls dropped out after class IV or V. Domestic chores in supporting a large family was the most often cited reason.

Quality of education leaves much to be desired.

It was found from the villagers that more often the teachers remained absent and when they came, they either did not teach or taught in a demotivated fashion.

Content and methodology is also very monotonous.

The main objectives of the proposed plan are :

Strengthening the primary education sector by providing more schools, more teachers, more and better quality infrastructure (sports kits, libraries etc.),

Strengthening network of middle and high schools,

Introducing higher education in the block through a degree college,

Emphasis on vocational education by setting up a polytechnic, and a college exclusively for women,

Most importantly stressing on information, education and communication, i.e., motivating students (through 'Mid-day Milk' Scheme, better facilities and more accessible schools) and also teachers (through motivational programmes in Teacher Training Institute).

Methodology and Database

Data was obtained from both primary and secondary sources. The secondary sources used were :

- Information with the block level officials,
- District Census Handbook,
- Dehradun District Database, and
- Perspective Plan for Dehradun District

However, a lot of importance was given to primary data collection for which efforts were made to ascertain the needs of the people and to ask for their priorities for development. This was achieved by selecting a few random, representative villages and then through an in-depth study of these villages. Wherever possible, Participatory Rural Appraisal techniques were employed. All efforts were made to make the villagers talk and prioritize their problems to bring out gender issues etc.

Norms widely accepted for location of schools were used,

- One Primary School within 1.5 km serving 200 village population.
- One Middle School within 3.0 km serving 5000 village population.
- One High School within 8.0 km serving 8000 village population.

An Overview of Existing Facilities in Vikasnagar

Vikasnagar block has a literacy percentage of 51 as per 1991 census. The number and percentage of male and female literates in the block Vikasnagar, as per 1991 census, are as follows.

Table 8.1 : Number and percentage of literates in Vikasnagar

	Male	Female	Total
Number	26606	13451	40057
Total population	52796	44975	97771
Population below 7 years	9529	8797	18326
Percentage	61.5	39	51

Primary Schools

Vikasnagar block has 83 primary schools. An interblock comparison (through "Dehradun District Database") reveals that amongst the 6 blocks it has the least number of primary schools. However, as it has 58 villages, and the number of schools per village is 1.44. However there are 1238 persons per primary school making it the worst served block by primary schools in the district as compared to Chakrata where there are 372 persons per primary school which is the best served block by primary schools.

On the basis of data collected through various sources – Dehradun District Database and from Block authorities and through the empirical findings it was seen that :

Availability and state of school buildings were very bad. In Teepuspur, there was only a two-room building. In other places in rainy season the buildings leak. Of the 83 schools, two are without buildings and 20 need repairs.

Facilities / Infrastructure in Schools: Though all schools have blackboards and some other sports kits etc., most do not have the rugs to be used as seating arrangement for the children. They also lack games, toys, music and other such facilities, necessary for the all-round development of the children.

Distance of Village from Primary School : There are six villages where the school was at an average distance of 2 km. and six villages where the primary school was less than one km. away.

Teachers

Table 8.2 : No. of Teachers in Primary Schools

	Male	Female	Total
Number	166	80	246
Percentage	67.5	32.5	100

The above Table 8.2 shows a slight bias in the appointment of female teachers in primary schools.

Enrolment Figures : The population in the age group of 6-10 years is 14902 students and those enrolled are 12680.

Visit to some representative villages revealed that enrolment was less in Muslim families, particularly the girls. Reasons cited by them were mainly :

Lack of interest by the children themselves,
Poverty and hence the need for more help at home and work,
Large families and, therefore, the need for girls to stay at home to look after the families.
Interaction with some Muslim girls, however, showed that they would have loved to study as is evident from the huge school they made on their map (Fig. 8.6).

Middle Schools

There are 23 Middle Schools in whole Vikasnagar block, i.e., 4614 persons per school. An inter-block comparison revealed that in Dehradun district, except Vikasnagar, all blocks have a bigger share of schools than their shares of population.

(a) Enrolment Pattern

	Pop.	Boys Enrol.	Rate	Pop.	Girls Enrol.	Rate	Pop.	Total Enrol.	Total Rate	SC%	ST%
Primary (0-11)	8347	7663	91.8	6555	5017	76.5	14902	12680	83.1	23	19
Middle (11-14)	5718	2471	43.2	4301	1793	41.7	10019	4264	42.6	23	23.7
High (15-17)	3454	1682	48.7	2366	763	32.2	5280	2445	42.0	23	43

Distance	No. of villages having middle schools
Within village	20
0-1 km	01
1-3 km	12
3.5 km	10
5 km	14

Buildings : Buildings Repairable	20
Buildings required	12

High Schools

The block has eight High Schools in the rural areas and three in Vikasnagar town; making it very underserved in this regard.

Residential school at Ambari (ST pocket).

Polytechnics : None in Vikasnagar. There are only two, both located in Dehradun city.

Degree Colleges – None in Vikasnagar, five in Dehradun and one each in Mussoorie and Rishikesh.

Adult Education – nine centres started on 1.4.87 and ended on 31.3.88.

Proposed Plan

It thus becomes evident that mere proliferation of schools or addition of teachers cannot serve by itself after the existing dismal scenario of education in the block. Therefore, efforts have to be made to motivate the children, their parents and the teachers to make school experience a true learning experience.

Data showed that two school buildings were less, 20 schools needed repairs and that there were six such villages which did not have a school within a km. radius. The plan provides for these 6+2 school buildings and also repairs of the 20 buildings needing repairs.

It was found that Vikasnagar block required 71 additional primary school teachers.

(*Source :* Draft Plan of Dehradun District). That has been provided for.

To improve the quality of education in all schools, provisions have been made for libraries, some furniture, sports kits and 50 sets of textbooks per school which will not be given out to students but can only be used by any student as and when required in the school itself. These would be managed by a students' council under the supervision of a teacher.

Vikasnagar has a sizable Muslim population who, for various cultural and social reasons often, are not motivated enough to go to schools. For them as well as for others a 'Motivation Drive' is proposed to be launched for which audio-visual aids will be used. Three 16 mm projectors, six tape recorders and few cassettes have been provided for in the budget. The drive would focus on :

(a) Health Education
(b) Family Planning
(c) Nutrition and Child Care
(d) Women Power

} Targeted for women

(a) NFDC Films on Bravery etc.
(b) On Good Qualities

} for children

(a) Alcoholism
(b) Literacy

A Mid Day Milk Scheme is proposed where in 250 ml of milk will be provided per child in primary schools for a period of 180 working days. The milk will be obtained from the local villagers. Heating etc. will be done on fuelwood to be provided by the villagers.

This scheme would not only act as an incentive for children to come to schools thus increasing the enrolment rate and decreasing the dropout rate, but also elevate the low health status of the children of this block.

Twentyfour villages have middle schools at a distance of more than 3 kms. from the village. Twelve more middle schools are provided for.

At present in the whole of Dehradun district there are only seven Degree Colleges with five in Dehradun, one each in Mussoorie and Rishikesh. The group felt the need for the setting up of a degree college in Vikasnagar, but since college is not a part of the district sector plan, therefore, no provision could be kept for the purpose.

Implementation Plan

The Mid Day Milk Scheme has to be implemented with full cooperation of local villagers and active participation of school children and teachers. The milk will be purchased from the IRDP beneficiaries of the village. The villagers are also expected to provide the fuelwood.

The school buildings have to be constructed within the stipulated time period to avoid cost and time overruns. Efforts will be made, wherever possible, to obtain land free of cost from government for the establishment of new schools.

Financial Allocation

*	Primary Schools :		
(a)	School buildings for 2 primary schools (2 x 3,00,000)	6,00,000	
(b)	Primary schools to be repaired (20		
	Major repairs (13 x 50,000)	6,50,000	
	Minor repairs (7 x 30,000)	2,10,000	
(c)	Expenditure for the establishment of 6 new primary schools in villages which have no primary schools within a radius of 2 kms.		
	6 acres of land (Rs. 25,000/acre)	1,50,000	
	6 schools bld. (Rs. 2,00,000/building)	12,00,000	
	Salaries of teachers (3/ school; Rs. 2000/month)	4,32,000	
	Salaries of attendants (1/ school, Rs. 1000/month)	72,000	
(d)	Salaries for 71 additional teachers for primary schools (Rs. 2000/month)		17,04,000
(e)	Mid Day Milk Scheme		
	Number of primary school children	= 12680	
	Milk provided/child/day	= 250 ml	
	No. of working days/year	= 180	
	Price of milk/litre	= Rs. 6/-	
	Total expenditure on Mid-day milk scheme		22,00,000
(f)	Provision of libraries to all 64 schools at Rs. 2,000/library		1,28,000
(g)	Sports kit to all primary schools at Rs. 5,000/school		3,20,000
(h)	Text book sets for all 64 schools 50 sets/ schools at Rs. 60/- set of text books		1,92,000
			78,58,000

* Middle Schools (12)	
Land (10 acre/ school at Rs. 25,000/acre)	3,00,000
Buildings (Rs. 2,00,000/building)	24,00,000
Salaries of teachers (3/school at Rs.2000/month)	8,00,000
Salaries of attendants (1/school at Rs.1000/month)	1,10,000
	38,28,000
* Teachers' Training Institute	2,00,000
* A polytechnic college for women is proposed to be set up at Vikasnagar and an initial provision of Rs. 2,50,000 was made for it in the first year	2,50,000

* **Audio visual equipment**	
16 mm projectors (2/block at a cost of Rs. 50,000/projector)	1,00,000
Tape recorders (6/block at Rs. 3,000/set)	18,000
Cassettes (60/block at Rs. 50/cassette)	3,000
* Miscellaneous expenditure	4,50,000
Total	1,27,07,000

Therefore, the total budgetary allocation for education sector of Vikasnagar block is Rs. 1,27,07,000.

FOREST – THE GREEN COVER

Ever since human civilization has evolved, the forest has been of great service to it by meeting its essential needs of food and shelter. Forest resources play a vital role in the evolution of human civilization. Accurate and comprehensive monitoring of forest resources is one of the major steps towards the prevention, control and management of ecology. So planning in the forestry sector is a must to attain the goal of environmental upgradation and related benefits. The future of mankind is interwined with the extent and nature of the forest cover. Keeping this in mind, an attempt has been made here to plan for forest resources at block level.

Dehradun district has a total forest cover of 219.5 thousand hectares (69 per cent of total geographical area). Scientific management of forest commenced in 1864 in the valley in areas of forests owned by Zamindars and ex-rulers, taken over by Government in 1952. Varieties of forest species, hundreds of minor forest produce and many kinds of wild animals highlight the forest wealth of the district.

The integral relationship of forest and common man is as true of Vikasnagar block as in the case of any other area in the world. The importance of the forest species in day to day living of local people is brought out in the utility matrix of forest products (See Fig. 8.11) by the villagers of village Timli, Vikasnagar block, Dehradun.

Through a utility matrix of forest trees and their uses the villagers of Timli demonstrated their dependence on forest produce. They scored each use of the trees with the help of seeds taken by us to the field. The scores in the matrix are out of 10 and show the number of seeds the people used to indicate the importance of each use of the tree concerned. To take one example (See Fig. 8.11), Bakli and Dhaman trees have maximum use as fuelwood in contrast to that of Amla and Bahra which are used for medicinal purposes and fruits. The analysis of the matrix is as follows :

NAME OF F.P. / USES	AMLA	SAL	SESUM	SAN	JINGAR	BAHR	MANGO	BAKLI-DHAMON	AMALTUS	SEM	CHAKOTRA JAMUN
FUEL WOOD	1	1	5	5	4	1	1	9	–	3	3
CONSTRUCT PURPOSES	2	6	7	4	3	3	4	8		2	4
FODDER USES	–	–	–	7	–	–	—	–	1	8	2
CONSUMPTION VALUE	7	–	–	—	—	4	8	-	5	—	5
FOR SHADE LEAF PLATES	—	6	7	8	2	—	5	8	3	5	6
MEDICINAL VALUE	10	—	—	—	3	9	2		10		2
COMMERCIAL VALUE	7	10	9	5	9	8	10	4	9	2	5
AS FRUITS	5	—	—	—	—	2	10	—	2	—	8

UTILITY RANKING OF MINOR FOREST PRODUCTS

SCORE: 1 To 10 (In order of utility

PREPARED BY. Villagers of Timli,

Fig. 8.11 : Utility Ranking of Minor Forest Products

Analysis of Utility Matrix

The villagers have highest use of Bakli and Dhaman trees for fuelwood purposes and for construction of kutcha houses.

San and Sem trees are mostly used for fodder purposes.

Leaves of Sal, Sesum, San and Jamun are used for shade and preparing leaf plates.

Mango, Amaltus, Amla, Bahra, Jamun, etc. are used as fruits, and are very popular among the villagers.

Sal and Sesum trees are of highest commercial value, but the people are not so keen about the use of Sal trees because most of these trees are found in the Reserved Forest (See Fig. 8.12) and they do not get any direct benefit from these trees.

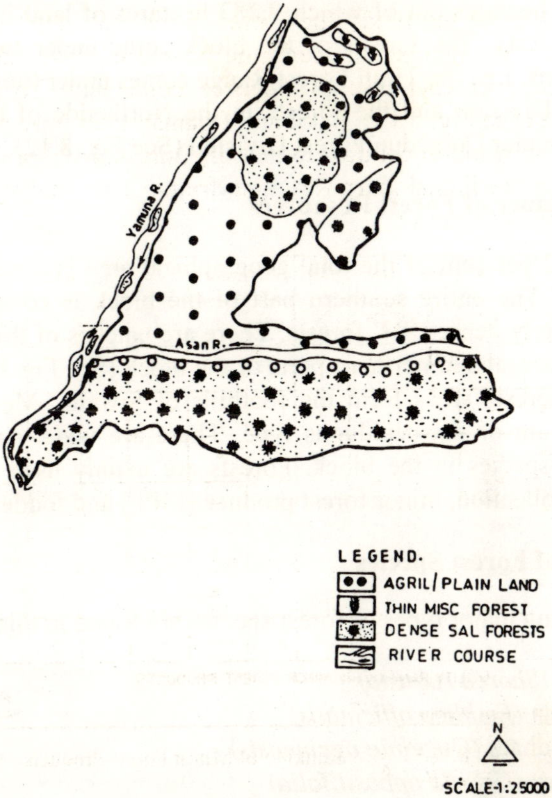

Fig. 8.12 : Forest Map of Vikasnagar

Methodology of Planning

Our planning strategy is directed towards involvement of people's participation in strengthening of natural resource base of the block. To begin with, we selected certain sample villages namely on the basis of availability of forest cover. People's initiative and participation were made key elements in the process of planning, instead of people acting as mere onlookers in the planning process. The sample villages were visited in small groups.

Vikasnagar block of Dehradun district is basically situated in the western-most corner of the Doon Valley. This block is partly covered with forests. The total geographical area of the block is

29,048 hectares out of which 9,282 hectares of land is covered with forests. The forests of the block come under two Forest Divisions, i.e., the Timli Forest Range comes under the Shiwalik Forest Division and the forests in the North-side of the block comes under Dehradun Forest Division (See Fig. 8.12).

Importance of Forest Resources

Only 32 per cent of the total geographical area is covered with forests. The entire southern part of the block is covered with moderately dense 'Sal' forests. There are patches of thin forests in the central and northern parts of the block (See Fig. 8.12). the entire forests areas form the foothills of Siwalik. Most of the forests are of dry-deciduous type. There are wide varieties of forests species in the block. Forests are mainly used for fuel-wood collection, minor forest produce (MPF) and fodder.

Types of Forest Species

Following major types of forest species are found in this block:

Sal *(Shorea robusta)*
Amla *(Emblica officinatis)*
Sandham *(Ougeinia ogeinensis)*
Moru *(Grewia opposititfolia)*
Chir *(Pine)*
Karu
Bakli *(Annogeissus lasifolia)*
Dhaman *(Grenia fillifolia)*
Sesum *(Dalbergia Sissoo)*
Amaltus *(Cassia fistula)*
Zingar *(Lannea coromandilica)*

This is not an exhaustive list of forest species in the area. The importance of these forest species in the life of local people has been drawn in the form of a PRA diagram (see Fig. 8.11).

Minor Forest Products and their Importance

Amla, Bahera, Zingar, Amaltas, Chakotra, Mango, etc. are the fruits found in the forests of this block. Th local people are very much dependent on these forest products. Some of these fruits are used for preparation of ayurvedic medicines.

Bakli, Dhaman, Kharpat, Barola, Kanju, etc. are some species which are exclusively used for fuel purposes by the local people.

Sal, Sagwan, Sissoo, Sesum, etc. are some valuable species which are useful for construction purposes. But these forest species are not allowed to be cut by the forest officials.

Many other trees like Malijan, Sem, San, Sandhan are used for preparing leaf plates. Varieties of M.F.P. and their utilities are shown in Fig. 8.12 as drawn by the villagers.

Wild Life

The dense sal forest in the sourthern side of this block in particular provides ideal habitat for a number of wild animals. As described by the local people, tigers and elephants were not uncommon a decade ago. Black bear, Sambhar, spotted deer, wild boar, Kakad, Chittal, Langoor, leopard, etc. are some of the wild animals found in the block. Similarly, birds like black patrige, crown patrige, black Bulbul can also be spotted in the valley area.

Problems of the Forestry Sector

Forest area in the block faced the onslaught of people in the recent past resulting in denudation of vegetation cover. This, in turn, created the problem of soil erosion and other related problems. Soil thickness is very less in this area and it can be eroded easily. Following problem areas can be identified so far as forestry sector is concerned. These are based on both the available secondary data and information through people's participation.

- Increasing population pressure on forest resources;
- Excessive human encroachments;
- Increasing demand for fuelwood, fodder and timber resulting in over-exploitation of minor forest products;

- Heavy grazing by livestock (of local villagers) in the forest area;
- Soil erosion and changing of hydrological conditions; and
- Loss of wild life due to thinning of forests.

How Ecological Imbalance is Caused due to Deforestation

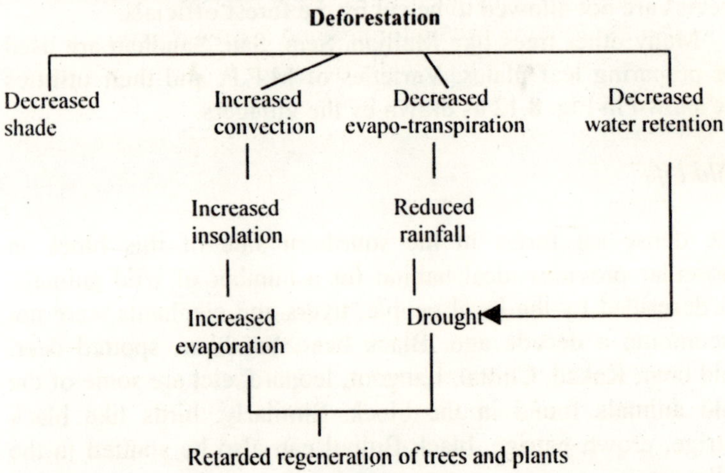

Strategy for Planning in Forestry Sector

The strategy for planning in this sector has been designed with the following objectives :

- To meet the requirements of fuelwood and other forest produce of the local people, especially womenfolk who go to collect them.
- To generate additional labour opportunity, particularly to landless / small farmers and women.
- To motivate villagers to plant trees and preserve them.
- To restore environment for its ecological preservation and maintenance.

The steps to be taken keeping this strategy in mind are as follows :

- Fodder development/pasture development so that local women have access to adequate fodder and pasture to meet their daily requirements.
- Plantation of species specifically useful for fuelwood purposes for convenience of women who gather them.
- Major thrust to be given on wasteland development and plantation in degraded forest area. Women groups from nearby villages can be formed and involved in this task.
- Plantation along village/district roads for benefit of local villagers.
- Ensuring people's participation in all these programmes especially small group participation whether facilitated by NGOs or the government.
- Emphasising soil conservation measures and plantation of such species which will be useful for conserving soil, again based on local priorities and needs.
- Fire protection to be ensured by forming small groups of local people for management of forests.
- Plantation of medicinal plants/herbs/grasses for local use to be based on local priorities and needs as expressed through participatory methods.
- Plantation of commercial species in certain areas keeping in view the long term benefits.

(*Source :* Divisional Forest Officer, Siwalik Division, Dehradun)

Financial Allocation for Various Programmes

Total allocation to this Sector = 103.5 lakhs

Scheme	Physical Target	Unit Financial Cost	Total Expenditure
Plantation in degraded forests	400 hect.	Rs.7,500	Rs. 30 lakhs
Plantation of commercial/medicinal species	300 hect.	Rs. 9,000	Rs. 27 lakhs
Plantation along village/district roads	50 km.	Rs. 5,000/km	Rs. 2.5 lakhs
Fuelwood species plant near villages	300 hectares	Rs. 8,000	Rs. 24 lakhs
Pasture/groundland level	500 hectares	Rs. 3,000	Rs. 15 lakhs
Dev. Of nurseries	2	Rs. 2.5 lakhs each	Rs. 5 lakhs

Conclusion

Forestry is a very important sector for overall planning of a particular area. Planning for an area is based on natural resources available in that area. Since forest resources form a vital component of natural resources, so it should be given adequate attention. After all, the livelihood patterns of the local people are intrinsically related to forest resources and they are totally dependent on such resources.

Accurate and comprehensive monitoring of forest resources is one of the major steps towards the prevention, control and management of ecology. So planning of forestry sector is a must to attain the goal of environmental upgradation with the benefits flowing to the local people. It may be repeated that the future of mankind is intertwined with the extent and nature of forest cover.

SOIL CONSERVATION

The Problem

Soil is one of the most important natural resources. The top soil takes 100 to 400 years to form but can be washed away in no times as can be witnessed by the silt laden torrents, streams and rivers during the rains. Erosion by rains depends upon the nature of the rain, the kind of soil, the climate changes and the way land is managed. It increases with the intensity of rain, and soil erodibility increases with the extremes of temperatures that are experienced in the area. The intense summer heat followed by heavy monsoon rains dislodges the soil particles and this process gets accelerated if the top soil is not protected by vegetation cover.

Average annual rainfall in Vikasnagar block is about 200 cm, 85 per cent of which is in the form of monsoon. The block witnesses heavy rainfall during the rainy season. The soil being of sandy loam type and with a substratum of doon gravel, its erodibility is very high. In the areas having a low green cover and on slopes, soil erosion is a major problem. The various types of soil erosion in the block as shown in Fig. 8.13 are:

- Sheet erosion on slopes having little vegetation,
- Gully erosion, and
- Bank erosion by streams and rivers.

While on the slopes, sheet erosion and gully erosion are the main problems, in the plain areas bank erosion is the major concern.

Impact of Soil Erosion

- Excessive damage to agricultural fields due to bank erosion by Asan river and its tributaries;
- Flooding of the areas on the sides of Asan river in case of heavy rainfall;
- Degradation of common property resources which affects women and weaker sections of society most adversely; and
- Scarcity of clean drinking water.

Strategy

The erosivity of rain and erodibility of soil can be measured but cannot be changed to reduce erosion and the only possibility is to manipulate and control the land management. Erosion can be manipulated in two ways depending on the management :

Biological Erosion Control : Land use has to be ecologically sound and crop management has to be such that maximum protective vegetation cover is provided so as to reduce water run-off and minimize splash erosion.

Mechanical Erosion Control : Physical control of soil and water movement by the use of mechanical devices.

At present most public finance in the field of soil conservation is devoted to the necessary remedial measures and treatment after the area has been eroded. However, the correct approach would be to adopt preventive practices in conjunction with treatment of degraded areas.

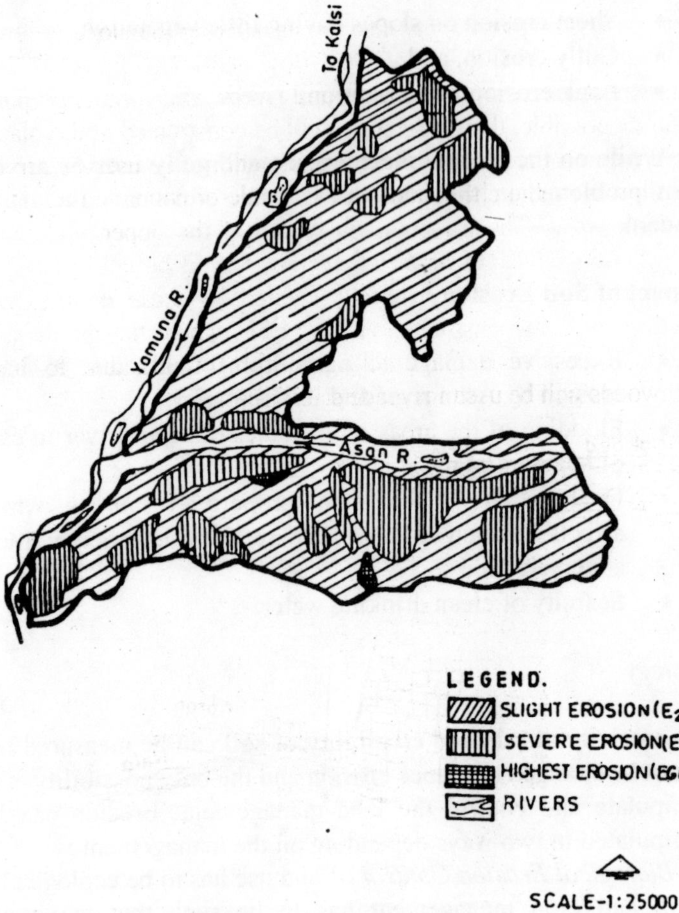

Fig. 8.13 : Soil Erosion Map

Measures to Control Soil Erosion

Plantation of vegetative checks barriers for preventing sheet erosion on slopes and erosion of agricultural fields. The species to be used for this purpose would be Khas (Vetevaria zizanioides), perennial rai (Lollium perenne), cocks foot (Dactylis glomerata), munj, etc.

Plantation of plants like Rambans and Utis on the sides of nalas to provide stability to the sides and on slopes.

Construction of vegetative / stone checkdams (see Figs. 8.14 and 8.15), cratewire dams, drop structures etc. on nalas (wherever the slope is more than 5 per cent) so as to bring the slope below 5 per cent and reduce the velocity of flow and check gully erosion. Cratewire structures (Galvanized Iron) will be used for this purpose. As far as possible, these structures will be constructed at the places where the nalas are narrow. Checkdams will not be used at curves. The slipway of the checkdams will be made of concrete (1:2:4) 10 cm thick walls. The minimum thickness of the upper section of these dams would be one metre. Aprons would be constructed to prevent erosion by the waterfalls created by these dams. Drop structures will be constructed at the places where the gradient of torrents is quite high. On small nalas with low gradient of flow, brushwoods will be used for grade stabilization.

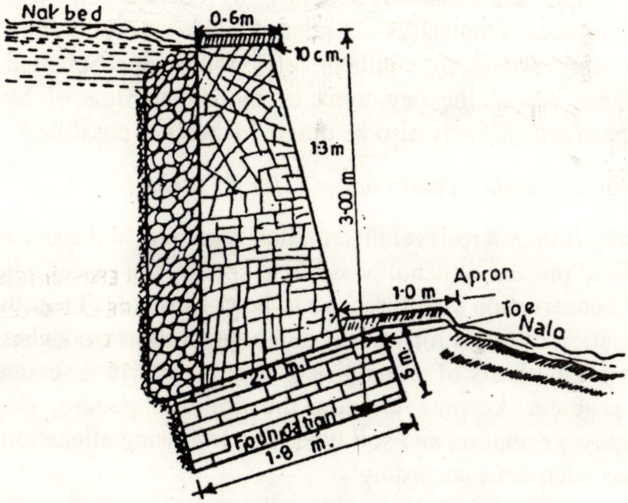

Fig. 8.14 : Retaining Wall or C.B. of a Check Dam

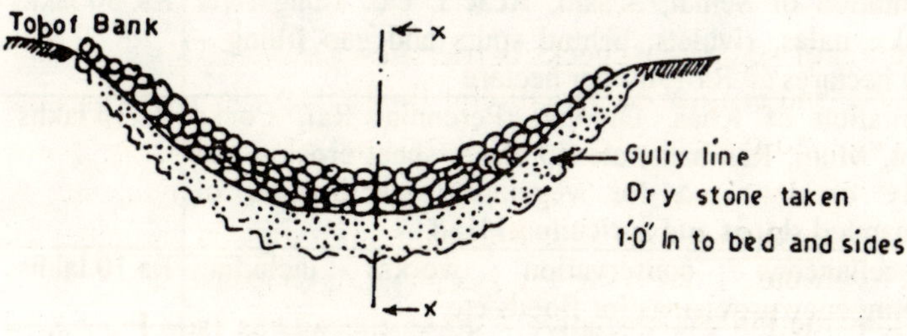

Fig. 8.15 : Dry Check Dam

Bank erosion is a serious problem in the block. It has resulted in large scale broadening of nalas, rivulets and river, and consequent loss of agricultural and forest land. This problem is more serious at the places where the course of the streams is curved. For controlling the flow of such nalas, rivulets and rivers, the method of channelization would be made use of. Spurs would be constructed wherever the problem of bank erosion is more serious.

All the mechanical structures would be supported / supplemented by vegetative structures, wherever possible. In the spaces between consecutive spurs and in the area behind the spurs, species like Sesam *(Dalbergia sisso),* Khair *(Acacia catechu),* Semal *(Bombax ceiba),* etc. will be planted which will take the places of mechanical structures as they weaken over the years. One metre long stalks of Gular *(Ficus racemosa),* Jhingan *(Lannea corrmandilica),* mulbery, etc. will also be planted at such places before the beginning of monsoon. Slips of Munj *(Erianthens mumja)* may also be planted wherever possible.

Allocation of Funds : Total Outlay = Rs. 85 lakhs

Since very little micro-level information regarding soil erosion is available at present, it is not possible to specify the places where the soil conservation structures are to be constructed. Therefore, the allocation of funds for various soil conservation works has to be done on the basis of an empirical and qualitative assessment of the problem, keeping in view the drainage pattern, slope, topography, vegetation and soil type. The following allocation of funds has been done accordingly :

Construction of checkdams, spurs, embankments, drop structures etc.	Rs. 30 lakhs
Plantation of Semal, Sesam, Acacia, etc. along river banks, nalas, rivulets, behind spurs and gap filling – 400 hectares @ Rs.7500 per hectare	Rs. 30 lakhs
Plantation of Khas, Didonia, Perennial Rai, Cocks Foot, Munj, Rambans, etc. to check sheet erosion and gully erosion and for vegetative stabilization of demanded slopes and agricultural land	Rs.10 lakhs
Miscellaneous conservation works including contingency provisions for floods etc.	Rs.10 lakhs
Publicity and creation of environmental awareness – through posters, pamphlets, leaflets and video shows in schools and villages.	Rs. 5 lakhs

Construction of soil conservation structures is to be done through Rural Engineering Service, Irrigation Department, Soil Conservation Department, etc.

Plantation works are to be done with active involvement of local people and schools. Special care has to be taken to ensure active involvement of women and weaker sections who are the worst sufferers of soil erosion, deforestation, loss of Common Property Resources, etc.

Limitations

Since micro-level data regarding the extent and types of soil erosion is not available, allocation of funds for various measures of biological and mechanical erosion control has been done on the basis of a qualitative assessment of the problem, keeping in view the drainage pattern, topography, vegetation and soil types of the block. As such the above allocation pattern may not be optimal.

Soil erosion in the block is caused also by the rivers, rivulets and torrents originating outside the block but flowing through it. As such our efforts to check soil erosion in the block would not yield the desired result unless appropriate steps are taken up to control run-off and soil erosion in the areas from which such rivers and rivulets originate.

INFRASTRUCTURE

Roads

The block headquarters of Vikasnagar is well connected with Dehradun, Saharanpur, Kalsi and Poanta Saheb (Himachal Pradesh). In fact, Herbertpur is the central point to which roads from all these places converge.

The total length of roads maintained by the Public Works Department (PWD) in the Vikasnagar block is 141 kilometres (Source : Centre for Micro Planning and Regional Studies, LBSNAA, Mussoorie). There are 59 villages in the block, out of which 51 are connected by all-weather roads. The other eight villages are connected with only fair weather roads (Source : BDO, Vikasnagar).

Our group members visited 12 of these villages and we found that approach roads to six of these villages are in bad shape. Going by random sampling method, we can safely assume that the approach roads to nearly 30 villages need repair and reconstruction. The length of these approach roads varies from 0.5 km to 2 kms from the main road. Taking an average length of 1 km, the total length of roads needing repairs comes to be around 30 kms.

Four of the villages requiring all-weather connections have to be provided with two causeways and three culverts. Ten lakh rupees are proposed to be set aside for improvement of existing roads inside the villages under the Jawahar Rozgar Yojana programme.

Financial Allocation

	Proposed Activity	Subsidy (amount in lakhs of Rupees)
1.	Repair of Approach Roads (30 kms) (@ Rs.1.51 lakhs / km.	45.3
2.	Culverts and Causeways	1.9
3.	Roads inside villages	10.0
	Total	57.2

Transport

Transport and communication is an integral part of the infrastructural facilities of a region. It is proposed to provide in our plans easy transport facilities to the main roads and also to improve the inter=village transport facilities in the block.

Financial Allocation

It is proposed to finance cycle rickshaws in the plain regions and horse drawn carriages in the hilly regions by providing easy credit to the prospective applicants. This would not only help in providing transport facilities in the block, but would also provide employment to the applicants.

(*In Rupees*)

	Activity	Subsidy	Loan
1.	Cycle rickshaws (200)		12 lakhs
2.	Horse driven carriages (50)	1 lakh	4 lakhs
	Total	1 lakh	16 lakhs

SOURCES OF RENEWABLE ENERGY

Interactions with the villagers revealed that domestic fuel is one of the major problems which they face in their day to day life. Women have to spend at least two to three hours a day for collecting fuelwood. Most of the cattle-dung is converted to dry cakes by the rural womenfolk and is used as domestic fuel.

We propose to tackle the problem of shortage of domestic fuel and reduce the drudgery of rural women by setting up of biogas plants on a massive scale. In the first year, we propose to set up 500 biogas plants in the block. At present, there are only 220 biogas plants in the block (*Source :* BDO, Vikasnagar). With a cattle population of nearly 34,000 (*Source :* Agricultural Census), the block has a potential of setting up over 4,000 biogas plants.

The JANATA model biogas plant, approved by the Ministry of Non-Conventional Energy Sources, Government of India, can be set up in various sizes as per the demands of the farmers. The size of the plant would depend on the size of the household and the number of cattle owned by the farmer. The cost of a plant of one cubic metre size is around Rs. 5000.

The biogas plants are proposed to be set up by a Non-Government Organization on a commission basis. The supervision shall be done by the technicians of the Uttar Pradesh Renewable Energy Development Agency (UPREDA). (Dehradun was in Uttar Pradesh at the time when the plan was prepared). The NGO shall also have the responsibility of maintaining the biogas plants for the next five years.

Benefits of Biogas Plants

The benefits from biogas plants are threefold :

- It reduces the drudgery of the rural women by making the domestic fuel available right at the doorstep.
- It releases a huge amount of bio-fertilizers in the form of slurry for the agriculture fields which will not only reduce the dependence of the farmer on chemical fertilizers but will also help in restoring the fertility of the degrading soil.

- The quality of cooking improves in matters of both efficiency and environment.

The second project envisaged by the group in this sector is popularization of smokeless *chullahs* among the people of the block. We propose to introduce smokeless *chullahs* in atleast 1,000 households of the block during the plan year. The benefits from smokeless *chullahs* are basically twofold :

- It increases the efficiency of fuel by ensuring effective combustion.
- It improves the atmosphere of the kitchen and thereby the cooking conditions for the women. As many of the households live in single or two-roomed houses, this also helps in improving the living conditions and health of the household in general.

Financial Allocation (in Rs. Lakhs)

Proposed Activity	Subsidy	Loan
Setting up of biogas plants (500 nos.)	12.5	12.5
Distribution of smokeless chullahs (500 nos.)	2.5	2.5
Motivation and publicity	1.0	
TOTAL	16.0	15.0

AGRICULTURE

Introduction

"Men does not live by bread alone!
But can he live without bread?"

Agriculture is the main economic activity for over 60 per cent of the workforce of the Vikasnagar block (Census 1991). Though the total area of the block is 29,048 hectares, the net sown area (NSA) of the block is only 10,486 hectares (*Source* : BDO office, See Fig. 8.16). The need for agriculture sector to be more productive is thus apparent from the fact that more than 60 per cent of the people depend for their sustenance on about 35 per cent of the land. Planning for increasing the agricultural productivity thus becomes an important priority in the whole planning scenario for the block as it will affect majority of the population of the block. Not only it is important from the point of affecting the majority population but also planning is necessary to increase the low productivity of crops that is visible in the block (please refer to the table on productivity of crops later in this section).

Objectives

- Increased agricultural productivity.
- Increased income of the farmers by crop diversification and suitable marketing facilities for the farmers.

These objectives were determined on the basis of the group's interaction with the villagers (12 villages were visited by the members of the group), the information provided by the block officials at the Block Headquarters and the information gathered from the secondary sources provided by Centre for Micro Planning and Regional Studies of Lal Bahadur Shastri National Academy of Administration, Mussoorie (both reports and data books).

Land-Use Pattern (*Source :* B.D.O. office) :

Present Scenario

- Thirty five per cent of the land in the block is exclusively devoted to agriculture (i.e. the Net Sown area).
- Thirty three per cent of the land is under forest cover.
- Twelve per cent of the land has been put to non-agricultural use.
- Four per cent of the land has been devoted to horticulture.
- Barren land, fallow land, permanent pasture, cultivable waste constitute rest of the land.

Distribution of Land Holdings (*Source :* Centre for Micro Planning and Regional Studies, LBS National Academy of Administration, Mussoorie):

- Seventy per cent of the land holders are small or marginal farmers (owning less than one hectare of land).

Fig. 8.16 : Agricultural Map of the Block

- Five per cent of the landholders are large farmers (owning more than 3 hectares of land).
- Small and marginal farmers own only 25 per cent of the net sown area.
- Large farmers own only 35 per cent of the net sown area.
- Census data of 1991 shows that 34 per cent of the main workers are cultivators and 28 per cent of them are agricultural labourers.

- Out of 18,179 households, nearly 11,120 households own land. The average landholding in the block is little less than one hectare.
- Interviews with villagers indicated that most of these holdings were fragmented and dispersed and that consolidation had not been undertaken in the block as the Government of U.P. (Dehradun was in Uttar Pradesh at the time when this plan was prepared) treats this block as a hilly block.

Irrigation [*Source :* Junior Engineer (I) Vikasnagar Block] :

Minor Irrigation (MI) projects (eight in number) constitute the bulk of the source of irrigation. Yamuna-Katapathar canal, Rudrapur canal, Harrawala canal are the important Minor Irrigation projects of the block. Total irrigated ayacut (or command area) of these MI projects equal to 7305 hectares.

Tubewells (twenty in number) installed by government form the second most important source of irrigation. With an average command area of 40 hectares, the command area from this source is 800 hectares.

Private tubewells (5 HP capacity) numbering 30 in the block have an aggregated command area of 60 hectares.

Community canals constructed under District Plan have an ayacut of 100 hectares.

Thus, the total command area (as it exists on records) of the block is about 8,300 hectares.

But, the information gathered from the block shows that only 5,252 hectares of land in Kharif and 4,871 hectares of land in Rabi season are irrigated. Thus, the discrepancy in data with respect to command area and actual irrigated area is to the tune of 3,000 hectares.

Supply of Inputs (*Source :* Block Development Officer, Vikasnagar) :

There are 8 centres for distribution of chemical fertilizers in the block, out of which 4 are located in Herbertpur and 3 are located in Vikasnagar.

Out of the 8 fertilizer distribution centres, 4 are run by government departments and the rest 4 are run by private individuals.

There are twelve banks in the block. Five of these banks are located in Vikasnagar.

There are 3 primary cooperative credit societies in the block.

There are 4 centres in the block for supply of High Yeiding Variety (HYV) seeds. Two of these are located in Herbertpur and one in Vikasnagar.

Mechanization (*Source :* Interviews with villagers) :

Use of traditional implements continues as many of the farmers lack the ability to buy modern implements because of small landholding size.

Some of the modern implements are unsuitable for hilly conditions (Portion of the block is hilly).

Crops Grown in the Block (*Source :* Block Development Officer, Vikasnagar) :

The net sown area of the block is 10,486 hectares. The gross cropped area (GCA) of the block is 15,500 ha. Therefore, the intensity of cropping in the block is 152 per cent.

The main crops of the block are cereals. Wheat (6970 ha.), rice (3103 ha.) and maize (3841 ha.) constitute over 80 per cent of the gross cropped area.

Other crops grown in the block are Jowar (cereal), Urad, Moong, Masoor, Arthar, Chana, Peanuts (in pulses), mustard, Til, groundnut and Soyabean in oilseeds, sugarcane and ginger (a recent introduction).

Basmati rice, which fetches a very high price in the market, is a special produce of the block.

The average production figures per hectare for various crops are as listed below:

Crop	Yield (in Qty./hectare)
Rice	18.44
Wheat	15.49
Maize	16.62
Jowar	16.00

Crop	Yield (in Qty./hectare)
Masoor	6.70
Chana	13.91
Peanuts	14.19
Arhar	9.59
Mustard	6.36
Til	2.13
Groundnut	12.71
Soyabean	13.14
Sugarcane	699.44

Source: BDO, Vikasnagar

Facilities for Marketing : (*Source* : Interviews)

- There is a Mandi in Vikasnagar for marketing of agricultural surplus of farmers.
- During the harvest season, middlemen/agents also roam in the villages to buy the produce. Farmers often sell to them at a lower price than what is prevailing at the Mandi but that also save them the cost of coming to Vikasnagar.
- As over 80 per cent of the gross cropped area is devoted to cereals, most of the marketable surplus is generated in cereals.

Problems of Farmers

On the basis of interaction with farmers, group interviews and PRA, following problems were short listed by the group. Priority Ranking methods were used to carry out group interviews. (See Fig. 8.17).

Inadequate Irrigation Facilities / Erratic Rainfall

Statistics from the block shows that only about 50 per cent of the Net Sown Area is irrigated.

With over 200 cm of rainfall per annum, the irrigation potential is there and can be utilized by proper water harvesting and soil conservation.

Soil Degradation

Decreasing soil fertility was ranked as the second most important problem by the farmers.

Consequences / Problems	Reduction	Increased Risk	Increase of Cost	Reduction of Income
Lack of Irrigation Facilities	8	9	1	6
Lack of HYV Seeds Fert. Pest	6	1	5	3
Lack of Modern Tools/Equpt.	6	2	3	4
Small Land Holding	1	1	5	5
Lack of Extd. Services	5	2	0	2
Degradation of Soil	7	2	5	5
Marketing Problems	0	1	0	7
This PRA Matrix was prepared by. Ninoo, Basiruddin, Mukesh, and 5 others of village Dhalipur				

Fig. 8.17 : Priority Ranking Matrix by Farmers

Low Level of Utilization of HYV Seeds / Chem. Fertilizer / Pesticides

One of the main reasons for low levels of utilization was non-availability of these inputs in adequate quantity at proper time. High cost of fertilizers was another reason for low consumption.

Use of Traditional Implements

Small holding size prevented farmers from going in for modern equipments.

Average holding size is around two acres.

High cost of these equipments also prevented the farmers from going in for them.

Marketing Problems

Some of the farmers had to sell their marketable surplus produce to the agents/middlemen at a low price than prevailing in the

Mandi. Because of the low surplus, it is not economical to go to the Mandi to sell the same.

Traditional Crops / Low Returns

It was no more profitable to grow cereals as the labour and fertilizer costs have gone up very high and make the cereal cultivation non-remunerative.

Poor Knowledge about Crop Diseases

New variety of seeds bring in new diseases.

Lack of extension services affect the productivity because pesticides cannot be applied at the right time due to lack of knowledge.

Strategies to Meet Problems

Increasing the command area under irrigation in the block from the present 50 per cent of net set sown area to 80 per cent by construction of water harvesting ponds, borewells and tube-wells.

Improving the fertility of soil by introduction of soil conservation methods and by total diversion of cow dung to the agricultural fields. This is possible only if biogas plants are introduced on a large scale.

Ensuring supply of seeds of proper quality and adequate quantity at the right time in the block.

Chemical fertilizers, pesticides and insecticides to be made easily available. Mobile units for such distribution to be introduced.

Mechanization can be introduced in a small way to start with. Power tillers, suitable for small holdings, can be introduced. So also seed-cum-fertilizer trills, threshers and proper storage bin can be introduced by arranging suitable credit tie-ups.

A couple of small demonstration farms can be started in two places with about 2-4 hectares of land where all the modern equipments and techniques shall be used. The farmers can be trained batch by batch in these farms.

Marketable surplus of the farmers can be collected by suitable government agencies like FCI. Alternatively, the communication to all the villages to be made by way of all-weather roads so that farmers can bring their produce to Vikasnagar Mandi.

Crop diversification to oilseeds, pulses and vegetables (from cereals) would not only ensure good fertility but also lessen the risk of farmers. Moreover, the new crops like vegetables, which have a higher value addition potential, can be introduced as marketing shall not be a problem with a bulging Dehradun city within 40 km radius.

Extension service to be made more service-oriented by way of regular meetings with farmers incentive to the village level workers to stay in the villages, etc.

Seed treatment before sowing can improve productivity as well as reduce the chances of diseases to the crop. Introduction of rizobium culture for certain crops like oilseeds can enhance the productivity of the same.

Weed control can improve the production by 20-30 per cent (*Source :* Centre for Micro Planning and Regional Studies report). So the use of weedicides needs to be promoted among the farmers.

Improving the storage facilities available with the small farmers by way of supply of small bins capable of storing 20-25 quintals of grains can go a long way in reducing the wastage in handling and damage (especially by rodents, insects etc.).

Consolidation of landholdings should be started in the block.

Principles of Plan Financing

Government to finance those projects fully which are a form of infrastructure and which benefit a community.

Subsidy is to be made available for farm mechanization, biogas plants, storage bins, private tubewells/pump sets, etc.

Some money to be kept aside for training, advertisement and motivational campaigns aimed at increasing the awareness of the farmers. For the existing staff of the agricultural department in the block same level of expenditure is to be maintained.

Physical Targets: Vikasnagar Block
(For the year 1994-1995)

Activity	Units	Fully Financed by Govt.	Partially Financed by Govt. and Banks
1. Minor Irrigation			
(a) Water Harvesting Ponds (1/4 acre)	50	50	
(b) Tubewells	5 (50 HP)		5
(c) Borings (5 hp)	50 (5 HP)		50
(d) Pumpsets (Diesel)	50		50
2. Farm Mechanization			
(a) Tractor	10		10
(b) Power Tiller	100		100
(c) Seed/Fert. Drill	200		200
(d) Storage Bins	2000		2000
3. Demonstration Farms (two of 3 ha. each)			
4. Storage Godown (one for seed and fertilizers)			
5. Awareness Campaign			
(a) Advertisements	20 sessions		
(b) Training			
(c) Incentives for Extension Personnel			

Note :

1. Subsidy for community tubewells shall be 75 per cent.
2. Subsidy for borings and pumpsets shall be 75 per cent.
3. Subsidy for tractors shall be Rs. 10,000.
4. Subsidy for power tillers shall be Rs. 8,000.
5. Subsidy for seed / fertilizer drill shall be 50 per cent and for storage bins 25 per cent.

Physical Targets: Vikasnagar Block
(For the year 1994-1995)

(*In Rs. Lakhs*)

Activity	*Subsidy*	*Loan*
1. Minor Irrigation		
(a) Water Harvesting Ponds	20	
(b) Tubewells	12	3
(c) Borings	3	9
(d) Pumpsets (diesel)	1.25	5
Total	36.25	17

Contd.

Activity		*Subsidy*	*Loan*
2.	Farm Mechanization		
(a)	Tractor	1	19
(b)	Power Tiller	8	72
(c)	Seed / Fert. Till	2	2
(d)	Storage Bins	40	120
	Total	**51**	**213**
3.	Demonstration Farms	10	
4.	Storage Godown	2	
	Total	**12**	
5.	Awareness Campaign		
(a)	Advertisements		
(b)	Training	2	
(c)	Incentives	5	
		1	
	Total	**8**	
	Grand Total	**107.25**	**230**

HORTICULTURE

The following villages, selected on the basis of their potential for horticultural activities, were visited for the study of horticulture and the potential for setting up of a processing plant in the region: Ambadi, Barwala, Jiwangarh, Katapatthar.

The agriculture in the block is characterized by small holdings, rainfed farming and low productivity. Planting of fruit trees not only helps in checking soil erosion, but also conserves water.

Characteristics of Orchard Farming

- High initial investment and longer gestation periods.
- Knowledge and experience to take right judgement in respect of site selection, land development, type of layout, variety and planting material because any error committed would come to light only after the gestation period (4-7 years) by which time a lot of labour and capital would have been invested by the orchardists.
- Opportunity cost of cultivation has to be foregone by the orchardists.
- Fruit crops give 5 to 10 times more yield as compared to cereal crops.

- Fruit trees have a long economic life of around 50 years.
- The soil required is well drained loam, sandy loam, clayey loam rich in humans.
- High humidity and temperature in the range of 10 to 45 degree centigrade is required.

Action Plan for Promoting Horticulture

People's Participation

Educating the people through conducting field days in existing orchards when fruit trees are in full bearing.

Organizing group meetings when progressive and existing orchardists share experience with small farmers.

Wide publicity through mass media about suitability of fruits to an area and its benefits.

Credit Support

Credit support to farmers from banks to tide away the high initial investment.

Infrastructural Facilities

Good quality planting material – Developing nurseries of repute in the region.

Irrigation facilities – Providing credit for building concrete irrigation tanks near orchards.

Fencing protection of plants from browsing, from trampling the irrigation systems by animals and from pilferage. Since barbed wire fencing is usually expensive, so other methods like building a live green hedge, stone walls, mud walls and trenches can come up.

Supply of inputs- Inputs like manures, fertilizers, growth hormones and plant protection chemicals are to be adopted.

Technical Knowhow

Since trees are perennial and have a long gestation period, chances of error are to be eliminated in the beginning by planning ahead. The right technology in respect of site selection, layout of the farm, procuring right planting material, maintenance of trees, irrigation, drainage, intercropping, application of organic and inorganic manures and availability of skilled labour is required.

Existing Scenario

The main fruits grown in this region are mangoes, litchis and guava. Besides, some amounts of Aaroo, Nashpati, Plum, Papita, Chikoo, Aonla and Citrus Lemon are also grown. The total area under horticulture cultivation in the block is 2,455 hectares and the number of cultivators is 250. Through extensive farmers' education, we intend to increase the area under orchards to 4,000 hectares in the block.

The layout of the fruit trees is at a distance of 30 ft. by 30 ft. Therefore, nine trees can be planted in an area of one bigha. A bigha is a piece of land measuring 90 ft. by 90 ft. The major fruit trees grown in the block are of mango and litchi. The most well known variety of mango is Dussehri, while the other popular varieties are Chausa, Langra and Fajli. The gestation period varies from 4 years for Fajli and Dussehri to 8 years for Chausa.

At present there is a training centre, Rajkiya Samudayik Phal Sanrakshan Kendra at Vikasnagar. A fruit processing plant of 10 MT capacity for making mango pickles, jam and jelly is located at Prithvipur, 4 km. from Vikasnagar. Another plant is located at Dhaula Kuan in Himachal Pradesh for mango, litchi and other fruit processing.

Existing Marketing Arrangements

At present, the entire orchards are leased out for a period of two years to the contractors at an average lease amount of Rs. 3,000 per bigha. 5.5 bighas roughly comprise an acre. The orchards are leased out for two years mainly because the fruits give high yields in a ratio of 3:2 in alternate years. These contractors mostly hire contractual labour during the plucking season from May to July at a flat rate between Rs. 1,000 and Rs. 1,500.

Usually the contractors and the labourers come from the district of Saharanpur. No labour is available locally as all operations require skilled hands, which is not available in the block.

The contractors pack the fruits in wooden boxes containing roughly 9 kg. of fruits, which is then sent by trucks to Azadpur Mandi in Delhi. The transportation cost is Rs. 5 per box, which comes to 50 P. per kilo of fruit transported. The fruits are sold through the Arhtiyas or the middlemen to the prospective buyers. The Arhtiyas usually get a commission anywhere between 6 – 8 per cent for the services. Besides, the rate at which the fruits are actually sold to the buyer is kept a closely guarded secret. Taking into account the labour charges for unloading at the Mandi, it is not surprising that the cost of selling comes out to a phenomenal 20 per cent of the selling price contracted.

Financial Allocations

	Subsidy	Loan
Publicity and education	5 lakhs	
Nursery	5 lakhs	
Concrete irrigation tanks	10 lakhs	20 lakhs
Credit support to new orchards (@Rs.7,500/- per hectare)		75 lakhs
Total	20 lakhs	95 lakhs

Note : 1,000 hectares of new orchards are assumed to come up in the year.

VIKASNAGAR FROZEN FOODS LIMITED

One processing unit identified as a potential for setting up at Vikasnagar is a plant for frozen fruits and vegetables. An integrated frozen fruit and vegetable farm is not only ecologically friendly and labour intensive, but would be also cost-efficient in Vikasnagar. At present, no large and medium units exist in Vikasnagar.

There are already existing fruit processing plants for making jelly, jam and pickles at Dhaula Kuan in Himachal Pradesh and at Prithvipur. The fruits consumed by such plants are of low quality for making of pulp. The fruits grown in this region are of very high quality and it is not economical to use these for making pulp. A good price can be obtained only if the fruits are sold for table purposes. Already Pepsi from Punjab comes to collect the low quality mangoes and litchis left after grading in the farmer's fields is over. The prevailing market prices in Delhi's Azadpur Mandi are as follows :

Chausa :	Rs. 150 to Rs. 200 per box
Dussehri :	Rs. 72 to Rs. 80 per box
Langra :	Rs. 70 to Rs. 75 per box
Fajli :	Rs. 32 to Rs. 40 per box
Litchi :	Rs. 70 to Rs. 75 per box (5 kg.)

Taking into account all the above factors, it is not economical to build an integrated fruit processing plant for making of jellies, jams and pickles in this region.

Therefore, it is proposed to set up a frozen fruit processing plant at Vikasnagar. The demand for frozen fruits and vegetables is growing day by day and is preferred over fresh fruits and vegetables mainly because :

(1) Price stability of frozen foods around the year.
(2) Good quality assured to the consumers.
(3) Availability throughout the year.

The plant would procure fruits at the farmers' fields and subject the fruit to a process of steam peeling which would destroy the enzymatic activity responsible for the degradation of the fruits. The fruit is then subjected to a cryogenic shock when it is passed through sub-zero temperatures. A thin crust of ice forms over it which is then packed for sale in the market.

Marketing of Plant Product

The processing plant would be of 60,000 MT capacity and would be set up at Dak Patthar. The command area of the project would cover an area of 15 km. radius. The product will be marketed in major North Indian cities and also exported to Europe, U.S.A. and the Gulf. Roughly, 60 per cent of the produce is proposed to be exported.

The detailed project report of the proposed plant is provided in the Appendix-A to this Chapter.

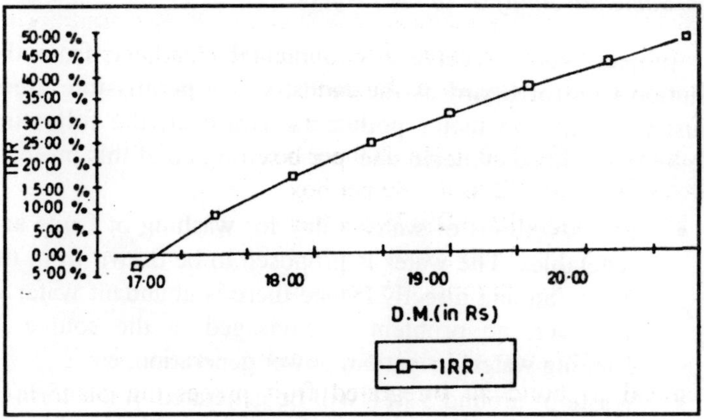

Fig. 8.18 : IRR of Project

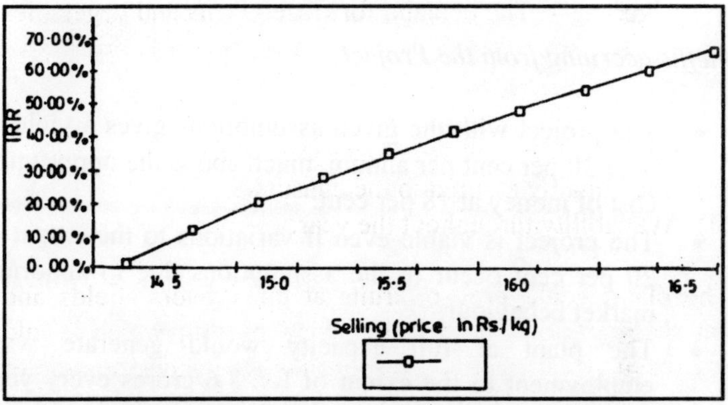

Fig. 8.19 : IRR Project AV Selling Price (in Rs. Kg.)

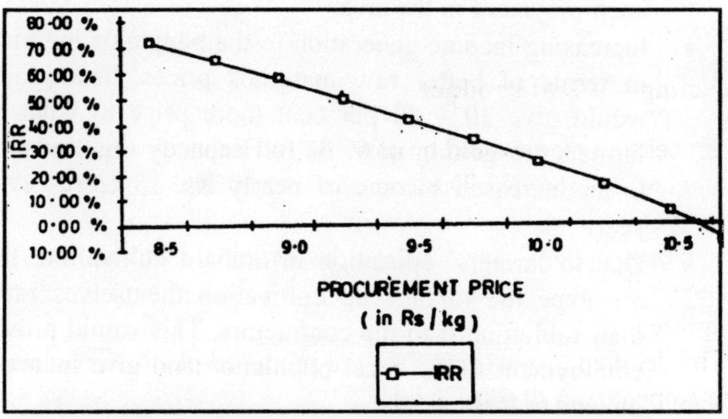

Fig. 8.20 : IRR Project AV Procurement Price (in Rs. Kg.)

Environmental Analysis of the Project

The project would receive environmental clearance from the Pollution Control Board as the industry is a permissible green industry causing no major pollutants. However, the following resources would be depleted due to the setting up of this project:

- 10,000 gallons of water a day for washing of fruits and vegetables. The water is proposed to be drawn from the river Yamuna directly. Since there is abundant water in the river, no problem is envisaged in the source of drinking water, irrigation, power generation, etc.
- Waste of around 5 MT will be generated in the form of outer peels of fruits and vegetables. The rubbish is proposed to be disposed of in the wasteland.

Benefits accruing from the Project

- The project with the given assumptions gives a yield of over 30 per cent per annum, much above the opportunity cost of money at 18 per cent.
- The project is viable even if variations to the extent of 20 per cent occur in the assumptions due to abnormal market behaviour.
- The plant at full capacity would generate wage employment to the extent of Rs. 3.6 crores every year, thereby reducing the extent of underemployment and unemployment in the area.
- Increasing income generation to the people of the block in terms of better raw materials prices. The project would give 30 – 40 per cent more price to what the farmers are getting now. At full capacity this translates to an increased income of nearly Rs. 15 crores every year.
- Due to farmers' education in orchard cultivation, they are expected to take up cultivation themselves rather than subletting it to the contractors. This would provide employment to the local population and give increased income to them.

- It will stabilize the prices of fruits and vegetables during the lean arrival season when prices shoot up. This would make the fruits accessible to the common consumers.

ANIMAL HUSBANDRY

Animal husbandry along with agriculture plays a dominant role in the socio-economic life of the rural poor of this country. Even the families living below the poverty line and owning no land usually keep a milch animal to support their daily milk requirements and supplement their income. Therefore, for the upliftment of the poorest of the poor, development of animal husbandry is perhaps even more important than agriculture. Animal husbandry is also very important from the point of providing gainful employment to the rural womenfolk while staying in their homes.

The following figures pertain to the statistics of animal population in the block:

Cows	20384 (local)
	3729 (cross bred)
Buffalo	11737
Goats	4989
Pigs	740
Horses	468
Poultry birds	38138
Sheep	2195
Others	4213
Block Milk Production Figures	
Total milk production	27,000 litres/day
Total consumption	17,000 litres/day
Surplus	10,000 litres/day

Current Facilities

There is one chilling plant at Dehradun where the surplus milk is sold. There are 3 veterinary surgeons, 3 veterinary hospitals and 9 stockman centres in the block.

An intensive animal husbandry programme is proposed to be launched in all the villages of the block with specific objectives.

Objectives of the Programme

- Changing the genetic composition of the milch animals in the block so that the yield improves substantially from the present 200 litres per lactation period to 1,800 litres.
- Optimum management, feeding and breeding practices for high yielding crossbred cows together with cultivation of nutritious green fodder to lower cost of milk production and to provide a package of dairy farming practices on varying sizes of farm holdings.
- Multiple cropping system of raising three or more crops in a year including grain, vegetable and fodder crops.
- Inculcating interest in a cooperative set-up since milk producers' cooperative societies are proposed to be built up in a phased manner.
- In all the villages to be adopted, the nerve centre of all activities would be a Dairy Vikas Kendra located at a central place within the village. Within the cluster itself, a village is identified as a headquarters village for purposes of directing and controlling the programme functionaries stationed there.

Strategies for Upliftment of Poor

Right from inception, the project would have a built-in bias towards improving the income and employment potential of the rural poor – the small and marginal farmers and the landless labourers. In order to meet this objective, the following steps would be taken :

- In determining the retail prices of improved seed varieties, the project would adopt a no-profit approach.
- Priority would be given to small and marginal farmers while choosing a site for crop and mini-kit and whole farm demonstrations.
- Equipment for crop pest control would be loaned to small farmers free of charge.

- Preference would be given to the landless labourers, small and marginal farmers in the sale of crossbred cows, at a fixed price.
- Landless labourers and marginal farmers to be advanced bank loans at differential rate of interest (4 %)
- Landless labourers belonging to Harijan community in the first year of the project to be provided free one kg. of concentrate ration for the first location of pregnant women.

Action Plan

The two major plant planks of the project programme would be crop productivity improvement and dairy development. Per hectare yield of various cereal, fodder, pulse and cash crops in the project area will be increased through the introduction of HYV's of crops and package of practices which is attempted through a network of crop demonstrations laid on marginal and small holdings. In the sphere of dairy development, Dairy Vikas Kendras (DVKs) would be set up throughout the project area which serve as the nerve centres for all the development activities of the project. Various facilities and services are provided to the farmers for artificial insemination, pregnancy diagnosis, examination and treatment of various reproductive disorders and other ailments, as also vaccination against contagious diseases like F.M.D., H.S., B.Q and R.P.

Education and guidance would be extended to the farmers to adopt improved and scientific practices on balanced feeding, rearing of calves, optimum use of fertilizers and plant protection chemicals. There would be provision for continuous monitoring of the progress and evaluation of the project programmes through systematic maintenance of records and conducting primary village survey, bench mark surveys, repeat surveys and Rapid Rural Appraisal (RRA) at suitable intervals in the project area.

Dairy Development Programmes

The major thrust in the project would be on crossbreeding. The targets for improving the genetic potential of local cattle through intensive artificial insemination is proposed at 50 per cent of the cattle population in the first year itself. The project would aim at the average lactation yield of a crossbred cow at about 3000 litres and that of buffalo at 1800 litres.

Women's Role

The availability of animal husbandry is expected to provide gainful employment to rural womenfolk. The women would collect and cut fodder, feed the animals and milk them two times a day. In this way, their contribution towards the family's income would improve their status within the family.

Problems Visualized during Implementation

Regular supply of liquid nitrogen cans to the rural centres. Otherwise, it would adversely affect the quality of semen leading to lower conception rate.

To remove the deep rooted prejudice against the efficiency of crossbred bullocks.

In view of the prevailing high cost of concentrates, poor cattle keepers fail to give balanced feed to the dairy animals with the result they do not get optimum yields and returns from the dairy enterprise.

In the absence of organized milk marketing facility in some villages/areas, the milk producers continue to suffer from the exploitation of the private milk vendors.

The price of milk offered by both public and private agencies for crossbred cow milk having lower fat content is not remunerative. This is one of the reasons why the crossbreeding programme has not picked up in certain areas.

It is very difficult to convince and motivate the families to follow a new technique or practice due to their conservative attitude and lack of education.

In the absence of certain benefits given to the households of weaker section, the medium and large farmers display hostile postures against the functionaries of the project and try to defame and harm them through various means. Such a situation creates great tensions amongst the village communities and the project staff.

Tradition-bound conservatism on the part of some orthodox families in the villages creates problems in the removal of scrub bulbs used for agricultural service in the area and successful implementation of crossbreeding programme.

Financial Allocations

The proposal is to build a stockman centre in each of the remaining 50 villages of the block at a cost of Rs. 50,000 each. The land for the building is proposed to be donated by the Panchayats.

Activity	Subsidy (figures in Rs. Lakhs)	Loan
Stockman Centre (50 villages)	25	
Equipments and other facilities	30	
Construction of silage pits (for preservation of green fodder)	10	
Demonstration farm at Vikasnagar (1 hectare 8 milch unit)	10	
Subsidy for concentrates	5	
Purchase support for cross breeds	50	450
Total	**130**	**450**

Note : 5,000 crossbreeds are assumed to be purchased with a subsidy amount of Rs. 1,000 per animal and a further credit support of Rs. 9,000 per animal.

Piggery

The programme of pig rearing has not been adopted in the block on a large scale by the people. This is evident if one notices that the population of pigs in the block is not even 1,000. The main reasons for apathy towards pig rearing is the lack of awareness of the economics of pig rearing. The extension workers must share the blame for this solely.

It is proposed that people would be encouraged to adopt the programme of piggery on a large scale. Pigs multiply exponentially during their life time. A sow can give birth every year upto 10-12 piglets in a single litter. These piglets grow very fast and can gain weight upto 20 kg. within a year. Pigs can be sold in the butcheries of Dehradun at not less than Rs. 20 a kilo. Pig rearing has a benefit in the sense that they can feed on anything, and the cost of pig rearing is almost nil. Pig rearing is the easiest means of supplementing the income of the rural poor.

Action Plan

It is proposed to widely publicize the benefits of pig rearing. Also, provisions for building stalls for stall feeding of pigs in every village would be taken up. Subsidy would be provided for the stall feeding of pigs. Stall feeding is essential to avoid the occurrence of any epidemic.

Financial Allocation

Publicity	Rs. 5 lakhs
Stalls (60)	Rs. 12 lakhs
Feed	Rs. 15 lakhs
Total	Rs. 32 lakhs

Note : Subsidy at the rate of Rs. 600 per annum per adult pig and Rs. 300 per annum for piglets would be given. It is expected that the population of adult pigs in the first year would be 1,500 and the population of piglets would be 2,000.

SUMMARY OF FINANCIAL ALLOCATION

	Activity	Subsidy (figures in Rs. Lakhs)	Loan (In Rs. Lakhs)
1.	Drinking water	79.5	0
2.	Health and sanitation	276.5	140
3.	Education	127.07	0
4.	Forests	103.5	0
5.	Soil conservation	85	0
6.	Roads	57.2	0
7.	Transport	1	16
8.	Renewable energy	16	15
9.	Agriculture	107.25	230
10.	Horticulture	20	95
11.	Animal husbandry	130	450
12.	Piggery	32	0
13.	Vikasnagar Industrial Development Cooperative	0	194
	Total Plan Outlay	**1,035.02**	**1,140**
	Funds allotted	**1,035**	**1,140**

CONCLUSION

Provision for drinking water and sanitation has been made for each village in Vikasnagar block. This was one of the main objectives of the plan. By providing safe drinking water and sanitation to all villages, we aim to prevent the common diseases prevalent in the villages as most of the diseases are waterborne.

The plan incorporates a multi-sectoral approach (consisting of health, education, agriculture, forestry, horticulture, animal husbandry and drinking water supply) to raise the standard of living in general, and status of women in particular. Family welfare would get a definite boost by raising female literacy.

Stress has been given for universalisation of primary education by motivating the people through a series of innovative motivational schemes including Mid-Day Milk Scheme to encourage the parents to send their children to school. Due stress has been laid on female education.

To restore and preserve the ecological balance of the region, the plan incorporates a massive afforestation programme covering an area of around 2,000 hectares. Soil erosion is proposed to be checked through construction of suitable mechanical structures like checkdams, embankments, spurs, drop-structures and gully-plugs, and through biological measures of control and vegetative stabilization.

A novel scheme of providing an optimum mix of subsidy and credit has been provided in the plan to make people adopt renewable sources of energy in their daily lives. A massive amount of Rs.16 lakhs as subsidy and Rs.15 lakhs as credit has been provided for the purchase of smokeless *chullahs* and installation of biogas plants.

Genetic breed improvement of the milch cattle and development of piggery are among the priority areas of the plan. The plan provides for a special subsidy of Rs. 10 lakhs to promote stall feeding of pigs to preserve a healthy environment.

The project on horticulture is a major income generating scheme which will also provide wage employment to a sizable section of the local population. It aims at training the farmers in orchard farming and doing away with the practice of subletting the orchards to the contractors. The setting up of a plant in the new area of frozen fruits has a great potential to earn valuable foreign exchange for the country.

The agricultural production is to be increased by a series of steps like increasing the area under irrigation, farm mechanization and crop diversification. A massive amount of plan funds has been allocated in farm mechanization which will not only reduce the drudgery of farmers, but also increase the farm production.

. A provision has been made for constructing roads (30 km.) and subsidy to people in the transportation sector for purchase of cycle rickshaws and horse-driven carriages.

Notes

1. Participatory Rural Appraisal : Methodology and Applications, Dr. Neela Mukherjee 1993 (New Delhi: Concept).
2. The State of the World's Children 1987, UNICEF.
3. Working Plan – Siwalik Forest Division
4. Evaluation of World Bank Aided Watershed Development Project, Rudra Prayag Sub Watershed.

APPENDIX – A

PROJECT REPORT – VIKASNAGAR FROZEN FOODS LIMITED

Project Cost

(Amount in Rs. Lakhs)

Particular	Amount
Land and Site Development	4
Building & Civil Work	8
Plant & Machinery – Imported	1254
Expenses of Foreign Technicians	8
Misc. Fixed Assets	30
Preliminary & Pro-operative Expenses	58
Contingencies & Cost Escalations	74
25% Margin Money for Working Capital	205
Total Cost	**1641**

Means of Finance

		Amount
Equity		
– V.I.D.C.	100	
– Financial Institutions	75	
– Public	56	
	—	231
Loans		
Foreign Currency Loan		
– Supplier's credit at 75% of total cost of P&M	941	
Rupee Term Loans		
– Financial Institutions	469	
(at a debt equity ratio of 2:1)	—	1409
		1640

Variables

Exchange Rate = Rs. 19 for 1 DM

Land and Site Development

For Plant at Vikasnagar, 5 acres of land @ Rs. 50,000 per acre	3
Site Development Charges	1
	4

Particular		**Amount**
Building & Civil Work		
Main building at Vikasnagar		5
Two motors of 50 H.P. each		1
Washing, grading and storage centers		2
		8
Plant and Machinery		
1. Hot dip galvanized execution steel frames for food production	800,000 DM	152
2. Complete insulation set for floor, wall, ceiling, doors for cold storage	1,200,000 DM	228
3. Refrigeration plant consisting of compressors, evaporative condensers, air unit coolers and ceiling evaporators, IQF tunnel	2,500,000 DM	475
4. Compressed air plant	500,000 DM	95
5. Equipment and material for kitchen processing lines and packing machinery	1,600,000 DM	304
		1254
Miscellaneous Fixed Assets		
Furniture and other accessories		2
6 trucks for collection of fruits and vegetables from P.A.C.S.		20
1 car and 2 vans		8
		30
Preliminary & Preoperative Expenses		
Publicity, advertisements, printing, stationery, farmer education		20
Cooperative floatation expenses		1
Establishment charges from conception stage till trial run		2
Travelling allowances		1
Miscellaneous expenses		
Interest and commitment charges on borrowings (loan of 1500 lakhs to be taken two months in advance)		30
Insurence charges		2
		56
Contingencies and Cost Escalations		
Land		1
Buildings		2
Plant and machinery		63
Tech. Knowhow fees		1
Misc. fixed assets		2
Preliminary & preoperative expenses		6
		75

Particular		Amount
Working Capital		
Raw material	(1 month)	
Stock in process	(1 month)	175
Finished goods	(1 month)	250
Receivables		400
Export receivables		50
Other current assets incl. cash and bank balances		500
		100
Total Current Assets		**1475**
Creditors for purchases of raw materials		500
Accrued expenses		50
Statutory liabilities		5
Other current liabilities		100
		655
Working capital gap		820
Bank loan (75% of working capital gap)		615

Profitability Projections

Assumptions

Average procurement price is Rs. 10,000 per kg.

Average nett S.P. is Rs. 15.12 per kg.

60% of the production is to be exported at an average price realization of DM 800 per M T, and the rest 40% is for domestic markets @ Rs. 15/- per kg.)

Installed Capacity is 60,000 MT

Year Nos.	1	2	3	4	5	6	7	8	9	10
Capacity utilization	60%	80%	90%	100%	100%	100%	100%	100%	100%	100%
Per cent quantity sold	50%	85%	95%	100%	100%	100%	100%	100%	100%	100%
A. Total Sales	4536	7711	8618	9072	9072	9072	9072	9072	9072	9201
B. Cost of production										
Raw materials	3600	4800	5400	6000	6000	6000	6000	6000	6000	6000
Packing charges	216	288	324	360	360	360	360	360	360	360
Transportation	144	192	216	240	240	240	240	240	240	240
Technicians' fees	1.6	1.6	1.6	1.6	1.6	0.0	0.0	0.0	0.0	0.0
Power and fuel	180	240	270	300	300	300	300	300	300	300
Direct labour and wages Wages	216	288	324	360	360	360	360	360	360	360
Consumable stores	72	96	108	120	120	120	120	120	120	120
Repair and maintenance	108	144	162	180	180	180	180	180	180	180
Other manu. expenses	180	240	270	300	300	300	300	300	300	300
Depreciation	116	116	116	116	116	116	116	116	116	116
Investment allowance	261	261	261	0	0	0	0	0	0	0
Preliminary expenses	12	12	12	12	12	0	0	0	0	0
Total cost of prod.	5106	6678	7464	7989	7989	7969	7976	7976	7976	7976
ADD opening work-in-process and finished goods	0	851	417	0	0	0	0	0	0	0
DEDUCT closing stock in process and finished goods	851	417	0	0	0	0	0	0	0	0
C. Cost of Sales	4255	7112	7881	7989	7989	7976	7976	7976	7976	7976
D. Gross Profit	281	599	737	1083	1083	1096	1096	1096	1096	1096
E. Interest and capital repayment										
(i) On foreign loans	137	137	137	137	137	137	137	137	137	137
(ii) On term loans	0	137	137	137	137	137	137	137	137	137
(iii) On W.C.	123	123	123	123	123	123	123	123	123	123

Note : Foreign loan at 7.5 per cent interest is repayable over a 10-year period. Term Loan is at 19.5 per cent interest with a 18-month moratorium period.
Working capital loan is at 20 per cent interest.

Calculations

Principal	6.86	6.3	5.8	5.3	4.6	4.0	3.3	2.6	1.8	0.9	0.0
		8	6	0	9	5	5	0	0	3	0
Interest	0.00	0.5	0.4	0.4	0.4	0.3	0.3	0.2	0.2	0.1	0.0
		1	8	4	0	5	0	5	0	3	7
(foreigh loan)	6.86	1.0	1.0	1.0	1.0	1.0	1.0	1.0	1.0	1.0	1.0
		0	0	0	0	0	0	0	0	0	0
	-	0.1	0.1	0.1	0.1	0.1	0.1	0.1	0.1	0.1	0.1
	1.00	5	5	5	5	5	5	5	5	5	5
Principal	3.43	4.1	3.9	3.6	3.3	3.0	2.6	2.1	1.5	0.8	0.0
		0	0	5	7	2	1	2	4	4	0
Interest	0.00	0.6	0.8	0.7	0.7	0.6	0.5	0.5	0.4	0.3	0.1
		7	0	6	1	6	9	1	1	0	6
(term loan)	3.43	0.0	1.0	1.0	1.0	1.0	1.0	1.0	1.0	1.0	1.0
		0	0	0	0	0	0	0	0	0	0
	-	0.0	0.2	0.2	0.2	0.2	0.2	0.2	0.2	0.2	0.2
	1.00	0	9	9	9	9	9	9	9	9	9
F. Selling, general and administrative expenses											
		3.5	3.5	3.5	3.5	3.5	3.5	3.5	3.5	3.5	3.5
		0	0	0	0	0	0	0	0	0	0
G. Net Profit		-	-	-10	336	336	349	349	34	34	47
		32	14						9	9	8
		9	7								
I. ADD		11	11	116	116	116	116	.116	11	11	11
Depreciation		6	6						6	6	6
Investment		26	26	261	0	0	0	0	0	0	0
allowance		1	1								
J. Net cash		48	23	367	452	452	465	465	46	46	59
accruals			0						5	5	4
K. Repayment		26	39	397	397	397	397	397	39	39	39
obligations		0	7						7	7	7
L. Debt Service		1.1	1.5	1.9	2.1	2.1	2.1	2.1	2.1	2.1	2.5
Ratio		8	8	3	4	4	7	7	7	7	0
M. Proposed		0	0	10	15	20	50	50	50	50	50
Dividend		%	%	%	%	%	%	%	%	%	%

Direct Labour and Wages

The plant will operate for 300 days a year in 3 shifts at 100 per cent capacity utilization.

This implies that 67 MT of fruits and vegetables will be processed in a shift

This would require 600 workers per shift for sorting, gradation, washing purposes assuming average wage level at Rs. 66.67 P./per day.

Daily wages for 3 shifts in a day	1.2 lakhs
Yearly wages at 100% capacity	360 lakhs

Assumption: Each worker can handle 1 quintal of vegetables working 8 hours a day.

Selling, general and administrative expenses

	Rs.	
Advertisement and development of markets		
Salary on administrative staff	300	
General Manager		
Operations Manager	1.25	
Sales Manager	1.00	
Purchases Manager	1.00	
Marketing Manager	1.00	
Head Accountant	0.75	
Development Officer (10)	5.00	
Marketing Officer (10) 5.00		
Staff (20)	5.00	
Drivers (12)	2.50	
Peons (6)	0.80	
		24
Other General Expenses		26
Total		350

Analysis of the Project

Assume discounted rate = 18.00%

Cash Flow Statement

Year	0	1	2	3	4	5	6	7	8	9	10
(I) From equity point of view											
Cash flows	-230.82	47.90	229.74	367.19	452.17	465.27	465.27	465.27	465.27	594.47	
Cum. Cash	-230.82	-182.92	46.81	414.00	866.17	1318.34	1783.61	2248.88	2714.15	3773.88	
Internal rate of return	85.99%										
Benefit cost ratio	6.59										
Net present value	1290 lakhs										
Payback period	2 lakhs										
(ii) From total capital point of view											
Cash flows	-1639.9	184.9	503.47	640.92	725.90	725.90	739.00	739.00	739.00	739.00	868.20
(Net Profit + Depreciation + Investment allowance)											
Cum. Cash flow	-1639.95	-1455.04	-951.57	-310.65	415.25	1141.15	1880.15	2619.15	3358.15	4097.15	4965.35
Internal rate of return	30.64%										
Benefit cost ratio	1.61										
Net present value	994.97 lakhs										
Payback period 4 lakhs											

Note: The worksheet has been built on the pattern of IDBI project refinancing form for banks.

9

A Tactical Plan for Appropriation of Benefits from Development of a Mini Hydro Power Plant through Public-Private Partnership Project

(At Cinta Mekar Village, Segalaherang Sub-District, Subang District, West Java Province, Indonesia)*

INTRODUCTION

A micro planning exercise was undertaken on July 24th and 25th 2003 as part of the implementation of a project for setting up a Mini Hydro Power Plant through a Public-private Partnership Project in Cinta Mekar Village in West Java, Indonesia. The micro-planning exercise was intended to facilitate decision making by the villagers on sharing of benefits and utilization of profits likely to be generated by the project. Though, the share of village community in the benefit and profit utilization was already agreed to between the public sector, private sector and the community (which was 50 per cent of profits), it was felt very important to let the community take decisions about how to use that 50 per cent share of the profits. It was also deemed important that decisions on who should be the beneficiaries and what should be the benefits come from the community's own will and decision making process.

A participatory micro plan produced by this process was also intended to act as an agreement that ties up the community (which was already aware of the project) to the project as the process puts the community at the centre stage of decision makers. This, it was hoped, will inculcate a sense of ownership

---

* Prepared by the people of Cinta Mekar. The Lead Facilitator was Dr. Amitava Mukherjee. Co-Facilitated by Hong Peng Liu, T.S. Rahaya, F. Subasman, S. Nugroho and A. Laksono.

and elicit commitment of the villagers in the development of their own community. Development of the community is one of the main purposes of this project.

AN INTRODUCTION TO CINTA MEKAR VILLAGE

Geographical Condition

Cinta Mekar Village is situated in a valley, surrounded by hills 500 meters above mean sea level. It covers an area of 238.85-km^2, comprises 132.85 km^2 of hilly area and 106 km^2 of flat terrain The village is divided into four sub-villages or "Dusuns", scattered over a fairly big hilly area, criss-crossed by a river and small streams. As one enters the village, the first sub-village is Dusun-I, then Dusuns II, III and IV follow. Thus, Dusun-I is the nearest from the road (indeed it is along the two sides of the village road), and Dusun-IV is furthest from the Road and in that perspective, is the most remote from amongst the four Dusuns of Cinta Mekar.

Cinta Mekar Village is bordered in the north by Kalijati Village; in the west by Cijengkol Village; in the South by Dayeuh Kolot Village and in the East by Leles Village. It belongs to Segalaherang Sub-district, Subang District, and West Java Province. The distance to the sub-district capital is 5 km; and to the district capital is 30 km, and takes about 15 minutes. Transportation is not a problem. There is regular public transportation passing though places near to the sub-district capital. Within the village, the mode of public transportation is motorcycles (so called *ojek*).

Vegetation and rainfall

The annual rainfall is 2000 mm and average temperature ranges between 28 °C – 30 °C. The village has an abundance of forests (which though is being foraged and cut by the villagers, both the poor and noon-poor, for their livelihoods). It has several high value fruit bearing trees such as coconuts, mangoes, palm and cashew nuts. Villagers also grow smaller fruit trees like banana, lemon and pomelow and some pineapple in their back yards and around homestead land.

Human Resources Characteristics

The demographic composition of Cinta Mekar is in Table-9.1. The village has 640 households and a total population of 2050. It is striking that the sex ratio is quite favourable with females outstripping males by a significant margin. It is also significant that people above 60 years of age constitute almost 25 per cent of the total population of the village. *Prima facie* this indicates a high life-expectancy at birth and an improved human development index for the village.

Table 9.1 : Cinta Mekar VillagePopulation By Age Groups

No.	Age Group	Sex		Total
		Male	Female	
1.	0 – 12 months	9	14	23
2.	13 months – 4 years	47	49	96
3.	5 – 6 years	36	42	78
4.	7 – 12 years	46	50	96
5.	13 – 15 years	105	110	215
6.	16 – 18 years	54	57	111
7.	19 – 25 years	62	67	129
8.	26 – 35 years	67	68	135
9.	36 – 45 years	72	75	147
10.	46 – 50 years	76	80	156
11.	51 – 60 years	164	175	339
12.	61 – 75 years	205	228	433
13.	More than 76 years	73	19	92
	TOTAL	**1016**	**1034**	**2050**

Source : Village Monographic, 2002

If we look at the illiteracy figures (Table 9.2) as well as the figure of people who are formally educated (Table 9.3), it is apparent that the system of education has delivered the "goods" for the people of the village. For a developing country, only 47 people being illiterate out of a population of 2050, is quite satisfactory. The favourable sex ratio also reflects the impact of literacy in reducing gender disparity.

Table 9.2 : Dynamics of population Cinta Mekar Village

Description	Sex		Total
	Male	Female	
A. Illiteracy			
1. Age 10 – 15 years	2	1	3
2. Age 16 – 18 years	3	1	4
3. Age 19 – 25 years	9	8	17
4. Age above 25 years	14	9	23
Total	**28**	**19**	**47**

Source : Village Monographic, 2002

Table 9.3 : Education level in Cinta Mekar

B. Formal Education (passed)	**Male**	**Female**	**Total**
1. Elementary school/equal	30	52	82
2. Junior High School	25	23	48
3. Senior High School	33	20	53
4. College	7	1	8
5. University	1	1	2
6. Total	96	97	213

Source : Village Monographic, 2002

Table 9.4 : Death & Birth in Cinta Mekar Village

Description	**Number**	
	Male	**Female**
Birth	9	14
Deaths	6	5
Immigrates	2	1
Emigrates	3	2
Total	**20**	**22**

The village is electrified and power connection to households is evident. However, about 130 households can not afford power connection due to poverty.

Occupational Structure and Means of Livelihood

The occupational structure of the Cinta Maker is in Table 9.5. About 10 per cent of the people are in gainful employment either with the government or with the private Sector or in self employment. The balance 90 per cent of the people depends upon agriculture or employment outside the village for their livelihood.

Dependence on agriculture is very high. Most of the people are either farmers or agricultural labourers. However, an overwhelming majority of the farmers are small and marginal farmers with land holdings below 0.1 hectares (Table 9.6). With small size of holdings, agricultural operations are mostly non-mechanized except for dehusking paddy which is carried in the Rice Mill in the village. The area receives rainfall for approximately 9 months in a year (and 2000 mm. of rainfall annually) and there is water available for both traditional and mechanized irrigation. Thus, though the major crop is paddy of different duration and yield, there is a mixture of both food and cash crops (such as ground nuts) in some farms. Generally the rainfall received enables the farmers to grow three crops in a year.

Table 9.5 : Occupational Structure Cinta Mekar Village.

Occupation		No. of People
Governmental/non-governmental service employee		
1.1.	Governmental service	
	a. Village officer	11
	b. Teacher	13
	c. Civil/military officer	5
	d. Medic officer	2
	e. Midwives	1
	f. Doctor	-
	Sub-Total of Government Service	**32**
1.2.	Retired civil/military officer	**5**
1.3.	Private employee	**20**
2. Financial services institution		
2.1.	Banking	30
2.2.	People Credit Bank	3
2.3.	Mortgage	6
	Sub-Total of Financial Services Providers	**39**
3. Transportation services		
3.1.	Motorcycle Operators (as part of public Transport)	**24**
4. Other services		
4.1.	Carpenter	44
4.2.	Bricklayer	35
4.3.	Tailor/embroidery	5
4.4.	Barber	3
	Total of other services	**87**
	Total	**207**

Source : Village Monographic, 2002

Additionally, there are off-farm employment opportunities in the village. Off-farm employment ranges from poultry farming, duckery, fishing, vending and running petty shops, transportation (motor-cycle), working in the Rice Mill, and cutting forest trees for sale as small timber. As we shall see later, there are additionally people engaged in traditional occupation such as carpentry, bricklaying, tailoring and embroidery, though their numbers may not be very large.

Most of the people in Cinta Mekar are, therefore, seemingly not poor but a mixture of economic strata, and are not hungry, though they are not well-off economically either. This is an issue which has been investigated by the villagers a length below. The villagers desire (*prime facie*) that project should be able to generate resources which will enable them to provide power connection to unconnected poor households, provide support to children whose parents can not afford education, build community infrastructure and create employment opportunities.

Table 9.6 : Land ownership structure in Cinta Mekar Village.

No.	Ownership of the Land	No. Of Owner
1.	Less than 0.1 hectare	1200
2.	0.1 – 0.5 hectare	166
3.	0.6 – 1.0 hectare	11
4.	1.1 – 1.5 hectare	9
5.	1.6 – 2.0 hectare	5
6.	3.0 – 5.0 hectare	-
7.	6.0 – 8.0 hectare	-
8.	9.0 – 10.0 hectare	-
9.	More than 10.0 hectare	-

Source : Village Monographic, 2002

The Planning Background and Objectives

It is with this back ground that Cinta Mekar was selected as a site for a demonstration project for increasing poor people's access to electricity energy, through a mini-hydro power plant being built by a partnership between the public sector, private sector, non-governmental organization and the community.

The participating Public Sector organizations in the project are the Directorate General of Electricity Energy Utilisation, Government of Indonesia and PLN, the Public Utility. While the Directorate General of Electricity Energy Utilisation, Government of Indonesia will provide the overall policy support for the venture, PLN the public utility will buy all the power that will be generated by the mini-hydro power plant being set up in Cinta Mekar, at an agreed price of Rupaiah 400 per unit.

The Private Sector partner is HIBS, with head quarters at Bandung, West Java. The company is providing 50 per cent of the capital outlay in addition to underwriting any cost overrun. The non-governmental organization, which will essentially be playing the role of a facilitator, is IBEKA, with Office in Banaruba, West Java. The community is participating in the project through a co-operative called Cinta Mekar Co-operative, which is providing 50 per cent of the project cost from funds provided by UNESCAP, Bangkok.

The project further provides that 50 per cent of the profit generated by the mini-hydro power plant being set up will go towards benefiting the poor of the village and the same will be utilized in the following order:

1. Providing power connections to those who can not afford to pay the cost of securing a connection (an estimated 102 households);
2. Providing support to children who can not go to school for want of resources to buy books, uniforms etc;
3. Providing support for better health facilities; and
4. Developing community infrastructure such as roads.

The issue was how will the profits from the project be equitably appropriated for the benefit of the poor in a village of over 640 households and having people in all categories of the poverty ladder (namely, poorest, poor, not so poor and non-poor), and for solving the problems of the community. It was in that perspective that a participatory micro-level planning exercise was undertaken in Cinta Maker.

Thus the ***objectives*** of the micro-planning exercise were:

1. Identifying the "poorest of the poor" and "poor households" in the village;
2. Locating the problem areas which inhibits development of the community and their inter-connections with the Mini-Hydro Power Plant;
3. Finding local solutions to local problems.

THE PARTICIPATORY PLANNING PROCESS

ıe planning process was conducted in a public place, namely, ɜ Village Hall and its premises. It was conducted over a period two full days, as agreed to by the villager - participants at the ginning of the planning process. The planning sessions were ended by 43 villagers on the first day, and 51 on the second y, including the head of the village, some of the village staff, men and elderly people. These participants were a fair ɪresentation of the village, and it consisted of villagers from all 4 sub-villages (called "Dusun" in local parlance) and from ious social strata.

Box 9.1

An Aware Member of the Community

n the afternoon at the first day's planning meeting, a *tan bakar* (grilled glutinous-rice snack) small vendor me to the ground of the village hall to sell his oduct. Since all the participants were inside the om and making curious noises, he took a look from e door. After awhile, he joined the group and unged whole hog into the process. He forgot that he ıd come to the place to sell his wares and earn his ead. On the second day, he gave up selling *ketan kar* and participated in the sessions for a whole day. n being enquired, he explained that he found this ıeeting so interesting that he sacrificed one day's sale *ketan bakar*. The meeting was important and also ɔncerned with his interest as a member of village ɔmmunity.

ablishment of Target Group

process began with a debate on the question about the ımunity's own criteria to determine which household can be categorized as a poor household. The debate was not about individuals but about households.

Several opinions were aired by the participants. These were written up by a member of the community on a white board. A large member of criteria was generated for categorizing households as poor. However, since a large number of criteria may make it difficult to identify which household is poor and which is not, it was decided by the participants to narrow down the number of criteria. The villagers then converged to agree on four main criteria for determining the status of any household. These criteria, were given in Table 9.7.

Those households which exhibit all these criteria would be categorized as poor. But the question arose that while some households may satisfy all the criteria in Table 9.7, others may only satisfy some of them and indeed there could even be some who meet one criteria only. How shall such such households exhibiting a variety of criteria be categorized? After considerable discussion it was decided that these criteria will be used to identify all households in the village, which satisfied one or more of these criteria. And then a decision will be taken on how to treat households which satisfied all the criteria and those that satisfied less than that number.

Table 9.7 : Criteria for determining Household Poverty

1. Households which have no land,
2. Households whose family members have no regular employment,
3. Households which cannot afford higher education. and
4. Households which have no capital to conduct a business.

All the criteria were deemed equally important and hence had the same weightage in determining the status of households as being poor or non-poor.

Identification of Beneficiaries

For the above exercise, the participants were grouped into four groups, which represented the number of the sub-villages in Cinta Mekar, viz., Dusun-I, Dusun-II, Dusun-III and Dusun-IV. (See Maps 9.1, 9.2, 9 3 and 9.4).

Identifying the Households

Each group was asked to write down on flash cards, the names of all the households that belong to the Dusun they represented. One card will have just one name of a household. Thus Group-I, wrote down the names of all the households of Dusun-I on flash cards and placed them on the floor. Similarly Groups-II, III and IV wrote down the names of all the households of Dusuns-II, III and IV respectively on flash cards and also placed them Dusun-wise on the floor of the Village Hall as also on the veranda. Once this exercise was completed by each group, all the groups were encouraged to visit the listing of households made by the other groups and see if all names have been included or not and suggest any deletion or addition, that they may deem necessary.

After the groups had checked each others work and additions made, the list of households was considered final. Thus *Name-cards* of all the households of Cinta Mekar were created by the villagers themselves.

Sticking *Criteria to Household Name-cards*

Having finalized the Name-cards of all the households, each group was asked to categorize these households based on the four criteria that had already been agreed to by the groups as shown in Table 9.7. The process followed was something as under.

- It was agreed that one specified colored sticker would represent one criterion from the identified criteria in Table 9.7. A Red sticker would indicate landlessness. A Green sticker would indicate lack of regular employment. An Orange sticker would be used to denote inability of the household to afford higher education. And a Pink sticker would indicate lack of capital in the household.
- For each household, that the respective Group knew in a Dusun, which meet **Criterion-1**, that is, *having no land*, a **red** coloured sticker was stuck on the card bearing the household's name.

- Similarly for each household that the respective Group knew in a Dusun which meet **Criterion-2**, that is, *households whose family members have no regular employment*, a **green** coloured sticker was stuck on the card bearing the household's name.
- For every household which meet **criterion-3**, that is, *households which cannot afford higher education* and **criterion-4**, that is, *households which have no capital to conduct business*, an **orange** coloured and a **pink** coloured sticker respectively were stuck on the card bearing the household's name.

It was understood that some households may not attract any sticker at all while some may attract all the stickers and so on, depending on the number of criteria that are applicable to a household.

Once all the groups had placed or stuck the stickers of different colours, all the participants were encouraged to look at what the other groups have done and they were free to suggest changes. There was some discussion amongst the villagers and some changes were suggested and made.

All the groups were also given a chance to review their own work once again and if they wished to make any change, they were given the option to do so after due consultation. Care was exercised to ensure that changes also reflected the respective groups' wisdom, not any one individual's preference.

Classifying the Household Name-cards

At the end of the exercise, a compilation of *Household Name-cards* bearing names of households with one, two, three or four, coloured stickers (signifying criteria for being poor) was generated. A Name-card, as we stated earlier, could have a maximum of four stickers and a minimum of no sticker at all. The accepted principle was that the larger the number of stickers that appeared on a *Household Name-card*, the larger the number of criteria for being poor the household satisfies and hence it was so much more poorer. *Household Name-cards* bearing no stickers and hence having no attributes of being poor, were excluded from the compilation, for these cards represented those households who are non-poor. The balance *House hold Name-cards* were then sorted out according to the number of stickers that they had. As the participants had agreed, these poor households groups were:

Miskin I (Poor I) : households that meet four criteria given.

Miskin II (Poor II) : households that meet three criteria given.

Miskin III(Poor III) : households that meet two criteria given.

Miskin IV (Poor IV) : households that meet one criterion given.

Based on the above criteria and the four fold classification of the households, the villagers decided that the utilization of the profits from the proposed project (Cinta Mekar Mini-Hydro Project) would be used first for those in Miskin-I, then for those which belonged to Miskin-II, then for those which were in Miskin-III and finally to those falling in to Miskin-IV. Table-08 is a summary of the number of households which met different criteria of poverty and hence attracted stickers of different colours in the different Dusuns.

The final list of names of households in the four categories is at *Annexure-I*. It would be apparent from *Annexure-I*, that:

(a) There are only four households (all in Dusun-IV) which satisfy all the four criteria and are in Miskin-I.

(b) There are 9, 7, 18 and 13 (totaling 47) households which were in Miskin-II in Dusun-I, Dusun-II, Dusun-III and Dusun-IV respectively.

(c) There are 15, 12, 42 and 37 households (totaling 100) which were categorized as being in Miskin-III in Dusun-I, Dusun-II, Dusun-III and Dusun-IV respectively.

(d) There are 45, 55, 63 and 54 households (totaling 217) falling in Miskin-IV in Dusun-I, Dusun-II, Dusun-III and Dusun-IV respectively.

Rest of the households (which bore no sticker at all) were non-poor and hence were not included in the Annexure-I. The names of these households and their categories were pasted on the walls of the Village Hall for everyone to see.

On the second day of the planning meeting, the participants were taken through this categorization of the households once again for their confirmation. The picture of the categorization as displayed in the wall is given on page no. 419.

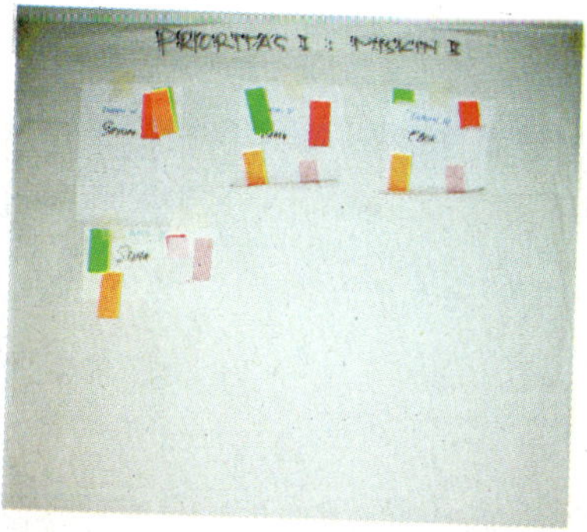

(A)
First priority (Miskin I/Poor I);

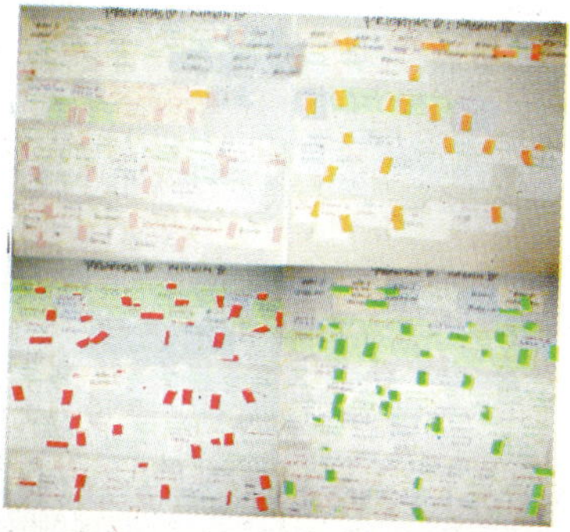

(B)
Second priority (Miskin II/Poor II)

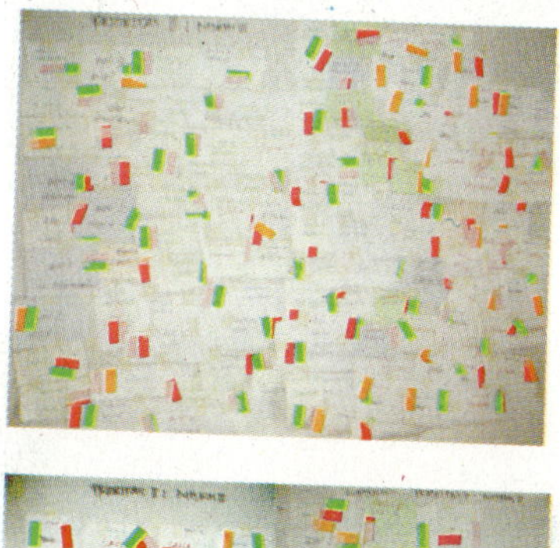

(C)
Third priority (Miskin III/Poor III);

(D)
Fourth priority (Miskin IV/Poor IV)

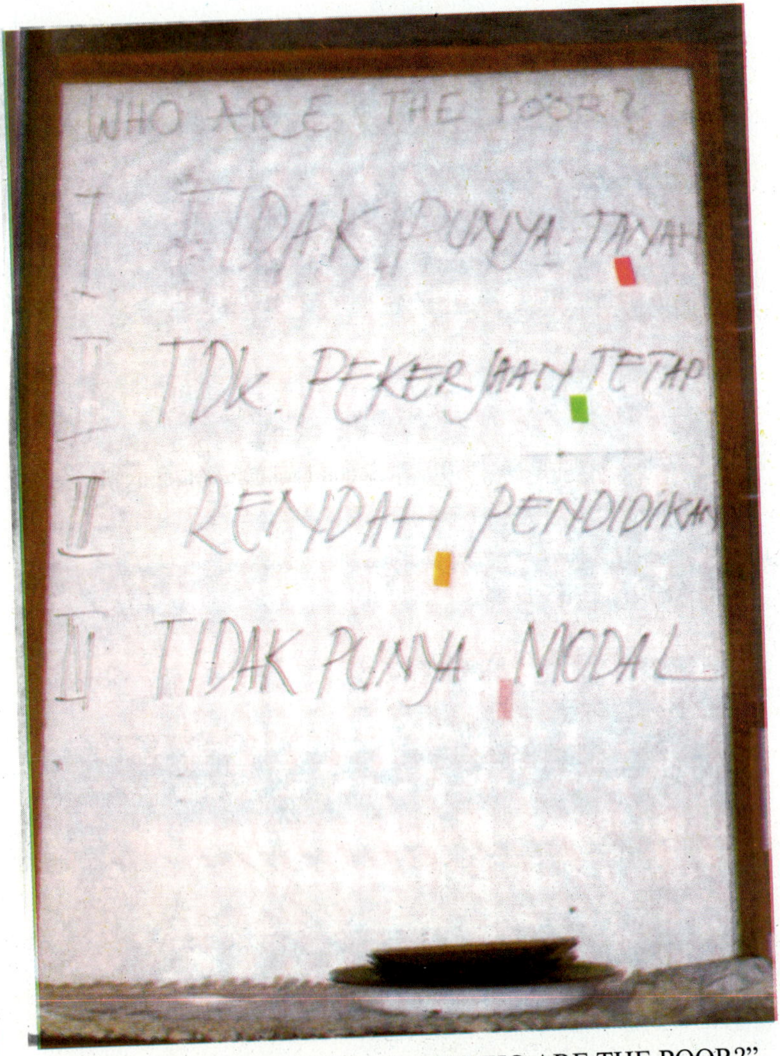

Plate 1 : Community"s Criteria of "WHO ARE THE POOR?"

Plate 2 : Community's Members Selecting "Poor-Poorest" Households in Cinta Mekar

Plate 3 : Community's Members Presenting Outcome of the Exercise to select "Poor-Poorest" Households in Cinta Mekar

Plate 4 : Community's Members Developing the Empowerment Circle in Cinta Mekar

Plate 5 : Community's Members Completing the Empowerment Circle in Cinta Mekar

Table 9.8 : Summary of the beneficiary identification result

Priority – Criteria/Sticker	Dusun I	Dusun II	Dusun III	Dusun IV	Total
Miskin IV (one criterion)					
Red	10	22	11	14	57
Green	7	15	24	26	72
Orange	10	6	9	5	30
Pink	17	11	16	10	54
Miskin III (two criteria)					
Red-Green	4	1	15	6	26
Red-Orange	-	-	1	5	6
Red-Pink	4	8	4	1	17
Green-Orange	3	1	-	8	22
Green-Pink	3	-	15	7	25
Orange-Pink	-	-	1	4	5
Miskin II (three criteria)					
Red-Green-Orange	4	-	3	4	11
Red-Green-Pink	2	4	10	5	21
Red-Orange-Pink	-	3	1	2	6
Green-Orange-Pink	3	-	4	2	9
Miskin I (four criteria)					
Red-Green-Orange-Pink	-	-	-	4	4
Non-poor					
No sticker	61	113	34	38	246
Total	**118**	**184**	**148**	**141**	**491**

Notes:

- *Red* : *have no land*
- *Green* : *have no regular job*
- *Orange* : *cannot afford higher education*
- *Pink* : *have no capital.*

The participants re-examined the classification of the households and confirmed that they were happy with the result of the exercise.

Box 9.2
A Profile of a Poor Household

As a sample, one household was picked up from the list o households which belong to the ***Miskin I*** group (first priorit beneficiary) for an interview. The interview was done with th wife as interviewee, because the husband was out for work.

The household belongs to ***Dusun IV*** (Sub-village IV). Thei house is located in the hilly area of the village, about 1.5 km fror the village office, 500 m from the main village road.

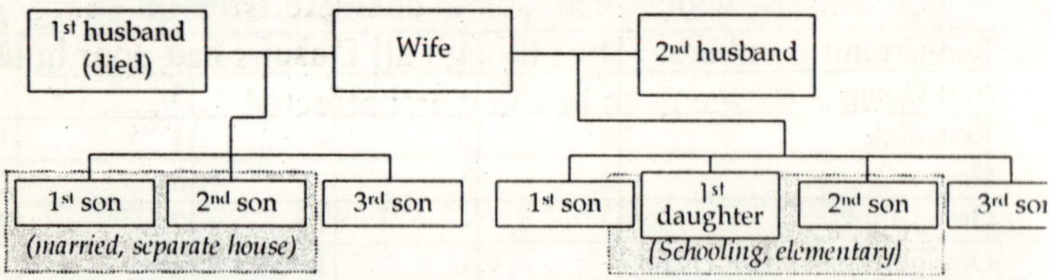

The husband's work is not a regular job, for he is a season farm labor. They do not have farmland. Between the season variation in availability of employment, the husband makes h living as log carrier: cutting logs from the forest and selling then For each log he carried, he earns Rp 5,000. Because of the distanc to the forest, he can only carry one log per day. The wife stays a home most of the time, except for sometimes in every three montl where there is need for women labor paddy transplanting an harvesting.

As for now they only use self-made simple kerosene lam for lighting in the night. They use fuel wood for cooking. The do like to have electricity connection to their house, given tha the cost is low enough. When she was asked about the cost, sh was doubtful if they can afford. She finally said that they coul afford an installation cost of Rp 50,000 but can not afford t pay the monthly bills.

The respondent admitted that she was not aware about th micro hydro project that will be implemented in the near futur for she or her husband never attend any meeting conducted in th village. When asked about their plans to improve their livin she said that they need to repair their house, and if financial aid provided she will use it as working capital to start a *busines* selling salted fish around the village.

In Table 9.8, which a summary of different households, having different characteristics warrants a few comments. If we further analyze Table 9.8, it will be seen that Dusun-IV has the highest number of landless households, and largest number of households which have no regular sources of employment. It is also the Dusun which can not afford higher education for their children and have no capital (presumably to commence livelihood activities). Thus in terms of poverty caused by "assetlessnes" as also capability poverty, Dusun-IV seems to be the most disadvantaged. However, all the Dusuns had households which had some characteristic of being poor, in varying numbers. Thus though all Dusuns had poor households, Dusun – IV seems to be the worst affected.

Problem Identification and Solutions

Having classified the households and the potential beneficiaries, the participants went on to examine the problems of the village as a whole. While eliminating the problems of landlessness, unemployment, lack of access to better education and lack of capital, would deal with issue relating to poverty reduction, it was important to know how these could be achieved. What were the villagers' ideas? What collective wisdom did they have to share? These were important issues to be decided.

Thus, one session was dedicated to identify problems the villagers of Cinta Mekar faces and suggest local solutions. In order to focus the groups' thinking on both problems and on solutions, at the beginning of the session, the facilitator introduced the concept of the Force Field Analysis. The Force Field Analysis introduced the concept of two sets of forces; one set of forces could bring the community down (negative forces), and the other that could lift the community up to a better condition (positive forces).

The participants were divided into two groups: Men's Group and Women's Group. Every Group was then asked to write down, on sheet(s) of paper or flash cards, problem(s) each of them thought may constrain, or, are constraining the village from accomplishing the condition they wanted to achieve. What were the impediarents to their realizing their dream Cinta Mekar? The problems raised by each group were to be subjected to group discussion.

Each group was asked to discuss every view that was expressed in the group and then record the problems identified by the group on a consensual basis. Each problem was recorded in different flash-cards. All the flash cards with problems written on them were laid on the floor and the Delphi Method used to club together similar cards or identical problems into one and then regroup the problems written in the basis of similarity. The process helped the groups to scale down from the numerous problems identified, for Cinta Mekar, to the following five:

Table 9.9 : Problems Confronting Cinta Mekar

Limited employment opportunities
Low economical status of the villagers
Low quality of human resources
Lack of unity of the community, especially in problem solving
Limited facility and infrastructure for economic activity

With five major problems, it was natural that the issue of which problem needs to be tackled first came up for discussion on. There was a need to prioritize. The number of participants was large, the opinions of the participants were varied. In order to prioritize the problems a system of voting was adopted. Each person had one vote which could be exercised by placing a sticker against the problem which she/he thought was most important for the community. Men and women would "vote" separately on their own list of problems identified.

The general principle agreed was that the problem which attracted the largest number of stickers would be taken as the most important problem and so on. The results from the exercise were as given in Tables 9.10 and 9.11.

Table 9.10 : Male Group's Prioritized Problems

Priority	*Problems*	*No. of Suggestion*	*No. of Votes*
1	Limited employment	11	18
2	Low economical status	7	5
3	Low quality of human resources	8	3
4	Unity of the community, especially in problem solving	2	2
5	Limited facility and infrastructure for economic activity	6	1

Table 9.11 : Women Group's Prioritized Problems

Priority	*Problems*	*No. of Suggestion*	*No. of Votes*
1	Limited capital for business	4	11
2	Limited employment	6	9
3	Low economical status	7	1
4	Agriculture failure	1	-
5	No permission from the husband to work outside	1	-

The perception of the worst problem for men and women differed very substantially. For men, the biggest problem was limited employment opportunities, but for women it was paucity of capital for business (which in Cinta Mekar represents petty trade, vending, village grocery store etc.) For women, lack of employment opportunities came only second. This difference in perception can be explained in terms of the social construct that prevail in Cinta Mekar today, where men like to seek employment outside the home, but women preferred being in off-farm employment within the households and certainly within the village. Given the economic structure of the village economy, women had only self-employment opportunities like making pickles, selling dried fish, vending provision etc. Lack of capital, naturally, posed the biggest stumbling block for them.

Finding Solutions

With the finalization of the results of the list of problems prioritized by men and women separately, the participants initiated a discussion on suggestions for seeking solutions, in order to achieve a better living condition for their village. The participants were grouped into two male's group and two female's group for a more effective discussion. Each group was requested to write their solutions on Flip Charts. The result from the exercise was encouraging.

The suggested solutions were as follows:

Box 9.3
Solutions
Group I (Male)

Solutions for "Limited Employment opportunities":

i. Create new self employment opportunities
ii. Improve education related to the available employment vacancies (meaning vocational education)
iii. Develop entrepreneurship
iv. Facilitate investment from outside
v. Community to inculcate willing to work hard
vi. Better utilization of natural resources
vii. Promote solidarity between the wealthy and the poor in the village

Solutions for tackling low economic status:

i. Capital fund introduction
ii. Improvement in communication
iii. Promoting investor's trust
iv. People should be honest/transparent
v. Community should inculcate a willingness to cooperate

For dealing with the problem of low quality of human resource:

i. Enhancement of education facility
ii. Conduct courses
iii. Scholarship
iv. Campaign for education awareness
v. Incentives for teachers

For Improving Unity

i. Promote awareness of in the community
ii. Promote "*Gotong-royong*" (literally meaning "hand on hand, shoulder to shoulder; a working together mechanism") mentality

For Improving Facility and infrastructure:

i. Promote "*Gotong-royong*"
ii. Introduction of a mutual development fund
iii. New facility development
iv. Refurbish/renovate non-functioning facilities

Box 9.4
Solutions
Group II (Male):

For Limited Employment opportunities in the village:

i. Create new employment in agriculture and industry
ii. Form a cooperative
iii. Improved utilization of natural resource
iv. Inculcate motivation for working hard
v. Introduction of capital aid
vi. Promoting unity among the community
vii. Facilitating investors from outside the village to come and invest in the village

Solutions for tackling low economic status:

No solution suggested

For dealing with the problem of low quality of human resource:

i. Create conditions where people can get basic nine years education
ii. Conduct skills training
iii. Elimination of illiteracy

For Improving Unity

i. Conduct routine community meeting
ii. Enhance the communication among the villager
iii. Enhance *Gotong-royong*

For Improving Facility and infrastructure:

No solution provided

Box 9.5
Solutions
Female Group I

For the problem of limited availability of capital:

i. More efforts, motivation and skills possessing
ii. More employment

For tackling the problem of limited employment opportunities

i. Development of entrepreneurship skill among women
ii. Development of a willing to work hard
iii. Creation of self-employment opportunities
iv. Promote the possession and development of some vocational skills

Box 9.6

Solutions

<u>Female Group II</u>

For dealing with the problems identified by the women's group

i. Generate a capital formation and facilities for setting up small business
ii. Imbibe willingness to work harder
iii. Practice "*Gotong-royong*".

Each group presented their results to the forum and clarifications sought and questions asked.

It would be apparent from reviewing the suggestions that the villagers of Cinta Mekar were suggesting, *on the one hand,* direct interventions (such as creating employment opportunities) and *on the other*, (in the livelihoods framework), proposing solutions primarily to seek betterment of human resources capital, social capital and financial capital. They were not as concerned with either physical capital or natural resources capital, (though they were concerned with their utilization, an issue to which we will return later).

Thus, the villagers sought, for improving their human capital base through better education, vocational and skills training, awareness generation programmes and incentives to teachers so that they maintained a high standard in the schools. For improving social capital, the suggestion was to inculcate *Gotong-royong* (meaning "hand on hand, shoulder to shoulder; a working together mechanism") mentality, motivation, willingness to work hard, enhanced communication in the community, transparency and honesty on the part of the villagers and so on. In case of financial capital, the prime focus was on provision of working capital.

The issue of better utilization of natural resources and awareness generation was significant because forests were being destroyed by both the poor and the non-poor. The poor cut logs and sell the same to etch out a living. The non-poor fell the trees to clear the land for growing what the people call "August paddy". The villagers were aware that these activities would jeopardize their long term interest but were unable to confront the problem as a collective. Hence, while on the one hand they need measures to better utilize their natural resources, on the other they needed social capital (unity, *Gotong-royong* and the rest of it) to deal with the problem at the community plane without personalizing the problem.

Location of Mini Hydro Power Plant through Public-private Partnership Project in Cinta Mekar Village

The establishment of the Mini Hydro Power Plant through Public-private Partnership Project in Cinta Mekar Village was given, as the decision to the effect was already taken. But the question in the micro – level planning process was of relating the same to two vital points: where would the Mini Hydro Power plant be located and two, how will it increase their well being in the context of the problems identified and solutions provided by the villagers themselves as discussed above?

Thus, at the end of the first day meeting, each group was asked to make their sub-village (Dusun) Map, to be brought at the next day's meeting. Volunteers were sought, who would co-ordinate the exercise in the different Dusuns. Four sets of volunteers were chosen by the participants for the purpose.

On the second day all the four groups brought their Maps to the planning session. The Maps were detailed and comprehensive. While one group concentrated on facilities (infra-structure), another concentrated on natural resources.

These four Dusun Maps (by four groups) were pasted on the wall of the Village Hall. All the participants could study them within the overall layout of the sub-village and the village as a whole. And all groups were encouraged to scrutinize each others work and certify, as it were, that they represented reality including the general layout of the settlement, public facility and geographical landmarks. There was a lot of interest and discussion and changes were made in all the Maps based on inputs received.

After the Maps were finalized, the group settled down and then a question was posed: where should the location of the proposed Mini-hydro Power Plant to be? The people were unanimous that it would be built in Dusun-I. The place was marked by the villagers on the Map of Dusun-I. There was, therefore, a general consensus built that though the Mini Hydro Power Plant through Public-private Partnership Project in Cinta Mekar will be located in Dusun-I, the benefits from the project will flow to people in all Dusuns who need support, starting from Dusun-IV where all the Miskin-I people lived, as discussed above.

Linking the Problems, Solutions and Mini Hydro Power Plant

On the second afternoon, a summary of what was achived thus far was presented: wealth ranking of all the households in the village (Miskin analysis as it were), identifying the beneficiaries, problems identification and their solutions, location of the Mini Hydro Power Plant and the "destination" of the benefits from the project. Now was the time to reflect on what the current state of their "well being" was and where and how would the Mini Hydro Power plant improve the same.

The participants first determined the characteristics of the community which in their opinion best describes "well-being" of the community/village. Several suggestions were raised and discussed amongst the participants. In the end, all the participants agreed, that to them the characteristics of *"well being"* would mean that:

(a) People can afford a three times daily meal.
(b) Villagers will have regular employment and income.
(c) All villagers possess large acreage of farmland.
(d) All households would own permanent (made of brick, stone, cement), "healthy" houses.
(e) All parents can afford higher education for their children.

Based on these well being characteristics, the participants were asked to develop a large "well-being" chart. On a large sheet of paper, a large circle with five radial lines was draw, in which each agreed well-being characteristic was represented by each of those radial lines. The respective well-being characteristic was written along the relevant radial line. Reference is invited to Figure 9.1.

The facilitator explained the chart. That each of the radial line represented one characteristic of well being the villagers had agreed. The length of the lines shows "scale" for each characteristic they represent. The center of the circle is the starting or zero point and the scale moves upwards towards the circumference of the circle. The point, at which the redial line meets the circumference, is the highest point of the scale, viz., 100 per ent. Thus the centre of the circle for any radial line is 0 per cent and the point on the circumference where the radial line meets the circumference represents the maximum point (100%) of the scale.

All the participants, then, were asked to give their individual opinion about the ***present condition*** of Cinta Mekar community with respect to each well being characteristic, on the chart. Each opinion was represented by a piece of specified colored sticker for each designated each characteristic, to be stuck at an appropriate point on the radial line. Thus if a participant felt that on the issue of villagers having regular job and income, Cinta Maker has achieved 100 per cent mark, he/she should stick the sticker at the point where the radial line (representing "villagers have regular job and income") meets the circumference. On the contrary if a participant felt that on the issue of villagers having regular job and income, Cinta Maker has achieved nothing in this regard, he/she should stick the sticker at the point where the radial line (representing "villagers have regular job and income") meets the centre of the circle and so on.

Participants were asked to freely express their opinion by sticking the coloured stickers provided. The process was carried out for each of the five well being characteristics in turn. And after every participant had stuck their sticker, they were asked to look at the result and if they wanted to change their minds, they were free to do so. Some changes were made.

The picture that came out of the process showed that on all accounts, Cinta Mekar was below the 50 per cent mark or so. That is the villagers perceived that the village was about half-way through to the ideal state to which the village should move.

After the current condition of the village was depicted, the participants were requested to depict what the state would be once the project is implemented successfully and the solutions identified by them were operationalised. This was done by the similar process but with stickers of different colours or stickers of the same colour marked with a black line. The process was repeated, except that pieces of stickers this time around would represent the participants "expectation" of the impact (rather than the actual state) that could be generated by the proposed project, in respect of the agreed well being characteristic.

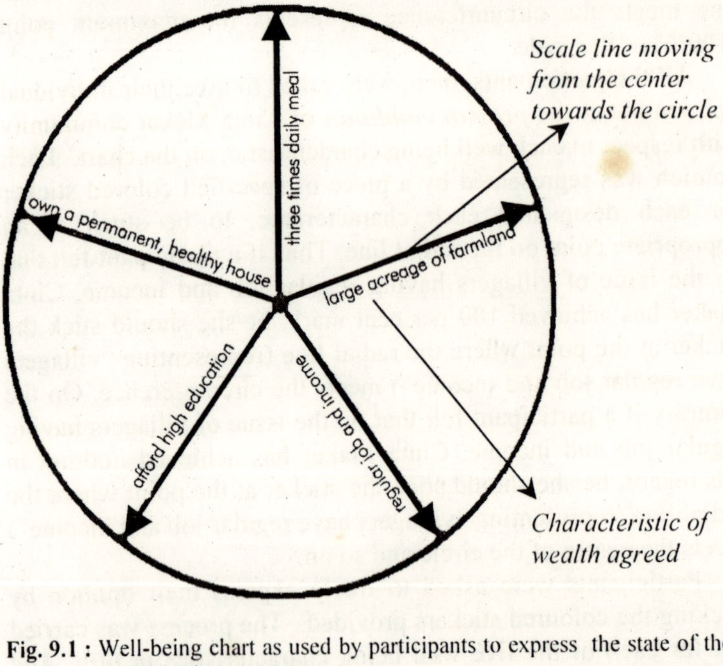

Fig. 9.1 : Well-being chart as used by participants to express the state of their wealth and expectancy.

The end result was then observed and studied by all the participants for ten minutes. Every participant was given a chance to check and correct the result, if they thought they had made a mistake or have changed their mind. However, every participant was only allowed to change one sticker in each characteristic scale line, before the final result was secured.

The final result is shown in Figure 9.3. The villagers felt that the proposed project would improve all the well-being characteristics of the Cinta Mekar on all fronts. From Figure 9.3, therefore, it seems that the community perceives that project will have significant impact in reducing poverty in the community.

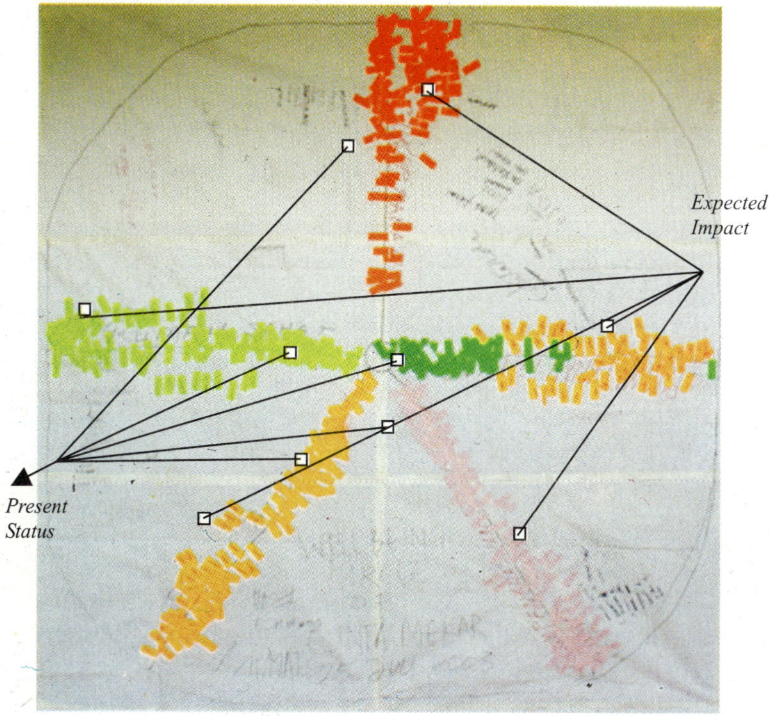

Fig. 9.2 : The present state of Well-being and the expected impact of the project on Cinta Mekar Village.

Once the well-being chart was completed, a discussion was initiated. The first question mooted was, how will the Mini Hydro Power project (which will generate power) help in ensuring three meals a day and all households would own permanent (made of brick, stone, cement) healthy house. There was no hesitation in getting a reply from the villagers. They were clear in their minds. The energy generated would be sold to the public utility, PLN. Out of the realizations from the energy sold to PLN, the villagers expect to create a fund for purveying working capital to the poor villagers. The poor villagers, with the working capital from the fund in conjunction with the capacity building/vocational and skill training they have proposed as solutions, can start their own enterprises, improve their earnings and then use the same for better food and housing. Power supply, the villagers noted, will be used to generate "capital" for inputs into income generation activities. They were also quick in identifying the connection between power generation and improvement in educational status of their children.

SOME ANALYSIS AND DISCUSSION OF THE RESULTS

A good and effective plan should serve the need of the targeted beneficiaries. The problems identified by the community itself form a very important basis for a good plan. The *problem identification* process has generated the following problems: limited employment, low economic status, limited capital for business, low quality of human resources, lack of unity, and limited facility/infrastructure for supporting economic activity in the village.

Problems, Solutions and Measures

Most of the problems identified by the villagers were in relation with their economic and social conditions. They indicated that their main motivation to participate in the project is to improve their economic condition. The need for employment and business capital could be an indication that agriculture was unable to contribute any further to their economic well-being. This possibly is caused by the limited ownership of land (Table 9.5), low level agricultural skill, and external uncertainties (like changes in product price, inputs prices, etc., which are common in the agricultural sector in Indonesia). Arguably, the villagers have suggested entrepreneurship/ business development (usually, to most of the villagers, *business* specifically means "vending or selling" goods) as a major solution to their problems, because agriculture can no longer do the trick.

The uncertainties in agriculture seem to have, especially affected the community in Cinta Mekar. That has necessitated the need to have *regular income/job*, which can be interpreted as working for a regular salary, as a coping mechanism where agriculture fails.

Despite all these, the fact that the issue of *land/farmland* appeared both in *criteria* to identify the poor and in *well-being characteristics,* indicates that agriculture is still regarded as important by the community. It shows that skills other than in agricultural operation is very limited in the community. In consequence, skills training/courses figured prominently in the list of solutions to the problems articulated by the villagers.

The point about *gotong-royong* (literally meaning "hand on hand", shoulder to shoulder; a working together mechanism) warrants a few comments. In the *problem identification* result, lack of unity among the community was raised as a major problem though ranked rather low in the prioritized list of problems. In the solutions suggested, *gotong-royong* - which requires unity amongst the villagers– appears in the suggested list of solutions coming from three of the four groups. It is seems that unity amongst the villagers is necessary to reduce social stratification but it is more important in solving their own problems through enhanced social capital. Thus despite "disunity", as it was, in the village, *gotong-royong* needs to be optimized and improved in Cinta Mekar.

Education (formal) is considered very important by the community, for it finds place both in the poverty criteria and in well-being characteristics. Table 9.3 shows that the level of education in the village is still low, though literacy levels are high. Examples from outside the village have demonstrated to the villagers how education can make a significant difference to their lives. Cinta Mekar is not a remote, isolated area. Transportation and communication are not problems, relatively speaking. The need of higher education articulated by the villagers signal that the orientation of the community is to seek employment outside the village as there is limited scope of employment in the village and agriculture can carry them only so far. These reasons, taken one with the other, provides the villagers with sufficient incentives to seek better education.

Impacts and Expectations

The result of the community's expectation as reflected in the well-being chart they generated (Figure 9.2) makes an interesting reading. As we discussed earlier, they expect that the Micro

Hydro Power Plant project would generate positive impact on all the *characteristics* of well-being identified by them. A few comments are in order here.

Three meals daily

Access to three meals a day is a very basic indicator of well-being. The reason that it is presented as one of elements in the well-being *characteristics* is possibly because there is still a significant portion in the community that cannot afford three meals daily. As is apparent from *well-being chart*, some participants really thought that Cinta Mekar has reached only the half way mark in providing three meals daily to all its inhabitants. The villagers expect the project would substantially improve this condition as was discussed earlier

Regular job/income

The villagers of Cinta Mekar also expect the project would create employment opportunities from income generating activities,, initiated with the help of working capital to be provided out of the fund that Cinta Mekar Co-operative wishes to create, from profits of the Mini-Hydro Power Plant. Employment would be generated not only through income such generating activities but also from the cooperative's own activities.

Farmland and Permanent, healthy house

When asked, how the Mini Hydro power project would enable all the villagers to access farmland, the participants reasoned that if the share of benefit from the Mini-Hydro Power Plant under reference could generate a substantial improvement in the overall income levels of the villagers, then it is possible for them to start saving, accumulate money and to buy some land some day. However, they realized that this was a long haul and the kind of impact expected would take quite some time. The craving for land reflects the importance that land holds for the villagers and the fact that most of them only own less than 0.1 hectare of land

- *not necessarily farmland.* That land is a basic resource, and possession of land is a status symbol came out in sharp focus. The case is similar for ensuring a permanent healthy house for all the villagers. From the well-being chart (Figure 9.2) it seems Cinta Mekar has presently reached only about the half way mark on the issue of providing permanent and healthy houses for all its inhabitants. With improvement in income, the inhabitants of Cinta Mekar expect, they can save and eventually have some resources to invest to better their houses. The condition of ones house is also considered a symbol of well being and high social standing in the community.

SUMMARY

The micro plan made by the community has demonstrated and signaled the start of a process of planning, monitoring and evaluation by the community itself. It produced wealth ranking of the households, list of prioritized classes of beneficiaries approved by the community, approval of the location of the Mini-Hydro Power Project, greater awareness and understanding about the project, agreement on the probable impact of the project, and the role of energy in economic livelihoods of villagers in Cinta Mekar and an estimated description of the impacts could affect the village's living.

Prioritized Beneficiaries

Category	Dusun	Name		
POOR I				
	IV	1. Sayun	3. Edok	
		2. Kama	4. Suha	
POOR II				
	I	1. Isak	4. Maman	7. Isud
		2. Sarmin	5. Adis	8. Jumid
		3. Kardi	6. Odik	9. Nanang
	II	1. Sartim	4. Somantri	7. Aop
		2. Uce	5. Suherman	
		3. Ojid	6. Oyok	
	III	1. Unib	7. Kastang	13. Amid
		2. Samsudin	8. Oyok Ading	14. Suhdi
		3. Maman	9. Sunandar	15. Rukana
		4. Dayat Ina	10. Ase M.	16. Sapdi
		5. Sofian	11. Cecep	17. Ruhyana
		6. Sahrum	12. Asri	18. Hasan
	IV	1. Nono	6. Dasmita	11. Sarya
		2. Daos	7. Rudi	12. Usep Yayat
		3. Sama	8. Kurni	13. Domoh
		4. Rusmid	9. Carmin	
		5. Dahwa	10. Atang Her	
POOR III				
	I	1. Dudi Budiman	6. U. Saprudin	11. Engkur
		2. Iim Rohimat	7. Aca	12. E. Sumyati
		3. Dahman	8. Cahdi	13. Udin
		4. Maman	9. Ukib	14. Adeh
		5. Isah	10. Didi	15. Arnesih
	II	1. Anemi	5. Amin	9. E. Permana
		2. Dadang	6. Ayo	10. Tata B.
		3. Maman	7. Mita	11. Rahmat
		4. Eman	8. Tata	12. Nara
	III	1. Rusli	15. Rohimat	29. Kastim
		2. Mahmudin	16. Dian	30. Ijah
		3. Jaya	17. Omo	31. Narlan
		4. Carmin	18. Sudin	32. Amin
		5. Suhar	19. H. Sahri	33. Ahyar
		6. Wawan	20. Husen	34. Dayat S.
		7. Odih	21. Ujum	35. Unam
		8. Urmita	22. Koswara	36. Didi
		9. Entim	23. Sarmid	37. Memet
		10. Dayat M.	24. Usdi	38. Rasmanta
		11. Jumri	25. Iwan	39. Rudi
		12. Taping	26. Herman	40. Suhata
		13. Rahmin	27. Usdia	41. Sahmat
		14. Sana	28. Rusmita	42. Erus
	IV	1. Pipih	15. Asmid	29. Adut
		2. Acum	16. Unirah	30. Dase
		3. Acim	17. Tarsono	31. Sapta
		4. Banda	18. Ono	32. Usup
		5. Juhari	19. Suryata	33. Kawir
		6. Karni	20. Sakirin	34. Amat
		7. Surni	21. Udin	35. Sabda
		8. Awir	22. Endang	36. Uri
		9. Sahri	23. Ija	37. Caman

		10. Taslan	24. Rohmin	
		11. Isna	25. Rasmid	
		12. Rukanah	26. Karosim	
		13. Odah	27. Usman	
		14. Sadmo	28. Mustopa	
POOR IV				
	I	1. Ucih	16. Endang	31. Isah
		2. Yadi	17. Lomri	32. Rukiah
		3. Udin Komarudin	18. O. Permana	33. Kenoh
		4. Udin Jaenudin	19. Tisna	34. Acem
		5. Endang Enut	20. Mas Adia	35. Emi
		6. Idi	21. Juhana	36. Ento
		7. Anemi	22. Bujang	37. Euis
		8. Kosim	23. Ade K.	38. Uneh
		9. Handi	24. Usmi	39. Yayat
		10. Ining	25. Sukandi	40. Toto
		11. Sulman	26. Unung	41. Atim
		12. Jajang	27. Karnapi	42. Dahrom
		13. Emen	28. Karna	43. Adik
		14. Endang Erum	29. Juhati	44. Bagja
		15. Wahyu	30. Yayah	45. Karwan
	II	1. Dase Permana	20. Yaya C.	39. Emah
		2. Nana	21. Icih	40. Eruk
		3. Rakus	22. Ade Sutisna	41. Amar
		4. Endi	23. Agus	42. Karmid
		5. Ata	24. Budiyana	43. Sanib
		6. Usdi	25. Lasmono	44. Tardi
		7. Andri	26. Ana	45. Umar
		8. Kahdi	27. Onoh	46. Datem
		9. Sanim	28. Pirdus	47. Ade Beres
		10. Aip	29. Atis	48. Sahmid
		11. Dulatip	30. Narya	49. E. Suhenda
		12. Yaya A.	31. Idus	50. Tomi
		13. Sahmi	32. U. Rahmat	51. Rosid
		14. Ene	33. Dahman	52. Mimin
		15. Rasmita	34. Kahmid	53. Atjeng
		16. Iris	35. Kardi	54. Asep Wawan
		17. Enco	36. Maman	55. Eman A.
		18. Tarsih	37. Arup	
		19. Ahtem	38. Atang	
	III	1. Idi	22. Daman	43. E. Sutardi
		2. Ana	23. Mahmud	44. Suhendi
		3. Jaenal Oji	24. Pendi	45. Sadang
		4. Cecep M.	25. Sarya	46. Mansur
		5. Nana	26. Enik	47. U. Pudin
		6. Amat	27. Kasni	48. Kusman
		7. Dayat R.	28. Tisna	49. Ase S.
		8. Atep	29. Ajud	50. Enda
		9. Ma Unung	30. Sahun	51. Taslim
		10. Cucu	31. Juarma	52. Cucu Wasita
		11. Suhlan	32. Nanang	53. Muslim
		12. Sajun	33. Sarna	54. Ayep
		13. Muksin	34. Suhir	55. Cahya
		14. Oman	35. Itas Solihin	56. Samo
		15. A. Suparman	36. Ruslan	57. Sasmita
		16. Ruhya	37. Ma Ining	58. Rukajat
		17. Idong	38. Ateng	59. Dahya

		18. Enco	39. Jadam	60. Ace
		19. Junata	40. Said	61. Waryana
		20. Atik S.	41. Sukmah	62. Andu
		21. Sahri S.	42. Apud	63. Ace I.
	IV	1. Tarlan	19. Nana	37. Onang
		2. Imis	20. Uhyana	38. Sarma
		3. Lili S.	21. Kotang	39. Wawan
		4. Ita	22. Saad	40. Oyok
		5. Rohmat	23. Iten	41. Ito
		6. Darya	24. Amsar	42. Anib
		7. Suherman	25. Onah	43. Abud
		8. Koko	26. Karsih	44. Muhdin
		9. Rahmat	27. Ujang Rahman	45. Sahman
		10. Rus'at	28. Badar	46. Ujang
		11. Mita	29. Ada	47. Ajo
		12. Sami	30. Carta	48. Sap'I
		13. Isuh	31. Kateng	49. Aceng
		14. Sarti	32. Mahmad	50. Isut Arkat
		15. Iwik	33. Ada K.	51. Ibul
		16. Atang	34. Udin	52. Sarwin
		17. Sahuri	35. Ono	53. Edi
		18. Kusep	36. Uner	54. Juneng

INDEX

Abu Lea natural forest, 271
advantages and disadvantages., 272
Accountability, 87
Achieving flexibility by empowering people, 69
Action Aid, Bangalore, 61
Action Planning, 117-19, 393-96
planning *per se*. 120
Activist participator research, 2-4
Activities, 135-37
Adult education, 356
Adult literacy campaign, 317
African regional workshop on participatory research, 3
Aga Khan Rural Support Programme, Pakistan, 4, 9, 10, 24, 63
Agricultural census operation, 121
Agricultural extension, 169
Agricultural management practices, 300
Agricultural production, problems of, 315-16
systems, 286
Agricultural production and protection, 252
Agricultural productivity, objectives of, 375-76
Agricultural system, 109-10
Agriculture, 29-30, 243-44, 248-51, 374-87
cash crops, 300
climate influence, 295-96
cropping pattern, 293-94
demonstration plots, 301
inter-cropping, 299
irrigation, 299-300
main problems, 301
problems and opportunities, 278-80
storage problems, 300-301
Agro-climatic zone, 248
Agro-economic details, 176-81, 187-94, 215-20
income, 191-92
irrigation scheme details, 188-91
land classification, 187-88
Agro-ecosystem analysis, 4-5
diagramming, 59-60
Agro-forestry, 164
Ahmadu Bello University, Northern Nigeria, 6
AKRSP, 32, 64
Alternative data bases, creation and maintenance of, 168-239
American Congress, 122
Amemo Peasant Association,
crops, pests and diseases, 297-99
findings of, 317-18
fuel sources of, 308-09
health post, 323-24
improved stoves, 318-19
introduction to, 290-92
issues in,
agriculture, 289-89, 292-301
Best Best for, 318-325
health and nutrition, 288-90, 309-13
livestock, 288-89, 301-303
natural resources, 288, 303-309
non-agricultural income generation activities, 290
problems and opportunities in, 315-18
main crop grown in, 292
problems in, 292
transect of, 296
Amstrong, Neil, 122
Analysis of preferences through Scor-

ing-ranking and matrix-ranking. 128
Analysis of relationship through Venn diagramming. 127
Analysis of space through social mapping. 127
Analysis of time through historical transect. 127
Ancharo,
agricultural proudction, 252. 254-64
agriculture-sector. problems and opportunities, 264
cropping pattern. 254
history of, 253-54
improved poultry breeds. 285
irrigation. 263-64
landuse in, 248
livestock resources in. 265-66
natural resources. 271-78
nutrition. health. income. 247-53
sources of. 274-78
preliminary Best Best. 281-82
recommendations. 264-65
transect of. 249-51
varieties of grain crops in. 256-58
vegetable garden development. 284-85
Ancharo weavers. small-scale spinning machines for. 281-83
Ancharo and Amemo Project Areas. 241
Animal husbandry. 169. 219. 391-92
Action Plan. 393-94
current facilities, 391-92
financial allocation. 395-96
objectives of. 392
problems visualised during implementation. 394-95
programmes. 391-96
Animal production. 266-67
Anti-poverty programmes. 37
Appalachia. 3
Application in Africa. objectives and activities. 241-45
Rapid rural appraisal in Amemo PA. 288-325
Rapid rural appraisal for local level planning Wollo Province. Ethiopia. 241-87
Application in India : Vikasnagar. district Dehradun. 326-405
Appleton, Judith. 30
Applied anthropology. 5-6
Arhtiyas. 387
Assessment. 124. 155. 164. 256
Attitudes in Application on PLA. 102-04
Australian Universities. 66
Authoritarianism, 70
Azadpur Mandi. Delhi, 387

Basic differences between participatory method. 112
Basic education. development of early curriculum, 158
Bee-keeping. 269. 319-20
Belgiam Survival fund. 310
Beliefs and behaviours, 112
Belshaw, D., 7
Bernades. C.N., 35
Best Judgement, 52-53
beyond farming system research, 53-54
Biases, 126
Bio-gas plant. 182. 381
benefits of, 373-74
Biological erosion control, 367
Bio-mass sub-system, 109
Block level planning. 135-36
porblems of, 329-30
Bovine-wealth sub-system. 109
Buchanan-Smith. M.. 54
Budgeting. 138-39
Bunch. R.. 63
Bureaucracy. 87

Campbell. G. J.. 33
Card sorting method. 132
Carruthers. Ian. 7
Cash crops. 292. 300, 314. 410
production. 319-20

Casteism. 130
Catchments. resources maps of, 158
Central Statistical Organisation. 121
Centralization. 70
Centrally/State sponsored schemes. 173
Challenges, 54
Chambers, Robert, 7, 28, 33, 53
Chapati diagramming, 43
Checkdams, 369
Checkland, P.B., 67
Chemical fertilizers, 260. 299. 381
Cinta Mekar Village,
  beneficiaries, identification of, 414-15
  death and birth rate, 409
  dusans, 407, 413-14
  dynamics of population, 408
  education level. 409
  geographical condition. 407
  household name cards, 415-18
  human resources characteristics. 407-08
  land ownership structure in. 411
  occupational structure. 409-10
  participatory planning process. 413-18
  planning background and objectives. 411-12
  public-private partnership project. 406
  target groups. establishment of. 413-14
  vegetation and rainfall. 407
Climate. influence of. 295-96
Collinson, Michael, 7, 34
Combination of Visual and Verbal. 45
Combolcha Rural Technological Centre. 283
Commanding heights. 88
Common property resources. 130. 152. 173
Commonality between PLA and micro-level planning. 114
Communication, 180. 214. 218
Community's dream. 126-27
Community Health Attendant (CHA), 277
Community health workers, 310
Comparisons, 33, 45
Comparison and training implication, 101-102
Competition, 293
Conflict resolution, 131. 132-33
Consolidated fund, 169
Constraints, 111. 140, 238, 281. 286, 287
Context in which local level planning operates, 99-100
Context in which PLA is used, 99-100
Contrast between verbal and visual models, 44-45
Conventional questionnaire survey comparison, 34-35
Conway, G., 3, 4, 38
Cooperative Societies, 185-86
Corbett. William. 159
Crop-combination. 254
Crop diseases, 381
Crop diversification, 382
Crops grown area, 248-49
Crop ranking, 293-94
Crop rotation, 259
Crop rotation and intercropping, benefit of, 260-61
Cropping pattern. 146, 252, 293-94
Crossbreeding. 393-95
Current political imperatives, 87
Dairy Development programmes. 393-94
  women's role in, 394-95
Dairy Vikas Kendras (DVK). 397
Data Collection. 112
Data requirement at Block Level planning, 212-16
  agro-economic details. 215
  demographic details, 215
  infrastructure details. 212-15
Data requirement at District level for planning. 216-20
  agro-economic details. 220

demographic details. 220
environmental and gender details, 222
infrastructure details, 216-20
Data requirment of village level for Micro-level planning, 175-212
Decentralised flexibility. 69
Decentralised planning. 87
Deforestation, 362
Dehradun. forest — the green cover. 359-66
Demographic details. 186-87, 215, 220
livestock and poultry, 187
population, 186
Demonstration farms. 381
Demonstration plots, 301, 310, 317
Determining allocation of the project, 133-34
Determining appropriateness for marginalised groups. 137-38
Determining the planning approach and the process, 125-26
Devaraj. S., 239
Development agencies. 148
Development programmes, planning and implementation of, 87
Dhakrain Village, health facility map, 341-44
seasonal food calendar. 344-45
Diagramming and Visual sharing. 22-23
Disaster prevention programme. 290
Disciplines. 68. 110
Discrimination against women. 344
Diseases, 343-44
District Co-operative Society. 219
Donor sector, 138
Donors. 60
Dream map, 122. 127
Drinking water. 178-79. 217, 321-22
planning alternatives. 337-38
problems of. 336-37
Drought Prone Areas programmes. Andhra Pradesh. 235
Dryland Development Board (DLDB). 234
Dunn. A.M.. 66

Economic services. 183-84. 214-15. 219-20
Education, 172-73, 213, 217
empirical observations. 350-52
existing facilities, 353-55
implementing plans. 357-58
methodology and database, 352-83
Educational institutions, 177-78
Elementary education. universalisation of. 172
Eliciting communal perception. 158
Employment. 158. 172. 180. 214-18. 390
opportunities, 411
Empowerment and equity, 58-60
Empowerment of people, 94
Environmental degradation. 153
Environmental details, 194-207
Environmental resources, suitability classification. 196-98. 200-206
Environmental resource availability classification, 194-96
Environmental resource depletability classification. 206-07
Erosion. 304
Erosion on farmland. 271
Exproducer's Cooperative (PC) land. 264
Extensive Farmers' education. 386
Familial social security system, 130
Family planning, 277
techniques. 350
Family welfare plan. funding for, 349-50
Farm and household surveys. 34-36
Farmers. credit support. 385
Farmer's problems. 379-80
Farmer's own extension, 63
Farming system research (FSR). 6
Female literacy. 174. 211
Female children. malnutrition. 211
Female wages. 210-11
Fertility management, 279
Field research on farming systems, 6-7

Fieldwork, preparation for. 243-45
  agriculture. 243-44
  health and nutrition. 244
  labour. 245
  livestock. 244
  marketing. 244
  natural resources. 244
  soil and water conservation. 244
Fieldwork programme. 245-52. 289-90
Financial allocation. 338-39. 365-66. 372-73
Financial generation. 535-36
Finding solutions.131-32
Five Year Plans. 100. 108
Fodder situation. 265-66
Fodder shortage. solve problems. 269-70
Fodder and feed production. 173
Food Corporation of India (FCI). 382
Food discrimination. 345
Food security problems. 544
  promotions of. 172
  structural adjustment programme on. 153. 164
Food security and nutrition assessment, 30
Food for work, 313
Forest sector. strategy for planning. 364-65
Forest species. 359
  types of. 362-63
Formulating strategies. 158
Franzel. Stevan. 34
Freire. Paulo. 3
Frozen fruit processing plant. Vikasnagar. 388
From RRA to PRA. 8-11
Frontiers. challenges and potentials. 53-67
Fruit processing plants. 386-87
Fruit trees. 386
Fuelwood problems. 317
Functional linkage matrix. 132
Future development. 70
Garhwal Himalays. 157
Gender bias. 126
Gender discrimination. 130
Gender issues. 352
Gender details. 207-12
  data on gender analysis. 207-12
German Commission of Justice and Peace. 56
Gibson. Tony, 44
Gill. Gerard, 39. 40
Gleick. J., 68
Global environmental issues. 68
Good quality planting material. 385
Gould, P., 20
Governance and planning. system of, 87
Government field organisations. 64-65
Government participatory methods. components of. 236-39
Gram Panchayats, 100, 140, 174
Gram Panchayat level to the Zilla Parishad/District level functionaries, 103
Gram and Town Panchayats. 174
Gram Sabhas, 170, 172
Grandin, Barbara, 37
Grandstaff. Terry B., 8, 13, 15, 25
Growford. Eric. 34
Green revolution, 109
Guijt. Irane. 241. 288
Gully problem. 271
  reclamation. 281
Gypmantasiri. 4

Hard systems approach, 143
Harijan (untouchables). 59
Harrawala canal. 377
Harwood. R., 6
Health, family welfare and sanitation. 339-50
Health problems and opportunities. 277-80
Health and nutrition. 30-32. 244-45. 309-13
Health services. 309-10

Hebbel Agricultural University. Bangalore, 66
Henry Ford's model & automobile. 60
Higher agricultural productivity, 174
Hill. Polly, 37
Hitecha nursery. 305-08, 317. 322
Home consumption. 300
Home gardens. 260-62
development. 281
Home improvement. 274-75
Homogenization. 70
Horticultural crops. 299, 326
Horticulture, 384-87
existing marketing arrangement, 386-87
Horticulture promoting. Action Plan for, 385-86
Household name cards. sticking criteria to. 415-16
classification of, 416-18
Housing, 182. 214
HYV seeds/chemical fertilizer/pesticides. 380-82

IBEKA, 412
Illiteracy. 408
IMF, 88
IRDP loans, 239
Income earning activities, 193
Income earning opportunities. ranking of, 275-76
Income generation, 313-15
activities. 281
Indian Institute of Forest Management. Bhopal. 66
Indigenous Technical Knowledge (ITK). 6
Indira Awas Yojana. 134
Industries. 182-83
Industrial cooperative societies, 183
Infant Mortality Rate (IMR). 212, 339
Infrstructural details. 176-186. 212-20
Infrastructural facilities. 371-72
Inglis, Andy, 35
Institute of Forest Management, Pokhara, Nepal, 66
Institutionalizing participatory methods. 236
Intercropping. 259-60. 209. 299-300. 322
Interface between economic and non-economic factors. 109
International Drinking Water Supply and Sanitation Decade. 347
Irrigation. 164, 299-300
facilities. 385
development. 281, 320-21
sources of, 377

Jamboni range. sal forest regeneration in, 164
Jamieson, N., 67
JANATA model biogas plant, 373
Jawahar Rozgar Yojana Programme, 352
JF Kennedy (JFK) episode, 122
Johari's window. 121, 125, 131
Joseph, Thomas. 30
Judicial and administrative services. 215-16

Kaplinsky, R., 68
Ketan bakar, 413
Khadi Village and cottage industries, 169
Kharif crops, 330
Khon Kaen International Conference. 9
Kolkata Metropolitan Development Authority. 100
Krishi Gram Vikas Kendras. Ranchi. 10

Lead Bank. 121
Learning mode. 141
Learning to unlearn, 236
Lecturing mode. 103. 141
Literacy. 172
Livestocks. 244-47. 252-53
diseases, 302

domestic animals. 301
fodder grasses collection, 303
income. 267
problems and opportunities. 278-80
Livestock census operation, 121
Livestock production. problems and opportunities. 269-70
LBS National Academy of Administration. Mussoorie. 10. 66. 334. 337. 371
Labour demand. 330
Labour migration, 330
Labour pattern. 274
Landholdings, distribution of. 375-76
Land policies, 55
Land reforms, 169
movement. 237
Land Tenure System. 263
Land use pattern. 152, 375-76
Local level planning. assessing environment for. 145
avoids the dangers associated. 92
for rural development. 88
limitations of. 100-101
plan for area development. 92-93
principles of. 93-94
obviates the difficulties. 91-92
principal classes of actors in. 99-100
relevance of PLA methods as tools for. 89-101
techniques of, 98-99
tools of. 96-98
Low External Input Sustainable Agriculture (LEISA), 153

Madagascar. 152
Major crops pests and diseases. 258-59
Male-female composition. 207-08
Marketable surplus. 382
Marketing. 244
Mascarenhas. J.. 20. 38. 40. 45
McCracken. J.. 9. 10
Mechanical erosion control. 367
Mechanization. 378. 381
Meet problems, strategies to, 381-82
Micro-environment. 195. 199-200. 205
Micro-level planning. data requirement categories. 175-200
agro-economic details, 187-94
demographic details. 186-87
environmental details. 194-207
gender details. 207-12
infrastructure deails, 176-86
Micro-level planning, data requirement of village level for. 175-212
Micro-level planning.
action planning. 116-19
activity prioritization, 132
assessing environment for, 143-44
communication dream, 126-27
conflict resolution. 131-33
hard system approach to, 143
implementation of. 135
nuts and bolts of. 115-16
components of. 115-16
parameters, 90
planning stage, 148-50
preplanning stages. 120-30
preparation steps. 120-21
potential problem identification, 129-30
problems prioritisation, 130-31
sensitizing the community, 124-25
stages of. 116-19
steps of tactical planning and action planning. 116-19. 119-40
your dream : your perspective, 122-24
use of participatory methods, 120-40
Micro-level planning for rural development, 87-160
inparticipatory framework, 108-40. 143-66
Micro-level planning for rural development and participatory learning and action techniques. 85-104
Micro-level planning/local level

planning. 91-92
Mid-day milk scheme. 352. 357
Mid-season droughts. 252
Mini-hydro power plant. 412
tactical plan for appropriation of benefits from development. 306-18
Minimimum needs programme, 174
Modern agricultural practices. 292
Modern animal husbandry. 292
Modes, reversals of. 41-46
Monitoring and evaluation system. 140
Monnapan. A.K.. 236
Moris, John R.. 33
Mother and child care. 277
MLA/MP local area development fund. 135
MSC-time matrix, 137
Muhalla, 145
Mukherjee, Amitava, 87, 108. 143. 168. 326
Mukherjee. Neela, 24
MYRADA, 9. 10, 37, 52. 59. 63

NABARD, 138
NTFP Collection and CPR Collection. 193-94
Narendra Dev University of Agriculture and Technology, Faizabad, 66
National Health Policy, 339, 347
National Plan. 96
Natural resources. 244, 247. 253. 303-308
problems and opportunities. 278-80
Natural Resources Management. 29
Need supportive leadership. 238
Neighbourhood Initiatives Foundation (NIF). 44
New economic policy, Ethiopean Government. 242
New research methods, development of. 109-10
Non-agricultural livelihoods. 164
Normal bureaucratic tendencies. 64
Nugu Dam, 39
Nutrition. 312-13

Occupational status of women. 208
ODA-supported Western Ghats programme. 31
Off-farm employment opportunities. 410
Open-ended plan. 125
Optimal ignorance in PLA terminology. 95
Optimizing trade offs. 14
Orchard farming, characteristics of. 384-85. 390
Organizations. types of. 64
Osner. Karl. 56
Oxen shortages, 267-68

Pakistan, 54. 152
Panchayat Bhavan. 225
Panchayat functions at the local levels. 171-75
Panchayat level planning. 108
Panchayati Raj Institutions (PRIs). 89, 99, 135, 145. 171, 172, 175, 225
Participating Public Sector Organisation, 411
Participation, kinds of, 126
Participative mode. 103
Participatory Action Research, 3
Participatory Data, 222-25
decision trees. 224
diagrams, 222
maps. 223
seasonal calendars, 223-24
time trends, 224
transects, 223
Venn diagrams. 224-25
Participatory Learning and Action (PLA). 108, 111
attitudes in application on. 102-04. 140-41
in micro-level planning. 114-20
methods. limitations of. 100-101
methods and local level planning. comparison and training implications. 101-102

PLA and Micro level planning. parameters, 90
PLA principles of, 93-94
problems, 90-91
schematic illustration of triangulation used in, 155-56
techniques of. 87-100, 144-46, 166
terminology, optimal ignorance in, 95
PLA tools, 164
planning stage use of. 148-50
PLA use in local level planning. 102
PLA *versus* other research methods. 112-14
Participatory Reflection and Action, 111
Participatory mapping and modelling. 20
Participatory methods in Governments. 225-239
adopting participatory methods. 234-36
government participatory methods. components of. 236-39
Participatory methodologies. 111-12. 114
Participatory Rapid Rural appraisal, importance elements, 111-12
Participatory Resource map. 24
Participatory Rural Appraisal (PRA), 108, 109, 221
additional principles stressed in, 14-15
background and features. 109-14
demand for training. 84
dangers and opportunities, 84
definition of, 11-13
discoveries of. 18-28
diagramming and visual sharing, 22-23
relaxed rapport, 21-22
sequences. 23-24
sharing and spread. 27-28
training and reorientation for outsiders. 25-26
village's knowledge and capabilities. 20-21
distinguishing features of. 110
in institutions. 64-67
methods. 339-42
methods in M&E Research, 62
paradigmatic significance of, 67-70
principles of, 13-15
relaxed rapport, 21-22
reversals and reality, 41-48
start, stumble. self-correct share, 84-86
sources of, 1-8
streams. 2-3
validity and reliability, 32-34
Participatory Rural Appraisal for Rural Development Planning, 168-239
Participatory Village Censuses, 38
Pelto, Perthi J., 2. 36
People bias, 126
People's perception and people's wisdom. 220-21
Personal behaviour, attitudes and learning. 56-57
Peters, Tom, 69
Piggery programme, 395
financial allocation, 396
Pisciculture, 185
PL Active and Customs, 94
Pl Active and unwritten laws. 95
Planning Commission, 102
Planning fodder crops, 323
Planning at district and intermediate level, 174-75
Planning at panchayat level, 172-73
Policy research and change, 54-56
Pollution Control Board, 390
Polytechnics, 356
Potential problem identification, 129-30
Pottier, Johann, 36
Poultry keeping area, 274
Poverty, 103, 117, 157
alleviation programmes, 169
Power, 181-82
Pretty, Jules N.. 29. 39, 44, 54
Pre-planning stage, 143-44
Preliminary Best Best, 281-82

Primary education. 174
Primary resource mapping. 146
Problem activity matrix. 132
Problem-Problem matrix. 131
Professional bias. 126
Professional credibility. 6
Programmes for equity. 30
Project benefit matrix. 137
Pronouncements. 89
Public distribution system. 170. 173. 184-85
Public-Private partnership project. 208-18, 406

Quality of life, improvement of. 172
Qualitative assessment. 370-71
Questionnair methods. 148

Rainfall data, 38-40
 distribution. 251-52
Rajkiya Samudayik Phal Sanrakshan Kendra, Vikasnagar. 386
Ramachandran. Vidya. 9. 37. 52
Ranking and scoring. 36-37
Rapid Assessment Procedures (RAP) 5, 8
Rapid Consumption Assessment. 164
Rapid Ethnographic Assessment (REA), 5
Rapid Fertilizer Assessment. 164
Rapid Rural Appraisal (RRA). 1. 7-8. 109. 290
 exercise. participants in. 245
 techniques issues. 243
RRA and PRA. comparison of. 11-18
RRA and PRA. continuum between
 principles shared by. 13-14
 menu of methods. 15-18
 policy and personal potential of. 37
 reversals and reality. 41-44
 utility : practical applications. 28-30
Recent decades. micro-level planning for rural development. 88-89
Reconnaissance. 155-57
Regional plan. 96
Regional Rural Banks. 134
Relaxed rapport. 21-22
Relevance of PLA methods as tools to local level planning. 89-100
Renewable energy. sources of. 373-75
Reversals and reality, 41-43
Reversals of Dominance, 46-49
 from extracting to empowering. 46-47
 from reserve to rapport. 47-48
 from Tedium to funn. 47-48
Rhoades, R.E.. 2. 23. 53
Rizobium culture. 382
Rochelean. Diane. 35
Rudrapur Canal. 377
Rural development. micro-level planning for. 88-89
Rural electrification. 169
Rural questionnaire surveys, 60-62
Russell. David B.. 67

Scheduled Castes and Scheduled Tribes. Welfare of the weaker sections. 170. 348
Scoones. Ian. 241, 288
Scrimshaw, S.. 5. 8
Seasonal bias. 126
Seasonal calendar. analysis of. 330-33. 343-44
Seasonal food calendar. 343-44
Seasonal diagrams. 158
Seasonal unemployment. 130
Seed treatment. 382
Second order science. 68
Sector activity matrix. 132
Sectoral budgets. 139
Sectoral plan. 125
Seedling support. 272
Selmer. R.. 69
Semi-structured key-informant interview. 125-27
Sensitizing the community. 124-25
Sequences. 23-24
Sex discrimination. 345
Shah, Anil. 57

Shah. M.. 29. 63. 64
Sharing and spread. 27-28
Sida Ager Villagisation area. 260
SIDA-Supported Vietnam-Sweden Forestry Cooperation Programme. Vietnam. 31
Silverman. Sydal. 36
Situation analysis. 127-28
Social anthropology. 5
Social mapping. 149-52
Soil conservation methods. 273-74. 336-71. 381
  allocation of funds. 370-71
  problems and opportunities. 273-74, 366
Soil erosion. 304
  control of. 367-68
  impact of. 367-68
Soil fertility, 259-60
Soil and Water Conservation. 244
Soil types. 303-04
Solar plants, 181-82
Somesh Kumar. 235
Sorghum varieties. 254-56
  ranking of. 257-58
Sources of information. 81-86
Spatial planning. 133
Species. 370
Spread by villages, 62-64
Spread with quality assurance, 57-58
Standard questionnaire method. 148
State Finance Commission. 175
State plan. 96
Storage problems. 300
Storage and processing facilities. 173. 382
Structural adjustment programme. 153
Subsidy. 382
Substituting for Surveys. 60-62
Sustainable agricultural programme. 81
Swift. Jeremy. 59. 68
73rd Constitutional Amendment Act. 89. 100. 108. 168. 170. 171

Tactical planning. 116-19
  planning *per se*. 119
  steps of. 119-133
Tectical Plan for Appropriation of Benefits from Development of a Mini Hydro Project Power Plant. 406-18
Tamil Nadu Agricultural University. 66
Tanzania. 54
Technical knowhow. 385
Teff Varieties. ranking of. 258
Three-dimensional model. 20
Top-down approach. 175
Traditional local level planning. techniques used in, 98-99
Training and reorientation for outsiders. 25-27
Transport, 179-80, 213. 217, 372-73
Tree Plantation. 271-72. 281, 304-05. 318
Triangulation. 38
Tubewells. 377

Umar. Abdi Noor, 59
Unemployment. 390
UNESCAP, Bangkok. 412
UNICEF. 344
Universal economic growth, 69
University of Khon Kaen. Thailand. 8. 25
University of Chiang Mai. 4
Upliftment of poor. stratgies for. 392-93
Upper Mile and cheleka catchment — Disaster prevention programme. 241
Use your own best judgement at all times. 84
Uttaranchal, 157
Uttar Pradesh Renewable Energy Development Agency (UPREDA). 373

Vaccine, 347
Vaccination against contagious diseases. 393
Vegetables. ranking of. 263

Vegetative check barriers. plantation of. 368
Venn diagrams. 146. 152. 155
Venn and chapati diagramming. 43
Vikasnagar Block
  agriculture. 374-86
  animal husbandry, 391-92
  drinking water problems. 336-37
  education quality. 350-59
  existing facilities. 353-55
  farmers' problems. 379-80
  financial allocation. 372
  forest resources. importance. 362
  forest species types, 362-63
  forest — the green cover. 359-66
  health family welfare and sanitation. 339-47
  implementation plan. 357-59
  infrastructural facilities. 371-72
  marketing facilities, 379
  methodology of planning. 361-62
  minor irrigation projects, 377
  objectives of plan. 334-35
  plan financing. principles of. 382
  prioritization of problems. 341-42
  renewable energy. sources of. 373-84
  soil conservation. 336-71
  sources of finance. 335-39
  statistical outline of health. 340
Vikasnagar Industrial Development Cooperative (VIDC). 335. 336
Vikasnagar Frozen Foods Limited. 387. 388
  project report. 399-405
Village area plan. dimensions of. 172-73
Village development plans. 164
Village *haats*. 173
Village income. 192-93
  primary sector. 192
  secondary sector, 192-93
  tertiary sector. 192-93
Village level planning. 108
Village volunteers. 63-64
Villager's knowledge and capabilities. 20-21
Visual literacy. 43
Voyce, M., 66

Wage employment, 336
Water and sanitation assessment, 30
Water-borne infections. 346
Water harvesting ponds. 381
Waterlogging areas, 263
Weed control. 382
Welbourne. Alice. 59
White. R., 20
Why local level planning used. 90-91
  problems of. 90-91
Why PLA used, problems. 90-91
Whyte. 2. 3
Widow-headed household. 157. 209
Wildlife reserve buffer zone. 29
Women's status within household. 209-12
  female-headed houschold. 209
  landless household. 209-10
  small and marginal farmers. 210
  widow-headed households. 209
Women's work patterns. 208-12
  occupational status. 208
Women and child development. 170
World Bank. 9. 68. 87. 88, 153
World Bank - IMF Combine. structural adjustment loans of. 152
World Development Report. 153

Xavier Institute of Social Services, Ranchi. 10. 66

Yamuna Hydel-Power Project. 326
Yamuna-Katapathar Canal, 377
Your dream : your perspective. 122-23
Youth for Action. Hyderabad. 10

Zimbabwe, 54
  structural adjustment programme on food security. 153
Zamindars. 359
Zilla Parishad. 140